Business Statistics by the Numbers

Jerome P. Keating
University of Texas at San Antonio

THOMSON
CUSTOM PUBLISHING

Custom Consultant: Colin Manly
Editor: Staci Powers
Director of Product Creation: Becky Schwartz
Manufacturing Supervisor: Donna M. Brown
Graphic Designer: Krista Pierson
Rights and Permissions Specialist: Kalina Ingham Hintz
Project Coordinator: Brian Schaefer

ISBN 0-759-34912-6

The Adaptable Courseware Program consists of products and additions to existing Custom Publishing products that are produced from camera-ready copy. Peer review, class testing, and accuracy are primarily the responsibility of the author(s).

Business Statistics by the Numbers

Jerome P. Keating

University of Texas at San Antonio
6900 North Loop 1604 West
Department of Management Science and Statistics
San Antonio, TX 78249-0632

"All knowledge is, in the final analysis, history.
All sciences are, in the abstract mathematics.
All methods of acquiring knowledge are essentially statistical."

C.R. Rao

"It is a truth very certain that when it is not in our power to determine what is true we ought to follow what is most probable."

Rene Descartes

"The quiet statisticians have changed our world-not by discovering new facts or technical developments but by changing the way we reason, experiment, and form our opinions about it."

Sir Ian Hacking

"When you can measure what you are speaking about, and express it in numbers, you know something about it; but when you cannot measure it, when you cannot express it in numbers, your knowledge is of a meager and unsatisfactory kind."

Lord Kelvin

Dedication

Words

In their inner offices, they
scrawl out notes that students
only half read or discard.
They must order more cabinets
to hold all these unwanted words
that few read, few hear.
They worry about
the waste of verbs.

At Vespers, they pray for a
few good words that will turn
their students from apathy,
to thoughts of better ways to live.

At the end of the divine office
they dream of Europe
united in peace …
Till then they view
life from the perch
of their separate fidelity
and wait for those
chosen to hear

Jerry Keating 1987

Dedicated to Victor Gillespie, OSB, who opened the world of mathematics to me through geometry and Abbot Denis Farkasfalvy, OCS, for the gift of teaching.

Recommended Course Outline

Week	Topic	Pages
1	Introduction	7-27
	Data & Statistics	
	Descriptive Statistics: Part I	28-45
2	Descriptive Statistics: Part II	45-58
3	Introduction to Probability	62-82
	Counting Rules	83-93
4	Probability Review	
	Exam I	
5	Discrete Distributions	94-98
	Binomial	99-114
6	Continuous Distributions	115-119
	Normal	120-138
7	Sampling Distributions	144-156
8	Exam II	
9-10	Hypothesis Testing	157-183
11-12	Comparison of Means & ANOVA	203-220
13	Exam III	
13	Chi-square Tests	
	Multinomial	189-196
14	Independence	197-202
15	Regression Analysis	221-240
	Final Exam	

Recommended Grading Policy:

Exam I	20%
Exam II	20%
Exam III	20%
Final Exam	25%
Instructor's Optional Points	15%

Instructors Optional Points: Instructor's Optional Points will be based on your attendance.

Course Objective: The goal of this course is to introduce the methods and uses of statistics in the business environment. Students need to demonstrate knowledge of the course concepts by knowing which decisions, comparisons, and inferences to make in the presence of uncertainty. Students need to demonstrate knowledge of the practical basis of the course by mastering and correctly applying the methods for making these decisions, comparisons, and inferences in business settings.

Nature of Course Content: Problem-based learning is used to provide the students with a hands-on and group-experience in learning the methods of statistics. The material will be illustrated through practical examples in business, economics, manufacturing, etc.

Table of Contents

Introduction

Many of us have some casual acquaintance with topics in Statistics such as probability, averages, percentages or other routinely reported descriptive information. We know that our chances of winning the lottery are related to probability and that the winnings are based on statistical notions such as risk. Today the discipline is deeply involved with the traditional physical sciences as well as economics, finance, genetics, marketing, meteorology, athletic competition, anthropology, engineering, history, poetic authorship, law and many other disciplines. In the last twenty-five years Statistics has emerged as a discipline apart from Mathematics and yet remains one inseparably linked to a vast spectrum of other disciplines. In this book, we examine its use in and impact.

Statistics and Mathematics

In the minds of many persons, Statistics is another area of Mathematics with a lot of formulas. Statistics has often been thought of in philosophical circles as an inverse process to Mathematics. Whereas Mathematics is deductive, Statistics is inductive. In geometry, we start with axioms about points, lines, circles and planes (e.g., two distinct points determine a straight line). Based upon the *assumed truth* of these axioms, results such as the Pythagorean Theorem are established by deductive reasoning. In Statistics, we start with the results from or outcomes of some scientific experiments, surveys, monthly sales trends for toys or other observations and try to hypothesize or infer what physical, economic, financial, or social model might be the basis for these outcomes.

This distinction between Statistics and Mathematics is not simply a way of drawing lines between disciplines; rather it reflects that *statisticians reason differently in that they infer from basic observations*. In this way, the statistician acts much like a detective by acquiring and synthesizing information, which statisticians call data.. He or she then analyzes the manner (known as sampling) in which the information is collected, summarizes the collected information by organizing and reorganizing the information according to different important characteristics.

Statistics in Experimental Science

Statistics has greatly influenced all scientific research in the modern era. As new theories are proposed, Statistics comes to the forefront of the debate to quantify how well the theory corresponds with observed information. If you have taken a class in physics, you are familiar with the experiment in which you drop a stainless steel ball bearing from a known height, say 16 feet, and time the descent of the bearing until it hits the floor. This experiment is the traditional way in which students are asked to estimate the effect of acceleration due to the mass of earth or as it is known more simply, gravity.

If you conducted this experiment then you know that the numbers *never exactly work* like they do in the textbooks. If h is the height from which you drop the bearing, Sir Isaac Newton (1686) said that the time t to impact is found from the formula: see Johnson and Kotz (1997) page 55.

$$h = \frac{1}{2} \times g \times t^2$$

where g is the gravitational attraction due to the mass of the earth. And the reason for the disparity between the theory of Newton and the information that we obtained is experimental or measurement error.

The experiment that you carried out may have been flawed from the outset because not all points on the surface of the earth are equidistant from its center of mass since the earth is not a perfect sphere. The experiment was probably not conducted at mean sea level. So the textbook answer for $g = 32\ ft/\sec^2$ may be slightly off depending upon your position on the earth's surface and the true elevation at which the experiment was conducted.

In the actual conduct of the experiment, was the height of the drop exactly sixteen feet? If it was a little more than sixteen feet, the corresponding descent time is longer. What mechanism did you use to release the bearing? If the mechanism produces a spin on the bearing this will lengthen the descent time. If you dropped it by hand then many effects can flaw the experiment. More importantly, how did you time the beginning and end of the experiment? Was it done on voice command? If you used a stopwatch, how accurate is it? Slight changes in the observed time t have a large effect on the estimate of g, denoted with a hat over the letter, $\hat{g}$, which is

$$\hat{g} = \frac{2 \times h}{t^2}$$

In this experiment if we know that $h = 16'$, then the formula tells us that the time required to travel the distance is about 1 second based on textbook values. Suppose for example, we set up an experiment, wherein we estimated this value by measuring the time required for the bearing to drop 16 feet.

In our one-time experiment, a laser measured the time as 0.987 seconds, an automated system at 0.99 seconds and a stopwatch measured the value at 1.0 seconds.

TABLE 1: Precision of Measurements and Their Effect on the Accuracy of Estimates

Method	**Time**	$\hat{g}$
Laser	0.987	32.848
Automated	0.99	32.65
Stopwatch	1.0	32

In a post examination, it was determined that the height was $15'7''$.

FIGURE 1: A sketch of Cavendish's 1797 apparatus to measure The Universal Gravitational Constant

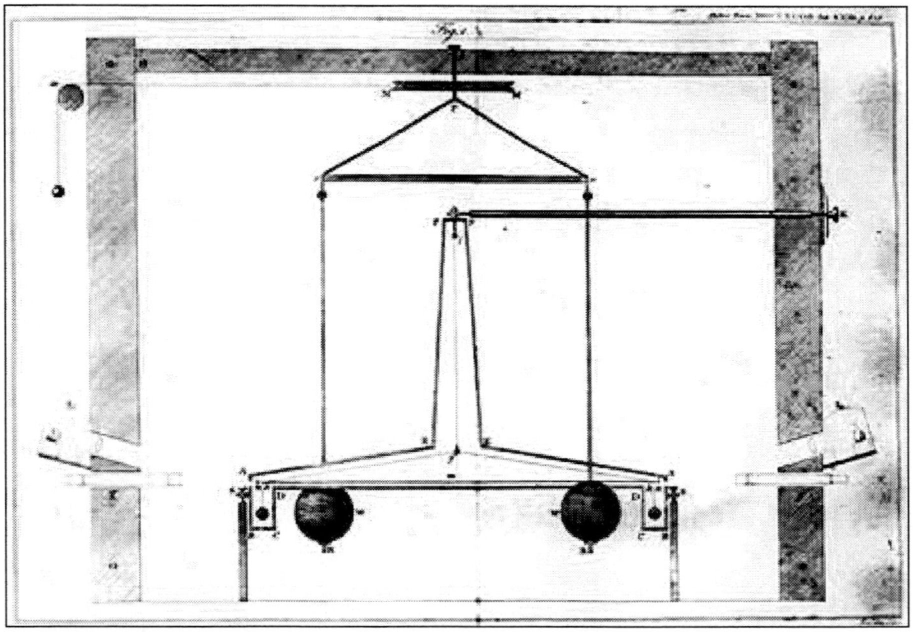

http://www.aip.org/physnews/graphics/html/newgrav.html

Thus we need a measurement process that can measure the time precisely (perhaps, to within a hundredth of a second but preferably to within a thousandth of a second). Clearly (in Table 1) this second type of experimental error questions: How well were we able to measure the quantities of distance and time? In the conduct of an experiment, it must be clear what is to be measured or counted and how will it be measured or counted. You may have missed a valuable lesson in experimental or measurement error if you modified your experimental errors to fit the textbook answer. Many scientists have fudged experimental evidence but that practice does not produce good science.

The Augustinian monk, Gregor Mendel (1866) first published the *"Laws of Heredity"* through probabilities based upon experiments crossing varieties of the *garden pea*. His results were not well received in the scientific community as noted from his correspondence with other prominent botanists. It is apparent they did not believe Mendel's probabilistic thesis of inherited traits and rather encouraged him to corroborate his findings on a species to which they did not apply. With his election as Abbott of the Augustinian monastery in Moravia, Mendel devoted most of the remainder of his life to official duties of the Church. See Stigler (1986).

Ludwig Boltzman, an Austrian like Mendel, gave a statistical explanation to properties of atoms such as mass, speed, and charge in 1866. In the following decade, he explained the *"Second Law of Thermodynamics,"* by jointly using laws of mechanics and concepts of probability to describe atomic motions. This theory, known as statistical mechanics, came under great scrutiny from scientists of the day. See Johnson and Kotz (1997) page 353.

In 1869, Adolphe Quetelet, a Belgian astronomer, published his treatise on *"The Average Man"* as a central value of human behavior about which values of others are grouped according to probability laws. He used the concept of chance to describe certain behaviors or outcomes and as such precipitated moral debate on free will versus determinism. As an example, he noted the *"propensity"* of committing a certain crime varied by age. See Johnson and Kotz (1997) page 64 and Stigler (1986).

The conjunction of their publications most likely initiated the modern age of statistical science. The astonishing result, that all these explanations are based on the ideas of probabilities gave credence to the concept that there was a level of uncertainty in all naturally occurring phenomena. The change was that fundamental laws of nature were inherently probabilistic and that the *"natural laws,"* such as Newton's laws of gravitational attraction, were expected behavior which one would anticipate to happen on the average. The Nobel Physicist, Max Born, eloquently stated this reversal of roles in the following passage:

> *"We have seen how classical physics struggled in vain to reconcile growing quantitative observations with preconceived ideas of causality, … , and how it fought a losing battle against the intrusion of chance. Today the order has been reversed: chance has become the primary notion, mechanics an expression of its quantitative laws."*

It should be noted that Mendel's (1870) theory of genetics was most likely based upon falsified data. The agreement between Mendel's prediction and the actual observation was indeed incredible. Sir R. A. Fisher (1936) pointed out in Science that Mendel's experimental results should have such good agreement with his theoretical expectations due to chance alone in about 7 out of 100,000 experiments. Fisher attributes the coincidence to an over zealous assistant, who knew what Mendel anticipated and did not disappoint his mentor. Perhaps, the culprit here is the lack of maturity of the scientific community in Mendel's time to understand the nature and magnitude of scientific uncertainty. Mendel's experiments were ultimately corroborated at the turn of the century by three other European botanists but some 16 years after his death.

> *"Accepted scientific theories are the best available approximations to phenomena that we do not fully understand."*

In this regard, engineering and the physical sciences have much less variability in their subjects than others such as psychology, sociology, or economics. An inanimate object such as a ball bearing has less uncertainty associated with it than does a person whose behavior is a product of free will as well as many other factors.

Statistics in the Social Sciences

The quantitative analysis of human behavior is a rather modern idea. From simple associations, such as state of sobriety and crime committed, social scientists try to quantify human behavior in many ways. Much has been learned about the human condition and our predilections for certain choices. Are left-handed persons more accident prone? Do we unknowingly prefer certain colors, letters, or numerals?

C. Radhakrishna Rao (1989) states in his treatise, Statistics and Truth, that:

> *"Since the acceptance of a theory depends on its verification by observed data, a scientist may be tempted to fudge experimental data to fit a particular theory and claim acceptance or establish priority of his ideas. No doubt, if a theory is wrong, it will be discovered sooner or later by other scientists conducting relevant experiments. However, there is a possibility of considerable harm being done to society by its acceptance in the meanwhile."*

Rao cites an example involving Cyril Burt, the father of Educational Psychology. His theory that differences in intelligence are largely inherited and unaffected by social factors, apparently supported by faked data, erroneously influenced government thinking on elementary education. Herrnstein and Murray (1994) resurrect the issue in their controversial volume, *The Bell Curve*, in which they profess that intelligence is between 40% and 80% inherited. They exonerate Burt of any data falsification based on accounts by others. The discipline of Statistics and the correctness of its procedures are at the center of this firestorm.

Statistics in Daily Life

How does statistics affect your life or is it just another subject to be learned in school and quickly forgotten. To see how the subject has become part of our everyday lives. Let's follow a typical day of a college student in an urban university trying to get to school or work. When you came to school or work today perhaps the meteorologist said that the chance of rain was 40% and therefore you brought an umbrella. Perhaps you drove to school or work. Was there anything unusual about the route that you drove? If you did not take the shortest route then perhaps you had some experience (or prior information) about potential traffic congestion at certain intersections, the possibility of a train crossing a road that you might take and thereby possibly making you late for class. The length of time that a traffic light is red, yellow, or green is usually determined by the flow of traffic, whether it is primarily North-South or East-West. Are the traffic lights along the road set up in a cascade effect?

Did you buckle your seat belt? Perhaps you should because of traffic fines and the information about different death rates in traffic accidents between those who buckle up and those that don't. In 1994, the average hospital bill of an injured person not wearing a seat restraint during an accident is $13,997 as opposed to $9,004 for those wearing one. You know that your driver's insurance premiums are higher than your parent's because persons in your age group are more likely to have accidents than persons in their fifties.

However, if you wanted $100,000 of term life insurance your premiums would be much less than your father's because persons in your age group are less likely to die than men in their fifties. If persons in your age group die they are most likely to have died accidentally, violently or due to the HIV virus, which causes AIDS. The AIDS virus is the leading cause of death among persons aged 25-44.

Statistics in Actuarial Science

The persons, who set these premiums, are well trained in statistics and known as *actuaries*. These topics interestingly fall within the domain of the statistician.

TABLE 2: Life Tables 1959-1961

AGE		Number Living	Number Dying
Beg	End	At Beginning	Within Interval
0	1	100,000	2,593
1	5	97,407	409
5	10	96,998	233
10	15	96,765	214
15	20	96,551	440
20	25	96,111	594
25	30	95,517	612
30	35	94,905	761
35	40	94,144	1,080
40	45	93,064	1,686
45	50	91,378	2,622
50	55	88,756	4,045
55	60	84,711	5,644
60	65	79,067	7,920
65	70	71,147	10,290
70	75	60,857	12,687
75	80	48,170	14,594
80	85	33,576	15,034
85	+	18,542	18,542

From Table 2, we can derive survival estimates for insurance purposes.
If a person aged 15 wants to buy a one-year term life insurance policy, how much should he or she pay based on the values in Table 2?

$$\Pr(X \leq 16 \mid X \geq 15) = \frac{440}{96{,}551} \times \frac{1}{5} = 0.000911435$$

Notice that of every 100,000 people born 18 years ago, 96,551 were still living at age 15. Of these 96,551 persons, 440 died before age 20. If we assume that persons expire uniformly over the interval then one-fifth of them would expire in the first year. We can extend this result by making some simplifying assumptions of uniformity.

In general it is most practical to apply the common mortality rates to everyone in the interval. This does ignore whether a person is near the beginning or near the end of an interval. In this age bracket, most persons die accidentally in traffic. However in the 75-80 age bracket, the distinction between 75 and 79 is probably quite significant. The common annual mortality rate for this age bracket is 91.1 per 100,000 individuals per year. So in this age bracket, we expect 91.1 persons to die and 99,908.9 to survive.

Assume that everyone in this age bracket buys a one-year renewable policy in the amount of $25,000. The company would expect to pay out

$$\$25{,}000 \times 91.1 = \$2{,}277{,}500$$

Thus just to break even each person must pay $22.78 per year or $1.90 per month. Note that the numbers cited above are averages and an individual company may have disproportionately more or less fatalities in this age group. How should the company arrive at a reasonable insurance premium? The consumer wants the company to remain solvent or otherwise his or her beneficiaries could not collect on the policy if the company goes bankrupt.

Suppose the company charges an annual rate $35, how many persons in this age group would have to expire before the company lost money on the group?

$$\frac{35 \times 100{,}000}{25{,}000} = 140$$

The actual methods used to set premiums involve complex factors in insurance, law, statistics, and interest theory. If we are 95% certain that in a group of 100,000 persons aged 15-20, that fewer that 140 would expire, then we are 95% certain of making a profit. The 5% would represent the company's risk of losing money on that age group.

In a general sense, Statistics is the art and science of:

- collecting
- analyzing
- presenting and
- interpreting information.

In the business sector, statistics are used to provide managers and decision makers with a better understanding of the business and economic environment to enable them to make better informed and better decisions in the presence of uncertainty. One can also provide an operational definition of statistics as:

Statistics:

1) uses methods to collect information through planned experiments and phenomenological observations;

2) organizes and summarizes information about a topic (e.g., stock market prices <Enron, WorldCom> , public concern over safety <Firestone>, flight schedules <United Airlines>, etc.), and

3) draws inferences about the topic through a subset of the information (e.g., bear or bull markets, fuel oil prices, gasoline prices, risk due to product safety <Scotchgard>, on time-arrival rates) known as data.

Statistics is a science because it uses the scientific method:

1) hypothesis (or conjecture), which is a statement about the nature of the issue. For example, the morbidity of diabetes cannot be diminished against the notion that morbidity can be reduced through diet, exercise, and medication.

2) experimentation (or planning/sampling).
What information should we gather to compare opposing hypotheses? Whom should we interview and what questions should we ask? Which characteristics should we measure?

3) conclusion (or inference).
What can we reasonably say about hypotheses based only on the information obtained in item 2? Do the results strongly favor either hypothesis? Are they simply inconclusive?

As business students we recognize the need to apply statistics to a variety of economical, financial, accounting and marketing endeavors.

<u>Business Applications</u>:

Accounting

- **Conducting audits**
    - In a post Enron and WorldCom environment, greater emphasis is placed on the conduct of independent audits.
- **Sampling from balance sheets**
    - In companies of such size, one cannot reasonably review every ledger page. So the audit accountant must sample form the available ledger pages. If he or she has some intuition as to where mistakes may be found then he or she can conduct stratified sampling plans discussed later.

Economics

- **Investment recommendations**
- **Use P/E ratios and dividends to predict to forecast financial viability**
    - Much emphasis has been placed on price to earnings ratios, especially in the light of the collapse of many dot-com companies, which were highly overvalued.
- **Unemployment rates, inflation rates, the producer price index, etc. are used to estimate GNP.**
    - The stock market fluctuates with the release of these numbers because they are viewed as signs of the financial well being of the country.

Marketing

- **Point of sale scanners AC Nielsen**
    - Can we use sales data to better market our products? Can we identify product lines that are ineffective?
- **Understanding market dynamics**

Production

- **Product Quality and Reliability**
    - Product Quality became associated with superior products produced by Japanese manufacturers. Product Reliability was originally associated with Military contracts through MIL-STD 817, NASA and NRC.

- **Quality Control Processes, x-bar charts, R-bar charts, and CUSUM charts**
  - W. Edward Deming used graphical methods such CUSUM charts and x-bar charts to monitor product quality, design of experiments to improve manufacturing processes
- **Control limits-fidelity in advertising**
  - Operating environments have been always been restricted but much emphasis is placed on disclosure of the conditions. For example, some vehicles have a much greater propensity to "rollover" such as SUVS.

Statistical Terms

A population is the complete collection of all elements (i.e., persons, items, or measurements) pertinent to the study. If we want to measure the financial effect of diabetes on families, then we want to know how frequently diabetes occurs, the frequency of each type such as geriatric diabetes, and the associated costs to families according to each type. In this context the families with a diabetic member would be the elements of the population.

In some cases, we must measure certain abstract items such as public sentiment for aggressive treatment of a disease. For example, consider the tremendous expenditures associated with finding a cure for the HIV virus, which previously affected a small part of the population. The elements of this population can be everyone, who is HIV^+. Certainly one of the most dangerous places worldwide is Africa, where as much as 20% of the adult population is HIV^+, implying that enormous numbers of children will be living without parents in the decades to come.

The population is determined by the topic of interest. If my major concern is student performance, then the population may be all UTSA students. If you want to make a broader inference about students in general, then the population may be taken as the set of all students at four-year colleges in Texas. The breadth of the population corresponds to the scope of the inference that you want to make. The students in this class could be taken as the population. The population is the statistical version of the universal set, from algebra.

A sample is any subset of a population (e.g., the academic performance of women in this class) or collection of elements. In the student example mentioned earlier, if the population consists of all UTSA students then the students in this class would form a sample of that population. If this class were the population then students seated in the second row would form a sample, as would the students seated on an aisle, as would the female students in the class.

A representative sample is one in which the characteristics observed in the sample occur with the same frequency that they do in the population.

"It is imperative to select representative samples to make meaningful inferences about the population."

Are all samples representative of the population? The obvious answer is no but it is helpful to have some examples as references. The *"Literary Digest"* Poll in the US Presidential election of 1936 exemplifies that large samples alone will not guarantee that the sample is representative.

- **Case Study: 1936 Presidential Election**

The history of statistics is filled with examples in which samples were not representative of the population at large and the consequent inferences were flawed. In the 1936 presidential election, Franklin Roosevelt was running for re-election against the Republican candidate Alf Landon. In the election year, Literary Digest, October 31, 1936, conducted a national poll of its readers in order to predict a winner. The poll had 1,293,669 votes in favor of Landon and 972,897 votes for President Roosevelt for 2.26 million voters from the 48 contiguous states in the poll and 54.69% preferred Landon.

TABLE 3: Literary Digest Poll versus Election Results

Candidate	LD Poll	Ballot	Difference
Landon	1,293,669	539,444	-754,225
Roosevelt	972,897	1,090,927	118,030
	2,266,566	1,630,371	-635,995

In the election, President Roosevelt received a landslide majority of 65.24% of the 1,672,175 ballots cast in the popular vote, whereas Landon received only 32.26%. A third candidate received most of the remaining ballots cast. What went wrong in the Literary Digest poll? Certainly the sample size was large enough and in fact more persons participated in the poll than actually voted in the election. Some national polls of the day sampled less than 25% of the number eligible voters but were much closer to the actual outcome. Why was the sample not representative of the population?

Recall that in 1936 the US was in the throes of the Great Depression. Literary Digest, in its November 14, 1936 issue, examined many issues from under representation of the "have-nots" to the source of its 10 million-ballot mailing list. We can say that Roosevelt supporters did not return their ballots in the same proportion as Landon voters. Literary magazines were not only the province of the literate and well educated but were also the convenience of those affluent enough to pay for such luxuries. Perhaps the ordinary blue-collar worker was less likely to return the preference ballot.

- **Case Study: 1969 Draft Lottery**

President Nixon signed the Selective Service Draft Lottery into law in November of 1969. In the legislation, the draft order was to be determined by a random selection sequence. The outcome of the first lottery, conducted December 1, 1969 received intense scrutiny from the public and the press. Much of the problem surfaced due to the inadequate mixing of the capsules used in the lottery.

Let us briefly describe the process and make some interesting observations. Each of the 366 days of a leap year was entered on a piece of a paper and placed in a capsule. The January dates were entered first followed by the February dates. The capsules were then mixed. The process continued until all the days of a leap year had been entered and mixed. Stephen Fienberg in Science, January 22, 1971, points out that the capsules containing January dates were mixed with the other months 11 times, the February dates 10 times, and continuing until the December dates were mixed once with capsules from the other months.

The capsules were then poured into a bowl from the end of the container that was originally faced down. This caused the earlier months to fall to the bottom of the bowl and the latter months to fall on top. Generally the capsules were chosen from the top of the bowl and no further mixing was allowed. To illustrate the outcome we show the average order number for each month in Table 4. For example, the date April 5 was the 269th day chosen. So the order number for April 5 is 269. The average order number for the month of April is found by averaging the draft lottery order numbers for the 30 days in April. On the average we would expect a month to have an average of 183. From Table 4, October is the month whose average order is the closest to the expected value. Notice that December has the lowest average order number, which means that male students born in December are on the average the ones most likely, drafted first. March has the highest average order number given in Table 4; so those male students born in March are on the average the least likely to be drafted.

The pattern generated by the mixing and pouring process was so pronounced that it produced a nearly linear descent in the average order number from March to December as depicted in Figure 2. Since this was a time in American history when the government came under tremendous public scrutiny, the lottery was proclaimed as everything from a debacle to a conspiracy. In those days, male students were required to successfully complete 30 semester credit hours per academic year or lose their deferments from the draft. Among students at UT campuses, the common response concerning the whereabouts of a student who didn't make the grades was: “He’s transferred to UT-Saigon.”

TABLE 4: Order Numbers for the Draft Lottery in 1970

	JAN	FEB	MAR	APR	MAY	JUN	JUL	AUG	SEP	OCT	NOV	DEC
1	305	86	108	32	330	249	93	111	225	359	19	129
2	159	144	29	271	298	228	350	45	161	125	34	328
3	251	297	267	83	40	301	115	261	49	244	348	157
4	215	210	275	81	276	20	279	145	232	202	266	165
5	101	214	293	269	364	28	188	54	82	24	310	56
6	224	347	139	253	155	110	327	114	6	87	76	10
7	306	91	122	147	35	85	50	168	8	234	51	12
8	199	181	213	312	321	366	13	48	184	283	97	105
9	194	338	317	219	197	335	277	106	263	342	80	43
10	325	216	323	218	65	206	284	21	71	220	282	41
11	329	150	136	14	37	134	248	324	158	237	46	39
12	221	68	300	346	133	272	15	142	242	72	66	314
13	318	152	259	124	295	69	42	307	175	138	126	163
14	238	4	354	231	178	356	331	198	1	294	127	26
15	17	89	169	273	130	180	322	102	113	171	131	320
16	121	212	166	148	55	274	120	44	207	254	107	96
17	235	189	33	260	112	73	98	154	255	288	143	304
18	140	292	332	90	278	341	190	141	246	5	146	128
19	58	25	200	336	75	104	227	311	177	241	203	240
20	280	302	239	345	183	360	187	344	63	192	185	135
21	186	363	334	62	250	60	27	291	204	243	156	70
22	337	290	265	316	326	247	153	339	160	117	9	53
23	118	57	256	252	319	109	172	116	119	201	182	162
24	59	236	258	2	31	358	23	36	195	196	230	95
25	52	179	343	351	361	137	67	286	149	176	132	84
26	92	365	170	340	357	22	303	245	18	7	309	173
27	355	205	268	74	296	64	289	352	233	264	47	78
28	77	299	223	262	308	222	88	167	257	94	281	123
29	349	285	362	191	226	353	270	61	151	229	99	16
30	164		217	208	103	209	287	333	315	38	174	3
31	211		30		313		193	11		79		100
Ave.	201.16	202.97	225.81	203.67	207.97	195.73	181.55	173.45	157.30	182.45	148.73	121.55

Notice the nearly linear descent in the monthly averages depicted in Figure 2:

FIGURE 2: Average Order Number by Month – 1970 Draft Lottery

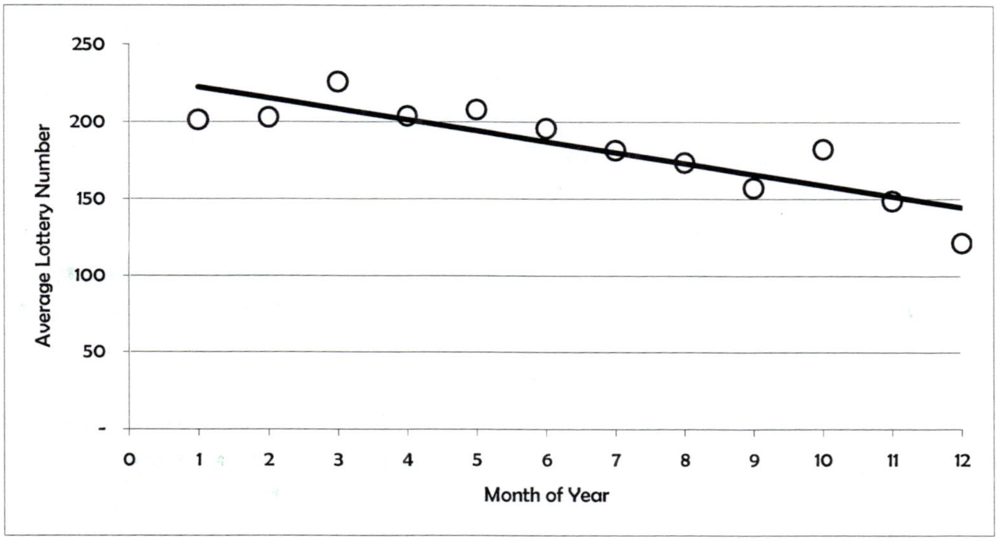

Designed Experiments

These examples show the complexity associated with sampling. How do you design an experiment to avoid many of the traps? Here are some suggestions:

- Identify the exact question to be answered and the relevant population to be sampled!
- Develop a plan for collecting data!
- Collect the data!
- Analyze the data and make inferences!

Samples result from either observational studies or planned experiments. In observational studies, we observe and measure characteristics but we don't attempt to modify the sample, (i.e., the subjects being sampled). In an experiment, we apply a treatment and then proceed to observe its effects on the sample. In the business sector we have many different sources of data from governmental agencies such as:

- Governmental Agencies
    - Bureau of the Census
    - Federal Reserve Board
    - Office of Management and Budget (GAO)
    - Department of Commerce
    - OSHA
    - EPA

- Companies maintain enormous databases or records
  - Employee records
  - Production records
  - Inventory records
  - Sales records
  - Credit records
  - Customer profiles
  - Preference surveys

A response variable is a characteristic of interest for each element of the population. Data are values of the variable for each element of the sample. See Diagram 1.

Some response variables are quantitative, and others are qualitative. Quantitative response variables imply that a measurement has been made. Qualitative response variables imply that a judgment or classification is made.

<**<u>Driver's License</u>**>	Height	Weight	DOB
	Hair Color	Eye Color	Restrictions

Data can also be classified according to measurement level.

The nominal level of measurement is characteristic of data, which are names, labels, or categories. For example, your response to a question of gender would be male or female. This is a nominal scale as is your response to a question about race or ethnicity.

The ordinal level of measurement involves data that can be arranged in order but differences between data values cannot be determined. For example, every semester you rate your instructors according a seven-point scale, from excellent, to very good, to meets expectations… etc. We know that excellent is better than very good but we cannot be certain that the difference between excellent and very good is the same as the difference between very good and meets expectations.

The interval level of measurement implies that we can determine meaningful amounts of differences among the data but there is no inherent starting point (or zero). For example, temperature can be measured according to a variety of scales. However, the fact that the temperature is 45° F versus 90° F does not mean that it is twice as hot as when the temperature is 90°.

DIAGRAM 1: Classifying Information

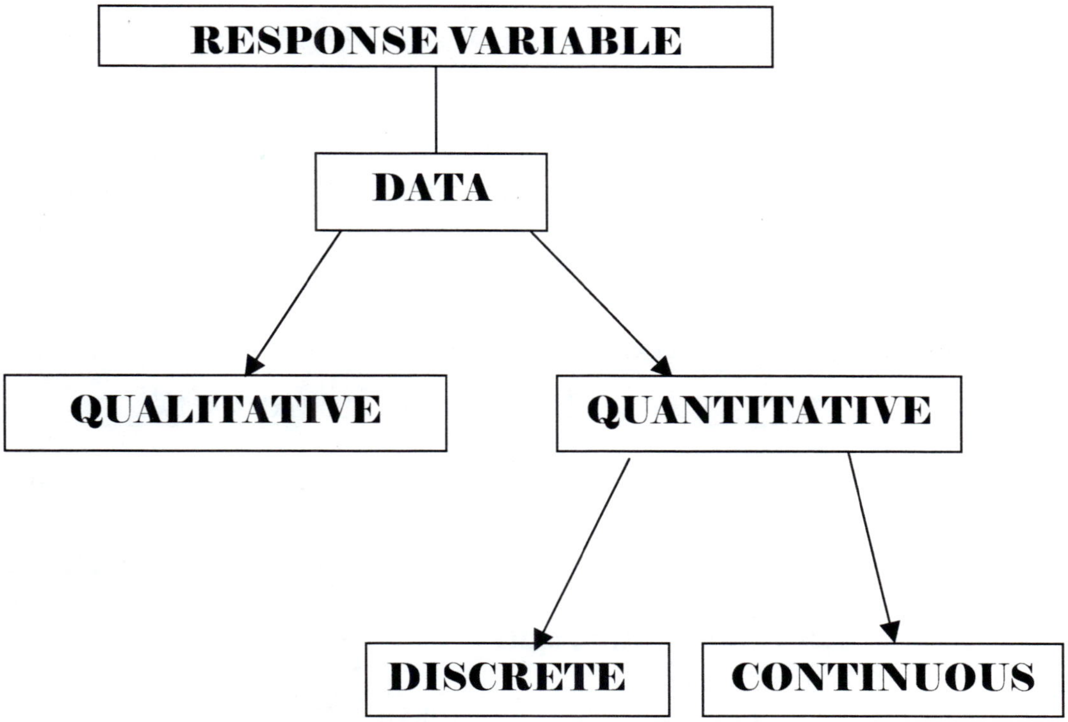

The ratio level is the interval level that has been modified to induce a zero or starting point (where zero indicates none of the quantity is present).

Quantitative response variables can also be classified according to whether they are discrete or continuous.

Continuous quantitative variables are ones that can attain any value between minimum and maximum values. For example student heights may attain any value between 4 feet and 7 feet or student weights may attain any value between 75 pounds and 300 pounds. So weight and height are continuous response variables.

Discrete variables imply that some values in an interval cannot be attained and frequently occur in the context of counts. For example, the number of sophomores in the class is a whole number. Other values that are often perceived as continuous are in fact discrete (e.g., stock market prices once only changed in multiples of 1/8 of a dollar). Most qualitative data are frequently converted into discrete scales.

Caveat: We discretize (make discrete) data, which are intrinsically continuous (Driver's License). Whenever we round the data, we are using a form for discretizing data.

In summarizing information, we develop statistical measures of the information in the population.

"A <u>parameter</u> is a numerical measure of a <u>population</u>."

If this class were a population, ***population parameters*** would be the average GPA of students in the class, the average amount of hours worked outside of class, the number of hours of mathematics classes taken in college, etc. We denote parameters by Greek letters, such as μ, α, β, and σ.

"A <u>statistic</u> is a numerical measure of a <u>sample</u> selected from the <u>population</u>"

(e.g., ***sample statistics*** would be the average GPA of students in the second row, the average number of hours worked by students who set in seats by the aisle, etc.). Statistics are traditionally denoted by symbols from our alphabet.

Liars, Damned Liars, and Statisticians:

The discipline is fraught with numerous problems of credibility that stems from the misuses of numerical information.

Abuses of Statistics

- Small Samples
  - Dental claims
    - Can we infer that a dentist is defrauding insurance companies based on a few claims?
  - Helicopter blades
    - Due to expense and time, most material fatigue tests of rotor blades involve six or fewer blades.
- Numbers
  - Precision is not synonymous with the number of decimal places of accuracy.
- Guesses
  - Papal crowd in San Antonio 9/13/1987

- Distorted Percentages
  - We decreased the number of bad tires by 100%
- Partial Pictures
  - 95% of the shareholders in Mobil-Exxon are ordinary middle-class people. However, they own less than 10% of the company.
- Loaded Questions
  - Would you say that lawn watering contributes more or less to the water shortage than rainfall?
- Misleading Graphs
  - Always look for an origin. Salary Figures!
  - Bayer aspirin commercial: "Stranded on a desert island."
- Pictographs

  Beware of icons used to represent items.
- Pollster Pressure

  Florida Ballot 2000

  - From obvious (hand washing) "Hawthorne_effect" to the Rosenthal effect.

Case Study: The Hawthorne Effect

Individual behavior changes if one knows that he or she is being observed. "This effect, known as The Hawthorne Effect, was first documented in a research project (1927 - 1932) of the Western Electric Company's (now AT&T) Hawthorne Plant in Cicero, Illinois (suburban Chicago). The study led by Harvard Business School professor Elton Mayo explored physical and environmental influences of the workplace such as lighting conditions, temperature, humidity, and other comfort factors. Psychological aspects, such work breaks, peer pressure, scheduling, and managerial style were explored later. The principal outcome of the study was, regardless of imposed external manipulation, worker productivity increased. Reasonable inferences are that workers were pleased to receive attention from the researchers, who expressed an interest in them or when workers were knowingly observed they tended to be more productive" resulting in a phenomenon known as the "Halo Effect."

See Clark, D (2002)
http://www.nwlink.com/~donclark/hrd/history/hawthorne.html

▪ **Case Study: Rosenthal effect**

An experimenter expectancy effect or Rosenthal effect, named for Robert Rosenthal, alludes to the impact of an experimenter's preconceived notion of participants expected behavior on their actual behavior. Experimenter expectation may influence participant behavior whether or not an experimenter has any intention to bias the results. The experimenter is usually unaware of the processes by which this phenomenon occurs. See:

http://www.apa.org/monitor/may02/hatsoff_1.html

This phenomenon manifests itself in many diverse ways. If your blood pressure is elevated when your physician or nurse takes but remains lower when you take it, your condition is being altered by the presence of the other party. The condition known as "white-coat hypertension" was thought to be harmless and perhaps a sign of social phobia. Italian researchers determined that individuals with the condition eventually have thicker heart muscles and impaired heart function. So while the cause of the phenomenon is unknown, we can say that its recurrence is associated with cardiac morbidity. See Parade Magazine August 25, 2002, page 6.

❖ Psychological Factors

Human Factors!!!
- Color
- Position

❖ Bad Samples

Nightline polls
- Beware of surveys that allow persons to respond. Recall the Literary Digest poll.

We are very concerned in statistics with several recurring problems.

Confounding occurs when the effects of two or more variables cannot be distinguished from one another. It is reasonable to examine the effects of ethnicity and age in the onset of diabetes. So suppose that a sample has persons from four ethnic groups including African-Americans and persons ranging in ages from 1-20, 21-40, 41-60, 61-80. However, if all the African-Americans were aged 61-80, we could not distinguish ethnic effect from that of age. In studies, which attribute academic performance to race, if members of one race are from mostly one segment of the SES, then we cannot determine whether the difference is due to race or SES.

Common Sampling Plans

- **Random** — Choose so that every group of size n has the same Chance of occurring. This method is usually implemented with a random number generator.
- **Stratified** — Separate the sampling units according to key characteristics such as age, gender, race, and class and sample proportionally from the strata.
- **Systematic** — Choose every k^{th} element from the population.
- **Cluster** — Separate the sampling units into groups (i.e., clusters) and sample all elements in the cluster. In the census the sampling units may be separated into clusters such as blocks and then every family in the block is sampled.
- **Convenience** — Use available sources of information.

Descriptive Statistics

There are two primary types of statistics:

1) Measures of central tendency
2) Measures of dispersion or scatter

Measures of Central Tendency

Measures of central tendency try in various ways to measure the center or middle of the data set. In the text that follows, values of the quantitative response variable are denoted by $x_1, x_2, \cdots, x_n$ from a sample of n measurements.

The *sample mean* $\bar{x}$ denotes the arithmetic mean of the n observations and is defined as

$$\bar{x} = \sum_{i=1}^{n} \frac{x_i}{n}.$$

- *Sample averages* describe the population well provided there are no excessively influential observations: Counterexample: family weights.

- The *sample mode* is the value of the sample that occurs most frequently. This is the most likely value to occur. Sometimes multiple modes appear and require special interpretation.

- The *sample median* is the middle of the sample when the values have been arranged in *ascending order*. If the sample size is odd then the median is unique, otherwise it is the average of the two middle observations. The sample median is not heavily influenced by an extreme observation, as we shall see later.

The following sample consists of the daily volume in gallons of Unleaded Plus sold by a Diamond Shamrock service station on nine days in July:

781 785 694 775 838 682 761 975 964

$$\bar{x} = \sum_{i=1}^{n} \frac{x_i}{n} = \frac{781 + 785 + \cdots + 964}{9} = 806.111.$$

The sample mode: The nine values occur with the same frequency. Some authors would say that these data exhibit no modal value, whereas others would say that they have 9 modes.

Notice that knowledge of the daily sales would help the company manage inventory and plan its delivery schedule. In Texas, gasoline trucks carry a maximum of 10,000 gallons typically separated into three 3 compartments, one containing 5,000 gallons and two containing 2,500. So based on the average use of 806.111 gallons per day by this station, a delivery of 2,500 gallons would be needed every three days.

FIGURE 3: Delivery and Inventory Scheduling

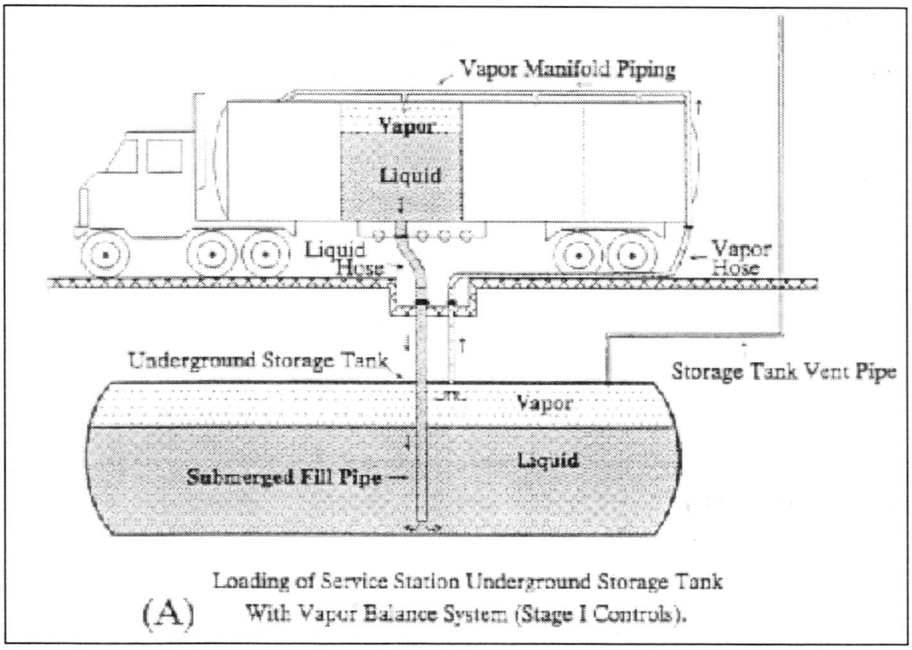

http://www.epa.state.oh.us/dapc/images/stage1.gif

To calculate the sample median, $\tilde{x}$, place the data in ascending order. Once the values are ordered, they are called the ordered statistics and denote them with subscripts around the parentheses by: $x_{(1)}, x_{(2)}, \cdots, x_{(n)}$:

<u>682</u> <u>694</u> <u>761</u> <u>775</u> 781 <u>785</u> <u>838</u> <u>964</u> <u>975</u>

$$x_{(1)} = 682, x_{(2)} = 694, x_{(3)} = 761,$$
$$x_{(4)} = 775, x_{(5)} = 781, x_{(6)} = 785,$$
$$x_{(7)} = 838, x_{(8)} = 964, x_{(9)} = 975$$

Notice that the fifth number when the data are placed in ascending order is the sample median. The *"order number"* of the *median* is denoted by

$$\frac{n+1}{2} = \frac{9+1}{2} = 5.$$

Since $n = 9$, then the order number of the median is 5.

$$\tilde{x} = x_{(5)} = 781.$$

Measures of Dispersion

Measures of dispersion attempt in various ways to quantify the spread or scatter in the values of the response variable for a particular sample.

The simplest measure of dispersion is the sample range, R, which is the difference between the largest and smallest values in the sample.

$$R = x_{(n)} - x_{(1)}$$

For the volumes of Unleaded Plus, we have that

$$\begin{aligned} R &= x_{(9)} - x_{(1)} \\ &= 975 - 682 \\ &= 293 \end{aligned}$$

A more common but more complicated measure of dispersion is given by the sample standard deviation, which is derived from the formula for the sample variance.

The sample variance is denoted by s^2 and given by

$$s^2 = \sum_{i=1}^{n} \frac{(x_i - \bar{x})^2}{n-1}.$$

To calculate s^2 by hand use the following columns from Table 5.

TABLE 5: Computations for the Sample Variance

i	x_i	$x_i - \bar{x}$	$(x_i - \bar{x})^2$
1	781	-25.111	630.562
2	785	-21.111	445.674
3	694	-112.111	12,568.876
4	775	-31.111	967.894
5	838	31.889	1,016.908
6	682	-124.111	15,403.540
7	761	-45.111	2,035.002
8	975	168.889	28,523.494
9	964	157.889	24,928.936
Total		0.000	86,520.889

The sample variance, s^2, is given by

$$s^2 = \frac{86{,}520.889}{8} = 10{,}815.111$$

The sample standard deviation s is then found by taking the principal square root of the sample variance:

$$s = \sqrt{\frac{86{,}520.889}{8}} = \sqrt{10{,}815.111} = 103.996.$$

Notice that sample values near $\bar{x}$ produce a smaller contribution to s^2 than do the extreme values of the sample. The contribution is magnified by the fact the difference is squared. From Table 5, the contribution to s^2 made by 785 is:

$$\frac{(785 - 806.111)^2}{9-1} = \frac{(-21.111)^2}{8} = \frac{445.674}{8} = 55.709$$

whereas the contribution made by 975 is:

$$\frac{(975 - 806.111)^2}{9-1} = \frac{(168.889)^2}{8} = \frac{28{,}523.494}{8} = 3{,}565.437$$

Thus extreme values make a larger contribution than central values and in this way the statistic measures scatter or dispersion in the data.

Why do we compute descriptive statistics? What do they mean?

"The goal of Statistics is to make meaningful inferences about values of population parameters based upon descriptive statistics calculated from representative samples."

Consider the grades of two students, who completed this course with an average grade of 73.5. The first student made grades of 92, 96, 94, and 12, whereas the latter student made grades of 72, 73, 74, and 75. The inference that the teacher makes is the assignment of final grades. Should both students receive the same grade in the class?

If we use the sample average as a designated measure of central tendency, then both students will receive "C's." If we use the *sample median* as a designated measure of central tendency, the first student will have a computed grade of 93.0 and an "A" in the course but the latter student will still have a median grade of

73.5 and will receive a "C" in the course. Before you jump on the bandwagon to campaign that all grades be computed based upon the *sample median*, remember the advice of Gloria Estefan:

"It cuts both ways."

To illustrate this duality, consider the procrastinating student with grades of 60, 69, 65, and 100. This person's sample average grade is 73.5 but the median grade is 67. If we used the median grading system the last student would receive the grade of "D." Notice that this student would have a median grade of "D" regardless of the outcome of his or her final grade.

We use the grades of these students to illustrate the necessity of other statistical measures, such as the scatter in the collected data. The statistician continues this pursuit of better descriptive statistics from the data through the technique of graphing.

Case Study: Electrical Power Consumption at the Consumer Level

The data in the Table 6 below represent the amount of electricity that we used in each month since 1983. We have lived in the same house since July 1982 and I have retained all of our electrical bills over that period.

TABLE 6: Electrical Use per Day by Month and Year

KWh	Y98	Y97	Y96	Y95	Y94	Y93	Y92	Y91	Y90	Y89	Y88	Y87	Y86	Y85	Y84	Y83
JAN	37.00	49.45	45.42	44.22	45.59	50.67	52.23	56.33	42.93	42.23	56.68	46.63	42.85	55.21	55.90	44.50
FEB	37.03	49.69	40.46	39.03	39.28	38.66	39.66	45.62	37.94	55.42	43.81	38.28	47.03	48.28	42.25	41.40
MAR	32.48	29.55	35.86	33.48	29.66	30.48	31.39	32.96	32.55	38.90	29.38	30.58	30.48	26.48	25.52	33.38
APR	29.67	30.75	26.93	28.38	24.87	24.43	30.00	30.24	30.17	37.93	30.63	32.33	33.09	28.19	30.59	26.81
MAY	46.91	35.16	36.82	40.03	38.03	35.09	34.03	37.90	42.83	49.48	38.83	35.67	37.67	37.27	40.43	27.90
JUN	62.36	50.54	53.27	50.79	55.10	47.62	49.65	52.10	63.09	59.16	41.88	44.35	44.66	49.43	48.93	38.93
JUL	66.13	65.63	58.83	54.40	57.83	64.60	57.13	53.59	53.50	57.23	63.47	48.53	59.30	54.39	52.72	45.09
AUG	50.41	52.55	52.32	55.87	54.97	59.00	52.86	51.34	63.72	49.45	60.10	59.93	48.64	55.93	47.72	50.73
SEP	45.71	51.03	40.53	47.97	40.43	47.53	45.66	46.33	49.28	50.16	51.69	46.87	40.07	51.03	42.80	41.77
OCT	27.66	33.55	23.79	33.17	34.76	32.86	28.10	33.21	39.28	36.72	34.38	25.90	41.72	31.38	27.69	30.68
NOV	19.91	30.90	23.10	27.73	24.67	34.45	28.93	39.65	26.65	27.97	28.45	28.24	28.31	29.84	27.91	29.52
DEC	34.80	33.13	39.86	42.50	34.20	36.07	45.60	32.20	46.61	61.10	38.37	32.26	33.65	39.19	30.90	56.82

Can you see patterns in these data based on the descriptive statistics? The mass of numbers makes this almost impossible. Try plotting the sample average by month. Plot the sample average by year. What did you find? How does the electrical use follow seasonal temperature variation? Do we have air conditioning? How do we heat our home in the winter? When we would go on vacation? You can answer all of these questions by cross-examining the data in different ways. Check out the answers in the answers at the back!

Statistical Graphing

A frequency histogram is a plot of the number of occurrences of the values of a response variable over a given interval. If the random (or response variable) is discrete then the plot of the number of occurrences against the discrete value of the response variable is called a frequency chart.

Example: How many siblings do you have? In this case, the response variable, X, is the number of siblings and the response is discrete.

In another class, I asked for this response and the results were:

6 persons came from families with 0 siblings,
30 persons came from families with 1 sibling,
31 persons from families with 2 siblings,
15 persons came from families with 3 siblings,
6 persons came from families with 4 siblings,
4 persons came from families with 5 siblings,
2 persons from families with 6 siblings,
2 persons from families with 7 siblings,
2 persons from families with 8 siblings, and
1 person came from a family with 10 siblings.

Let X = # of siblings and Y = # of persons with X siblings.

X	0	1	2	3	4	5	6	7	8	9	10
Y	6	30	31	15	6	4	2	2	2	0	1

FIGURE 4: Histogram of the Number of Siblings

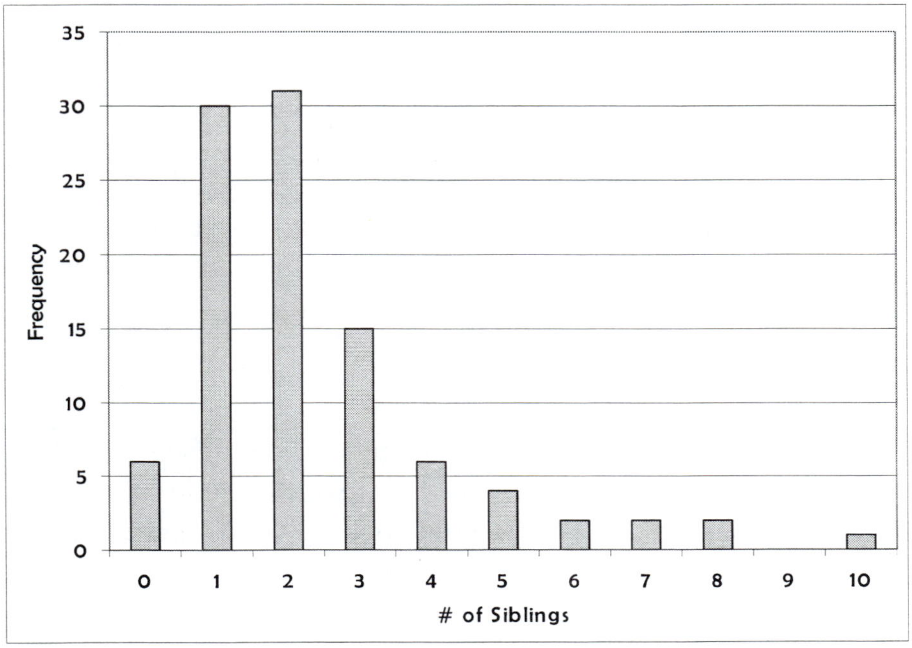

However, for some data we would not have much of picture to look at if we simply used the frequency chart. If we use individual GPA as the response variable, we would not anticipate that many persons have the same GPA due to the facts that numbers of semester credit hours differ by students and the courses have different weights according to the number of credit hours per course. To obtain a better picture we separate the data into intervals called classes, which have a fixed width. The statistics community is divided on how to graph the data (i.e., determine the class width and the beginning of the graph). Graphs vary considerably depending upon one's choices of class width and starting point.

Frequency Polygons

We use a method developed by David Scott of Rice University in his article "Frequency Polygons: Theory and Application," Journal of the American Statistical Association, **80**, 348-354 (1984). In this approach, Scott suggests:

1) starting at some arbitrarily chosen starting point, such as "0" and

2) develop a fixed class width, w, that is a function of the value of the sample standard deviation, s, and the sample size, n, from one of the two choices below.

- $$w_1 = \frac{2.15 \times s}{n^{1/5}}$$
  This width is best whenever one is concerned about fitting the tails of the distribution

- $$w_2 = \frac{3.49 \times s}{n^{1/3}}$$
  This width is best whenever one is trying to identify the mode(s) of the distribution

The constants given here are not arbitrary but are rather obtained through an optimality known as maximizing the goodness of fit. In particular, notice that

$$3.49083 \approx 2 \times 3^{1/3} \pi^{1/6}.$$

For most of the data sets that we encounter, we will see little differences in the polygons obtained by using the first or second width. However, we will introduce a method that will combine two polygons and the combined polygons formed by using either method will differ very little.

We use the frequency polygon in the following way.

1) Separate the data into classes determined by w
   (i.e., 0 to w, w to $2\times w$, $2\times w$ to $3\times w$, etc.)
2) Count the number, f_i, of occurrences
   (known as the class frequency) in each class
3) Plot the number of occurrences, f_i, against the
   midpoint, m_i, of the interval or class
4) Connect the adjacent pairs of points to form the
   vertices of the frequency polygon

Example: The following data are scores on an introductory Statistics test by fifty-nine students in 1987. We can computer descriptive statistics but a graph might better convey the information contained in the data.

TABLE 7: Student Grades on First Statistics Exam (1987)

86	87	78	66	62	66	72	74	54	71	82	62
93	98	56	80	80	87	77	70	87	51	60	85
97	80	86	82	93	63	76	81	81	43	45	70
62	87	89	63	65	68	91	43	68	78	74	82
88	44	76	85	100	81	79	93	67	91	82	

The average score on this exam was $\bar{x} = 75.2$ with a standard deviation of $s = 14.22$. The median class score is $\tilde{x} = 79$. Using Scott's method of drawing frequency polygons, we calculate the class width as:

$$
\begin{aligned}
w &= \frac{2.15\times s}{n^{1/5}} \\
&= \frac{2.15\times 14.22}{59^{1/5}} \\
&= 13.53
\end{aligned}
$$

Intervals Widths and Starting Points

Using this width of 13.53 and starting at zero, we produce the following table with the beginning, ending and mid points, and the frequencies of the class intervals. Recall that we move in fixed intervals of 13.53 and we must continue until we have counted all the data. Mandatory rules require that we begin our bins at least one width less than the minimum value and continue to produce intervals, until our last interval begins at least one width after the maximum value in the sample.

See Scott's frequency polygon in Figure 5 below. Notice that we use b_i to denote the beginning value of the ith interval, e_i to denote the ending value of the ith interval, m_i to denote the midpoint of the ith interval and f_i to denote the frequency of the ith interval.

TABLE 8: Beginning, Ending, and Mid Points and Frequencies for Grade Data

Beginning b_i	Ending e_i	Midpoint m_i	Frequency f_i
0.00	13.53	6.765	0
13.53	27.06	20.295	0
27.06	40.59	33.285	0
40.59	54.12	47.355	6
54.12	67.65	60.885	11
67.65	81.18	74.415	20
81.18	94.71	87.945	19
94.71	108.24	101.475	3
108.24	121.77	115.005	0

This method is an excellent one for most data sets because we let the data determine the size of the interval rather than a subjective choice.

FIGURE 5: Scott's Frequency Polygon for Grades with a Zero Starting Point

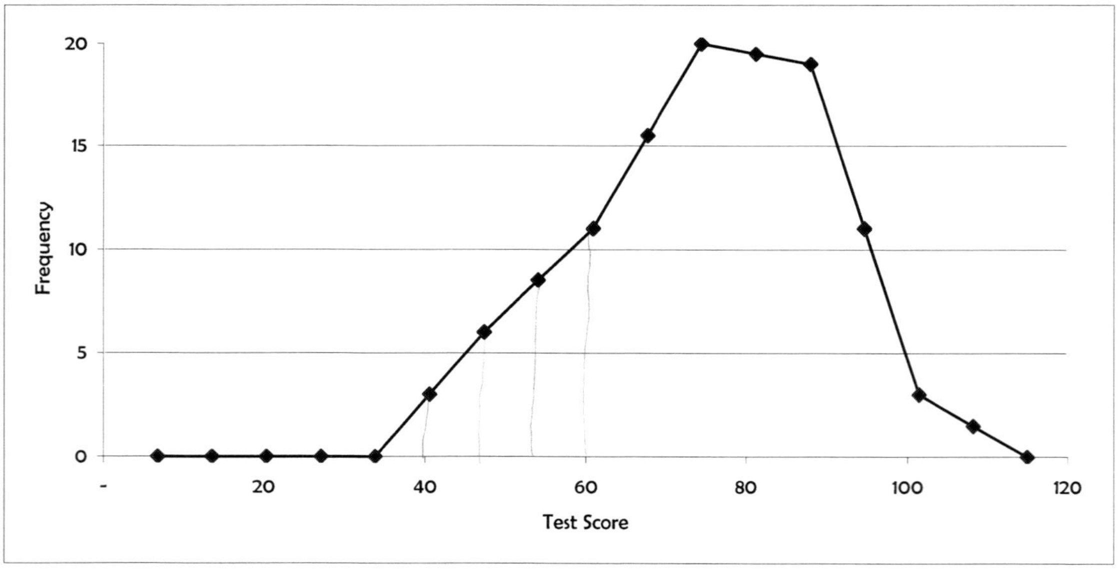

One can also average several of these frequency polygons with starting points between 0 and 13.53. The resultant average graph will no longer be sensitive to the chosen starting point.

TABLE 8a: Beginning, Ending, and Mid Points and Frequencies for Grade Data Starting at 6.765

Beginning b_i	Ending e_i	Midpoint m_i	Frequency f_i
6.765	20.295	13.53	0
20.295	33.285	27.06	0
33.285	47.355	40.59	4
47.355	60.885	54.12	4
60.885	74.415	67.65	17
74.415	87.945	81.18	24
87.945	101.475	94.71	10
101.475	115.005	108.24	0

In the Figure 5a, we started our graph not at 6.765, the midpoint of the first interval of the preceding Scott's polygon. This second graph produces a decidedly different picture. These differences illustrate the effect of the starting point on the actual frequency polygon. To remove the effect of the starting point let's average the two graphs and view the outcome.

FIGURE 5a: Scott's Frequency Polygon for Grades with a 6.765 Starting Point

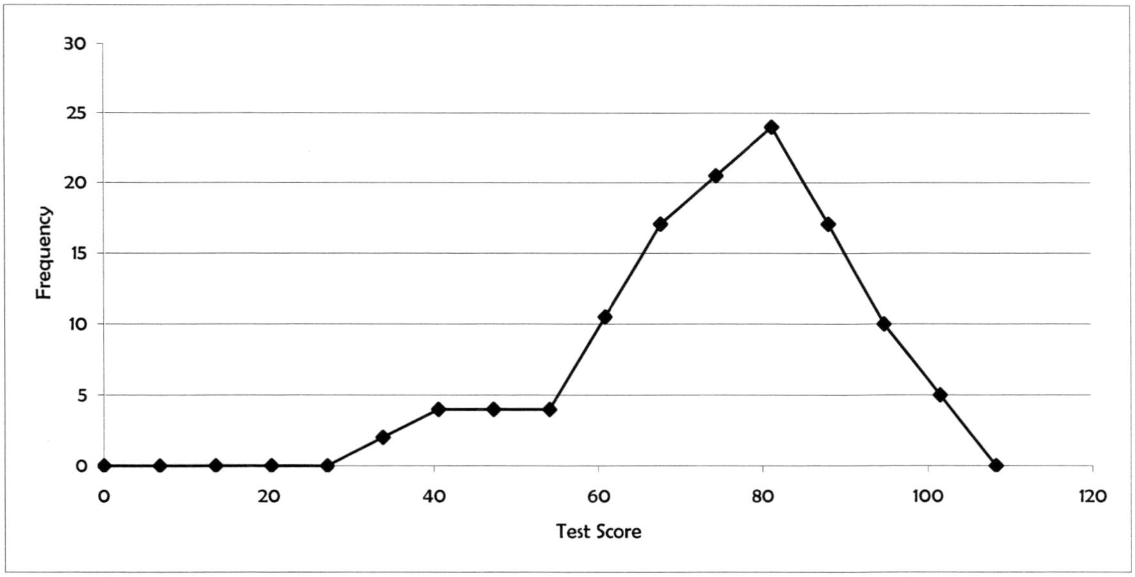

We obtain a more accurate graph by averaging the two graphs or polygons. We produce a polygon that is smoother and less sensitive to the starting point. In doing so, we address the practitioner's second concern of the subjective choice of a starting point.

In Table 9, look at every other row of the first three columns beginning with the first entry. Notice that these are identical to those in Table 8. If one start at 6.765

instead of zero as in Table 8a, he or she will produce a table that consists of every other row in Table 9 beginning with the second row. The intermediate values are obtained by averaging or interpolating within the table for each of the two tables. By starting the second table at the midpoint of the first interval, the midpoints of the first table become the endpoints of the second table and vice versa.

TABLE 9: Intervals and Frequencies for Combining Polygons

b_i	e_i	m_i	$f_i(1)$	$f_i(2)$	$\bar{f}_i$	b_i	e_i	m_i	$f_i(1)$	$f_i(2)$	$\bar{f}_i$
0.00	13.53	6.77	**0**		0.00	60.89	74.42	67.65	15.5	**17**	16.25
6.77	20.30	13.53	0.0	**0**	0.00	67.65	81.18	74.42	**20**	20.5	20.25
13.53	27.06	20.30	**0**	0.0	0.00	74.42	87.95	81.18	19.5	**24**	21.75
20.30	33.83	27.06	0.0	**0**	0.00	81.18	94.71	87.95	**19**	17.0	18.00
27.06	40.59	33.83	**0**	2.0	1.00	87.95	101.48	94.71	11.0	**10**	10.50
33.83	47.36	40.59	3.0	**4**	3.50	94.71	108.24	101.48	**3**	5.0	4.00
40.59	54.12	47.36	**6**	4.0	5.00	101.48	115.01	108.24	1.5	**0**	0.75
47.36	60.89	54.12	8.5	**4**	6.25	108.24	121.77	115.01	**0**	0.0	0.00
54.12	67.65	60.89	**11**	10.5	10.75						

The actual counts are boldfaced, shaded in gray, and given in whole numbers without decimals. The interpolated or average frequencies are shown with decimals. The last column is obtained by averaging the frequencies of the first two graphs. The final graph is dubbed an averaged shifted histogram (ASH) or an averaged shifted frequency polygon. The term shifted is used to denote that we shifted the starting point of our bins but kept the same bin width throughout. We averaged the interpolated frequencies and by so doing produced a graph that has smoother characteristics than either of the two polygons with which we started.

Notice that the two polygons formed by starting first at zero and then at 6.765 differ considerably in appearance. When students see such differences they know that the graphing process is subject to much variability. In this case we only change the starting points. The combined graph is said to be "robust" to the starting point. By the term robust we mean that we tend to produce similar results (in this case a graph) regardless of where we start as long as we use the two-stage procedure. Notice that the combined polygon actually captures features of both individual polygons. Notice that in the combined graph a prominent mode begins to appear. The graph is clearly skewed to the left. Try this method but start one polygon at 10 and another at 16.765.

Truth in Advertisement

Notice that the method is imperfect in this case because natural bounds of 0 and 100 exist for the test scores. These graphs tend to average or round off the curve, see Silverman (1986) for details. One can modify the procedure via transformation to remove this complication but it is essential to mention this shortcoming.

FIGURE 6: Combined Frequency Polygon for Grades with Starts of 0 and 6.765

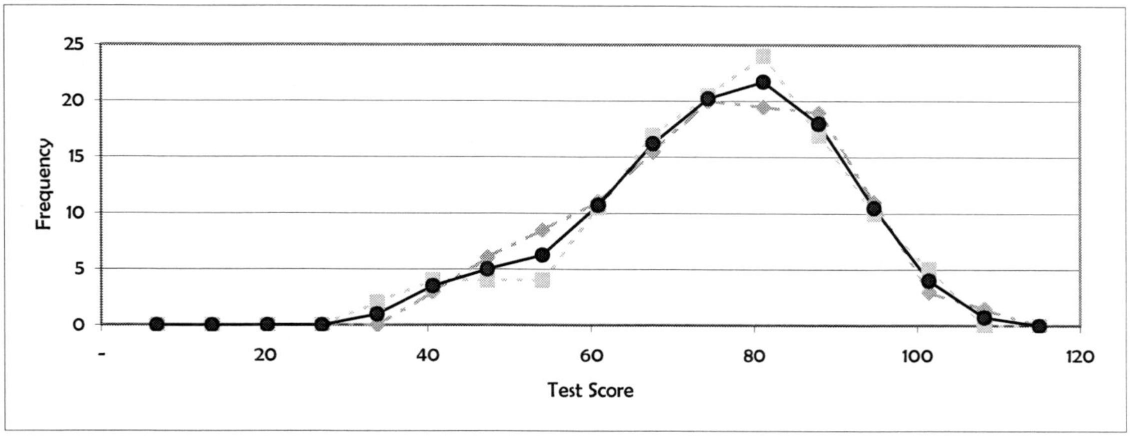

Case Study: Describing Toxicity Levels

The following data are the cadmium concentrations found in the livers of 57 starlings found in the Monk Woods** in the United Kingdom. See Sparks (2000).

0.79	1.35	1.47	1.89	1.95	1.95	2.02	2.08	2.13	2.27	2.30	2.41
2.45	2.46	2.53	2.56	2.56	2.73	2.78	2.82	2.91	2.93	2.93	3.05
3.06	3.30	3.39	3.45	3.45	3.49	3.56	3.59	3.73	3.76	4.09	4.17
4.28	4.37	4.40	4.55	4.62	4.81	4.82	4.93	5.12	5.16	5.31	5.58
5.92	6.06	6.10	6.62	7.29	7.39	8.12	9.23	11.38			

** Monk Woods is a collection of ancient woodlands, cloaking both sides of a hidden valley in Avon.

The intent of this assay is the determination of the distribution of ingested cadmium resident in the livers of the starlings. Now let's use the second width-see Wand (1997).

$$w = \frac{3.49 \times s}{n^{1/3}} = \frac{3.49 \times 2.0237}{57^{1/3}} = 1.8352$$

The distribution of Cadmium concentrations or levels in these starlings would give us a profile of Cadmium levels in the species. We could determine the magnitude of the toxicity in the species and whether a significant environmental problem existed. In business, we would be concerned about this situation if we were putting Cadmium into a factory effluent, which then migrated into the ecosystem of this species. Using the Scott's process, we form intervals of width w beginning at some fixed starting point. In this case, we choose to start at –1.8352 and the reason for this negative choice is based on the proximity of the data to zero. In Table 10, we provide the beginning, mid, and ending points of intervals in column 1 and associated frequencies in column 2. In column 4 we attach frequency to the endpoints by averaging the adjacent midpoints. This process is appropriate since part 4 of Scott's process draws straight lines connecting the adjacent frequencies plotted against their corresponding midpoints.

TABLE 10: Intervals and Frequencies for Cadmium Levels Starting at –1.8352

Cadmium Level	f-1		Cadmium Level	Interpol f-1
-1.8352			-1.8352	0.0
-0.9176	0		-0.9176	0.0
0.0000			0.0000	1.5
0.9176	3		0.9176	3.0
1.8352			1.8352	16.0
2.7528	29		2.7528	29.0
3.6705			3.6705	22.0
4.5881	15		4.5881	15.0
5.5057			5.5057	10.5
6.4233	6		6.4233	6.0
7.3409			7.3409	4.0
8.2585	2		8.2585	2.0
9.1761			9.1761	1.5
10.0938	1		10.0938	1.0
11.0114			11.0114	1.0
11.9290	1		11.9290	1.0
12.8466			12.8466	0.5
13.7642	0		13.7642	0.0
14.6818			14.6818	0.0

From this set of intervals and frequencies we draw a graph of the frequency polygon. This frequency polygon is sensitive to the arbitrarily chosen starting point of –1.8352. To obtain a different perspective, let us repeat this process but start at -.9176 and move over in increments of 1.8352. We shift the bins by one-half the width of the interval. From this set of intervals and frequencies we can draw another graph of the frequency polygon. This frequency polygon is sensitive to the chosen starting point: -.9176. Notice that in the interpolated graphs, the x – coordinates are perfectly aligned from Tables 10 and 11 because we chose to shift the bins by one-half the width of the interval. In this way the endpoints of Table 10 become the midpoints of Table 11 and vice versa.

TABLE 11: Intervals and Frequencies for Cadmium Levels Starting at –0.9176

Cadmium Level	f-2	Cadmium Level	Interpol f-2	Cadmium Level	f-2	Cadmium Level	Interpol f-2
-0.9176		-0.9176	0.0	7.3409	**4**	7.3409	4.0
0.0000	**1**	0.0000	1.0	8.2585		8.2585	2.5
0.9176		0.9176	9.0	9.1761	**1**	9.1761	1.0
1.8352	**17**	1.8352	17.0	10.0938		10.0938	1.0
2.7528		2.7528	19.5	11.0114	**1**	11.0114	1.0
3.6705	**22**	3.6705	22.0	11.9290		11.9290	0.5
4.5881		4.5881	16.5	12.8466	**0**	12.8466	0.0
5.5057	**11**	5.5057	11.0	13.7642		13.7642	0.0
6.4233		6.4233	7.5	14.6818	**0**	14.6818	0.0

We can average the effect of these different starting points by averaging the frequencies at each of the x – coordinates. So in Table 12, we form the average in the last column from the interpolated frequencies in the preceding columns.

TABLE 12: Intervals and Frequencies for Scott's Polygon for Cadmium Levels

Cadmium Level	**Interpol. f-1**	**Interpol. f-2**	**Average frequency**
-0.9176	0.0	0.0	0.00
0.0000	1.5	1.0	1.25
0.9176	3.0	9.0	6.00
1.8352	16.0	17.0	16.50
2.7528	29.0	19.5	24.25
3.6705	22.0	22.0	22.00
4.5881	15.0	16.5	15.75
5.5057	10.5	11.0	10.75
6.4233	6.0	7.5	6.75
7.3409	4.0	4.0	4.00
8.2585	2.0	2.5	2.25
9.1761	1.5	1.0	1.25
10.0938	1.0	1.0	1.00
11.0114	1.0	1.0	1.00
11.9290	1.0	0.5	0.75
12.8466	0.5	0.0	0.25
13.7642	0.0	0.0	0.00
14.6818	0.0	0.0	0.00

These data can be found in "Statistics in Ecotoxicology." The combined graph is not sensitive to the natural lower bound of zero. The smoothed graph known as an averaged shifted histogram (ASH) produces a frequency polygon that is much less sensitive to the starting point. One could continue this process repeatedly and develop an even smoother curve.

FIGURE 7: Averaged Shift Histogram (ASH) of the Cadmium Levels

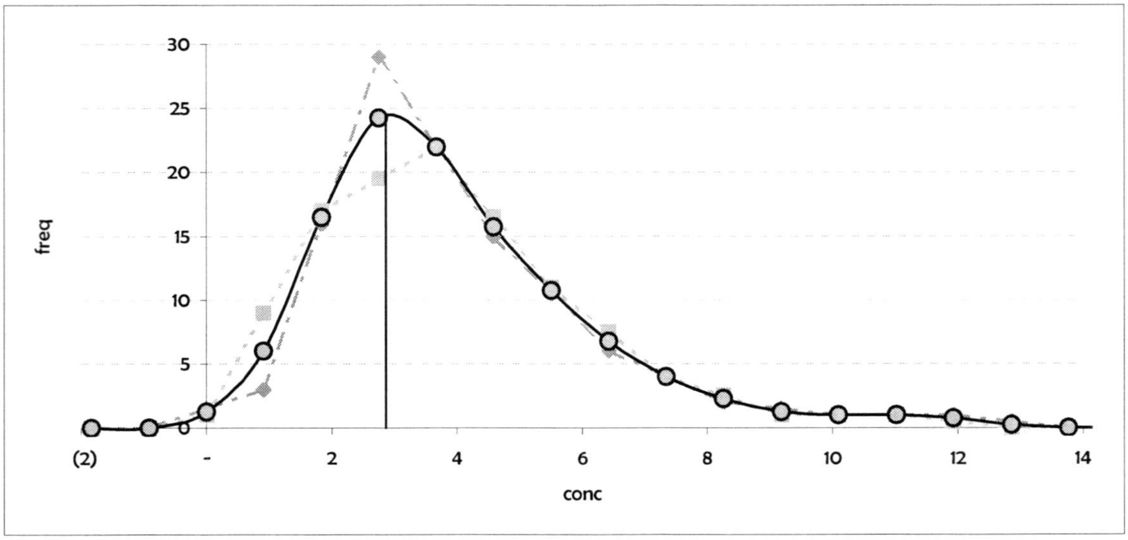

Mitchell Lake in southern Bexar County was once a sewage dump for San Antonio. It is one of the most important bird sanctuaries in Texas because migratory birds and insects (such as the Monarch butterfly) use this spot as a resting place on their journeys from as far north as Canada to Mexico. If we knew the toxicity of cadmium in Starlings then we could clearly see that part of the distribution of Starlings that would be in danger. The mode has also been depicted and we can see that the distribution tends to have a long right tail just as the distribution of grades tended to have a longer left tail.

Case Study: Quality Control Piston Rings

The data in Table 13 are taken from Montgomery (2001) and represents 125 inner diameters in mm of forged piston rings used in automobile engines. The data were collected in 25 random samples of five observations each. The large amount of data makes it very difficult to detect any patterns in the data so we will attempt the Scott's frequency polygon method as a means to display the distribution of these data. In this case let's use the width suggested by Marcel Wand (1997) so that

$$\begin{aligned} w &= \frac{3.49 \times s}{n^{1/3}} \\ &= \frac{3.49 \times 0.010007}{125^{1/3}} \\ &= \frac{3.49 \times 0.010007}{5} = 0.0070288 \end{aligned}$$

Notice that the width of the interval is extremely small because the data are highly concentrated about 74mm, which was the design size of the inner diameter. We would hope that the inner diameters of the forged piston rings fall within acceptable bounds for the engines in which they will be used. If we proceed as before but start at 73.9505, we produce Table 14 for the polygon.

TABLE 13: Inner Diameters of Forged Piston Rings

Sample	Item-1	Item-2	Item-3	Item-4	Item-5	s-ave	Sample	Item-1	Item-2	Item-3	Item-4	Item-5	s-ave
1	74.030	74.002	74.019	73.992	74.008	74.010	**14**	74.006	73.967	73.994	74.000	73.984	73.990
2	73.995	73.992	74.001	74.011	74.004	74.001	**15**	74.012	74.014	73.998	73.999	74.007	74.006
3	73.988	74.024	74.021	74.005	74.002	74.008	**16**	74.000	73.984	74.005	73.998	73.996	73.997
4	74.002	73.996	73.993	74.015	74.009	74.003	**17**	73.994	74.012	73.986	74.005	74.007	74.001
5	73.992	74.007	74.015	73.989	74.014	74.003	**18**	74.006	74.010	74.018	74.003	74.000	74.007
6	74.009	73.994	73.997	73.985	73.993	73.996	**19**	73.984	74.002	74.003	74.005	73.997	73.998
7	73.995	74.006	73.994	74.000	74.005	74.000	**20**	74.000	74.010	74.013	74.020	74.003	74.009
8	73.985	74.003	73.993	74.015	73.988	73.997	**21**	73.988	74.001	74.009	74.005	73.996	74.000
9	74.008	73.995	74.009	74.005	74.004	74.004	**22**	74.004	73.999	73.990	74.006	74.009	74.002
10	73.998	74.000	73.990	74.007	73.995	73.998	**23**	74.010	73.989	73.990	74.009	74.014	74.002
11	73.994	73.998	73.994	73.995	73.990	73.994	**24**	74.015	74.008	73.993	74.000	74.010	74.005
12	74.004	74.000	74.007	74.000	73.996	74.001	**25**	73.982	73.984	73.995	74.017	74.013	73.998
13	73.983	74.002	73.998	73.997	74.012	73.998							

TABLE 14: Intervals and Frequencies for the ASH of Inner Diameters

Width (mm)	*Interpol f-2*	*Interpol. f-1*	*Average*	*Width (mm)*	*Interpol f-2*	*Interpol. f-1*	*Average*
73.9505	0.00	0.00	0	73.9962	30.00	28.50	29.25
73.9541	0.00	0.00	0	73.9997	32.50	30.00	31.25
73.9576	0.00	0.00	0	74.0033	35.00	31.50	33.25
73.9611	0.00	0.50	0.25	74.0068	29.50	33.00	31.25
73.9646	0.50	1.00	0.75	74.0103	24.00	23.50	23.75
73.9681	1.00	0.50	0.75	74.0138	17.50	14.00	15.75
73.9716	0.50	0.00	0.25	74.0173	11.00	9.50	10.25
73.9751	0.00	0.50	0.25	74.0208	6.50	5.00	5.75
73.9787	4.00	1.00	2.5	74.0243	2.00	3.00	2.5
73.9822	8.00	7.00	7.5	74.0279	1.50	1.00	1.25
73.9857	10.50	13.00	11.75	74.0314	1.00	0.50	0.75
73.9892	13.00	20.00	16.5	74.0349	0.50	0.00	0.25
73.9927	21.50	27.00	24.25	74.0384	0.00	0.00	0

As one can see from the Figure 8, the inner diameters are not symmetrically distributed about the design value of 74 mm and are slightly skewed to the left. There also appear to be some forged piston rings with abnormally small inner diameters. If we knew the design tolerances for the inner diameters then we could assess the proportion of non-conforming piston rings.

FIGURE 8: Averaged Shift Histogram (ASH) of Inner Diameters

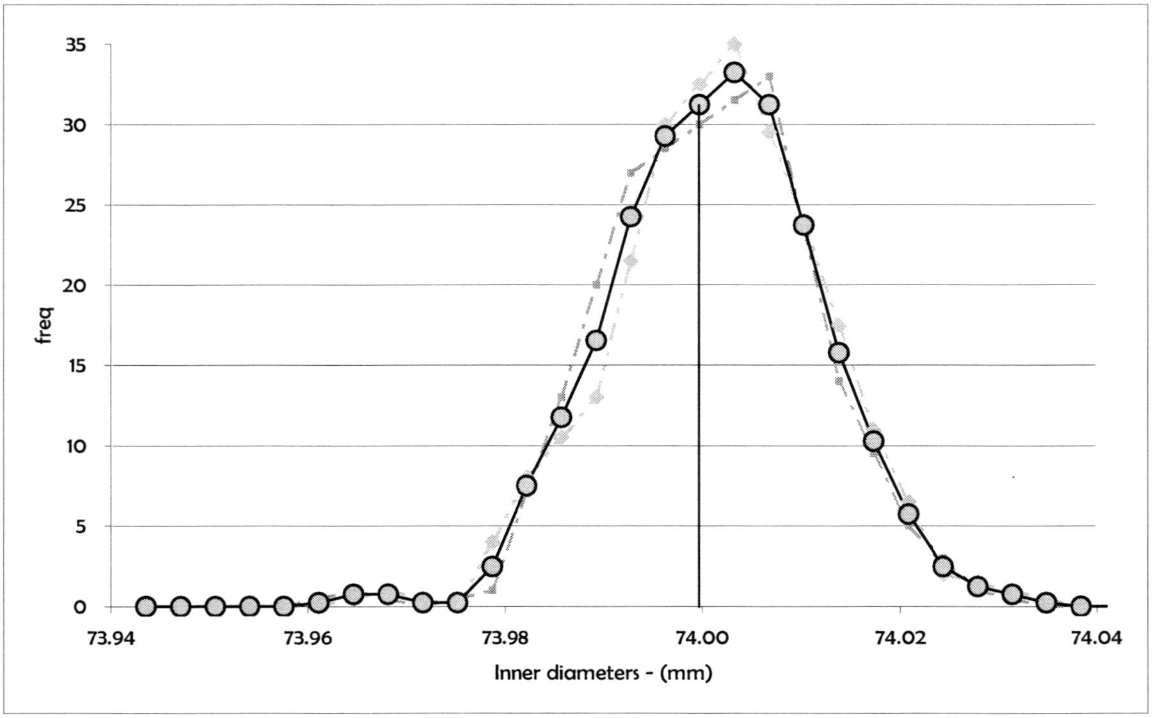

Dot Diagrams

The student grades, see Table 7, are plotted as circles along the grade axis in Figure 9. The multiple observations are plotted atop one another to indicate the frequency with which a particular temperature occurred. This linear graph known as a dot-diagram conveys our first look at the data in graphical form. The dot-diagram is quite similar to the frequency histogram and herein we notice that our graph does not suggest patterns as well as it did for the sibling data set.

FIGURE 9: Dot Diagram of Student Grades

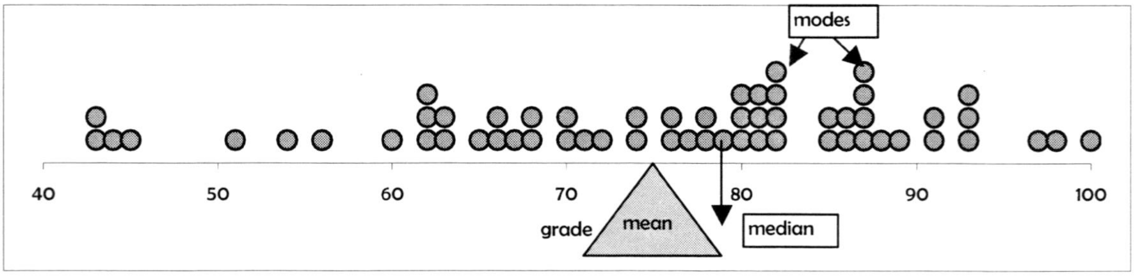

Notice that the sample mean has a physical interpretation as the center of mass of the data assuming that each observation has the same mass. The sample mean is the position on the horizontal axis where the base of a fulcrum would leave the axis balanced or in equilibrium. The sample median is similar to the scales of justice so that we center in such a way that the same number of observations lie to its right and left.

The modes in the dot diagram appear to be numerous. Remember that a sample is a snapshot of a population. So in this particular snapshot the primary modes appear at 82 and 87. The second most frequently occurring values, or secondary modes, occur at 62, 80, 81, and 93. We can continue and enumerate the tertiary modes at 43, 63, 66, 74, 76, 78, 85, 86, and 91. The multiplicity of these values and their placement along the axis reflect sample specific phenomena that may or may not accurately reflect the population. From the frequency polygon method we conjecture that the data are unimodal and that the population mode is estimated to be 81.18 or about 81.

FIGURE 6-Revisited: Combined Frequency Polygon for Grades

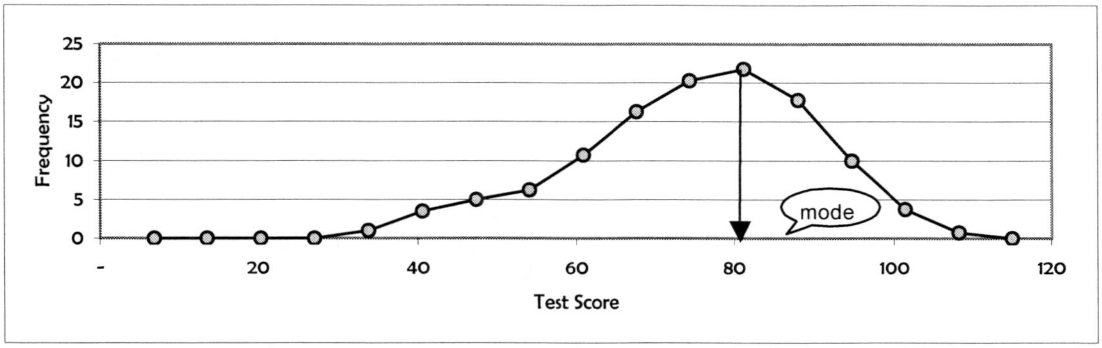

Stem and Leaf Plots

The stem and leaf plot, which was developed by John Tukey in his 1977 ground breaking book Exploratory Data Analysis, is a special case of the frequency polygon approach in which, the width, w, and the beginning points are chosen arbitrarily.

Example:

Reconsider the student grades in which 59 students took an exam in 1987. Order the scores so that the tens place becomes the stem and the units place becomes the leaf. The leaves are listed next to the stem in ascending order in Table 15 below.

TABLE 15: Stem and Leaf Plot for Student Grades

Grades	
40	3 3 4 5
50	1 4 6
60	0 2 2 2 3 3 5 6 6 7 8 8
70	0 0 1 2 4 4 6 6 7 8 8 9
80	0 0 0 1 1 1 2 2 2 2 5 5 6 6 7 7 7 7 8 9
90	1 1 3 3 3 7 8
100	0

While the direct method of Tukey may seem common sense today, it was a bold step to take thirty years ago. Most of the suggestions of these esteemed statisticians, Mosteller and Tukey (1968), would have been dismissed as rubbish, if persons of lesser academic caliber submitted it. Exploratory data analysis is a critical turning point in the discipline of statistics, as the discipline began to separate from mathematics and forge its own identity. A great need was surfacing in economics, psychology, marketing, and management; the need was spurred by the use of computers. Such exploratory methods were unthinkable without modern-day computing. Imagine the complexity of finding the standard deviation of a set of one thousand data points. Yet census figures consisted of millions of records.

For the grading example, notice that the frequency becomes the number of leaves, the width is ten and the beginning value is 39.5. If we transpose this graph, we obtain a plot in Figure 10 like our frequency histogram or polygon plot.

FIGURE 10: Transposed Stem and Leaf Plot for Student Grades

	40	50	60	70	80	90	100
20					9		
					8		
					7		
					7		
					7		
15					7		
					6		
					6		
			8	9	5		
			8	8	5		
10			7	8	2		
			6	7	2		
			6	6	2		
			5	6	2	1	
			3	4	1	1	
5			3	4	1	3	
	5		2	2	1	3	
	4	6	2	1	0	3	
	3	4	2	0	0	7	
	3	1	0	0	0	8	0
Grades	**40**	**50**	**60**	**70**	**80**	**90**	**100**

Example

Reconsider the gasoline sales of super-unleaded gasoline at the Diamond Shamrock service station on Judson Road. Order the sales so that the hundreds place becomes the stem and the last two units become the leaf. The leaves are then listed next to the stem in ascending order in Table 16.

TABLE 16: Stem and Leaf Plot for Unleaded Gas Sales

Sales				
600	82	94		
700	61	75	81	85
800	38			
900	64	75		

Case Study Revisited: Quality Control - Piston Rings

Recall the data that were 125 inner diameters in millimeters (mm) of forged piston rings used in automobile engines. The large amount of data can be condensed by means of a stem and leaf plot. In this case, the stem is reduced to the hundredths place, i.e., 73.96, 73.97, and so on to 73.03. The leaf is the thousandths place in the diameter measurement. We list the last digit here without its preceding decimals in Table 17.

TABLE 17: Stem and Leaf Plot of Inner Diameters of Forged Piston Rings

mm	
73.96	7
73.97	
73.98	2 3 4 4 4 4 5 5 6 8 8 8 9 9
73.99	0 0 0 0 2 2 2 3 3 3 3 4 4 4 4 4 4 5 5 5 5 5 5 6 6 6 6 7 7 7 8 8 8 8 8 9 9
74.00	0 0 0 0 0 0 0 0 0 1 1 2 2 2 2 2 3 3 3 3 4 4 4 4 5 5 5 5 5 5 5 6 6 6 6 7 7 7 7 7 8 8 8 9 9 9 9 9 9
74.01	0 0 0 0 1 2 2 2 3 3 4 4 4 5 5 5 5 7 8 9
74.02	0 1 4
74.03	0

The stem and leaf plot does pick up the striking concentration of the values at about 74.00 mm as designed. We can also detect outliers at both extremes of the data set, one at 73.967 mm and one at 74.030 mm.

Sample Percentile Rankings

When you received your SAT scores in Mathematics a percentile was given next to your score. The percentile indicates your relative rank within the group of persons, who took the exam. For example, if you made a score that produced a 90th percentile ranking then 90% of those persons who took the test made a lower score than you and 10% made a higher score. In general, if we let p denote a probability in question, where $0 < p < 1$, the sample $100 \times p\%$-percentile, x_p, is the number so that $100 \times p\%$ of the sample values were less than x_p and $100 \times (1-p)\%$ of the sample values were greater than the number.

> When $p = 0.50$, we have the sample median, $\tilde{x}$, when $p = 0.25$, we have the first quartile, Q_1, and when $p = 0.75$, we have the third quartile, Q_3, and if p is a multiple of 10%, we produce the sample deciles.

In general the value of the $100 \times p$ percentile, x_p, is determined from the following formula, where p falls between $\frac{i}{n+1}$ and $\frac{i+1}{n+1}$:

SAMPLE PERCENTILE FORMULA

$$x_p = x_{(i)} + [(n+1)p - i] \times [x_{(i+1)} - x_{(i)}]$$

Example: Determine the 78th sample percentile of the gasoline sales.

Notice, that for some integer, i:

$$\frac{i}{n+1} \le p < \frac{i+1}{n+1}$$
$$where \quad i = 1, \cdots, n$$

Since $p = 0.78$ and $n = 9$, then

$$\frac{i}{9+1} \le 0.78 < \frac{i+1}{9+1}$$
$$\frac{i}{10} \le 0.78 < \frac{i+1}{10}$$
$$i \le 7.8 < i+1$$

Thus the 78th percentile, in this case, is located between the 7th and 8th largest values in the sample, which are $x_{(7)} = 838 - and - x_{(8)} = 964$. In Figure 11, one can see geometrically how these proportions were developed.

$$\begin{aligned}
x_p &= x_{(i)} + ((n+1)p - i) \times (x_{(i+1)} - x_{(i)}) \\
x_{0.78} &= x_{(7)} + ((9+1) \times 0.78 - 7) \times (x_{(8)} - x_{(7)}) \\
&= 838 + (7.8 - 7) \times 126 \\
&= 838 + 0.8 \times 126 \\
&= 838 + 100.8 \\
&= 938.8
\end{aligned}$$

FIGURE 11: Seventy-Eighth Percentile of Gasoline Sales

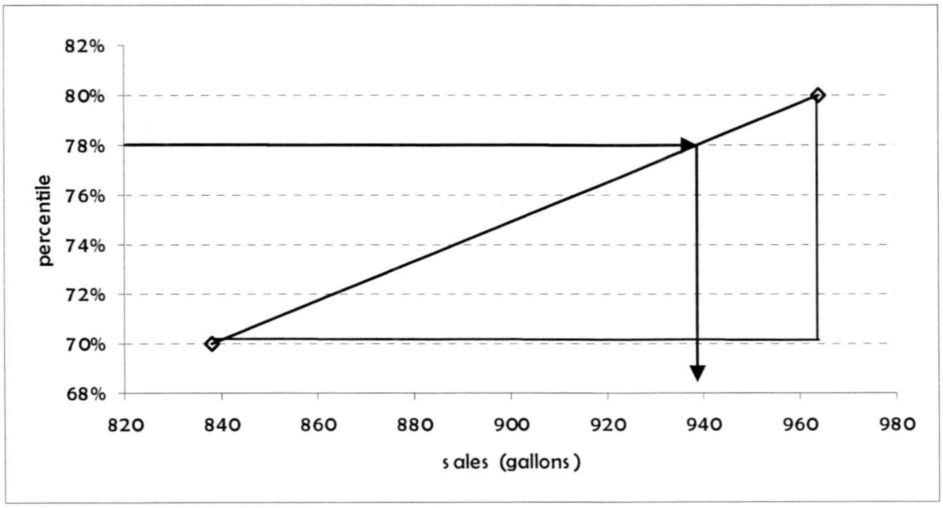

We cannot, based on these data, make estimates about sample percentiles which are less than $\frac{1}{n+1}$ or greater than $\frac{n}{n+1}$

Boxplots

Boxplots provide a graphical summary of the descriptive statistics obtained from a sample. The boxplot contains:

- The center of the data
- Where most of the data fall
- The spread of the unquestionably good data
- Possible outliers

Boxplots were used in the context of the standard deviation and the sample mean.

- **The Empirical Rule**

- The center of the data is taken to be $\bar{x}$.

- Most of the data fall between $\bar{x} - s$ and $\bar{x} + s$. So the data fall within plus or minus one standard deviation of the mean. In the normal distribution (bell shaped curve), the proportion of sample observations falling within this range is about 68%.

- The spread of the unquestionably good is bounded by $\bar{x} - 2s$ and $\bar{x} + 2s$. So the preponderance of data falls within plus or minus two standard deviation of the mean. In the normal distribution (bell shaped curve), the proportion of sample observations falling within this range is about 95.44%.

- Values that fall outside $\bar{x} \pm 2s$ are considered to be suspect whereas values that fall outside $\bar{x} \pm 3s$ are considered to highly suspect and therefore possible outliers.

This technique often referred to as the empirical distribution is impaired by the fact that any outlier (extreme value) affects the mean and inflates the variance and the sample standard deviation. So actually finding such values in practice is complicated by this inherent problem.

To avoid this complication, Tukey sought robust estimates of dispersions that were not adversely effected by outliers. Earlier we discussed both crude and complicated measures of dispersion such as the sample range and the sample standard deviation, which heavily effected by possible outliers. An alternative measure is the inter-quartile range, *IQR*, given by:

$$IR = Q_3 - Q_1$$
$$step = 1.5 \times IR$$

In bell-shaped distributions, the sample inter-quartile range is approximately 1.349 times the sample standard deviation (see Keating and Scott, 1999).

$$IR \cong 1.349 \times S$$

A box on a vertical scale, in which the bottom of the box starts at Q_1 and the top of the box ends at Q_3, depicts the range containing the middle 50% of the data. For clarity we will place a solid horizontal bar in the box at the median value, $\tilde{x}$, which represents the middle of the data set. This box extends vertically by means of whiskers, which are calculated using the step value given above. The inner fences are given by

$$UIF = Q_3 + step$$
$$LIF = Q_1 - step$$

The range, of unquestionably good data, is shown by extending the box vertically: the lower inner fence lies on a vertical scale, in which the bottom end starts at LIF and extends upward to meet the bottom of the box. Another line emanates from the box's top and ends at UIF. Points outside these inner fences can be scrutinized as outliers.

$$\begin{aligned} UIF &= Q_3 + step \\ &= Q_3 + 1.5 \times (Q_3 - Q_1) \\ &= 2.5 \times Q_3 - 1.5 \times Q_1 \\ &= .5 \times (Q_3 + Q_1) + 2 \times (Q_3 - Q_1) \\ &= \ddot{x} + 2 \times IR \\ &\cong \tilde{x} + 2 \times IR \end{aligned}$$

In this case, we have made the approximation that $\tilde{x} \cong \frac{1}{2}(Q_3 + Q_1)$. The latter expression is called the midhinge, $\ddot{x}$, and is another measure of central tendency.

The boxes obtained in this way are similar to those obtained using the sample mean and sample standard deviation except that we are using more robust estimates. The farther outside the inner-fences that a point falls reflects its extreme nature. The bounds of the reasonably good data are: $\tilde{x} \pm 2 \times IR$. So the preponderance of data falls within plus or minus two inter-quartile ranges of the sample median, where we have approximated the sample median with the average of the first and third quartiles.

Data that fall outside the outer-fences, which are another step away from the inner-fences, are highly suspect. The outer fences are given by the equations below.

$$UOF = Q_3 + 3 \times step = \ddot{x} + 3 \times IR \cong \tilde{x} + 3 \times IR$$
$$LOF = Q_1 - 3 \times step = \ddot{x} - 3 \times IR \cong \tilde{x} - 3 \times IR$$

The outer bounds of the data are $\tilde{x} \pm 3 \times IR$. So empirically the analyst anticipates that almost all data fall within plus or minus three inter-quartile ranges of the sample median.

Example: Reconsider the gasoline sales data, in which sample median, $\tilde{x} = 781$. The quartiles are $Q_1 = 727.5$ and $Q_3 = 901$. The inter-quartile range and step are:

$$\begin{aligned} IR &= Q_3 - Q_1 \\ &= 901 - 727.5 \\ &= 173.5 \\ step &= 1.5 \times IR \\ &= 1.5 \times 173.5 \\ &= 260.25 \end{aligned}$$

The inner fences are then given by:

$$\begin{aligned} UIF &= Q_3 + step \\ &= 901 + 260.5 \\ &= 1{,}161.25 \\ LIF &= Q_1 - step \\ &= 727.5 - 260.25 \\ &= 467.25 \end{aligned}$$

The boxplot in Figure 12 conveys that there are no extreme observations in this sense that the sample mean is slightly larger that sample median.

The outer fences are then given by:

$$\begin{aligned} UOF &= Q_3 + 2 \times step \\ &= 901 + 520.5 \\ &= 1421.5 \\ LOF &= Q_1 - 2 \times step \\ &= 727.5 - 520.5 \\ &= 207 \end{aligned}$$

FIGURE 12: Boxplot of Unleaded Gasoline Sales

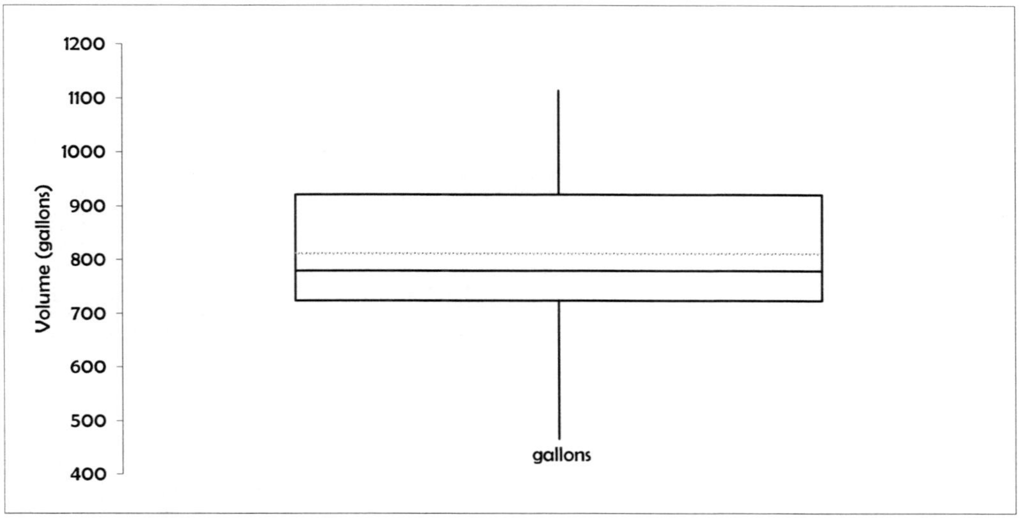

Case Study Revisited: Quality Control Piston Rings

Recall the data that were 125 inner diameters in mm of forged piston rings used in automobile engines. The large amount of data can be condensed into a boxplot as well that contains numerous descriptive statistics. Recall in the stem and leaf plot, we became suspicious of extreme observations 73.967 and 73.030. The lines for the sample mean and sample median are virtually superimposed upon one another. The boxplot in Figure 13 supports our intuition about the extreme nature of these observations. Each extreme value is shown to fall outside the inner fences.

FIGURE 13: Boxplot of Inner Diameters of Forged Piston Rings

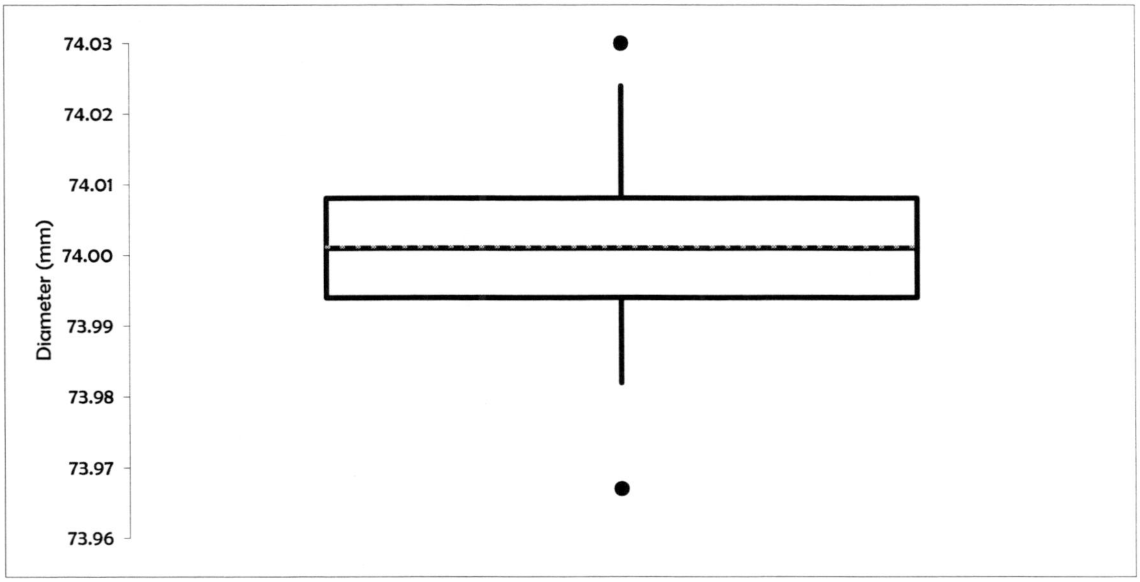

Skewness

When the long tail in a frequency histogram or polygon is on the left side of the data as in the test scores, we say that the data are skewed to the left (see Figure 6a). Notice that this longer left tail occurs because some very low grades occurred on this exam. The effect of very low grades tends to decrease the sample average 75.2 below the sample median of 79. This ordering of the sample average and sample median is characteristic of unimodal data, which are skewed to the left.

When the long tail in a frequency polygon or histogram is on the right side of the data, as in the cadmium levels, see Figure 7a, in the Starling data set, we say the data are skewed to the right. Notice that some Starlings had significantly high levels of cadmium, whereas most were clustered at much lower levels. This tends to increase the sample average cadmium level above the sample median. In data sets, which are skewed to the right, the sample median is less than the sample average. Sometimes the frequency polygon or histogram is symmetric about a central value. In the symmetric case, the sample average and sample median should be equal. The grades of the consistent student, 72, 73, 74, and 75, are symmetric about 73.5. The grades of the procrastinator are skewed to the right because the sample median, 67, is less than the sample average, 73.5. The test grades of the first student are skewed to the left since the sample median grade 93 is greater than the sample average grade. One can also detect Skewness graphically in unimodal distributions with finite bounds. In such distributions, measure the distance from the unique mode to each finite bound. If the distance to the upper bound exceeds the distance to the lower bound then the data are skewed to the right. If the opposite ordering occurs then the data are skewed to the left as in the students' grade data, where we had several very low scores that caused the sample average to fall below the sample median.

FIGURE 6a: Skewness (to the left) of Student Grades

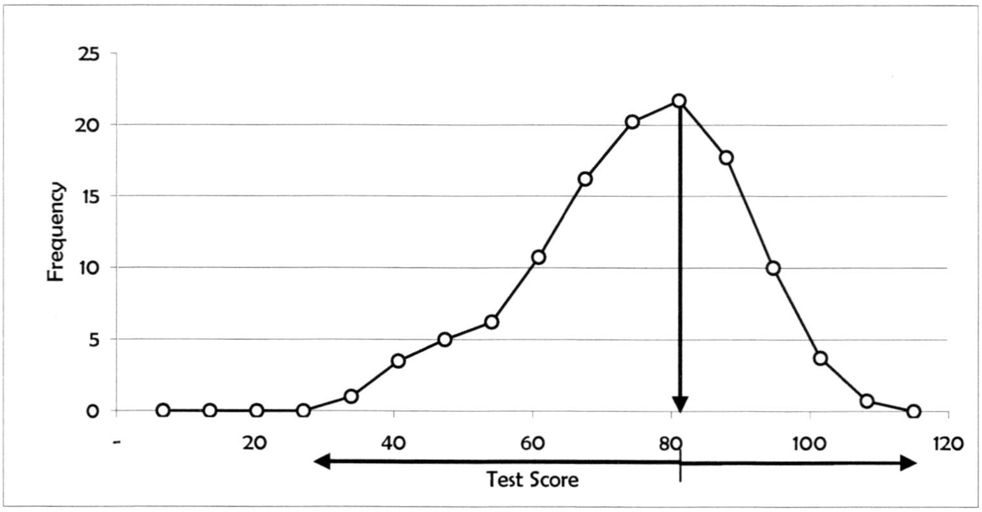

FIGURE 7a: Skewness (to the right) of Cadmium Levels

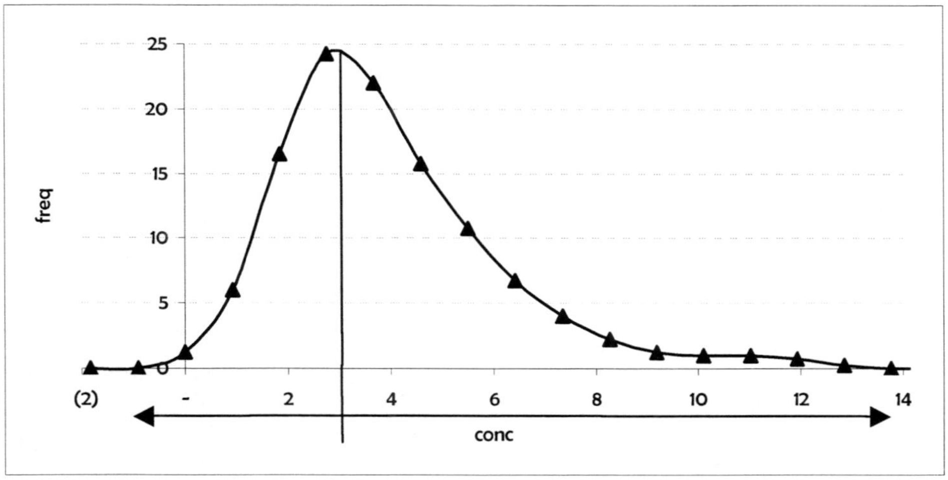

Grouped Data

Many times when we read a newspaper, a magazine article or a research paper, the data may be grouped as in a report for incomes of families of 4 persons, or the value of a family's home. In a certain geographical area, a newspaper may report the number of families with incomes between \$20,000 and \$29,000. There are many reasons for reporting the data in this way and most of the reasons are simply practical.

1) When there are many observations in the data set, the analyst will find it very difficult to report every income in a brief article. This grouping procedure allows the statistician to report the data in a less exact way.

2) This procedure allows for a more honest reporting of the data. For example, a person may not want to report his or her exact income as \$11,249 but will report that he or she has an annual income between \$10,000 and \$19,000.

3) Since you have completed many questionnaires, you know that frequently data are requested in this way for simplicity of computation.

For these and many other reasons we need to analyze grouped data. Grouped data are formed when the values of the response variable are subdivided into r groups. Each group has a beginning value, b_i, and an ending value, e_i, for each $i = 1, \cdots, r$. The midpoint, m_i, of the ith class is

$$m_i = \frac{b_i + e_i}{2}$$

The number of values in the sample that fall in the ith interval is called the frequency of the interval and is denoted by f_i.

Example: Program Success

In 1989 UTSA conducted a review of an MS program. One component of the review is directed at measuring the financial success of its graduates. In the 7 years preceding 1989, 15 persons graduated from the program. Suppose their salaries are given in Table 18 below:

TABLE 18: Class Intervals for Salary Data of Graduates in 1987

Beginning b_i	Ending e_i	Midpoint m_i	Frequency f_i
\$0	\$9,000	\$4,500	3
\$10,000	\$19,000	\$14,500	2
\$20,000	\$29,000	\$24,500	0
\$30,000	\$39,000	\$34,500	5
\$40,000	\$49,000	\$44,500	2
\$50,000	\$59,000	\$54,500	3

We can still compute a sample average, a sample mode, and a sample standard deviation. These estimates are cruder than those obtained using the actual salaries. The sample mode of grouped data is the midpoint of the interval, which occurs most frequently. In this case, the interval from \$30,000 to \$39,000 has a frequency of 5 and therefore occurs more frequently than the others. So the midpoint, \$34,500, of this interval is the grouped mode.

The sample average, $\bar{x}_g$, of grouped data is given by

$$\bar{x}_g = \frac{\sum_{i=1}^{r} f_i m_i}{n-1}, \textit{where} \qquad n = \left(\sum_{i=1}^{r} f_i \right)$$

For the MS graduates, we calculate a sample average of the grouped data as

$$\bar{x}_g = \frac{3 \times 4{,}500 + 2 \times 14{,}500 + \cdots + 3 \times 54{,}500}{15} = \$31{,}166.67$$

The sample variance, s_g^2, for grouped data is given by

$$s_g^2 = \frac{\sum_{i=1}^{r} f\left(m_i - \bar{x}_g\right)^2}{n-1}$$

For the MS Statistics graduates, we obtain the following value:

$$s_g = \sqrt{\frac{3\times(4{,}500-31{,}166.67)^2 + 2\times(14{,}500-31{,}166.67)^2 + \cdots + 3\times(54{,}500-31{,}166.67)^2}{14}}$$
$$= \$18{,}387.37$$

The sample average salary reflects a salary of $31,166.67 and a sample standard deviation of $18,387.37. These values indicate that the amount of scatter in the data is considerable. We can also plot the frequency of the intervals against their respective midpoints as we did in Scott's approach. Notice in this case, we get a much cruder graph that we *cannot make smoother* because we have this one and only one grouping. Notice the virtual bimodality of the data that reflects graduates as being in of two groups. Those at the lower salaries might be PhD students or stay at home moms whereas the ones at higher salaries might be working in Corporate America.

FIGURE 14: Frequency Plot of Salaries

Cross-validation and Corroboration with Polygon Data

Recall that we had earlier taken a set of complete data and converted it into grouped data using "Scott's method." The discerning student might inquire about the accuracy of the grouped methods for these complete data sets. Our first example concerned the student grades; let's use the polygon-interval data and see how consistent the sample statistics for the grouped set are with those obtained from the complete set.

TABLE 8-Revisted: Grouped Grade Data-Beginning at Zero.

Beginning b_i	Ending e_i	Midpoint m_i	Frequency f_i
40.59	54.12	47.355	6
54.12	67.65	60.885	11
67.65	81.18	74.415	20
81.18	94.71	87.945	19
94.71	108.24	101.475	3

$$\bar{x}_g = \frac{6\times 47.355 + 11\times 60.885 + 20\times 74.415 + 19\times 87.94 + 3\times 101.475}{59} = 74.874$$

The group mode from the original polygon is 74.415. In a similar way, the grouped standard deviation is $s_g = 14.425$. Notice that the values are in fairly good agreement with the complete data. $\bar{x} = 75.2$ and $s = 14.22$. We are not surprised by the fact that the estimate of the standard deviation is larger in that we knew the grouping would produce cruder less precise results.

TABLE 8a-Revisted: Grouped Grade Data-Beginning at 6.765.

Beginning b_i	Ending e_i	Midpoint m_i	Frequency f_i
33.825	47.355	40.59	4
47.355	60.885	54.12	4
60.885	74.415	67.65	17
74.415	87.945	81.18	24
87.945	101.475	94.71	10

$$\bar{x}_g = \frac{4\times 40.59 + 4\times 54.12 + 17\times 67.65 + 24\times 81.18 + 10\times 94.71}{59} = 74.988$$

The group mode from the second polygon is 81.18. In a similar way, the grouped standard deviation is $s_g = 14.503$. Notice that the values are in good agreement with the complete data, in which $\bar{x} = 75.2$ and $s = 14.22$. Again the grouped estimate of the standard deviation exceeds that of the complete sample. We again confirm that the grouping leads to cruder estimates of the complete sample mean and the complete sample standard deviation.

Problem Set 1

Complete the following sentences with the **most appropriate answer**.

1) The goal of statistics involves ____________
   a) representative samples b) appropriate sample statistics
   c) inference about population parameters d) all of these

2) A __________ is a numerical measure of a population.
   a) statistic b) parameter c) sample mean d) sample

3) Sampling errors cannot arise from ______________________
   a) personal bias b) omission of a subset of the population
   c) large samples d) none of these

4) The population is always a ______
   a) sample space b) set of UTSA students
   c) sample d) set of real numbers

5) Which of the following data are often discretized?
   a) height b) weight c) age d) all of these e) none of these

(6-12) The following data are the low temperatures of 17 major cities in Texas taken on Saturday February 12, 1994. A meteorologist wants to use these data to make inferences about the low temperature in the state.

45	39	33	26	38	39	46	48	53
57	56	46	47	38	46	43	47	

6) The average low temperature of the sample is ________
   a) 41.50 b) 43.94 c) 46.00 d) 44.06

7) The mode of the sample of low temperatures is .
   a) 38 b) 39 c) 46 d) 47

8) The range of the sample of low temperatures is ______
   a) 7.70 b) 7.75 c) 7.94 d) 31.00

57 - 26 =

9) The standard deviation of the sample of low temperatures is _______
   a) 7.70 b) 7.75 c) 7.94 d) 63.06

10) The median low temperature of the sample data is _________
   a) 43 b) 46 c) 53 d) 57

$\frac{17+1}{2} = 9$

11) In order to construct a frequency polygon for these low temperatures, Scott would suggest using an interval width of size ________

a) 4.02 b) 4.14 c) 9.39 d) 9.69

12) Based on the measures of central tendency one would conclude that the data are_____

a) skewed to the right b) symmetric
c) skewed to the left d) cannot be determined.

(13-15) The following table shows the monthly water use (in hundreds of ft^3) of the Keating household for three consecutive years.

Monthly Use	Frequency
8-14	23
15-21	10
22-28	1
29-35	1
36-42	1

13) The grouped average of the sample of water use is _________

a) 14.63 b) 16.53 c) 25.00 d) 14.69

14) The grouped standard deviation of the sample of water use is ______

a) 7.11 b) 6.28 c) 39.43 d) 6.37

15) The grouped mode of the sample of water use is __________

a) 23 b) 14.63 c) 25 d) 11

16) Plot Scott's frequency polygon for the temperature data for question 6.

(17-18) Consider the following sample that contains 5 observations.

12 17 20 30 36

17) If we delete an observation from this sample to create a sample of size 4, which observation should we delete to **change** its average the most?

a) 12 b) 17 c) 20 d) 30 e) 36

18) If we delete an observation from this sample to produce a sample of size 4, which observation should we delete to **decrease** the sample standard deviation the most?

a) 12 b) 17 c) 20 d) 30 e) 36

19) Let a population consist of all UTSA Business majors. If we select a sample of Accounting majors from this population, their average GPA is a:
a) parameter b) statistic c) measure of dispersion d) response variable

Complete the following sentence, which is in two parts:
I. The goal of statistics is to make meaningful inferences about values of:

20) a) population parameters b) measures of central tendency
c) measures of dispersion d) response variables

II. based on descriptive statistics chosen from _____.

21) a) random samples b) the population
c) representative samples d) surveys

(22-27) The following data are the electrical uses of a household for the month of February in seven years. Consider these values as a sample of size 7.

1,150 1,323 1,176 1,718 1,358 1,110 1,364

22) The sample average electrical use for the month of February is:
a) 1,314.14 b) 1,323 c) 1,718 d) 1,414

23) The sample median electrical use for the month of February is:
a) 1,414 b) 1,718 c) 1,314.14 d) 1,323

24) The sample range of electrical use for the month of February is:
a) 825.09 b) 608.00 c) 395.00 d) 214.00

25) The sample standard deviation of electrical use for February is:
a) 152.00 b) 190.97 c) 206.27 d) 214.00

26) The width of Scott's frequency polygon for theses data is:
a) 300.51 b) 278.217 c) 167.621 d) 9.051

27) Which observation in this sample contributes most to the sample standard deviation?
a) 1,110 b) 1,176 c) 1,364 d) 1,718

(28-31) In a class of 50 students, the teacher reports grades in the following way:

Grade	Frequency
40-49	1
50-59	4
60-69	8

70-79	12	74.5
80-89	15	84.5
90-99	10	94.5

28) The grouped mode of these data is given by:
a) 15 b) 79.5 c) 84.5 d) 44.5

29) The grouped mean of these data is given by:
a) 69.5 b) 77.7 c) 79.5 d) 84.5

30) The grouped standard deviation of these data is given by:
a) 13.01 b) 12.87 c) 11.80 d) 14

31) These data are:
a) skewed to the right b) skewed to the left Mean > Median
c) symmetric d) none of these

32) Plot Scott's frequency polygon for the February electrical data. Scale and label the axes. Start the plot at zero!

Probability and Counting Principles

A statistical experiment is the process of:
1) selecting a sample from the population and
2) measuring the value of the response variable for each element in the sample.

The sample space, $\mathscr{S}$, is the set of all possible outcomes of the experiment. An event is any outcome or collection of outcomes of an experiment. Two events, A and B, are said to be mutually exclusive provided they cannot occur simultaneously. Mathematically, we say that the events are disjoint. For instance, you can't be a freshman and a senior at the same time.

$$A \cap B = \phi$$
(A and B)

Recall that $A \cap B$ is the event of all outcomes of an experiment, which occur in event A **and** in the event B. Each event A and each event B has a rule that determines membership in the event. In order for an outcome of an experiment to fall in the intersection, the outcome must satisfy the rule that determines membership in A and satisfy the rule determining membership in B. In other words, the outcome must satisfy both conditions. When the events are mutually exclusive, they have no elements in common; that is, there are no outcomes of the experiment that satisfy both conditions. Recall that the intersection of events in S is defined as:

$$A \cap B = \{E \mid E \in A - and - E \in B\}$$

$A \cup B$ is the event of all outcomes of an experiment, which occur in an event A or in an event B. In order for an outcome of an experiment to fall in the union, the outcome must satisfy the rule that determines membership in A or the rule that determines membership in B. In other words, the outcome has to satisfy only one of the two conditions. It can satisfy both conditions but membership in one or the other assures membership in the union. Mathematically, we define $A \cup B$ as

$$A \cup B = \{E \mid E \in A - or - E \in B\}$$

In the material that follows, we introduce the concept and definition of probability by example. In this context probability is put forth as the relative frequency of occurrence of an event. That is, how frequently do we expect the event to occur?

Example:

From the fall semester of 1990, the gender composition of UTSA students is recorded in Table 19 by:

TABLE 19: UTSA Undergraduate Students classified by Gender and Rank (1990)

	Fresh	Soph.	Junior	Senior	Total
Women	2,235	1,529	1,475	2,005	7,244
Men	1,981	1,222	1,350	1,867	6,420
Total	4,216	2,751	2,825	3,872	13,664

Let $A = \{\text{the event that a person from this population of students is a Woman}\}$. If we randomly choose a student from the population, what's the probability that the chosen student is a woman?

$$\begin{aligned}\Pr(A) &= \frac{\#\text{–}women}{total\text{–}\#\text{–}students} \\ &= \frac{7{,}244}{13{,}664} \\ &= 0.530\end{aligned}$$

This value, probability, is the ratio of the number of women and the number of students in the population. Note that 53.0% of UTSA undergraduates were women.

If we let $B = \{\text{the event that a person from this population is a Sophomore}\}$ and randomly select a student from this population, what is the probability that the chosen student is a sophomore?

$$\begin{aligned}\Pr(B) &= \frac{\#\text{–}sophs}{total\text{–}\#\text{–}students} \\ &= \frac{2{,}751}{13{,}664} \\ &= 0.201\end{aligned}$$

This probability is the ratio of the number of sophomores and the number of students. Note that 20.1% of UTSA undergraduates were sophomores.

If we randomly select a student from the population, what is the probably that a randomly chosen student is a sophomore and a woman?

$$\begin{aligned}\Pr(A \cap B) &= \frac{\#\text{–}soph.\text{–}women}{total\text{–}\#\text{–}students} \\ &= \frac{1{,}529}{13{,}664} \\ &= 0.112\end{aligned}$$

This value is the ratio of the number of students that satisfy the compound event to the total number of students in the population. So that women-sophomores compose 11.2% of the undergraduate student population.

Probability, much like Geometry, is based on a few fundamental axioms from which all other results can be obtained through deductive reasoning. **Andrei Kolmogorov** formalized this method in 1933 and he is one of the great Russian probabilists (with **Markov** and **Chebyshev**), who laid the path for probability theory and statistics. His career spanned more than half a century and included many applied topics such as the strategic placement of barrage balloons around Moscow during the German invasion of 1941. He died in 1987. He established that one must only assume the truth of the following three axioms. There is a fourth axiom that addresses the probability of infinitely many mutually exclusive events, when the number of infinite events can be placed in one-to-one correspondence with the positive integers. This axiom is beyond the scope of this presentation. See more about Kolmogorov in Johnson and Kotz (1997) pg 255.

The Axioms of Kolmogorov

1) For any event A in $\mathcal{S}$, $\Pr(A) \geq 0$.

2) $\Pr(\mathcal{S})=1$, and

3) If A and B are mutually exclusive events in $\mathcal{S}$ then

$$\Pr(A \cup B) = \Pr(A) + \Pr(B).$$

Note Intersection = ϕ (See Figure 12)

The last property, which is known as the finitely sub-additive condition can be illustrated via **Venn diagrams** as in the figure that follows. The fact that A and B are mutually exclusive is illustrated by the fact that they do not overlap; they are disjoint. Hence the probability of their union is simply the sum of their probabilities. Use the analogy of area: if we had two non-overlapping regions, the total area (i.e., the union) would be the sum of the areas of the individual regions.

FIGURE 15: Two Mutually Exclusive Events in the Sample Space, $\mathcal{S}$

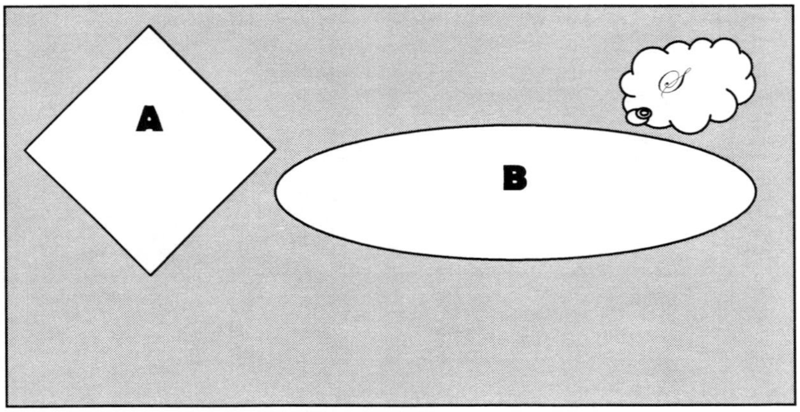

Suppose we randomly select a student from the student population. What is the probability that a randomly selected student is a freshman or a sophomore?

Let A_1, A_2, A_3, and A_4 be respectively the events that a student is a freshman, sophomore, junior, or senior. Then the event, C, that a student is a freshman or a sophomore is

$$C = A_1 \cup A_2$$

So use the third axiom to compute the probability of this compound event.

$$
\begin{aligned}
\Pr(C) &= \Pr(A_1 \cup A_2) \\
&= \Pr(A_1) + \Pr(A_2) \\
&= \frac{4{,}216}{13{,}664} + \frac{2{,}751}{13{,}664} \\
&= 0.50988
\end{aligned}
$$

It follows that about 51% of all undergraduates are underclassmen. Notice that probability within this context is simply proportional by representation. This can be extended to the union of several events.

What is the probability that a randomly chosen student is a freshman, junior or senior? The event, D, that a student is a freshman, junior, or senior is

$$D = [A_1 \cup A_3] \cup A_4$$

Now using the associative rule, we can determine the probability of the event D. This situation can again be illustrated via Venn Diagrams as in the one given in Figure 16 below.

FIGURE 16: Four Mutually Exclusive Classes

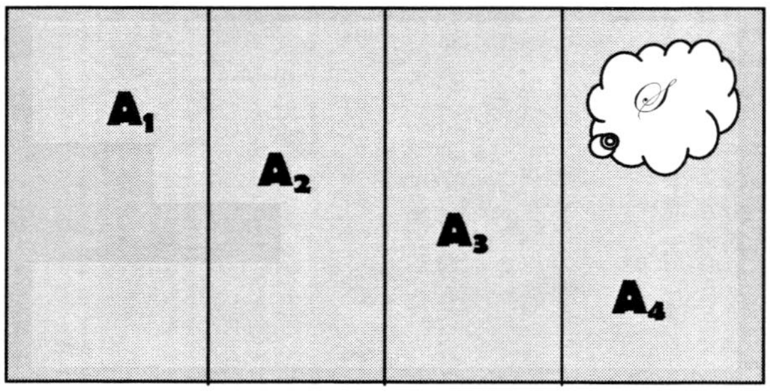

$$
\begin{aligned}
\Pr(D) &= \Pr([A_1 \cup A_3] \cup A_4) \\
&= \Pr(A_1 \cup A_3) + \Pr(A_4) \\
&= \Pr(A_1) + \Pr(A_3) + \Pr(A_4) \\
&= \frac{4{,}216}{13{,}664} + \frac{2{,}825}{13{,}664} + \frac{3{,}872}{13{,}664} \\
&= 0.799
\end{aligned}
$$

Often in probability it is simpler to use the complement of an event to compute probability rather than calculating the probability directly. The complement of an event A is the set of all outcomes in the sample space, $\mathscr{S}$, that are not in A and we denote the complement of A by A'.

TABLE 19A: 1990 UTSA Undergraduate Students

	Fresh	**Soph.**	**Junior**	**Senior**	**Total**
Women	2,235	1,529	1,475	2,005	7,244
Men	1,981	1,222	1,350	1,867	6,420
Total	4,216	2,751	2,825	3,872	13,664

Complement Rule of Probability

Let A be an event in the sample space, $\mathscr{S}$, and let A' be the complement of the event. Then it follows from axioms 2 and 3 that

$$P(A') = 1 - P(A).$$

The truth of this rule can be illustrated via Venn Diagrams, in which the sample space acts as the universal set in the Venn diagram in Figure 17 below. Everything, which is not in A, is shaded in dark gray: $A \cup A' = \mathscr{S}$.

FIGURE 17: An Event and its Complement in a Sample Space, $\mathscr{S}$

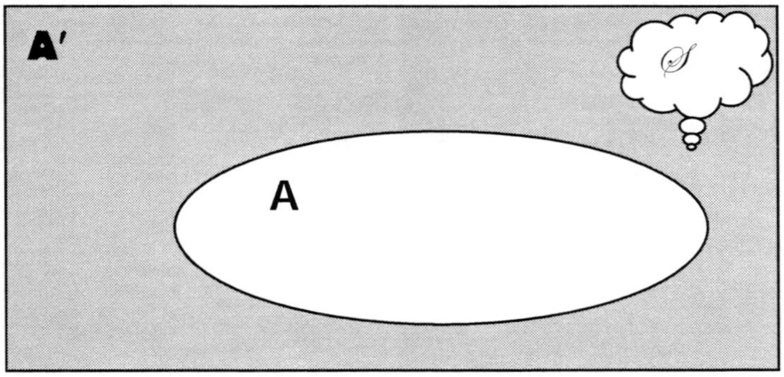

$$\Pr(A \cup A') = \Pr(\mathscr{S}) = 1$$

In the event D in the preceding example, we could have asked for the probability that the chosen student is not a sophomore. So that

$$D = A_2'.$$

By the **Complement Rule of Probability**, we have

$$
\begin{aligned}
P(D) &= 1 - P(A_2) \\
&= 1 - 0.201 \\
&= 0.799
\end{aligned}
$$

Notice that the null set (or empty set) is the complement of the sample space; so that, we have as a corollary that:

The following formula allows us to compute the probability of the union of any two events. Notice that **Axiom 3 of Kolmogorov** showed us how to compute the probability of the union of two mutually exclusive events. So we want to develop a formula that works whether the events are mutually exclusive or not.

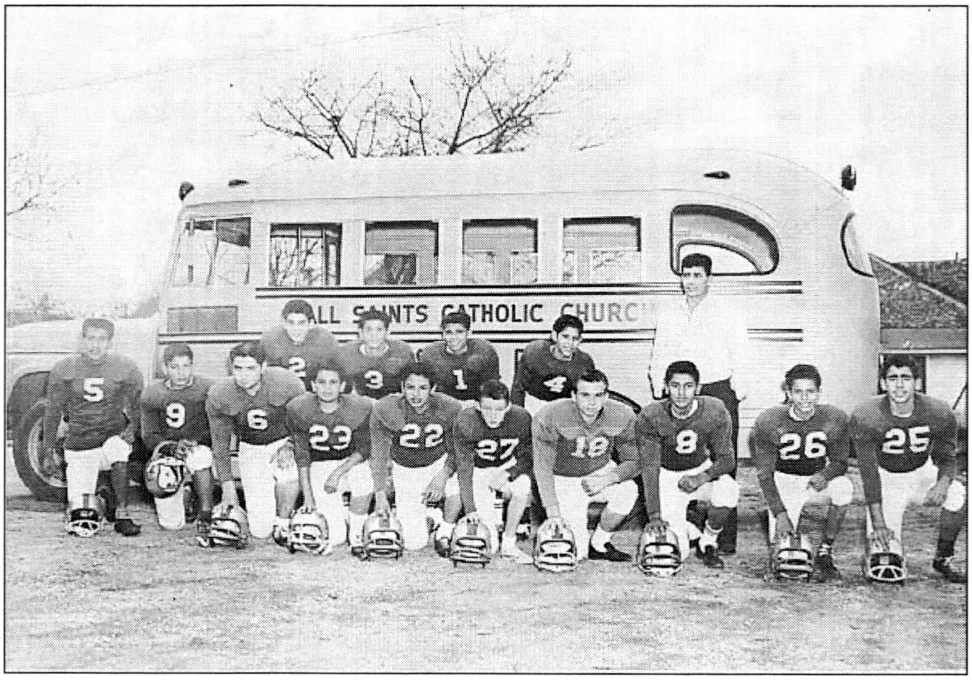

Can you find my number? Guess the date of the picture?

Μψ νυμβερ ισ 27. Τηε πιχτυρε ωασ τακεν ον Δεχεμβερ 7, 1961 ιν Φορτ Ωορτη

The Additive Rule of Probability (ARP):

Let A and B be events in the sample space, $\mathscr{S}$. Then it follows from **axioms 2 and 3 of Kolmogorov** that

$$\Pr(A \cup B) = \Pr(A) + \Pr(B) - \Pr(A \cap B).$$

This additive rule generalizes **Kolmogorov's third axiom**. Whenever, the events are mutually exclusive, their intersection by definition is the **null set**. Moreover, the probability of the null set is zero by **Axiom 2** and **the complement rule**.

FIGURE 18: The Additive Rule

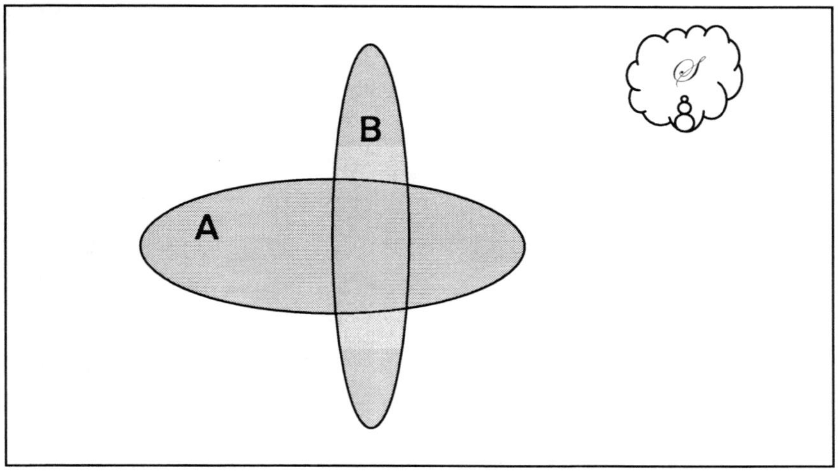

The gist of the **Additive Rule of Probability** is that when we count $\Pr(A)$, we count the probability of the intersection once, and if we add to that $\Pr(B)$, we count the intersection twice. In computing the probability of the union to avoid over-counting, we subtract the probability of the intersection.

Example: Using the same definitions as before that A is the event of a woman and B is the event of a sophomore, what is the probability that a randomly chosen student in this population is a sophomore or a woman?

TABLE 19A: UTSA Undergraduate Student Classification (1990)

	Fresh	Soph.	Junior	Senior	Total
Women	2,235	**1,529**	1,475	2,005	**7,244**
Men	1,981	1,222	1,350	1,867	6,420
Total	4,216	**2,751**	2,825	3,872	13,664

In the Table 19A above notice that the row total for women is highlighted in light gray, whereas the column total for sophomores is highlighted in a darker gray. The intersection of the row and column is the cell of sophomore women.

$$\begin{aligned} \Pr(A \cup B) &= \frac{7{,}244}{13{,}664} + \frac{2{,}751}{13{,}664} - \frac{1{,}529}{13{,}664} \\ &= 0.530 + 0.201 - 0.112 \\ &= 0.619 \end{aligned}$$

Conditional Probability

Sometimes it is useful to update the probability of an event given that we have new information. This process of updating probability is called conditional probability. With the same example as before, denote the event that a student is a woman given that a student is a sophomore as $A \mid B$. The new event is conditioned on knowledge that the student is a sophomore. This event may have a different probability than the event that the student is a woman.

The process of conditioning occurs frequently in daily business practice. If a stock goes up today, will the stock go up tomorrow? Many experts claim that the best predictor of tomorrow's stock price is today's stock price. If a person smokes, his or her life or health insurance premiums will increase. If a person is less than 25 years old, he or she will pay a higher car insurance premium than someone who is older. The company is assigning premium as a function of certain adverse circumstances that vary by age.

Definition of Conditional Probability

Let A and B be two events in the sample space, $\mathscr{S}$, then

$$\Pr(A \mid B) = \frac{\Pr(A \cap B)}{\Pr(B)}, \qquad \textit{where} \ \Pr(B) \neq 0.$$

(Read as: Probability of *A* **given** *B*)

Since the event B is known to have occurred then we restrict our universe to the set B. We see that $\Pr(A \mid B)$ is just the probability that A occurs within B.

FIGURE 19: Conditional Probability of A within B

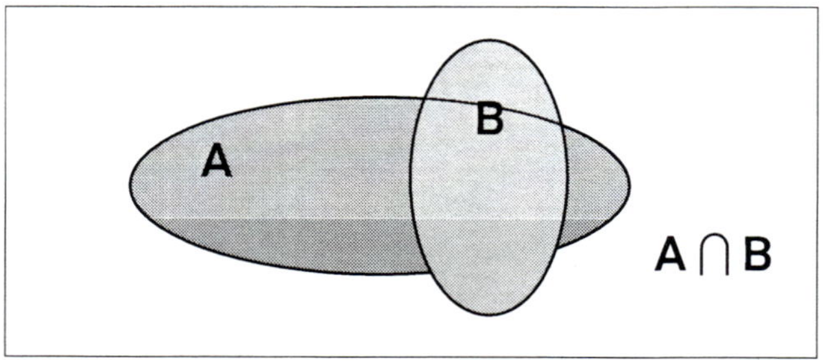

TABLE 19A: UTSA Undergraduate Student Classification (1990)

	Fresh	Soph.	Junior	Senior	Total
Women	2,235	**1,529**	1,475	2,005	7,244
Men	1,981	1,222	1,350	1,867	6,420
Total	4,216	**2,751**	2,825	3,872	**13,664**

In the example, previously mentioned, if we know that a student was a sophomore then the student must come from the column headed by Soph. Within the sophomore class, the number of women is 1,529 highlighted.

$$\Pr(\,A \mid B\,) = \frac{\dfrac{1{,}529}{13{,}664}}{\dfrac{2{,}751}{13{,}664}} = \frac{1{,}529}{2{,}751} = 0.556$$

Notice that this number differs from the probability of being a woman in the general population. This simply says that the proportion (55.6%) of women in the sophomore class is slightly higher than the proportion (53.0%) of women in the population.

The conditioned event dictates the reduced sample space, that is, the conditioned event is very important. If we exchange the two events, that is, condition upon the other event, we may get very drastic differences in the condition probabilities. What is the probability that a student is a sophomore given that the student is a woman?

TABLE 19A: UTSA Undergraduate Student Classification (1990)

	Fresh	Soph.	Junior	Senior	Total
Women	2,235	**1,529**	1,475	2,005	**7,244**
Men	1,981	1,222	1,350	1,867	6,420
Total	4,216	2,751	2,825	3,872	13,664

$$\Pr(\,B \mid A\,) = \frac{1{,}529}{7{,}244}$$
$$= 0.211$$

The proportion (21.1%) of sophomores among the women is slightly higher than the proportion (20.1%) of sophomores in the population. So that sophomore representation among women is greater than in the general population.

Definition of Independence

Two events, A and B, in the sample space, $\mathscr{S}$, are independent provided

$$\Pr(A \mid B) = \Pr(A)$$

Two events are independent when the proportion of one event is equal to the proportion of the second event. The events of being a woman and a sophomore are independent provided the proportion of women in the sophomore class is the same as the proportion of women in the population. In spoken and written English we develop connotations associated with the traditional meaning of a word. If we have a mathematical definition, which produces connotations that are at variance with traditional connotations then misunderstanding is a likely outcome. I much prefer the term, proportional representation, as it better captures the spirit of the definition. In the examples given previously the unconditional and the conditional probabilities are not equal so the events are dependent. But these values are nearly equal and so the events are nearly independent but not exactly independent.

In the class given below at Utopia U., observe that the event of a woman and the event of a sophomore are independent but the event of a woman and the event of a junior, are dependent.

TABLE 20: Undergraduate Student @ Utopia U.

	Fresh	Soph.	Junior	Senior	Total
Women	245	180	115	60	600
Men	155	120	85	40	400
Total	400	300	200	100	1,000

The next rule provides a way to always compute the probability of an intersection.

Multiplicative Rule of Probability (MRP)

Let A and B be events in the sample space, $\mathscr{S}$, then

$$\Pr(A \cap B) = \Pr(A \mid B) \times \Pr(B).$$

The probability of being a sophomore and a woman has already been computed. Let's check this formula to make certain the answers agree.

TABLE 19A: UTSA Undergraduate Student Classification (1990)

	Fresh	Soph.	Junior	Senior	Total
Women	2,235	**1,529**	1,475	2,005	7,244
Men	1,981	1,222	1,350	1,867	6,420
Total	4,216	**2,751**	2,825	3,872	**13,664**

Recall that

$$\Pr(B) = \frac{2{,}751}{13{,}664} = 0.201 - and$$

$$\Pr(A \mid B) = \frac{1{,}529}{2{,}751} = 0.556 - so - that$$

$$\Pr(A \mid B) \times \Pr(B) = 0.112,$$

which agrees with $\Pr(A \cap B)$.

Multiplicative Rule of Probability (MRP):

Special Case – Independent Events

In the special case, in which A and B are independent, computing the probability of an intersection is found by taking the product of the individual (or marginal) probabilities.

$$\Pr(A \cap B) = \Pr(A) \times \Pr(B)$$

In this case, we say that the compound probability is a product of the marginal information. Notice in the tables given above for UTSA and Utopia U. if we knew that gender and class rank were independent events we could construct the values in each gender-class rank cell from the marginal information

---

Example

Twenty (20) UTSA graduates apply for two vacancies at a local company. Among the 20 graduates, 11 are Hispanics, 8 are Anglos, and 1 is an African-American. Assuming that all 20 are (equally) qualified, what is the probability that both persons hired are Anglo-Americans?

Let B be the event that the first person hired is Anglo and A be the event that the second person hired is Anglo. Then the intersection of A and B is the event that both persons hired are Anglo-Americans.

$$\begin{aligned}\Pr(A \cap B) &= \Pr(A \mid B) \times \Pr(B)\\ &= \frac{7}{19} \times \frac{8}{20}.\\ &= \frac{14}{95}.\\ &= 0.147\end{aligned}$$

Statistics in the Courts

Is the hiring practice discussed in the example above discriminatory? The legal system has been slow to adopt statistical methods as criteria in litigation. In Castañeda v. Partida (1977), which was a jury discrimination case in the Rio Grande Valley, the U.S. Supreme Court ruled that "gross statistical disparities" alone could be prima facie proof of discrimination. This case is based upon the Civil Rights Act of 1964 and protects African-Americans, Hispanic Americans, Native-Americans, and Women as protected groups.

*The statistical ruling is that events, such as hiring practices, which produce a hiring mix expected to occur "rarely" (in less than **5%** of such cases) by chance, are forms of systematic discrimination provided the disparaged group is protected by the Civil Rights Act.*

In this case the burden of proof is reversed and the hiring entity must establish that each person hired is more qualified than every member of a protected group that was not. We will examine this situation in greater detail later.

Note: Earlier in the semester we mentioned the 1969 draft lottery. Even after the lottery was imposed cities were able to pool draftees across several districts and by filling their allotted quotas in January through May, a disproportionate number of draftees still came from lower-income neighborhoods because college students had yet to graduate.

TABLE 20A: Undergraduate Student Classification @ Utopia U.

	Fresh	**Soph.**	**Junior**	**Senior**	**Total**
Women	245	180	115	60	600
Men	155	120	85	40	400
Total	400	300	200	100	1,000

Example

In the Table 20 A, we can see that the event A of being a woman and the event B of being a sophomore are independent. So the probability of being a woman and a sophomore is

$$\begin{aligned}\Pr(A \cap B) &= \Pr(A) \times \Pr(B). \\ &= \frac{600}{1,000} \times \frac{300}{1,000} \\ &= 0.180\end{aligned}$$

Case Study: On Invasion of Privacy

There are many valid reasons for asking sensitive personal questions such as have you smoked marijuana, snorted cocaine, or cheated on your income taxes. The answers to the substance abuse questions would inform us of how widespread the practices are in the college population. However, since these practices are illegal, a person will think twice about his or her response to such a question. The questions are routinely asked for government jobs and military appointments. If there is no record of conviction on the person he or she may want to conceal his or her practice.

If the intent of our inference is the formation of public policy then there are ways of asking the questions so that the privacy of the individual is protected and the policy maker has greater assurance that the responses are truthful. In the following example, we use an example adapted from C.R. Rao's monograph, **Statistics and Truth**, to illustrate a way of asking delicate questions without invading one's right to privacy.

Case Study: Screening Questions in Questionnaires

If your mother's birthday falls on an even-numbered day of the month answer question number 1, otherwise answer question number 2.

Response Questions

1. Does your birthday fall on an even numbered day of the month?
2. Have you smoked marijuana?

Your response will be simply "Yes" or "No" and the questioner will not know which response question you answered. Here's how this information can be used. In a year with 365 days, I know that 178 days are even-numbered and 187 are odd-numbered. Let A be the event that your mother's birthday is even numbered. So the probability that you answered the first response question is 178/365.

$$\Pr(A) = \frac{178}{365} = 0.488$$

By the **complement rule (CRP)**, it follows that the probability that one answered the second response question is:

$$\Pr(A') = 1 - \frac{178}{365} = \frac{187}{365} = .512$$

Let π_0 = probability of smoking marijuana, which is unknown; π_0 can be interpreted as the proportion of college students who have smoked marijuana. The probability that one answers "Yes" to first response question remains 178/365=0.488. The probability that the screening issue led you to question answer the second response question is 187/365=0.512 and therefore we expect on the average that 187 out of 365 persons would answer this question.

Let Y be the event that a person answered yes to the response question. Then one can answer yes after responding to the first question, A_1 or one can answer yes after responding to the second question, A_2.

$$\Pr(Y) = \Pr(Y \cap A_1) + \Pr(Y \cap A_2)$$

The first event on the right hand side is the event of replying "Yes" and answering the first response question and the second event is the one of replying "Yes" and answering the second response question. These are the only ways of replying "Yes" and they are mutually exclusive. Using the (MRP), we simplify this expression into:

$$\begin{aligned}\Pr(Y) &= \Pr(Y \mid A_1) \times \Pr(A_1) + \Pr(Y \mid A_2) \times \Pr(A_2) \\ &= \frac{178}{365} \times \frac{178}{365} + \pi_0 \times \frac{187}{365}\end{aligned}$$

Let p be the known proportion of persons that answer "Yes" out of a group of n persons questioned. Equate the empirical fraction, p, in the group that answers "Yes" to $\Pr\{Yes\}$. This substitution reduces the previous equation to one, whose only unknown value is the probability, π_0.

$$p = \frac{178}{365} \times \frac{178}{365} + \pi_0 \times \frac{187}{365}$$

Given p, we can solve for an estimate of π_0. To exemplify this procedure, suppose that 120 persons responded "Yes" out of 200 students.

$$\frac{120}{200} = \frac{178}{365} \times \frac{178}{365} + \pi_0 \times \frac{187}{365}$$
$$0.6000 = 0.2378 + \pi_0 \times 0.5123$$
$$\frac{0.3622}{0.5123} = \pi_0$$
$$\pi_0 = 0.7070$$

Obviously this answer is an estimate because the class could have an unusually high percentage of students whose mothers had even-numbered birthdays but the estimate here is that 70.7% of the students have tried marijuana. We cannot, however, know whether students answered the question truthfully or not.

The estimate is very sensitive to the number of persons who respond "Yes." For the circumstance given above, about 60% of the students respond "Yes" but this produces an estimate of 70.7% who have tried marijuana.

To see the reactive nature of the estimate, let's assume that 60 of the 200 persons responded "Yes."

$$\frac{60}{200} = 0.3000 = .2378 + \pi_0 \times 0.5123$$
$$\textit{yielding}$$
$$\pi_0 = 0.1214$$

Notice that the estimate is much smaller than the 30% who respond "Yes" in our sample since one expects almost 25% of the participants to answer, "Yes," because they answer the first question. In this case one would estimate that 12.14% of the students had tried marijuana.

The screening question is very important!! Its impartiality directly effects whether persons will answer the question truthfully. But beware of screening issues, which seem impartial but are in fact highly predisposed to forcing most persons to answer the second response question. For example, let me replace the birthday screening question with a seemingly impartial one.

> *"If the first number in your social security number is odd numbered then answer response question 1, otherwise answer response question 2."*

Historical experience tells me that 90-95% of my students have social security numbers that begin with an even number, most likely 4. By posing the screening question in this manner, most of the population would answer the second response question. This would be advantageous if it did not cause individuals to be suspicious.

Bayes' Theorem

The events $C_1, C_2, \cdots, C_r$ in a sample space, $\mathscr{S}$, form a partition of $\mathscr{S}$ provided

- •{ These Events Are Mutually Exclusive, for each i = 1, ... , r
- ••$\{\Pr(C_i) > 0$

and

- •••$\{\Pr(C_1 \cup C_2 \cup \cdots \cup C_r) = 1$

The purpose of the second condition is to guarantee that the partition has been screened of any unnecessary events. In practice, this happens rarely so we focus our discussions on the first and third properties.

In our initial example in probability, we had two partitions of the student population at UTSA one by gender and one by class rank. The events G_1 and G_2 formed a partition of the undergraduate student population by gender. Notice that the first condition (mutually exclusive) is satisfied because a student cannot be of both genders. The third condition is satisfied since each student must be of one gender or the other. An event and its complement form the simplest partition of just two events. The student population was also partitioned by class rank: freshman, sophomore, junior, or senior. So events A_1, A_2, A_3, and A_4 form a partition of the sample space of UTSA students. The first condition (mutually exclusive) is satisfied because a student cannot simultaneously be a freshman and a junior, or a sophomore and a junior. The third condition is satisfied because every undergraduate must be in one of the four groups.

Bayes' Theorem: Let $C_1, C_2, \cdots, C_r$ be a partition of the sample space, $\mathscr{S}$, and let A be an event in $\mathscr{S}$ such that $\Pr(A) > 0$. Then

$$\Pr(C_j \mid A) = \frac{\Pr(A \mid C_j) \times \Pr(C_j)}{\Pr(A \mid C_1) \times \Pr(C_1) + \cdots + \Pr(A \mid C_r) \times \Pr(C_r)}$$

This theorem was discovered by Reverend (Anglican) Thomas Bayes and published after his death in 1761. See Johnson and Kotz (1997) pg 11.

Case Study: AIDS A Question of Mandatory Testing

In 1989, U., the National College Newspaper, ran an article on a study of 20 American universities that revealed that three out of every one thousand-college students were HIV positive. The study was conducted by the National Center for Disease Control (CDC) with the American College Health Association. The study consisted of testing 1,000 anonymous blood samples from each of the 20 universities.

Much public discussion associated with this virus centers around the controversial subject of mandatory testing. The members of the U.S. Military and some health professionals are required to be tested for this virus. Most Americans are quite naive about medical tests and presume their infallibility (i.e., if a person tests positively then the person must have the disease). Despite the miracles of modern medicine the health professions are still staffed by humans who are capable of mistakes. In fact, the military has found that many false positives have occurred due to incorrect labeling of the blood vials. This frightening observation means that the infected individual went undetected because of the same personnel error.

A blood test, conducted on patients known to be HIV positive, was 99% accurate in declaring the presence of the virus among those known to have it. Among a control group of persons known to be free of the virus, the same blood test falsely declared that 2% were HIV positive. This mistake is known in medicine as a <u>false positive</u>. This mistake can be quite damaging to one's personal reputation, and the associated social stigma is all too well known. If this blood test is used on all college and university students in a national mandate, what is the probability that a person has the HIV virus given that the test is positive?

Let

- $C_1 = \{\text{event that a college student is the HIV}^+\}$ and
- $C_2 = \{\text{event that a college student is not HIV}^+\}$.

Because they are complements, C_1 and C_2 form a partition of the college students. Let $A = \{\text{event that a college students blood tests positive}\}$. Then the simple question stated above can be written as $\Pr(C_1 \mid A)$. From Bayes' theorem, we have that r=2 and j=1. So we can express the probability as

$$\Pr(C_1 \mid A) = \frac{\Pr(A \mid C_1) \times \Pr(C_1)}{\Pr(A \mid C_1) \times \Pr(C_1) + \Pr(A \mid C_2) \times \Pr(C_2)}$$

The term $\Pr(A \mid C_1)$ is the probability that a student tests positively for the virus given that the student has it. The 1989 historical medical evidence indicates that

$\Pr(A \mid C_1) = 0.99$. The term $\Pr(A \mid C_2)$ is the probability that a student tests positively given that the student does not have the virus. The 1989 medical evidence indicates that $\Pr(A \mid C_2) = 0.02$. Among the population of college students, the study conducted by the CDC indicates that the probability that a college student is HIV positive is:

- $\Pr(C_1) = 0.003$ and
- $\Pr(C_2) = 0.997$

So the given information allows us to substitute into **Bayes' theorem**:

$$\begin{aligned}\Pr(C_1 \mid A) &= \frac{\Pr(A \mid C_1) \times \Pr(C_1)}{\Pr(A \mid C_1) \times \Pr(C_1) + \Pr(A \mid C_2) \times \Pr(C_2)} \\ &= \frac{0.99 \times 0.003}{0.99 \times 0.003 + 0.02 \times 0.997} \\ &= \frac{0.00297}{0.00297 + 0.01994} \\ &= 0.1296\end{aligned}$$

This alarming result is correct. Given that a college student tests positively, there is roughly a 13% chance that the student is HIV positive. Do you want mandatory testing for college students? What are the costs to a health system?

Let's see if we can sort out the cause for this unusual rate. Consider a representative group of 100,000 college students (i.e., a group in which exactly 0.3% are HIV positive). Then we would expect 300 of these students to have AIDS according to the CDC study and 99,700 to be HIV negative. We expect our test to indicate that 99% of the 300 are positive, which produces 297 positives from those known to have HIV. Of the 99,700 students, who are HIV negative, we expect our test will falsely declare 2% (or 1,994) as positive. This produces a total of 2,291 persons who will test positive on the average and of these we expect 297 to be HIV positive. The resulting probability is 297/2,291=0.1296.

When you read about such a discrepancy, the natural inclination is to accuse the health profession of quackery. However, it is the mandatory nature of the test that produces these suspect results and not the medical profession. The Surgeon General C. Everett Koop, argued adamantly against a mandatory test because of this problem of false positives. In my illustration of 100,000 college students there would be 1,994 false positives. A physician will only recommend the blood test provided the student exhibits symptoms of the virus, or has behavioral patterns, which place one at risk (e.g., one is an IV drug user, a hemophiliac, a homosexual man, sexually active with an AIDS patient, etc.). If the physician is only 70% accurate in diagnosing the disease, how does this physician screening process change the odds?

Case Study: Underground Storage Tanks (UST)

In an effort to limit the contamination of underground water supplies such as the Edwards Underground Aquifer, the Environmental Protection Agency (EPA) sought legislation to include leak detection systems in underground gasoline storage tanks. However, the EPA actively sought statistical advice before informing Congress. The agency recommended that any leak detection system had to be able to demonstrate:

- A probability of detecting a leak of 0.2 gallons per hour, of 95% within a month while
- Maintaining a false alarm rate of 5%

These probabilities can be found in **The Federal Register** dated September 23, 1988.

In 1986 the EPA conducted a nationwide study to determine the prevalence of leaking tanks, UST's. The results were done on a regional basis and then combined to form a national leak rate for UST's of 35%. In other words, the EPA suspects that 35% of the underground storage tanks are leaking nationwide. The Central region had the highest leak rate of 46%, whereas the Pacific region had the lowest rate of 28%.

Let $L_1 = \{\text{event that a UST leaks}\}$ and $L_2 = \{\text{event that a UST does not leak}\}$. As complements L_1 and L_2 form a partition of the UST. Let LDS be the acronym for a leak detection system and $A = \{\text{event that a LDS indicates a leak}\}$. Then the simple question stated above can be written as $\Pr\{L_1 \mid A\}$, that is the probability that an underground storage tank is leaking given that the system has indicated an alarm.

From Bayes' theorem, this probability is

$$\Pr(L_1 \mid A) = \frac{\Pr(A \mid L_1) \times \Pr(L_1)}{\Pr(A \mid L_1) \times \Pr(L_1) + \Pr(A \mid L_2) \times \Pr(L_2)}$$

The term $\Pr\{A \mid L_1\}$ from Bayes' theorem is the probability that a LDS indicates a leak given the UST leaks. For a leak of 0.20 gallons per hour, federal law requires that a LDS have a minimum probability of 0.95 or $\Pr\{A \mid L_1\} \geq 0.95$. The term $\Pr\{A \mid L_2\}$ is the probability that a LDS indicates a leak given that the UST is not leaking. Again federal law requires that a LDS have a maximum probability of 0.05 or $\Pr\{A \mid L_2\} \leq 0.05$. Among USTs in the United States Central Region, which includes Texas, the 1986 EPA study indicates that the probability that a UST leaks is $\Pr(L_1) = 0.46$ and $\Pr(L_2) = 0.54$. So the EPA information given and federal law, allows us to compute the probability that an EPA certified system has of detecting a leak of 0.20 gallons per hour by substituting these values into Bayes' theorem.

$$\begin{aligned}\Pr(L_1 \mid A) &= \frac{\Pr(A \mid L_1) \times \Pr(L_1)}{\Pr(A \mid L_1) \times \Pr(L_1) + \Pr(A \mid L_2) \times \Pr(L_2)} \\ &= \frac{0.95 \times 0.46}{0.95 \times 0.46 + 0.05 \times 0.54} \\ &= 0.9418\end{aligned}$$

It is necessary for this conditional probability to be high. The laws in place for the US guarantee us a practical leak detection rate of 94.18% for leaks of 0.20 gallons. The tendency among station operators would be to ignore a system that has a high false alarm rate. This is the technical analogue of the little boy who cried wolf. Let's compute the probability that that a tank is not leaking given an alarm.

$$\begin{aligned}\Pr(L_2 \mid A) &= \frac{\Pr(A \mid L_2) \times \Pr(L_2)}{\Pr(A \mid L_1) \times \Pr(L_1) + \Pr(A \mid L_2) \times \Pr(L_2)} \\ &= \frac{0.05 \times 0.54}{0.95 \times 0.46 + 0.05 \times 0.54} \\ &= 0.0582\end{aligned}$$

It is necessary for this conditional probability to be low. The laws in place for the central US guarantee a practical false-alarm rate of 5.82% for leaks of 0.20 gallons per hour. Notice what happens if a system has a 99% of detecting leaks as small as 0.20 gallons per hour when the tank is leaking but has a false alarm rate of 10%.

$$\begin{aligned}\Pr(L_1 \mid A) &= \frac{\Pr(A \mid L_1) \times \Pr(L_1)}{\Pr(A \mid L_1) \times \Pr(L_1) + \Pr(A \mid L_2) \times \Pr(L_2)} \\ &= \frac{0.99 \times 0.46}{0.99 \times 0.46 + 0.10 \times 0.54} \\ &= 0.8940\end{aligned}$$

Notice that the probability of observing a true leak of at least 0.20 gallons per hour when the system produces a warning decreases due to the higher false alarm rate.

$$\begin{aligned}\Pr(L_2 \mid A) &= \frac{\Pr(A \mid L_2) \times \Pr(L_2)}{\Pr(A \mid L_1) \times \Pr(L_1) + \Pr(A \mid L_2) \times \Pr(L_2)} \\ &= \frac{0.1 \times 0.54}{0.99 \times 0.46 + 0.1 \times 0.54} \\ &= 0.106\end{aligned}$$

So such a system guarantees a practical false-alarm rate of 10.6% for leaks.

Counting Rules

Multiplicative Counting Rule (MCR)

Let $A_1, A_2, \cdots, A_r$ be r finite sets with $n_1, n_2, \cdots, n_r$ elements, respectively. Then there are, N, ways

$$N = n_1 \times n_2 \times ... \times n_r$$

of selecting one element from each of $A_1, A_2, \cdots, A_r$.

Example: Group Selection by Gender

Consider a student group, which consists of 23 women and 27 men. How many different ways can one man and one woman be chosen from the group?

In this case let A_1 denote the set of women in the group and the A_2 set of men. Then $n_1 = 23$ and $n_2 = 27$. By the **MCR**, we know that there are

$$\begin{aligned} N &= n_1 \times n_2 b \\ &= 23 \times 27 \\ &= 621. \end{aligned}$$

different ways of selecting one man and one woman from the group.

Example: Group Selection by Class Rank

In the same student group, we want to select a subcommittee, which consists of one freshman, one sophomore, one junior, and one senior. Suppose that the group of 50 students has 17 freshmen, 13 sophomores, 12 juniors, and 8 seniors. Let A_1, A_2, A_3, A_4 denote the sets of freshmen, sophomores, juniors, and seniors, respectively. Then we have $n_1 = 17, n_2 = 13, n_3 = 12 - and - n_4 = 8$. So it follows by the **MCR** that there are

$$\begin{aligned} N &= n_1 \times n_2 \times n_3 \times n_4 \\ &= 17 \times 13 \times 12 \times 8 \\ &= 221 \times 96 \\ &= 21{,}216. \end{aligned}$$

different ways of choosing one freshman, one sophomore, one junior and one senior from the group.

We use the **MCR** to count the number of occurrences of several arrangements that frequently occur in practical settings. The ones that we will address are permutations and combinations.

Permutations

Let A be a set of n distinct elements. A permutation of r elements chosen (without replacement) from the n elements is a specific arrangement of these r elements. To be explicit, two permutations differ if

1) The elements in the two arrangements differ, or
2) If the order of the elements differ.

Let A be the set of vowels, $A = \{a, e, i, o, u\}$. Suppose that from this set of five vowels that we choose three vowels. In this case, $n = 5$ and $r = 3$. Let's list all the distinct arrangements of size 3 from this set of 5 vowels.

{a, e, i}, {a, e, o}, {a, e, u}, {a, i, o}, {a, i, u},
{a, o, u}, {e, i, o}, {e, i, u}, {e, o, u}, {i, o, u}.

These ten arrangements differ because no two groups of three contain the same vowels (i.e., they differ by an element). Moreover, from each arrangement we can create more permutations by merely changing the order of the elements in the arrangement. For example, the permutation {a, e, i} produces 5 more permutations:

{a, i, e}, {i, a, e}, {i, e, a}, {e, a, i}, and {e, i, a}.

So altogether there are 60 distinct permutations of the 5 vowels if we choose 3 of them. In general, there is a formula for the calculation of the number permutations of size r chosen from a set with n elements. The number is denoted by ${}_nP_r$ and given by

$$ {}_nP_r = \frac{n!}{(n-r)!} $$

So in this example,

$$ {}_5P_3 = \frac{5!}{(5-3)!} = \frac{5!}{2!} = \frac{120}{2} = 60. $$

The formula comes from the **MCR**. Notice that in a permutation there are n distinct ways to choose the first element in the arrangement, $n-1$ ways to choose the second element, and so on, until there are $n-r+1$ ways of choosing the rth element in the permutation.

Each time we choose another element there are fewer from which to choose from because we choose without replacement. By the **MCR**,

$$_nP_r = n \times (n-1) \times \cdots \times (n-r+1).$$

Combinations

Once again start with a set A, which has n distinct elements. A combination of r elements chosen from the n elements in A is an arrangement of r of the n elements chosen without replacement. However, combinations differ if and only if the arrangements contain different elements. In the example of vowels, the ten original arrangements are different combinations but changing the order of the arrangement does not produce a new combination.

The number of distinct combinations of size r chosen from a set with n elements is denoted by $_nC_r$ and given by

$$_nC_r = \frac{n!}{(n-r)! \times r!}$$

In the example of the set of vowels, we have that $n=5$ and $r=3$, so that

$$\begin{aligned} _5C_3 &= \frac{5!}{(5-3)! \times (3!)} \\ &= \frac{5!}{2! \times 3!} \\ &= 10. \end{aligned}$$

We can also derive the formula for the number of distinct combinations from the one for the number of distinct permutations as

$$_nC_r = \frac{_nP_r}{r!}$$

This observation reveals that for a given arrangement of size r, there are $r!$ ways of rearranging the elements in a given combination. In the example of the set of vowels, the combination {a, e, i}, could be arranged into 3!=6 permutations.

Example: Class Elections

In a group of 36 students, how many different ways can the group elect a President, Vice President, and Treasurer? Since the order of the offices is important, the choices represent distinct permutations. The total number of ways is given by

$$_{36}P_3 = 36 \times 35 \times 34 = 42{,}840.$$

Example: Group Selection-Stratified by Gender

In a group of 45 students of whom 25 are men and 20 are women, how many different ways can you select a group of 5 students so that 3 are men and 2 are women?

Since there is no ranking within the three men, the number of choices of 3 men from the 25 available is a combination. For the same reason, the choice of the two women is a combination. The number, n_1, of ways of selecting 3 men from the 25 is given by

$$n_1 = {}_{25}C_3 = \frac{25!}{22! \times 3!} = 2{,}300.$$

The number, n_2, of ways of choosing the two women from the 20 available is:

$$n_2 = {}_{20}C_2 = \frac{20!}{18! \times 2!} = 190.$$

By the **MCR**, the total number of ways of selecting three men and two women is:

$$N = n_1 \times n_2 = 2{,}300 \times 190 = 437{,}000.$$

Example: Probabilities of Stratified Samples

What's the probability that a group of 5 students, chosen from the 45 available, will consist of exactly 3 men and two women? In this problem, we found the total number of ways of selecting 3 men and 2 women from the population of 25 men and 20 women. To compute the probability we must divide the number of favorable outcomes by the total number of ways of selecting 5 students from the 45. The number of such ways is

$$_{45}C_5 = 1{,}221{,}759.$$

So the probability becomes

$$\begin{aligned}\Pr(\text{3 men and 2 women}) &= \frac{_{25}C_3 \times {_{20}C_2}}{_{45}C_5} \\ &= \frac{437{,}000}{1{,}221{,}759} \\ &= 0.358.\end{aligned}$$

Thus in 35.8% of such selections should we expect see a selection of exactly 3 men and 2 women.

Example: Stratified Selection of Committee Members

An employer advertises vacancies for 6 CPA's and receives an applicant pool of 30 persons, who meet the advertised qualifications. Among the applicants are 20 women and 10 men. The employer ends up hiring 2 women and 4 men.

$$\begin{aligned}\Pr(\text{2 women and 4 men}) &= \frac{_{20}C_2 \times {_{10}C_4}}{_{30}C_6} \\ &= \frac{190 \times 210}{593{,}775} \\ &= 0.0672\end{aligned}$$

Thus in only 6.72% of such cases should we expect see a hiring outcome with such a disproportionate outcome by gender.

Example: Stratified Selection of Basketball Lineups

Coach Carter has 3 centers, 5 forwards, and 4 guards on the Roadrunner men's team. How many different lineups can he field assuming no one plays out of position?

- A basketball team has 1 center, 2 forwards, and 2 guards. So the number, n_1, of ways choosing one center from the 3 available is
  - $n_1 = {_3C_1} = 3.$

- Each team has two forwards, so the number n_2 of ways of picking two forwards from the 5 available is
    - $n_2 = {}_5C_2 = 10.$
- A team has two guards, so the number, n_3, of ways of picking two guards is:
    - $n_3 = {}_4C_2 = 6.$

Consequently the total number of lineups would be the product of these numbers by the **MCR**:

$$N = n_1 \times n_2 \times n_3 = 3 \times 10 \times 6 = 180.$$

Example: Stratified Committee Representation

A small business in San Antonio has 30 Hispanic, 20 Anglo, and 10 Black employees. The company wants to establish a representative grievance committee, which consists of 3 Hispanics, 2 Anglos and 1 Black. How many ways can the company select a representative committee?

- So the number, n_1, of ways choosing 3 Hispanics from the 30 available is
    - $n_1 = {}_{30}C_3 = 4{,}060.$
- The number, n_2, of ways of picking two Anglos from the 20 available is
    - $n_2 = {}_{20}C_2 = 190.$
- The number, n_3, of ways of picking one Black employee from the 10 available is
    - $n_3 = {}_{10}C_1 = 10.$

The total number of representative committees is the product by the **MCR**.

$$N = n_1 \times n_2 \times n_3 = 4{,}060 \times 190 \times 10 = 7{,}714{,}000.$$

Example (First Texas Lottery)

Each time the lottery was played 6 winning numbers are chosen and 44 numbers are not chosen because originally 50 numbers were used. On each ticket, we choose 6 numbers. How many ways are there of picking 6 numbers from the 50 available?

$$n_0 = {}_{50}C_6 = 15{,}890{,}700.$$

How many ways are there of matching exactly 4 of the 6 winning numbers? Notice that we must choose the 4 winning numbers from the 6 available and the two losing numbers from the 44 available. The number, n_1, of ways of matching 4 winning numbers is

$$n_1 = {}_6C_4 = 15.$$

The number, n_2, of ways of choosing the two losing numbers is

$$n_2 = {}_{44}C_2 = 946.$$

So the probability of matching exactly 4 winning numbers is

$$\Pr(4\text{ matches and 2 mismatches}) = \frac{15 \times 946}{15{,}890{,}700} = 0.000892975.$$

So the chance of matching exactly 4 numbers is slightly less than one out of a thousand.

Case Study: Statistics and the Law- Discriminatory Hiring Practices

The reader should note that the Civil Rights Act of 1964 recognizes Women, Blacks, Hispanics, and Native Americans as protected groups. The protection afforded these groups extends to a form of statistical discrimination known as *"systematic discrimination."* In this form of discrimination, the plaintiffs (a protected group) can shift the burden of proof to the defendants provided the protected group can show that the hiring process resulted in an unrepresentative hire which was highly unlikely to occur due to chance alone. The courts have defined how rare an event must be to come under legal scrutiny.

The legal system has been slow to adopt statistical methods as criteria in litigation. However, in **Castañeda vs. Partida (1977)**, which was a jury discrimination case, the U.S. Supreme Court adopted criteria that *"gross statistical disparities"* alone could be **prima facie proof of discrimination**. This Texas case originated in the South Texas region and was initiated by Hispanics. Meier, Sacks, and Zabell (1986) give an in depth discussion of this *"systematic discrimination."*

An employer advertises vacancies for six CPAs and receives an applicant pool of 30 people meeting the minimum qualifications for the positions. Among the 30 applicants, 20 are women and 10 are men. The employer completes its hiring and hires five men and one woman. Does this hiring practice constitute *"systematic discrimination"* against women, who are a protected group under the Civil Rights Act of 1964?

We know that the number of ways of choosing five men and one woman from the group is given by

$$ {}_{10}C_5 \times {}_{20}C_1 = 252 \times 20 = 5{,}040 $$

The total number of ways of selecting the six CPAs is given by

$$ {}_{30}C_6 = 593{,}775 $$

The subsequent probability would be the ratio of the two counts which is

$$ \begin{aligned} \Pr(\text{hiring one woman}) &= \frac{{}_{10}C_5 \times {}_{20}C_1}{{}_{30}C_6} \\ &= \frac{252 \times 20}{593{,}775} \\ &= \frac{5{,}040}{593{,}775} \\ &= 0.008488 \end{aligned} $$

The probability of this event happens rarely due to chance alone but would it qualify for the process of *"systematic discrimination."* To invoke this statute we need to compute the probability that none of the six persons hired were women as well.

In a similar way the probability of hiring no women due to chance alone is given by

$$
\begin{aligned}
\Pr(\text{hiring no women}) &= \frac{{}_{10}C_6 \times {}_{20}C_0}{{}_{30}C_6} \\
&= \frac{210 \times 1}{593{,}775} \\
&= \frac{210}{593{,}775} \\
&= 0.000353669
\end{aligned}
$$

So the probability that a hiring practice would have resulted in at most one woman being hired due to chance alone is the sum of these two probabilities

$$
\begin{aligned}
\Pr(\text{hiring at most one woman}) &= \underbrace{\Pr(\text{hiring no women})}_{} + \underbrace{\Pr(\text{hiring one woman})}_{} \\
&= 0.000353669 + 0.008488064 \\
&= 0.008841733.
\end{aligned}
$$

Since the probability that such a practice would have occurred due to chance alone is so remote, in a class action suit the women would be able to invoke *"systematic discrimination."* The legal test on the probability value of a remote event was set at 0.05 in **Palmer vs. Schultz (1989)**. We don't know whether discrimination took place or not; only the participants may know. In the courts, the roles of plaintiffs and defendants would then be reversed so that the firm would be forced to show that each of the five men selected was better qualified than each of the 19 women who were not hired. The down side to this process is that companies can do the calculations as well and find the minimum number of women that they must hire to escape the invocation of *"systematic discrimination."* The company, not the court, creates a *"veiled quota."* This practice was redressed in the case of **Hazelwood vs. the State of New Jersey (1980)**.

Case Study: LOTTO TEXAS

In examining the updated game, *LOTTO TEXAS*, the odds of winning can be determined from combinations. There are now 54 numerals used in the game of which 6 are chosen. The participant in turn chooses 6 numerals as well and compares his or her selections with the numbers chosen by the lottery. Let x *be the number of matches* and of course then $6-x$ *is the number of mismatches*.

The number of ways of making x *matches* is given by ${}_6C_x$ since the matches must be made with the 6 numerals chosen in the drawing. The number of ways or making $6-x$ mismatches is ${}_{48}C_{6-x}$ because the $6-x$ *mismatches* must be made with the 48 not chosen in the drawing.

To compute the probability we determine the number of ways of making x matches and $6-x$ matches and this number is divided by ${}_{54}C_6 = 25{,}827{,}165$ ways of picking 6 numbers from the 54 available lottery numbers.

$$P(none) = \frac{{}_6C_0 \times {}_{48}C_6}{{}_{54}C_6} = \frac{1 \times 12{,}271{,}512}{25{,}827{,}165} = 0.475139722$$

$$P(one) = \frac{{}_6C_1 \times {}_{48}C_5}{{}_{54}C_6} = \frac{6 \times 1{,}712{,}304}{25{,}827{,}165} = 0.397791395$$

$$P(two) = \frac{{}_6C_2 \times {}_{48}C_4}{{}_{54}C_6} = \frac{15 \times 194{,}580}{25{,}827{,}165} = 0.113008919$$

$$P(three) = \frac{{}_6C_3 \times {}_{48}C_3}{{}_{54}C_6} = \frac{20 \times 17{,}296}{25{,}827{,}165} = 0.01339365$$

$$P(four) = \frac{{}_6C_4 \times {}_{48}C_2}{{}_{54}C_6} = \frac{15 \times 1{,}128}{25{,}827{,}165} = 0.000655124$$

$$P(five) = \frac{{}_6C_5 \times {}_{48}C_1}{{}_{54}C_6} = \frac{6 \times 48}{25{,}827{,}165} = 0.000011151$$

$$P(six) = \frac{{}_6C_6 \times {}_{48}C_0}{{}_{54}C_6} = \frac{1 \times 1}{25{,}827{,}165} = 0.000000039$$

Case Study: The Birthday Problem

Suppose that there are r persons, born in 1985, in a room. What is the probability that at least two of these r persons have the same birthday? It is very difficult to solve this problem directly. It is easier to determine the probability of the complement of this event. The complement of this event is that each of the r persons has a different birthday. If there are three persons born in 1985 in the room then the number of ways in which the three persons can have different birthdays is given by:

$$\begin{aligned} n_1 \times n_2 \times n_3 &= 365 \times 364 \times 363 \\ &= 48{,}228{,}180 \\ &= {}_{365}P_3 \end{aligned}$$

The number of ways in which the three persons born in 1981 can have birthdays regardless of whether they are different are not is given by:

$$m_1 \times m_2 \times m_3 = 365 \times 365 \times 365$$
$$= 48{,}627{,}125$$
$$= (365)^3$$

So the probability that three randomly chosen people born in 1981 have different birthdays is:

$$\pi(3) = \frac{{}_{365}P_3}{(365)^3}$$
$$= \frac{48{,}228{,}180}{48{,}627{,}125}$$
$$= 0.991795834$$

So the probability that at least two of the three persons born in 1981 have the same birthday is 0.008204166. In general, the probability that r randomly chosen people born in 1981 have different birthdays is:

$$\pi(r) = \frac{{}_{365}P_r}{(365)^r}$$

We can calculate the probabilities for various values of r. The break-even point is $r = 23$.

TABLE 21: Probabilities that r persons have different birthdays

r	$\pi(r)$	r	$\pi(r)$
4	0.9836	20	0.5886
5	0.9729	21	0.5563
6	0.9595	22	0.5243
7	0.9438	23	0.4927
8	0.9257	24	0.4617
9	0.9054	25	0.4439
10	0.8831	26	0.4135
11	0.8589	27	0.3841
12	0.8330	28	0.3557
13	0.8056	29	0.3274
14	0.7769	30	0.3014
15	0.7471	31	0.2766
16	0.7164	32	0.2531
17	0.6850	33	0.2309
18	0.6531	34	0.2101
19	0.6209	35	

Discrete Distributions

We have devoted the first part of this course to data analysis including descriptive statistics for both complete and grouped data. We followed this introduction with a discussion of probability and the axioms that allow us to implement its computation.

We introduce the notion of a probability distribution for a discrete random variable, X. We assume that the variable, X, has r possible outcomes, $\{x_1, x_2, \ldots, x_r\}$, known as the range space (or domain) of X. Recall the example of the number of siblings, X, of persons in this class had a range space in which, $\{x_1 = 0, x_2 = 1, \ldots, x_r = 17\}$.

The **probability distribution** of a random variable is a function that assigns a probability to each value of the range space. So for each $i = 1, \cdots, r$,

$$p(x_i) = \Pr[X = x_i]$$

and

$$p(x) = 0, -for - all - x \neq x_i - for - some - i = 1, \ldots, r$$

The probability distribution of the random or response variable, X, can be expressed in three ways:

- Tabular (table)
- Graphical (frequency histogram)
- Mathematical Function

The **probability distribution** $p(x)$ is subject to two constraints that are consequences of the **axioms of Kolmogorov**.

$$p(x) \geq 0$$

$$\sum_{i=1}^{r} p(x_i) = 1 \qquad \text{Axioms 1 \& 2}$$

Example

Consider the typical American family with two children. Let the random variable X be the number of girls in the family. Then there are exactly four possible outcomes:

$$\{\text{GG, GB, BG, BB}\},$$

where G represents the birth of a girl and B represents the birth of a boy. If we assume that birth order is independent of gender and that a child is as likely to be a boy as a girl then each of the four events are equally likely to occur and have probabilities of ¼.

Then the **range space** of X is {0, 1, and 2}. The outcome, {BB}, is the event that yields $X = 0$. The event $X = 1$ is equivalent to the event {GB, BG} and the event $X = 2$ is equivalent to the outcome {GG}. Then the distribution of X given in tabular form in Table 22 is:

TABLE 22: Probability distribution of number of girls in families with 2 children

x	0	1	2
$p(x)$	¼	½	¼

The graphical form of the probability distribution, X, of the number of girls in families with two children is given in Figure 19 by:

FIGURE 19: Probability distribution of the number of girls as a graph

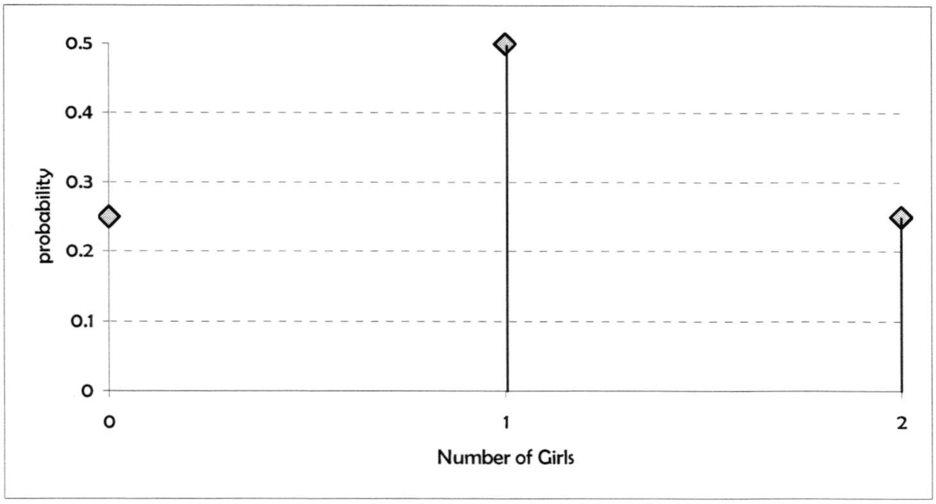

We can describe the distribution of X via a mathematical formula for $x = 0, \cdots, 2$.

$$p(x) = \frac{{}_2C_x}{4}, x = 0, \cdots, 2.$$

Recall that the random variable is a characteristic of interest about each of the population. We can now reintroduce the notion of parameters.

<u>Parameters</u> are numerical measures of the population.

The population mean μ is the population analog to the sample mean. It is defined by for a discrete response variable X as:

$$\mu = \sum_{i=1}^{r} x_i \times p(x_i)$$

This definition is virtually identical to the one for grouped data where the value x_i has replaced the midpoint m_i and $p(x_i)$ replaces the relative frequency f_i/n.

The population mode θ is the population analog to the sample mode. It is defined by for a discrete response variable X as:

$$\begin{aligned} &\theta = x_i - such - that \\ &p(x_i) \geq p(x), - for - all - x. \end{aligned}$$

Notice that this value may not be unique.

Example:

The population mean μ of the number of girls X is given by

$$\mu = 0 \times \frac{1}{4} + 1 \times \frac{2}{4} + 2 \times \frac{1}{4} = 1.$$

This means that the expected number of girls in families with two children is one. In this case, we see that the entire population is being sampled. In finite populations this is called an exhaustive sample or a census.

The population mode θ of the number of girls X is given by

$$\begin{aligned} &\theta = 1, - because - \\ &p(1) = \frac{2}{4} > p(x) - for - all - x \neq 1 \end{aligned}$$

The population variance, σ^2, of the discrete response variable X is given by

$$\sigma^2 = \sum_{i=1}^{r} (x_i - \mu)^2 p(x_i)$$

Example:

The population variance σ^2 of the number of girls X is given by

$$\sigma^2 = (0-1)^2 \times \frac{1}{4} + (1-1)^2 \times \frac{2}{4} + (2-1)^2 \times \frac{1}{4} = \frac{1}{2}.$$

The population standard deviation σ is the principal square root of the population variance, and in this example: $\sigma = 0.707$. The parameter measures scatter within the distribution.

Example:

Consider the response variable X which is the number of times it takes an MS 1013 student to complete the course with a grade of C or better so that he or she can declare a major in Business. Suppose that the probability distribution $p(x)$ is given by

$$p(x) = \frac{(4-x)^2}{14}, x = 1,2,3$$

Determine the expected number of times that a student must take this class to declare a Business major.

$$\mu = 1 \times \frac{(4-1)^2}{14} + 2 \times \frac{(4-2)^2}{14} + 3 \times \frac{(4-3)^2}{14}$$
$$= \frac{9}{14} + \frac{8}{14} + \frac{3}{14}$$
$$= \frac{20}{14} = \frac{10}{7}$$

The expected number of times μ required to complete MS 1013 to declare a Business major is 1.429 attempts.

The population mode θ of the number of attempts, X, needed to pass MS 1013 successfully and declare a Business major is:

$$\theta = 1,-because-$$
$$p(1) = \frac{9}{14} > p(x) - for - all - x \neq 1$$

Also we can find the population standard deviation from the population variance as

$$\sigma^2 = \left(1-\frac{20}{14}\right)^2 \times \frac{9}{14} + \left(2-\frac{20}{14}\right)^2 \times \frac{4}{14} + \left(3-\frac{20}{14}\right)^2 \times \frac{1}{14}$$

$$= \frac{324}{14^3} + \frac{256}{14^3} + \frac{484}{14^3}$$

$$= \frac{1,064}{2,744} = \frac{133}{343}$$

The population standard deviation σ is 0.6227 attempts

The distribution given here can be converted into a **pseudo-sample** that is completely representative of the population. The **pseudo-sample** for this problem is given by

$$\{\underbrace{1, 1, 1, 1, 1, 1, 1, 1, 1}_{9} \quad \underbrace{2, 2, 2, 2,}_{4} \quad \underbrace{3}_{1}\}$$

In this way we can use our calculators on the pseudo-sample to compute the population mean μ and the population standard deviation σ. Notice that the sample mean of the representative sample is exactly the population mean of the distribution. This should call to mind the goal of statistics to use descriptive statistics calculated from representative samples to make inferences about the values of population parameters. If we had used the value of n in the denominator of the formula for the sample variance instead of $n-1$, the sample variance would equal the population variance of the distribution.

Creation of **representative pseudo-samples** emphasizes the inherent link between **sample descriptive statistics** and the values of **population parameters**.

Binomial Distribution

Binomial Experiment:

In certain situations, the form of an experiment actually dictates the underlying **discrete probability distribution**. In the text below we specify four conditions, which dictate that the associated discrete random variable will have a binomial distribution.

- The outcome of an experiment is **dichotomous**, which allows only one of available two responses. A response variable is assigned a value of *1*, provided the item has the **characteristic** and *0* if it does not. In the terms that follow, we say that an experimental item is a *"success"* provided it has the characteristic, or is a *"failure"* if the experimental unit doesn't have the attribute.

- The experiment is repeated in "n" **independent** trials.

- The "success probability," which we denote by p **remains constant** from trial to trial of the experiment.

- The count Y of the **number of successes** has a **binomial distribution** with **success probability** p and a **sample size** of n trials. The "success" probability is denoted by p, whereas the "failure" probability is denoted by $(1-p)$.

The probability distribution of a *binomial* random variable, Y, is the probability of observing exactly y *successes* in n *trials* of the experiment and is given by:

$$\begin{aligned} p(y;n,p) &= \Pr[Y=y] \\ &= {}_nC_y p^y (1-p)^{n-y}, \end{aligned}$$

for each y = 0, 1, …, n.

The probability of *"success"* is p and the probability of *"failure"* is $1-p$. Because successive trials are independent, the probability of any one **combination** of y *successes* and $n-y$ *failures* is

$$p^y(1-p)^{n-y}.$$

However, all permutations, which result in exactly y *successes* and $n - y$ *failures*, produce the same combination of which there are ${}_nC_y$. So the probability of obtaining exactly y *successes* and $n - y$ *failures* is the product of these values.

Example:

In assessing product quality a manufacturer is concerned about the quality of its products. This topic has high visibility with business executives in the automotive industry, the electronics industry, and the home entertainment industry (e.g., TVs, VCRs, CDs). Consumer dissatisfaction undermines consumer confidence and provides marketing ammunition to one's competitors. Many Japanese companies carved a niche in U.S. markets by providing components of better quality. So we construct a product specific indicator variable, where I=1, if the product is **acceptable**, and I=0 if **defective**.

Marketing surveys often contain a sequence of questions about consumer preferences. To simplify the tabulation and reduce confusion, the responses are simply: yes or no. The marketing department of a large automotive firm may ask your preference about its products. For example, do you prefer a car with an anti-lock braking system? Do you prefer a car with front wheel drive? Do you prefer a car with four-wheel steering? Do you prefer a car with side impact air bags? In each case an answer of yes would indicate that the consumer prefers the feature of this car. So we can develop a preference-specific indicator variable, I=1, if the consumer wants the feature and I=0, otherwise. In this way, the marketing firm can begin to assess its share of the market.

Ethnic issues are quite common in the business community. We sometimes hear of marketing items for ethnic minorities. In our culture, issues of interest to Hispanics are quite important in San Antonio and the South Texas Region. So we introduce an ethnic-specific indicator variable I=1, if the person is of Hispanic descent and I=0, otherwise.

Example:

Suppose that a child, (not precocious), takes a statistic exam that consists of ten multiple-choice questions each of which has five possible answers. If the child is merely guessing, what is the probability that he or she gets exactly 3 correct answers out of ten?

The child's answers are **dichotomous** in that each is either **correct or incorrect**. Each question represents a new and independent trial of the experiment; the exam consists of 10 questions for a **sample of size** of $n = 10$. Since the child has 5 possible answers per question and we assume that the child is guessing, **the probability of a success is** $p = 0.20$ **(or 1-out-of-five)**. Then Y the number of correct answers has a **binomial distribution** because the experiment satisfies the conditions of a **binomial experiment**.

$$\begin{aligned} p(3;10,0.20) &= {}_{10}C_3(0.20)^3(1-0.20)^{10-3} \\ &= 120 \times (0.008) \times (0.2097152) \\ &= 0.201326592. \end{aligned}$$

So if the child guesses, he or she should get 3 exactly correct in 20.13% of the cases just due to chance alone, see Table 23.

What is the probability that he or she gets at most 3 correct? In this case, we want to know the probability that Y is no more than 3 correct (or 3 or fewer correct). This situation corresponds to $\{Y \leq 3\}$.

$$\begin{aligned} \Pr\{Y \leq 3\} &= \Pr\{Y = 0\} + \Pr\{Y = 1\} + \Pr\{Y = 2\} + \Pr\{Y = 3\}. \\ &= p(0,10,0.20) + p(1,10,0.20) + p(2,10,0.20) + p(3,10,0.20) \end{aligned}$$

So to answer this question, we must calculate $p(0), p(1), p(2), -and-, p(3)$.

1) First compute $p(0)$: Table 23.

$$\begin{aligned} p(0;10,0.20) &= {}_{10}C_0(0.20)^0(0.80)^{10-0} \\ &= 0.107374182 \quad . \end{aligned}$$

2) Next compute $p(1)$: Table 23.

$$\begin{aligned} p(1;10,0.20) &= {}_{10}C_1(0.20)^1(0.80)^{10-1} \\ &= 10 \times (0.20) \times (0.134217728 \ ) \\ &= 0.268435456 \ . \end{aligned}$$

3) Finally compute $p(2)$: Table 23.

$$\begin{aligned} p(2;10,0.20) &= {}_{10}C_2(0.20)^2(0.80)^{10-2} \\ &= 45 \times (0.04) \times (0.16777216) \\ &= 0.301989888. \end{aligned}$$

So we can compute the **compound event** of at most 3 correct answers.

$$\begin{aligned}\Pr\{Y \leq 3\} &= \Pr\{Y=0\} + \Pr\{Y=1\} + \Pr\{Y=2\} + \Pr\{Y=3\}.\\ &= p(0,10,0.20) + p(1,10,0.20) + p(2,10,0.20) + p(3,10,0.20)\\ &= 0.10737418 + 0.26843546 + 0.30198989 + 0.20132659\\ &= 0.87912612.\end{aligned}$$

What is the probability that the child got at least 3 correct (i.e., 3 or more correct)? In this case, the event corresponds to $\{Y \geq 3\}$.

$$\begin{aligned}\Pr\{Y \geq 3\} &= \Pr\{Y=3\} + \Pr\{Y=4\} + \cdots + \Pr\{Y=10\}.\\ &\text{or by the complement rule}\\ &= 1 - \Pr\{Y < 3\}\}\\ &= 1 - \{p(0,10,0.20) + p(1,10,0.20) + p(2,10,0.20)\}\\ &= 1 - \{0.107374182 + 0.268435456 + 0.301989888\}\\ &= 0.32220474.\end{aligned}$$

Fortunately, we have tables in the back of the section, for $n = 10$, which provides the probabilities for small values of n and specific values of p.

TABLE 23: Binomial Probabilities for sample sizes of 10 for various values success probability

Y\p	0.10	0.15	0.20	0.25	0.30
0	0.3487	0.1969	0.1074	0.0563	0.0282
1	0.3874	0.3474	0.2684	0.1877	0.1211
2	0.1937	0.2759	0.3020	0.2816	0.2335
3	0.0574	0.1298	0.2013	0.2503	0.2668
4	0.0112	0.0401	0.0881	0.1460	0.2001
5	0.0015	0.0085	0.0264	0.0584	0.1029
6	0.0001	0.0012	0.0055	0.0162	0.0368
7	0.0000	0.0001	0.0008	0.0031	0.0090
8	0.0000	0.0000	0.0001	0.0004	0.0014

To use a binomial table find the particular table for the specified sample size. Locate the probability of interest by scanning the first row until you find the column headed by the specific probability p (0.20 in this case). The values in that column form the probability distribution for various values of Y. To find the probability that $Y = 5$, scan down the first column until you arrive at the row headed by $Y = 5$ and then scan across that row until you fall in the column headed by the appropriate value of p (0.20 in this case). In the event that the value of n exceeds 20 or if the specific probability is not one in the table then we must compute the probabilities using the formula. Notice that the values in the table concur with our individual calculations and we understand how the tabled values can be computed.

Example Fidelity in Advertising

It is well known that the chances that a *12-ounce Dr. Pepper* can is under-filled are 0.32 (I am assuming this from professional experience). What is the probability that a six-pack will contain exactly 2 under-filled cans?

The event is **dichotomous** because each can is under-filled or it isn't. The experiment is **repeated in** $n = 6$ **independent trials** (i.e., each can represents a trial of the experiment). A *success* is defined as an *under-filled can*. The **probability of success is, therefore** $p = 0.32$. So Y the count of under-filled cans has a binomial distribution.

$$\begin{aligned} p(2;6,0.32) &= \Pr[Y = 2] \\ &= {}_6C_2 \times (0.32)^2 \times (1-0.32)^{6-2} \\ &= {}_6C_2 \times (0.32)^2 \times (0.68)^4 \\ &= 15 \times (0.1024) \times (0.21381376) \\ &= 0.328417935 \end{aligned}$$

This example relates to the manner in which one would test for truth in advertising, for example, does the product contain as much as the label claims? Either the product has at least the stated amount or less. Notice that $p = 0.32$ is not in the table and so the probabilities must be computed by hand. We could use the table for $n = 6$ on page 109, to see if the number we calculate makes sense or is somewhat close to the table value. In this case, the agreement is obvious.

$$\Pr\{Y = 2 \mid n = 6 \text{ and } p = 0.30\} = 0.3241$$

If someone makes a claim about having a superior product, he or she can compare products side by side. The outcome is dichotomous (i.e., the Energizer lasts longer than the Coppertop, or Excedrin stops pain faster, etc.) We especially see statistics playing a more prominent role in product advertising and marketing as producers are being held to standards of accountability through the fidelity in advertising legislation.

Example: Extra Sensory Perception

An Unlikely Application: A person claims to have ESP! Can we determine whether the person's claim has any validity? The following experiment is often conducted to reduce the number of persons claiming to have ESP. Consider a regular deck that contains 26 red cards and 26 black cards. We ask the *candidate* to cut the deck and identify the color of the card. He or she then returns the card to the deck; the deck is shuffled; and the process is repeated 15 times.

The experiment is binomial because the outcomes are **dichotomous—the person either correctly identifies the color** or does not. By **returning the card to the deck**, the number of red and black cards in the deck remains equal so that p, the **probability of identifying the correct color remains constant** from trial to trial. By **shuffling the deck one does induce some randomness between trials** but not completely (see Persi Diaconis).

What is the probability that someone without ESP identifies 12 more cards correctly? We are making an assumption that the person has no ESP.

1) Let $Y = \#$ of cards correctly identified;
2) Let $n = 15$, the number of trials
   [This number can be changed by the tester]; and
3) Let $p = 0.50$, (50%) (The success value if he or she is only guessing).

Remember: p = *probability of successes in one trial!*

$$\Pr(Y \geq 12) = \sum_{y=12}^{15} p(y;15,0.50) = 0.014 + 0.003 + 0.000 \cdots + 0.000 = 0.017$$

From the table on page 112, we can add the values correctly to four decimal places.

y	0.50
12	0.0139
13	0.0032
14	0.0005
15	0.0000

If we assume that a seer merely guesses then he or she should get 12 or more correct only about 17 times in every 1,000 repeats of the experiments, and 13 or more correct only 3 times in every 1,000 repeats of this experiment. Is the candidate seer a charlatan? We don't know but this process is able to document the frequency with which we should observe such extreme occurrences due to chance alone.

Population Parameters

The **mean** μ of the population characteristic of a **binomial random variable** is given by

$$\mu = n \times p$$

Note that p is the **probability of success per trial** and n is the **number of trials**, so that np is the **expected number of successes in the n trials**. The corresponding variance σ^2 of the population characteristic, is given by

$$\sigma^2 = n \times p \times (1 - p).$$

The name for the binomial distribution comes from the binomial theorem in algebra. The theorem tells us how to exponentiate a binomial term.

Binomial Theorem:

Let a and b be real numbers and let n be a positive integer. Then

$$(a+b)^n = \sum_{r=0}^{n} {}_nC_r a^r b^{n-r}$$

A special case of this theorem is a result that everyone remembers.

$$(a+b)^2 = a^2 + 2ab + b^2$$

You may also recall the following cubic formula:

$$(a+b)^3 = a^3 + 3a^2b + 3ab^2 + b^3$$

The British scientist, **Sir Isaac Newton**, (for more information on Newton see Johnson and Kotz (1997) page 55) first established this theorem in 1665 at the age of 23. Newton had time to devote to his personal interest during this year because European universities were closed throughout 1666 due to the **Bubonic Plague**, which claimed the lives of one of out every three Europeans. The reader should recall that the **binomial coefficients** ${}_nC_r$, come from **Pascal's triangle**. For more information on Blaise Pascal, see Johnson and Kotz (1997) page 61.

TABLE 24: Pascal's Triangle

n							r					
1						1		1				
2					1		2		1			
3				1		3		3		1		
4			1		4		6		4		1	
5		1		5		10		10		5		1
…	1		…		…		…		……		…	

The French mathematician **Blaise Pascal** wrote this result in 1653, but published it in 1665. So Newton was unaware of it.

The entries in Pascal's triangle are determined as follows. The first row is started with entries 1 and 1 and a column between them is left blank. The entries in successive rows are found from the entries in the row above. Recall that in entering the coefficients one always skips a column between entries in the same row. Each row is started with 1 in the column preceding the first column in the row above. The next entry (don't forget to skip a column) is determined by adding the entries in the adjacent columns in the row above. Also, each row ends with 1. For example, the fourth row begins with 1, the next entry, 4, is found by adding 1 and 3 (in the row above) which are the entries in the columns next to the new entry but in the row above it.

The binomial coefficients can be obtained from this triangle as follows. The sample size determines the row number to use in the triangle, whereas the column within the row determines the value of r+1. Thus, the value in the fourth row (n=4) and third column (r+1=3 or =2) gives ${}_4C_2=6$.

This theorem is needed to prove that all the binomial probabilities sum to 1.

$$\sum_{y=0}^{r} p(y) = \sum_{r=0}^{n} {}_nC_r p^r (1-p)^{n-r} = \left(p + [1-p]\right)^n = 1^n = 1$$

The theorem is also needed to prove that

$$\mu = \sum_{y=0}^{n} y \times p(y) = n \times p$$

and:

$$\sigma^2 = \sum_{y=0}^{n} (y-\mu)^2 \times p(y) = n \times p \times (1-p).$$

Case Study: Product Quality - MRE

Star Food Processing is a San Antonio based firm, which produces meals-ready-to-eat (**MRE**) for the U.S. Army. In December 1990, this company was awarded a contract with the U.S. Army to increase its production of MRE. The military sets limits on the level of bacteria present in order to prevent food poisoning of military personnel. The product is acceptable provided the levels of bacteria do not exceed those specified by the military. Based on inspection records, we can conservatively say that the company has an acceptance record of 0.999. In each two-hour period the company produces a lot containing 5,000 MRE.

Each MRE either has **acceptable bacteria levels** or it does not, and each MRE represents **an independent trial**. The probability of acceptance is $p = 0.999$ (i.e., the contamination probability is 0.001). Then Y is the **count of the number of acceptable MRE** in the lot of $n = 5{,}000$. With this high value of product quality and large sample size, the textbook tables are not helpful. Likewise many approximation are really not applicable because of the small value of $1 - p$. Even routines in EXCEL can produce incorrect results or values that cannot be computed.

Using the methods suggested on recursive relations, we know that the mode of the binomial should occur for y between $np \pm 1$. In the case of MRE,

$$np \pm 1 = 5{,}000 \times 0.999 \pm 1 = 4{,}995 \pm 1.$$

First, we calculate the probability for 4,996 successes from the binomial probability equation. The result is tedious to do but is within our capacity, provided one uses creative calculations.

$$\Pr\{Y = 4{,}996\} = {}_{5{,}000}C_{4{,}996} \times (0.999)^{4{,}996} \times (0.001)^{4} = 0.1755200$$

Recursion formulas are useful in competing probabilities of successive events given a particular probability. The first formula below allows us to compute the probability of the following (or next) value of the binomial random variable based on the probability of a specific (current) value. The second formula allows us to compute the probability of the preceding (or prior) value of the binomial random variable based on the probability of a specific (current) value.

$$\Pr\{Y = y + 1\} = \Pr\{Y = y\} \times \frac{p \times (n - y)}{(y + 1) \times (1 - p)}$$

$$\Pr\{Y = y - 1\} = \Pr\{Y = y\} \times \frac{y \times (1 - p)}{p \times (n - y + 1)}$$

It follows that we can compute the $\Pr\{Y = 4{,}997\}$ from the first recursion formula based on the value of $\Pr\{Y = 4{,}996\}$.

$$\Pr\{Y = 4{,}996 + 1\} = \Pr\{Y = 4{,}996\} \times \frac{0.999 \times (5{,}000 - 4{,}996)}{(4{,}996 + 1) \times (1 - 0.999)}$$

$$\Pr\{Y = 4{,}997\} = (0.1755200) \times \frac{0.999 \times (4)}{(4{,}997) \times (0.001)} = 0.1403598 .$$

In a similar way, we obtain probabilities for the last three values in the range as

$$\Pr\{Y = 4{,}998\} = 0.0841653$$
$$\Pr\{Y = 4{,}999\} = 0.0336392$$
and
$$\Pr\{Y = 5{,}000\} = 0.0067211$$

We can compute the $\Pr\{Y = 4{,}995\}$ from the second recursion formula based on the value of $\Pr\{Y = 4{,}996\}$.

$$\Pr\{ Y = 4{,}996 - 1\} = \Pr\{ Y = 4{,}996 \} \times \frac{4{,}996 \times (1 - 0.999)}{(5{,}000 - 4{,}996 + 1) \times (0.999)}$$

$$\Pr\{ Y = 4{,}995 \} = (0.1755200) \times \frac{4{,}996 \times 0.001}{(5) \times (0.999)} = 0.1755552 .$$

In a similar way the reader can verify the following binomial probabilities:

$$\Pr\{Y = 4{,}994\} = 0.1462960$$
$$\Pr\{Y = 4{,}993\} = 0.1044762$$
$$\Pr\{Y = 4{,}992\} = 0.0652715$$
$$\Pr\{Y = 4{,}991\} = 0.0362402$$
$$\Pr\{Y = 4{,}990\} = 0.0181056$$

We can use these probabilities to calculate probability statements on the number of acceptable MRE in a lot of 5,000. What threshold would you set for testing product quality? If the producer meets the government's specification of an acceptance rate of 99%, the probability of observing at least 4,990 successes is 0.9863501 or equivalently the probability of observing less than 4,990 successes due to chance alone is 0.0136499. If the Army subjected the producer to a test of 5,000 MRE in which the company had to have at 4,990 successes to pass contract agreements on quality, they would succeed in 98.635% of all such tests but they could fail such a test in 1.365% of all such tests. So the chance that the producer's acceptable product under this scenario is rejected is 1.365%. This value is known as the producer's risk.

Binomial Tables

Binomial probabilities for a specified sample sizes and various values success probability

$n = 6$ p

y	0.01	0.05	0.10	0.20	0.25	0.30	0.40	0.50	0.60	0.70	0.80	0.90	0.95	0.99
0	0.9415	0.7351	0.5314	0.2621	0.1780	0.1176	0.0467	0.0156	0.0041	0.0007	0.0001	0.0000	0.0000	0.0000
1	0.0571	0.2321	0.3543	0.3932	0.3560	0.3025	0.1866	0.0938	0.0369	0.0102	0.0015	0.0001	0.0000	0.0000
2	0.0014	0.0305	0.0984	0.2458	0.2966	0.3241	0.3110	0.2344	0.1382	0.0595	0.0154	0.0012	0.0001	0.0000
3	0.0000	0.0021	0.0146	0.0819	0.1318	0.1852	0.2765	0.3125	0.2765	0.1852	0.0819	0.0146	0.0021	0.0000
4	0.0000	0.0001	0.0012	0.0154	0.0330	0.0595	0.1382	0.2344	0.3110	0.3241	0.2458	0.0984	0.0305	0.0014
5	0.0000	0.0000	0.0001	0.0015	0.0044	0.0102	0.0369	0.0938	0.1866	0.3025	0.3932	0.3543	0.2321	0.0571
6	0.0000	0.0000	0.0000	0.0001	0.0002	0.0007	0.0041	0.0156	0.0467	0.1176	0.2621	0.5314	0.7351	0.9415

$n = 7$ p

Y	0.01	0.05	0.10	0.20	0.25	0.30	0.40	0.50	0.60	0.70	0.80	0.90
0	0.9321	0.6983	0.4783	0.2097	0.1335	0.0824	0.0280	0.0078	0.0016	0.0002	0.0000	0.0000
1	0.0659	0.2573	0.3720	0.3670	0.3115	0.2471	0.1306	0.0547	0.0172	0.0036	0.0004	0.0000
2	0.0020	0.0406	0.1240	0.2753	0.3115	0.3177	0.2613	0.1641	0.0774	0.0250	0.0043	0.0002
3	0.0000	0.0036	0.0230	0.1147	0.1730	0.2269	0.2903	0.2734	0.1935	0.0972	0.0287	0.0026
4	0.0000	0.0002	0.0026	0.0287	0.0577	0.0972	0.1935	0.2734	0.2903	0.2269	0.1147	0.0230
5	0.0000	0.0000	0.0002	0.0043	0.0115	0.0250	0.0774	0.1641	0.2613	0.3177	0.2753	0.1240
6	0.0000	0.0000	0.0000	0.0004	0.0013	0.0036	0.0172	0.0547	0.1306	0.2471	0.3670	0.3720
7	0.0000	0.0000	0.0000	0.0000	0.0001	0.0002	0.0016	0.0078	0.0280	0.0824	0.2097	0.4783

$n = 8$ p

y	0.01	0.05	0.10	0.20	0.25	0.30	0.40	0.50	0.60	0.70	0.80	0.90	0.95	0.99
0	0.9227	0.6634	0.4305	0.1678	0.1001	0.0576	0.0168	0.0039	0.0007	0.0001	0.0000	0.0000	0.0000	0.0000
1	0.0746	0.2793	0.3826	0.3355	0.2670	0.1977	0.0896	0.0313	0.0079	0.0012	0.0001	0.0000	0.0000	0.0000
2	0.0026	0.0515	0.1488	0.2936	0.3115	0.2965	0.2090	0.1094	0.0413	0.0100	0.0011	0.0000	0.0000	0.0000
3	0.0001	0.0054	0.0331	0.1468	0.2076	0.2541	0.2787	0.2188	0.1239	0.0467	0.0092	0.0004	0.0000	0.0000
4	0.0000	0.0004	0.0046	0.0459	0.0865	0.1361	0.2322	0.2734	0.2322	0.1361	0.0459	0.0046	0.0004	0.0000
5	0.0000	0.0000	0.0004	0.0092	0.0231	0.0467	0.1239	0.2188	0.2787	0.2541	0.1468	0.0331	0.0054	0.0001
6	0.0000	0.0000	0.0000	0.0011	0.0038	0.0100	0.0413	0.1094	0.2090	0.2965	0.2936	0.1488	0.0515	0.0026
7	0.0000	0.0000	0.0000	0.0001	0.0004	0.0012	0.0079	0.0313	0.0896	0.1977	0.3355	0.3826	0.2793	0.0746
8	0.0000	0.0000	0.0000	0.0000	0.0000	0.0001	0.0007	0.0039	0.0168	0.0576	0.1678	0.4305	0.6634	0.9227

$n = 9$ p

Y	0.01	0.05	0.10	0.20	0.25	0.30	0.40	0.50	0.60	0.70	0.80	0.90	0.95	0.99
0	0.9135	0.6302	0.3874	0.1342	0.0751	0.0404	0.0101	0.0020	0.0003	0.0000	0.0000	0.0000	0.0000	0.0000
1	0.0830	0.2985	0.3874	0.3020	0.2253	0.1556	0.0605	0.0176	0.0035	0.0004	0.0000	0.0000	0.0000	0.0000
2	0.0034	0.0629	0.1722	0.3020	0.3003	0.2668	0.1612	0.0703	0.0212	0.0039	0.0003	0.0000	0.0000	0.0000
3	0.0001	0.0077	0.0446	0.1762	0.2336	0.2668	0.2508	0.1641	0.0743	0.0210	0.0028	0.0001	0.0000	0.0000
4	0.0000	0.0006	0.0074	0.0661	0.1168	0.1715	0.2508	0.2461	0.1672	0.0735	0.0165	0.0008	0.0000	0.0000
5	0.0000	0.0000	0.0008	0.0165	0.0389	0.0735	0.1672	0.2461	0.2508	0.1715	0.0661	0.0074	0.0006	0.0000
6	0.0000	0.0000	0.0001	0.0028	0.0087	0.0210	0.0743	0.1641	0.2508	0.2668	0.1762	0.0446	0.0077	0.0001
7	0.0000	0.0000	0.0000	0.0003	0.0012	0.0039	0.0212	0.0703	0.1612	0.2668	0.3020	0.1722	0.0629	0.0034
8	0.0000	0.0000	0.0000	0.0000	0.0001	0.0004	0.0035	0.0176	0.0605	0.1556	0.3020	0.3874	0.2985	0.0830
9	0.0000	0.0000	0.0000	0.0000	0.0000	0.0000	0.0003	0.0020	0.0101	0.0404	0.1342	0.3874	0.6302	0.9135

$n = 10$ p

y	0.01	0.05	0.10	0.20	0.25	0.30	0.40	0.50	0.60	0.70	0.80	0.90	0.95	0.99
0	0.9044	0.5987	0.3487	0.1074	0.0563	0.0282	0.0060	0.0010	0.0001	0.0000	0.0000	0.0000	0.0000	0.0000
1	0.0914	0.3151	0.3874	0.2684	0.1877	0.1211	0.0403	0.0098	0.0016	0.0001	0.0000	0.0000	0.0000	0.0000
2	0.0042	0.0746	0.1937	0.3020	0.2816	0.2335	0.1209	0.0439	0.0106	0.0014	0.0001	0.0000	0.0000	0.0000
3	0.0001	0.0105	0.0574	0.2013	0.2503	0.2668	0.2150	0.1172	0.0425	0.0090	0.0008	0.0000	0.0000	0.0000
4	0.0000	0.0010	0.0112	0.0881	0.1460	0.2001	0.2508	0.2051	0.1115	0.0368	0.0055	0.0001	0.0000	0.0000
5	0.0000	0.0001	0.0015	0.0264	0.0584	0.1029	0.2007	0.2461	0.2007	0.1029	0.0264	0.0015	0.0001	0.0000
6	0.0000	0.0000	0.0001	0.0055	0.0162	0.0368	0.1115	0.2051	0.2508	0.2001	0.0881	0.0112	0.0010	0.0000
7	0.0000	0.0000	0.0000	0.0008	0.0031	0.0090	0.0425	0.1172	0.2150	0.2668	0.2013	0.0574	0.0105	0.0001
8	0.0000	0.0000	0.0000	0.0001	0.0004	0.0014	0.0106	0.0439	0.1209	0.2335	0.3020	0.1937	0.0746	0.0042
9	0.0000	0.0000	0.0000	0.0000	0.0000	0.0001	0.0016	0.0098	0.0403	0.1211	0.2684	0.3874	0.3151	0.0914
10	0.0000	0.0000	0.0000	0.0000	0.0000	0.0000	0.0001	0.0010	0.0060	0.0282	0.1074	0.3487	0.5987	0.9044

$n = 11$ p

y	0.01	0.05	0.10	0.20	0.25	0.30	0.40	0.50	0.60	0.70	0.80	0.90	0.95	0.99
0	0.8953	0.5688	0.3138	0.0859	0.0422	0.0198	0.0036	0.0005	0.0000	0.0000	0.0000	0.0000	0.0000	0.0000
1	0.0995	0.3293	0.3835	0.2362	0.1549	0.0932	0.0266	0.0054	0.0007	0.0000	0.0000	0.0000	0.0000	0.0000
2	0.0050	0.0867	0.2131	0.2953	0.2581	0.1998	0.0887	0.0269	0.0052	0.0005	0.0000	0.0000	0.0000	0.0000
3	0.0002	0.0137	0.0710	0.2215	0.2581	0.2568	0.1774	0.0806	0.0234	0.0037	0.0002	0.0000	0.0000	0.0000
4	0.0000	0.0014	0.0158	0.1107	0.1721	0.2201	0.2365	0.1611	0.0701	0.0173	0.0017	0.0000	0.0000	0.0000
5	0.0000	0.0001	0.0025	0.0388	0.0803	0.1321	0.2207	0.2256	0.1471	0.0566	0.0097	0.0003	0.0000	0.0000
6	0.0000	0.0000	0.0003	0.0097	0.0268	0.0566	0.1471	0.2256	0.2207	0.1321	0.0388	0.0025	0.0001	0.0000
7	0.0000	0.0000	0.0000	0.0017	0.0064	0.0173	0.0701	0.1611	0.2365	0.2201	0.1107	0.0158	0.0014	0.0000
8	0.0000	0.0000	0.0000	0.0002	0.0011	0.0037	0.0234	0.0806	0.1774	0.2568	0.2215	0.0710	0.0137	0.0002
9	0.0000	0.0000	0.0000	0.0000	0.0001	0.0005	0.0052	0.0269	0.0887	0.1998	0.2953	0.2131	0.0867	0.0050
10	0.0000	0.0000	0.0000	0.0000	0.0000	0.0000	0.0007	0.0054	0.0266	0.0932	0.2362	0.3835	0.3293	0.0995
11	0.0000	0.0000	0.0000	0.0000	0.0000	0.0000	0.0000	0.0005	0.0036	0.0198	0.0859	0.3138	0.5688	0.8953

$n = 12$ p

12	0.01	0.05	0.10	0.20	0.25	0.30	0.40	0.50	0.60	0.70	0.80	0.90	0.95	0.99
0	0.8864	0.5404	0.2824	0.0687	0.0317	0.0138	0.0022	0.0002	0.0000	0.0000	0.0000	0.0000	0.0000	0.0000
1	0.1074	0.3413	0.3766	0.2062	0.1267	0.0712	0.0174	0.0029	0.0003	0.0000	0.0000	0.0000	0.0000	0.0000
2	0.0060	0.0988	0.2301	0.2835	0.2323	0.1678	0.0639	0.0161	0.0025	0.0002	0.0000	0.0000	0.0000	0.0000
3	0.0002	0.0173	0.0852	0.2362	0.2581	0.2397	0.1419	0.0537	0.0125	0.0015	0.0001	0.0000	0.0000	0.0000
4	0.0000	0.0021	0.0213	0.1329	0.1936	0.2311	0.2128	0.1208	0.0420	0.0078	0.0005	0.0000	0.0000	0.0000
5	0.0000	0.0002	0.0038	0.0532	0.1032	0.1585	0.2270	0.1934	0.1009	0.0291	0.0033	0.0000	0.0000	0.0000
6	0.0000	0.0000	0.0005	0.0155	0.0401	0.0792	0.1766	0.2256	0.1766	0.0792	0.0155	0.0005	0.0000	0.0000
7	0.0000	0.0000	0.0000	0.0033	0.0115	0.0291	0.1009	0.1934	0.2270	0.1585	0.0532	0.0038	0.0002	0.0000
8	0.0000	0.0000	0.0000	0.0005	0.0024	0.0078	0.0420	0.1208	0.2128	0.2311	0.1329	0.0213	0.0021	0.0000
9	0.0000	0.0000	0.0000	0.0001	0.0004	0.0015	0.0125	0.0537	0.1419	0.2397	0.2362	0.0852	0.0173	0.0002
10	0.0000	0.0000	0.0000	0.0000	0.0000	0.0002	0.0025	0.0161	0.0639	0.1678	0.2835	0.2301	0.0988	0.0060
11	0.0000	0.0000	0.0000	0.0000	0.0000	0.0000	0.0003	0.0029	0.0174	0.0712	0.2062	0.3766	0.3413	0.1074
12	0.0000	0.0000	0.0000	0.0000	0.0000	0.0000	0.0000	0.0002	0.0022	0.0138	0.0687	0.2824	0.5404	0.8864

$n = 13$ p

y	0.01	0.05	0.10	0.20	0.25	0.30	0.40	0.50	0.60	0.70	0.80	0.90	0.95	0.99
0	0.8775	0.5133	0.2542	0.0550	0.0238	0.0097	0.0013	0.0001	0.0000	0.0000	0.0000	0.0000	0.0000	0.0000
1	0.1152	0.3512	0.3672	0.1787	0.1029	0.0540	0.0113	0.0016	0.0001	0.0000	0.0000	0.0000	0.0000	0.0000
2	0.0070	0.1109	0.2448	0.2680	0.2059	0.1388	0.0453	0.0095	0.0012	0.0001	0.0000	0.0000	0.0000	0.0000
3	0.0003	0.0214	0.0997	0.2457	0.2517	0.2181	0.1107	0.0349	0.0065	0.0006	0.0000	0.0000	0.0000	0.0000
4	0.0000	0.0028	0.0277	0.1535	0.2097	0.2337	0.1845	0.0873	0.0243	0.0034	0.0001	0.0000	0.0000	0.0000
5	0.0000	0.0003	0.0055	0.0691	0.1258	0.1803	0.2214	0.1571	0.0656	0.0142	0.0011	0.0000	0.0000	0.0000
6	0.0000	0.0000	0.0008	0.0230	0.0559	0.1030	0.1968	0.2095	0.1312	0.0442	0.0058	0.0001	0.0000	0.0000
7	0.0000	0.0000	0.0001	0.0058	0.0186	0.0442	0.1312	0.2095	0.1968	0.1030	0.0230	0.0008	0.0000	0.0000
8	0.0000	0.0000	0.0000	0.0011	0.0047	0.0142	0.0656	0.1571	0.2214	0.1803	0.0691	0.0055	0.0003	0.0000
9	0.0000	0.0000	0.0000	0.0001	0.0009	0.0034	0.0243	0.0873	0.1845	0.2337	0.1535	0.0277	0.0028	0.0000
10	0.0000	0.0000	0.0000	0.0000	0.0001	0.0006	0.0065	0.0349	0.1107	0.2181	0.2457	0.0997	0.0214	0.0003
11	0.0000	0.0000	0.0000	0.0000	0.0000	0.0001	0.0012	0.0095	0.0453	0.1388	0.2680	0.2448	0.1109	0.0070
12	0.0000	0.0000	0.0000	0.0000	0.0000	0.0000	0.0001	0.0016	0.0113	0.0540	0.1787	0.3672	0.3512	0.1152
13	0.0000	0.0000	0.0000	0.0000	0.0000	0.0000	0.0000	0.0001	0.0013	0.0097	0.0550	0.2542	0.5133	0.8775

$n = 14$ p

y	0.01	0.05	0.10	0.20	0.25	0.30	0.40	0.50	0.60	0.70	0.80	0.90	0.95	0.99
0	0.8687	0.4877	0.2288	0.0440	0.0178	0.0068	0.0008	0.0001	0.0000	0.0000	0.0000	0.0000	0.0000	0.0000
1	0.1229	0.3593	0.3559	0.1539	0.0832	0.0407	0.0073	0.0009	0.0001	0.0000	0.0000	0.0000	0.0000	0.0000
2	0.0081	0.1229	0.2570	0.2501	0.1802	0.1134	0.0317	0.0056	0.0005	0.0000	0.0000	0.0000	0.0000	0.0000
3	0.0003	0.0259	0.1142	0.2501	0.2402	0.1943	0.0845	0.0222	0.0033	0.0002	0.0000	0.0000	0.0000	0.0000
4	0.0000	0.0037	0.0349	0.1720	0.2202	0.2290	0.1549	0.0611	0.0136	0.0014	0.0000	0.0000	0.0000	0.0000
5	0.0000	0.0004	0.0078	0.0860	0.1468	0.1963	0.2066	0.1222	0.0408	0.0066	0.0003	0.0000	0.0000	0.0000
6	0.0000	0.0000	0.0013	0.0322	0.0734	0.1262	0.2066	0.1833	0.0918	0.0232	0.0020	0.0000	0.0000	0.0000
7	0.0000	0.0000	0.0002	0.0092	0.0280	0.0618	0.1574	0.2095	0.1574	0.0618	0.0092	0.0002	0.0000	0.0000
8	0.0000	0.0000	0.0000	0.0020	0.0082	0.0232	0.0918	0.1833	0.2066	0.1262	0.0322	0.0013	0.0000	0.0000
9	0.0000	0.0000	0.0000	0.0003	0.0018	0.0066	0.0408	0.1222	0.2066	0.1963	0.0860	0.0078	0.0004	0.0000
10	0.0000	0.0000	0.0000	0.0000	0.0003	0.0014	0.0136	0.0611	0.1549	0.2290	0.1720	0.0349	0.0037	0.0000
11	0.0000	0.0000	0.0000	0.0000	0.0000	0.0002	0.0033	0.0222	0.0845	0.1943	0.2501	0.1142	0.0259	0.0003
12	0.0000	0.0000	0.0000	0.0000	0.0000	0.0000	0.0005	0.0056	0.0317	0.1134	0.2501	0.2570	0.1229	0.0081
13	0.0000	0.0000	0.0000	0.0000	0.0000	0.0000	0.0001	0.0009	0.0073	0.0407	0.1539	0.3559	0.3593	0.1229
14	0.0000	0.0000	0.0000	0.0000	0.0000	0.0000	0.0000	0.0001	0.0008	0.0068	0.0440	0.2288	0.4877	0.8687

$n = 15$ p

y	0.01	0.05	0.10	0.20	0.25	0.30	0.40	0.50	0.60	0.70	0.80	0.90	0.95	0.99
0	0.8601	0.4633	0.2059	0.0352	0.0134	0.0047	0.0005	0.0000	0.0000	0.0000	0.0000	0.0000	0.0000	0.0000
1	0.1303	0.3658	0.3432	0.1319	0.0668	0.0305	0.0047	0.0005	0.0000	0.0000	0.0000	0.0000	0.0000	0.0000
2	0.0092	0.1348	0.2669	0.2309	0.1559	0.0916	0.0219	0.0032	0.0003	0.0000	0.0000	0.0000	0.0000	0.0000
3	0.0004	0.0307	0.1285	0.2501	0.2252	0.1700	0.0634	0.0139	0.0016	0.0001	0.0000	0.0000	0.0000	0.0000
4	0.0000	0.0049	0.0428	0.1876	0.2252	0.2186	0.1268	0.0417	0.0074	0.0006	0.0000	0.0000	0.0000	0.0000
5	0.0000	0.0006	0.0105	0.1032	0.1651	0.2061	0.1859	0.0916	0.0245	0.0030	0.0001	0.0000	0.0000	0.0000
6	0.0000	0.0000	0.0019	0.0430	0.0917	0.1472	0.2066	0.1527	0.0612	0.0116	0.0007	0.0000	0.0000	0.0000
7	0.0000	0.0000	0.0003	0.0138	0.0393	0.0811	0.1771	0.1964	0.1181	0.0348	0.0035	0.0000	0.0000	0.0000
8	0.0000	0.0000	0.0000	0.0035	0.0131	0.0348	0.1181	0.1964	0.1771	0.0811	0.0138	0.0003	0.0000	0.0000
9	0.0000	0.0000	0.0000	0.0007	0.0034	0.0116	0.0612	0.1527	0.2066	0.1472	0.0430	0.0019	0.0000	0.0000
10	0.0000	0.0000	0.0000	0.0001	0.0007	0.0030	0.0245	0.0916	0.1859	0.2061	0.1032	0.0105	0.0006	0.0000
11	0.0000	0.0000	0.0000	0.0000	0.0001	0.0006	0.0074	0.0417	0.1268	0.2186	0.1876	0.0428	0.0049	0.0000
12	0.0000	0.0000	0.0000	0.0000	0.0000	0.0001	0.0016	0.0139	0.0634	0.1700	0.2501	0.1285	0.0307	0.0004
13	0.0000	0.0000	0.0000	0.0000	0.0000	0.0000	0.0003	0.0032	0.0219	0.0916	0.2309	0.2669	0.1348	0.0092
14	0.0000	0.0000	0.0000	0.0000	0.0000	0.0000	0.0000	0.0005	0.0047	0.0305	0.1319	0.3432	0.3658	0.1303
15	0.0000	0.0000	0.0000	0.0000	0.0000	0.0000	0.0000	0.0000	0.0005	0.0047	0.0352	0.2059	0.4633	0.8601

$n = 16$ p

y	0.01	0.05	0.10	0.20	0.25	0.30	0.40	0.50	0.60	0.70	0.80	0.90	0.95	0.99
0	0.8515	0.4401	0.1853	0.0281	0.0100	0.0033	0.0003	0.0000	0.0000	0.0000	0.0000	0.0000	0.0000	0.0000
1	0.1376	0.3706	0.3294	0.1126	0.0535	0.0228	0.0030	0.0002	0.0000	0.0000	0.0000	0.0000	0.0000	0.0000
2	0.0104	0.1463	0.2745	0.2111	0.1336	0.0732	0.0150	0.0018	0.0001	0.0000	0.0000	0.0000	0.0000	0.0000
3	0.0005	0.0359	0.1423	0.2463	0.2079	0.1465	0.0468	0.0085	0.0008	0.0000	0.0000	0.0000	0.0000	0.0000
4	0.0000	0.0061	0.0514	0.2001	0.2252	0.2040	0.1014	0.0278	0.0040	0.0002	0.0000	0.0000	0.0000	0.0000
5	0.0000	0.0008	0.0137	0.1201	0.1802	0.2099	0.1623	0.0667	0.0142	0.0013	0.0000	0.0000	0.0000	0.0000
6	0.0000	0.0001	0.0028	0.0550	0.1101	0.1649	0.1983	0.1222	0.0392	0.0056	0.0002	0.0000	0.0000	0.0000
7	0.0000	0.0000	0.0004	0.0197	0.0524	0.1010	0.1889	0.1746	0.0840	0.0185	0.0012	0.0000	0.0000	0.0000
8	0.0000	0.0000	0.0001	0.0055	0.0197	0.0487	0.1417	0.1964	0.1417	0.0487	0.0055	0.0001	0.0000	0.0000
9	0.0000	0.0000	0.0000	0.0012	0.0058	0.0185	0.0840	0.1746	0.1889	0.1010	0.0197	0.0004	0.0000	0.0000
10	0.0000	0.0000	0.0000	0.0002	0.0014	0.0056	0.0392	0.1222	0.1983	0.1649	0.0550	0.0028	0.0001	0.0000
11	0.0000	0.0000	0.0000	0.0000	0.0002	0.0013	0.0142	0.0667	0.1623	0.2099	0.1201	0.0137	0.0008	0.0000
12	0.0000	0.0000	0.0000	0.0000	0.0000	0.0002	0.0040	0.0278	0.1014	0.2040	0.2001	0.0514	0.0061	0.0000
13	0.0000	0.0000	0.0000	0.0000	0.0000	0.0000	0.0008	0.0085	0.0468	0.1465	0.2463	0.1423	0.0359	0.0005
14	0.0000	0.0000	0.0000	0.0000	0.0000	0.0000	0.0001	0.0018	0.0150	0.0732	0.2111	0.2745	0.1463	0.0104
15	0.0000	0.0000	0.0000	0.0000	0.0000	0.0000	0.0000	0.0002	0.0030	0.0228	0.1126	0.3294	0.3706	0.1376
16	0.0000	0.0000	0.0000	0.0000	0.0000	0.0000	0.0000	0.0000	0.0003	0.0033	0.0281	0.1853	0.4401	0.8515

$n = 17$ p

y	0.01	0.05	0.10	0.20	0.25	0.30	0.40	0.50	0.60	0.70	0.80	0.90	0.95	0.99
0	0.8429	0.4181	0.1668	0.0225	0.0075	0.0023	0.0002	0.0000	0.0000	0.0000	0.0000	0.0000	0.0000	0.0000
1	0.1447	0.3741	0.3150	0.0957	0.0426	0.0169	0.0019	0.0001	0.0000	0.0000	0.0000	0.0000	0.0000	0.0000
2	0.0117	0.1575	0.2800	0.1914	0.1136	0.0581	0.0102	0.0010	0.0001	0.0000	0.0000	0.0000	0.0000	0.0000
3	0.0006	0.0415	0.1556	0.2393	0.1893	0.1245	0.0341	0.0052	0.0004	0.0000	0.0000	0.0000	0.0000	0.0000
4	0.0000	0.0076	0.0605	0.2093	0.2209	0.1868	0.0796	0.0182	0.0021	0.0001	0.0000	0.0000	0.0000	0.0000
5	0.0000	0.0010	0.0175	0.1361	0.1914	0.2081	0.1379	0.0472	0.0081	0.0006	0.0000	0.0000	0.0000	0.0000
6	0.0000	0.0001	0.0039	0.0680	0.1276	0.1784	0.1839	0.0944	0.0242	0.0026	0.0001	0.0000	0.0000	0.0000
7	0.0000	0.0000	0.0007	0.0267	0.0668	0.1201	0.1927	0.1484	0.0571	0.0095	0.0004	0.0000	0.0000	0.0000
8	0.0000	0.0000	0.0001	0.0084	0.0279	0.0644	0.1606	0.1855	0.1070	0.0276	0.0021	0.0000	0.0000	0.0000
9	0.0000	0.0000	0.0000	0.0021	0.0093	0.0276	0.1070	0.1855	0.1606	0.0644	0.0084	0.0001	0.0000	0.0000
10	0.0000	0.0000	0.0000	0.0004	0.0025	0.0095	0.0571	0.1484	0.1927	0.1201	0.0267	0.0007	0.0000	0.0000
11	0.0000	0.0000	0.0000	0.0001	0.0005	0.0026	0.0242	0.0944	0.1839	0.1784	0.0680	0.0039	0.0001	0.0000
12	0.0000	0.0000	0.0000	0.0000	0.0001	0.0006	0.0081	0.0472	0.1379	0.2081	0.1361	0.0175	0.0010	0.0000
13	0.0000	0.0000	0.0000	0.0000	0.0000	0.0001	0.0021	0.0182	0.0796	0.1868	0.2093	0.0605	0.0076	0.0000
14	0.0000	0.0000	0.0000	0.0000	0.0000	0.0000	0.0004	0.0052	0.0341	0.1245	0.2393	0.1556	0.0415	0.0006
15	0.0000	0.0000	0.0000	0.0000	0.0000	0.0000	0.0001	0.0010	0.0102	0.0581	0.1914	0.2800	0.1575	0.0117
16	0.0000	0.0000	0.0000	0.0000	0.0000	0.0000	0.0000	0.0001	0.0019	0.0169	0.0957	0.3150	0.3741	0.1447
17	0.0000	0.0000	0.0000	0.0000	0.0000	0.0000	0.0000	0.0000	0.0002	0.0023	0.0225	0.1668	0.4181	0.8429

$n = 18$ p

y	0.01	0.05	0.10	0.20	0.25	0.30	0.40	0.50	0.60	0.70	0.80	0.90	0.95	0.99
0	0.8345	0.3972	0.1501	0.0180	0.0056	0.0016	0.0001	0.0000	0.0000	0.0000	0.0000	0.0000	0.0000	0.0000
1	0.1517	0.3763	0.3002	0.0811	0.0338	0.0126	0.0012	0.0001	0.0000	0.0000	0.0000	0.0000	0.0000	0.0000
2	0.0130	0.1683	0.2835	0.1723	0.0958	0.0458	0.0069	0.0006	0.0000	0.0000	0.0000	0.0000	0.0000	0.0000
3	0.0007	0.0473	0.1680	0.2297	0.1704	0.1046	0.0246	0.0031	0.0002	0.0000	0.0000	0.0000	0.0000	0.0000
4	0.0000	0.0093	0.0700	0.2153	0.2130	0.1681	0.0614	0.0117	0.0011	0.0000	0.0000	0.0000	0.0000	0.0000
5	0.0000	0.0014	0.0218	0.1507	0.1988	0.2017	0.1146	0.0327	0.0045	0.0002	0.0000	0.0000	0.0000	0.0000
6	0.0000	0.0002	0.0052	0.0816	0.1436	0.1873	0.1655	0.0708	0.0145	0.0012	0.0000	0.0000	0.0000	0.0000
7	0.0000	0.0000	0.0010	0.0350	0.0820	0.1376	0.1892	0.1214	0.0374	0.0046	0.0001	0.0000	0.0000	0.0000
8	0.0000	0.0000	0.0002	0.0120	0.0376	0.0811	0.1734	0.1669	0.0771	0.0149	0.0008	0.0000	0.0000	0.0000
9	0.0000	0.0000	0.0000	0.0033	0.0139	0.0386	0.1284	0.1855	0.1284	0.0386	0.0033	0.0000	0.0000	0.0000
10	0.0000	0.0000	0.0000	0.0008	0.0042	0.0149	0.0771	0.1669	0.1734	0.0811	0.0120	0.0002	0.0000	0.0000
11	0.0000	0.0000	0.0000	0.0001	0.0010	0.0046	0.0374	0.1214	0.1892	0.1376	0.0350	0.0010	0.0000	0.0000
12	0.0000	0.0000	0.0000	0.0000	0.0002	0.0012	0.0145	0.0708	0.1655	0.1873	0.0816	0.0052	0.0002	0.0000
13	0.0000	0.0000	0.0000	0.0000	0.0000	0.0002	0.0045	0.0327	0.1146	0.2017	0.1507	0.0218	0.0014	0.0000
14	0.0000	0.0000	0.0000	0.0000	0.0000	0.0000	0.0011	0.0117	0.0614	0.1681	0.2153	0.0700	0.0093	0.0000
15	0.0000	0.0000	0.0000	0.0000	0.0000	0.0000	0.0002	0.0031	0.0246	0.1046	0.2297	0.1680	0.0473	0.0007
16	0.0000	0.0000	0.0000	0.0000	0.0000	0.0000	0.0000	0.0006	0.0069	0.0458	0.1723	0.2835	0.1683	0.0130
17	0.0000	0.0000	0.0000	0.0000	0.0000	0.0000	0.0000	0.0001	0.0012	0.0126	0.0811	0.3002	0.3763	0.1517
18	0.0000	0.0000	0.0000	0.0000	0.0000	0.0000	0.0000	0.0000	0.0001	0.0016	0.0180	0.1501	0.3972	0.8345

$n = 19$ — p

y	0.01	0.05	0.10	0.20	0.25	0.30	0.40	0.50	0.60	0.70	0.80	0.90	0.95	0.99
0	0.8262	0.3774	0.1351	0.0144	0.0042	0.0011	0.0001	0.0000	0.0000	0.0000	0.0000	0.0000	0.0000	0.0000
1	0.1586	0.3774	0.2852	0.0685	0.0268	0.0093	0.0008	0.0000	0.0000	0.0000	0.0000	0.0000	0.0000	0.0000
2	0.0144	0.1787	0.2852	0.1540	0.0803	0.0358	0.0046	0.0003	0.0000	0.0000	0.0000	0.0000	0.0000	0.0000
3	0.0008	0.0533	0.1796	0.2182	0.1517	0.0869	0.0175	0.0018	0.0001	0.0000	0.0000	0.0000	0.0000	0.0000
4	0.0000	0.0112	0.0798	0.2182	0.2023	0.1491	0.0467	0.0074	0.0005	0.0000	0.0000	0.0000	0.0000	0.0000
5	0.0000	0.0018	0.0266	0.1636	0.2023	0.1916	0.0933	0.0222	0.0024	0.0001	0.0000	0.0000	0.0000	0.0000
6	0.0000	0.0002	0.0069	0.0955	0.1574	0.1916	0.1451	0.0518	0.0085	0.0005	0.0000	0.0000	0.0000	0.0000
7	0.0000	0.0000	0.0014	0.0443	0.0974	0.1525	0.1797	0.0961	0.0237	0.0022	0.0000	0.0000	0.0000	0.0000
8	0.0000	0.0000	0.0002	0.0166	0.0487	0.0981	0.1797	0.1442	0.0532	0.0077	0.0003	0.0000	0.0000	0.0000
9	0.0000	0.0000	0.0000	0.0051	0.0198	0.0514	0.1464	0.1762	0.0976	0.0220	0.0013	0.0000	0.0000	0.0000
10	0.0000	0.0000	0.0000	0.0013	0.0066	0.0220	0.0976	0.1762	0.1464	0.0514	0.0051	0.0000	0.0000	0.0000
11	0.0000	0.0000	0.0000	0.0003	0.0018	0.0077	0.0532	0.1442	0.1797	0.0981	0.0166	0.0002	0.0000	0.0000
12	0.0000	0.0000	0.0000	0.0000	0.0004	0.0022	0.0237	0.0961	0.1797	0.1525	0.0443	0.0014	0.0000	0.0000
13	0.0000	0.0000	0.0000	0.0000	0.0001	0.0005	0.0085	0.0518	0.1451	0.1916	0.0955	0.0069	0.0002	0.0000
14	0.0000	0.0000	0.0000	0.0000	0.0000	0.0001	0.0024	0.0222	0.0933	0.1916	0.1636	0.0266	0.0018	0.0000
15	0.0000	0.0000	0.0000	0.0000	0.0000	0.0000	0.0005	0.0074	0.0467	0.1491	0.2182	0.0798	0.0112	0.0000
16	0.0000	0.0000	0.0000	0.0000	0.0000	0.0000	0.0001	0.0018	0.0175	0.0869	0.2182	0.1796	0.0533	0.0008
17	0.0000	0.0000	0.0000	0.0000	0.0000	0.0000	0.0000	0.0003	0.0046	0.0358	0.1540	0.2852	0.1787	0.0144
18	0.0000	0.0000	0.0000	0.0000	0.0000	0.0000	0.0000	0.0000	0.0008	0.0093	0.0685	0.2852	0.3774	0.1586
19	0.0000	0.0000	0.0000	0.0000	0.0000	0.0000	0.0000	0.0000	0.0001	0.0011	0.0144	0.1351	0.3774	0.8262

$n = 20$ — p

y	0.01	0.05	0.10	0.20	0.25	0.30	0.40	0.50	0.60	0.70	0.80	0.90	0.95	0.99
0	0.8179	0.3585	0.1216	0.0115	0.0032	0.0008	0.0000	0.0000	0.0000	0.0000	0.0000	0.0000	0.0000	0.0000
1	0.1652	0.3774	0.2702	0.0576	0.0211	0.0068	0.0005	0.0000	0.0000	0.0000	0.0000	0.0000	0.0000	0.0000
2	0.0159	0.1887	0.2852	0.1369	0.0669	0.0278	0.0031	0.0002	0.0000	0.0000	0.0000	0.0000	0.0000	0.0000
3	0.0010	0.0596	0.1901	0.2054	0.1339	0.0716	0.0123	0.0011	0.0000	0.0000	0.0000	0.0000	0.0000	0.0000
4	0.0000	0.0133	0.0898	0.2182	0.1897	0.1304	0.0350	0.0046	0.0003	0.0000	0.0000	0.0000	0.0000	0.0000
5	0.0000	0.0022	0.0319	0.1746	0.2023	0.1789	0.0746	0.0148	0.0013	0.0000	0.0000	0.0000	0.0000	0.0000
6	0.0000	0.0003	0.0089	0.1091	0.1686	0.1916	0.1244	0.0370	0.0049	0.0002	0.0000	0.0000	0.0000	0.0000
7	0.0000	0.0000	0.0020	0.0545	0.1124	0.1643	0.1659	0.0739	0.0146	0.0010	0.0000	0.0000	0.0000	0.0000
8	0.0000	0.0000	0.0004	0.0222	0.0609	0.1144	0.1797	0.1201	0.0355	0.0039	0.0001	0.0000	0.0000	0.0000
9	0.0000	0.0000	0.0001	0.0074	0.0271	0.0654	0.1597	0.1602	0.0710	0.0120	0.0005	0.0000	0.0000	0.0000
10	0.0000	0.0000	0.0000	0.0020	0.0099	0.0308	0.1171	0.1762	0.1171	0.0308	0.0020	0.0000	0.0000	0.0000
11	0.0000	0.0000	0.0000	0.0005	0.0030	0.0120	0.0710	0.1602	0.1597	0.0654	0.0074	0.0001	0.0000	0.0000
12	0.0000	0.0000	0.0000	0.0001	0.0008	0.0039	0.0355	0.1201	0.1797	0.1144	0.0222	0.0004	0.0000	0.0000
13	0.0000	0.0000	0.0000	0.0000	0.0002	0.0010	0.0146	0.0739	0.1659	0.1643	0.0545	0.0020	0.0000	0.0000
14	0.0000	0.0000	0.0000	0.0000	0.0000	0.0002	0.0049	0.0370	0.1244	0.1916	0.1091	0.0089	0.0003	0.0000
15	0.0000	0.0000	0.0000	0.0000	0.0000	0.0000	0.0013	0.0148	0.0746	0.1789	0.1746	0.0319	0.0022	0.0000
16	0.0000	0.0000	0.0000	0.0000	0.0000	0.0000	0.0003	0.0046	0.0350	0.1304	0.2182	0.0898	0.0133	0.0000
17	0.0000	0.0000	0.0000	0.0000	0.0000	0.0000	0.0000	0.0011	0.0123	0.0716	0.2054	0.1901	0.0596	0.0010
18	0.0000	0.0000	0.0000	0.0000	0.0000	0.0000	0.0000	0.0002	0.0031	0.0278	0.1369	0.2852	0.1887	0.0159
19	0.0000	0.0000	0.0000	0.0000	0.0000	0.0000	0.0000	0.0000	0.0005	0.0068	0.0576	0.2702	0.3774	0.1652
20	0.0000	0.0000	0.0000	0.0000	0.0000	0.0000	0.0000	0.0000	0.0000	0.0008	0.0115	0.1216	0.3585	0.8179

Continuous Distributions

The probability distributions considered so far have been for discrete random variables in that only integer values could be attained with positive probability. For continuous random variables, we know that any value in an interval from a to b can be obtained from an experiment (for example, heights $\mathbf{a} = \mathbf{4'}$ and $\mathbf{b} = \mathbf{7'}$).

For continuous response variables:

- **Positive probability is assigned only to intervals** and
- **Probability is defined as the area under the probability distribution over the interval.**

Let $\mathbf{X}$ be a continuous random variable with probability distribution $p(\mathbf{x})$. This function $p(\mathbf{x})$ represents the likelihood of occurrence of a random variable $\mathbf{X}$.

- It follows that:
  - $p(\mathbf{x}) \geq 0$

  for all values of $\mathbf{x}$,
- and the probability of an interval $I = [a,b]$ is defined as:
  - $\Pr[a \leq \mathbf{X} \leq b] = \int_I p(\mathbf{x})\mathbf{dx} = \int_a^b p(\mathbf{x})\mathbf{dx}$
- where $\int_a^b p(\mathbf{x})\mathbf{dx}$ is the **definite integral** of the probability distribution over the interval $I = [a,b]$.

The **definite integral computes area under the curve** $y = p(\mathbf{x})$ above the $x-$axis and between the lines $x = a$ and $x = b$.

This event is depicted in the following figure, Figure 21 for an arbitrary function: $p(\mathbf{x})$.

FIGURE 21: Probability for Continuous Response Variables

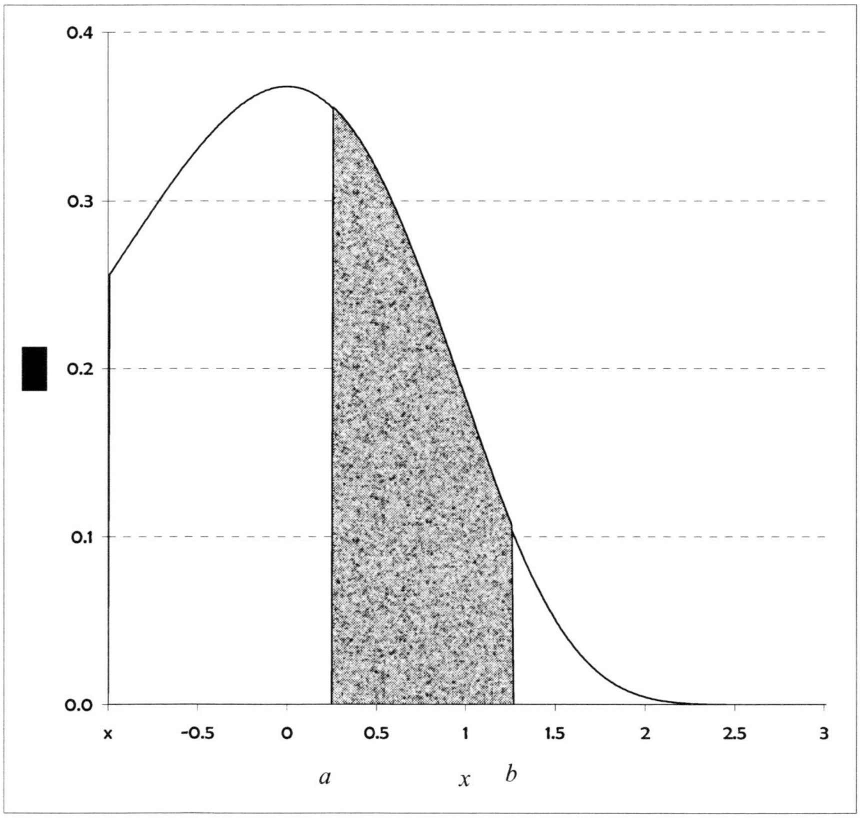

- In continuous distributions, **the use of area for probability implies** that for an individual point

  - $\Pr\{\mathbf{X}=a\}=\int_a^a p(\mathbf{t})\mathbf{dt}=0.$

- From **Kolmogorov's second axiom**, it follows that

$$\int_{-\infty}^{+\infty} p(\mathbf{t})\mathbf{dt}=1.$$

- This second condition **forces the area under the probability distribution to be 1**.

- Notice that if I and J are disjoint intervals (non-overlapping) then

$$\Pr(I\cup J)=\Pr(I)+\Pr(J)$$

because the area of their union is the sum of their areas whenever the regions do not overlap. Therefore, I and J are mutually exclusive.

Example: Hiring Experienced Workers

Suppose a company wants to hire someone for an entry-level position. However, the company advertises that some experience, 1-2 years, is preferred. The company will not hire someone with more than two years experience because they will want to advance more rapidly than the company is prepared to do at this time. If we assume that the likelihood of being hired increases linearly with experience until the second year, the probability distribution would be given by:

$$p(\mathbf{x}) = \begin{cases} \dfrac{\mathbf{x}}{2}, & 0 \le \mathbf{x} \le 2 \\ 0, & \text{elsewhere} \end{cases}$$

Note that $\int_0^2 \frac{\mathbf{x}}{2}\mathbf{dx} = \mathbf{1}$, so that $p(\mathbf{x})$ is a **legitimate continuous probability distribution** according to the **axioms of Kolmogorov**. The probability distribution is graphed in Figure 22 and defines a triangle with a base of length 2 and an altitude of length 1. So the total area of the triangle is 1.

FIGURE 22: Probability Distribution for experience of new-hires

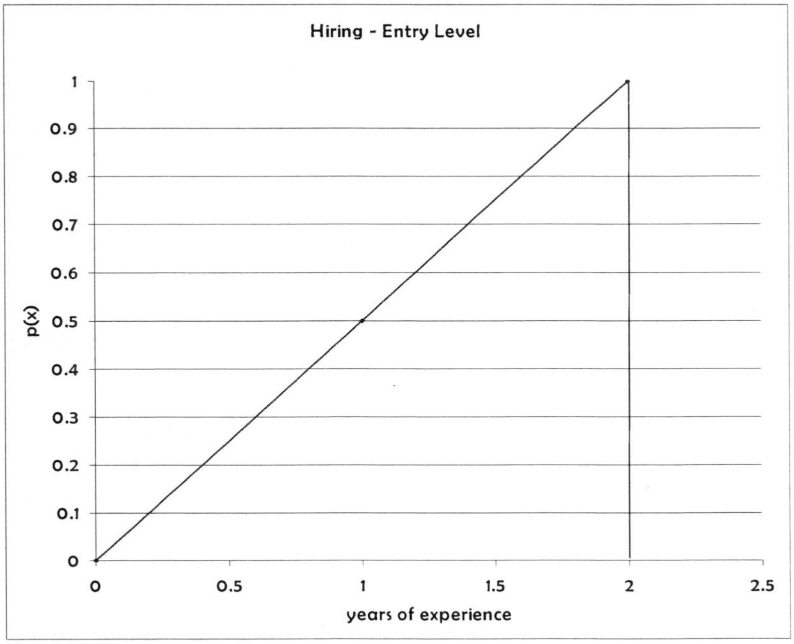

What is the probability that the company hires someone with at least 6 months (or 0.5 years) but no more than 15 months (or 1.25 years) experience? The region is

depicted in Figure 23. Since the probability distribution is given in terms of years, we convert the statement into years.

$$
\begin{aligned}
\Pr(0.50 < \mathbf{X} < 1.25) &= Area(Trapezoid) \\
&= \frac{1}{2}(b_1 + b_2) \times h \\
&= \frac{1}{2}(0.25 + 0.625) \times (0.75) \\
&= {}^{21}\!/_{64}.
\end{aligned}
$$

FIGURE 23: Probability that a new-hire has at least six but no more than 15 months experience

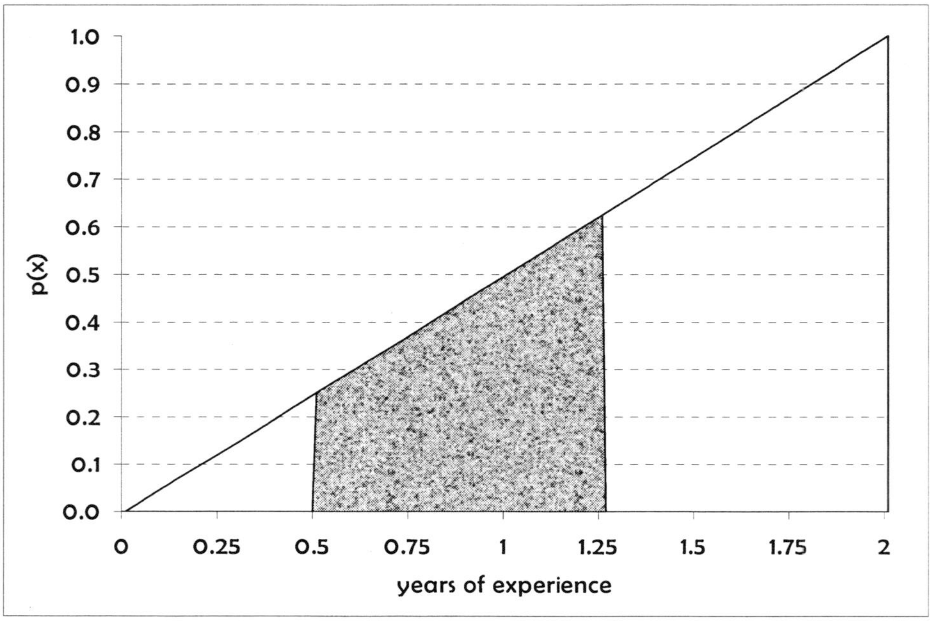

Case Study: Choosing Store Locations

Many factors are used in corporate decisions to choose locations for new stores. Factors of importance include population density, distribution of wealth, access to highways, access to modes of transportation such as a train, cost of real estate and so on. A paramount factor is the distance of the customer from the store. With all other things being equal, most consumers will choose the store closest to home. The consumer's concept of closeness is however, affected by available modes of transportation (see Keating and Mason 1988).

Economists developed models known as "**gravity models**" for such settings. The model states that the likelihood that a consumer will frequent a store is

inversely proportional to the distance from the store squared. The model is known as a Pareto distribution, in honor of the Swiss-born economist, **Vilfredo Pareto** (1897) and the parameter d is the buffer zone associated with the store.

$$p(\mathbf{x}) = \begin{cases} \dfrac{d}{\mathbf{x}^2} & ,\mathbf{x} \geq d \\ 0 & ,0 \leq \mathbf{x} < d \end{cases}$$

If the **buffer zone** is 0.10 miles then $d = 0.10$ and the distribution becomes:

$$p(\mathbf{x}) = \begin{cases} \dfrac{0.10}{\mathbf{x}^2} & ,\ \mathbf{x} \geq 0.10 \\ 0 & ,\ 0 \leq \mathbf{x} < 0.10 \end{cases}$$

FIGURE 24: A Pareto Distribution for choosing a store

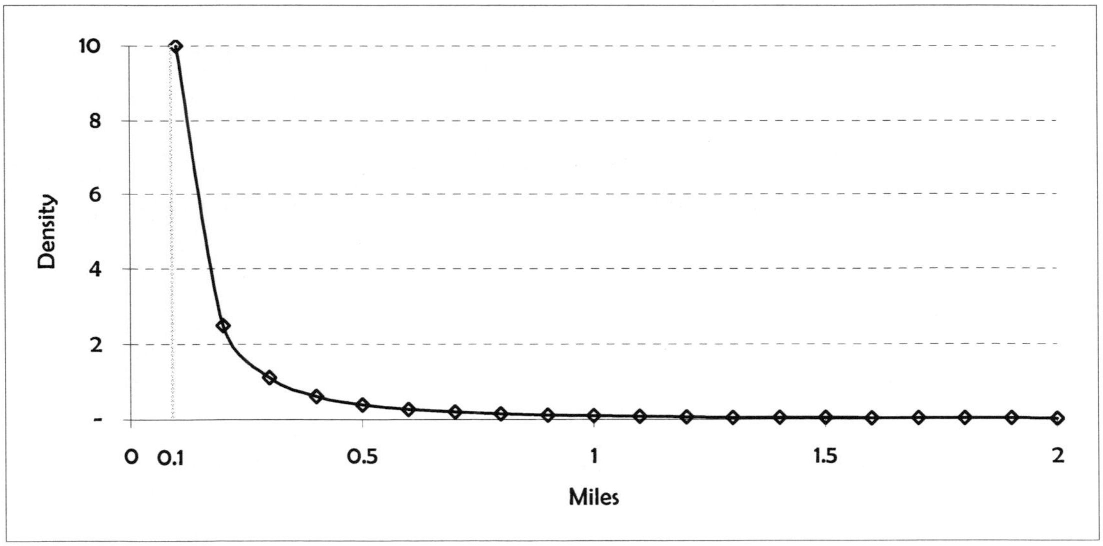

Compute the probability that a person who lives within a mile of the store frequents the store.

$$\Pr(\mathbf{X} \leq 1) = \int_{0.1}^{1} \frac{0.1}{\mathbf{x}^2} \mathbf{dx} = -\frac{0.1}{\mathbf{x}} \Big|_{x=0.1}^{x=1.0} = -0.1 - \left(-\frac{0.1}{0.1}\right) = -0.1 + 1 = 0.90.$$

So this model implies that a person who lives within a mile of the store will frequent the store with a 90% probability. However, what is the probability that someone who lives more than 2 miles from the store will visit?

$$\Pr(\mathbf{X}>2)=1-\Pr(\mathbf{X}\leq 2)=1-\int_{0.1}^{2}\frac{0.1}{\mathbf{x}^2}\mathbf{dx}=1+\frac{0.1}{\mathbf{x}}\Big|_{x=0.1}^{x=2.0}=1+\left[\frac{0.1}{2}-\left(\frac{0.1}{0.1}\right)\right]=0.05$$

So the chances that someone, who lives more than two miles from the store, actually shops there, are only 5%.

Normal Distribution

A continuous random variable $\mathbf{X}$ has a **normal distribution** $p(\mathbf{x})$ with distribution given by:

$$p(\mathbf{x})=\frac{\exp\left[-\frac{1}{2}\left(\frac{\mathbf{x}-\mu}{\sigma}\right)^2\right]}{\sqrt{2\pi}\times\sigma}.$$

The random variable $\mathbf{X}$ is a real-valued, μ is the **mean** of the population characteristic, and σ is the **standard deviation** of the population characteristic. We denote this property as:

$$\mathbf{X}\sim\mathbf{N}(\mu,\sigma)$$

The number e is the base of the natural logarithm, and approximated by $e \doteq \mathbf{2.718281828459045}$. A graph of the normal distribution is given below.

FIGURE 25: A Normal Distribution or Bell-Shaped Curve

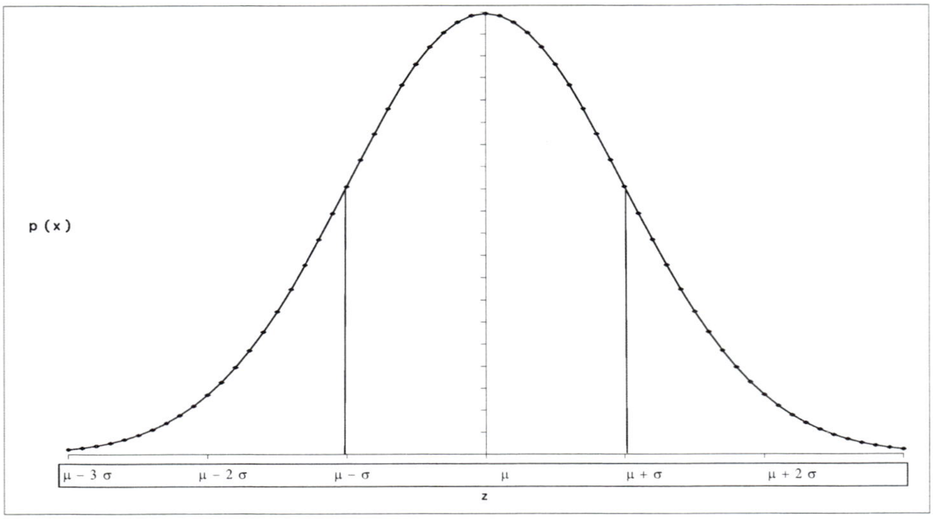

The exponential function is defined by $\mathbf{exp}(\mathbf{x})=e^{\mathbf{x}}$.

The graph has a characteristic bell-shape and is frequently referred to as the bell-shaped distribution. It was first discovered by **Abraham DeMoivre** in 1733 (see Johnson and Kotz (1997) pg 26) but was later popularized by **Karl Friedrich Gauss** (1809) (see Johnson and Kotz (1997) pg 361) and is commonly referred to as a Gaussian distribution and is depicted on the infamous book, **The Bell Curve**, authored by Herrnstein and Murray (1994).

Mathematical properties of the graph of $p(x)$:

- At $\mathbf{x} = \mu$, the graph of $p(x)$ attains a **relative maximum** of $\frac{1}{\sqrt{2\pi}\sigma}$.
- Consequently, the value of μ is the **mode** of the random variable X (i.e., its distribution is highest at μ).
- The graph of $p(x)$ is **symmetric** about the line $x = \mu$. The property of symmetry assures that $x = \mu$ is the **median of the distribution**.
    - In this symmetric case, the **mode = median = mean**.
- At $x = \mu \pm \sigma$, the graph of $p(x)$ changes its **concavity**. Between these values, the graph is **concave downward**, and outside these values, **concave upward**.

Standard Normal Distribution:

When $\mu = 0$ and $\sigma = 1$ the random variable has a **standard normal distribution** and we refer to this random variable as $\mathbf{Z}$. The standard normal probability density function is given by

$$p(\mathbf{z}) = \frac{1}{\sqrt{2\pi}} e^{-\mathbf{z}^2/2}$$

A graph of this probability distribution is seen in Figure 26 on the following page. The graph is symmetric about the line $\mathbf{z} = 0$, attains a relative maximum at $\mathbf{z} = 0$, and has points of concavity at $\mathbf{z} = \pm \mathbf{1}$.

FIGURE 26: A Standard Normal Distribution

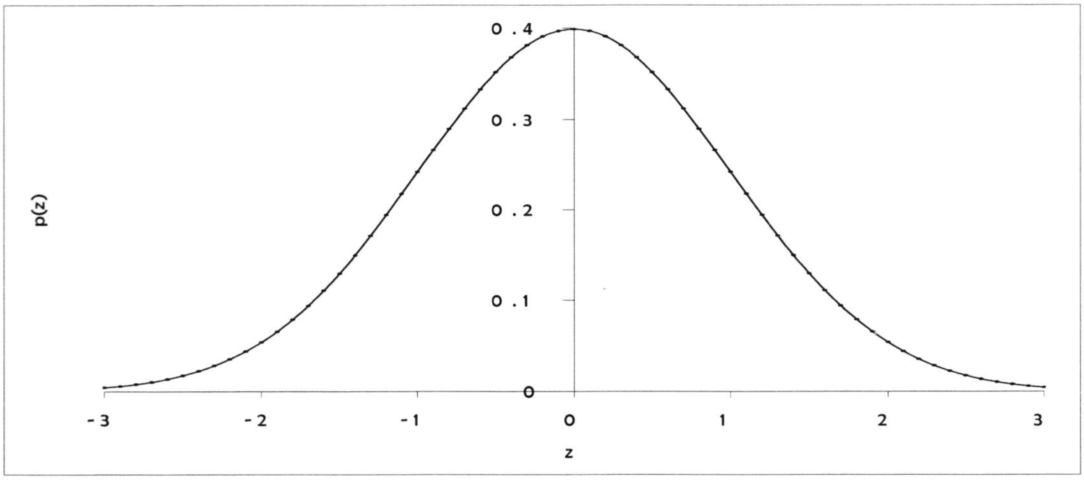

Finding probabilities (or areas) under the standard normal distribution must be done numerically because the probability distribution has no closed form antiderivative.

Finding Standard Normal Probabilities:

The **lack of a closed form antiderivative** implies we must use Table 25 on page 138 to compute these probabilities. In general, we have formulas to compute such probabilities but the area under the curve in the standard normal distribution must be solved for numerically.

Tables are given on page 138 listing the area under the curve $p(\mathbf{z})$ between $\mathbf{z} = 0$ and $\mathbf{z} = a$. To illustrate this concept, let's evaluate $\Pr\{\mathbf{0} \leq \mathbf{Z} \leq \mathbf{1.25}\}$. A graph of this situation is given in the Figure 27.

FIGURE 27: A Standard Normal region between 0 and 1.25.

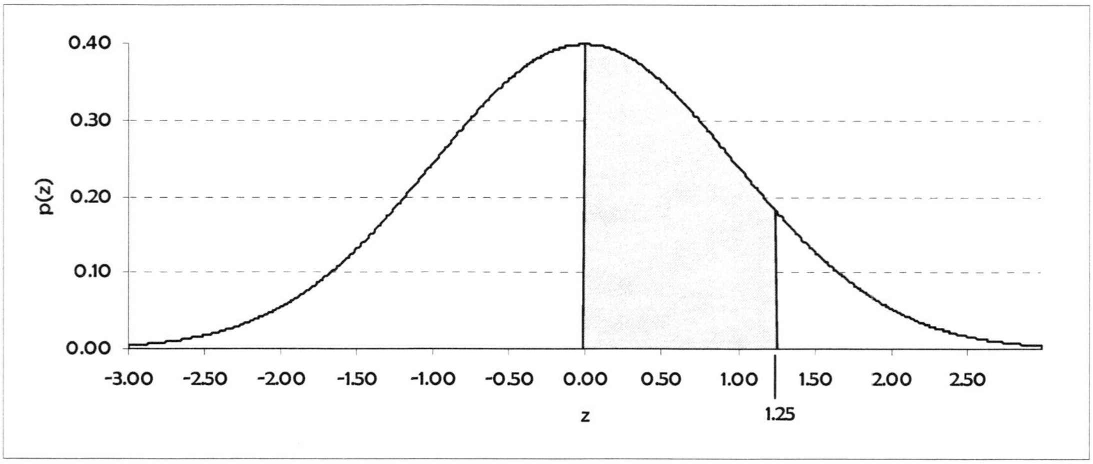

TABLE 25A: Excerpt from a Standard Normal table

z	0.00	0.01	0.02	0.03	0.04	0.05	0.06	0.07	0.08	0.09
1.1	.3643	.3665	.3686	.3708	.3729	.3749	.3770	.3790	.3810	.3830
1.2	.3849	.3869	.3888	.3907	.3925	**.3944**	.3962	.3980	.3997	.4015
1.3	.4032	.4049	.4066	.4082	.4099	.4115	.4131	.4147	.4162	.4177

To find the *area* or *probability*, scan down the first column headed by $\mathbf{z}$, to find the row, which contains **1.2**. Then scan across this row until you find the column headed by **0.05**. The appropriate probability is located in the corresponding row and column. So it follows that

$$\begin{aligned}\Pr\{0 \le \mathbf{Z} \le 1.25\} &= \mathbf{T}(1.25) \\ &= 0.3944\end{aligned}$$, where $\mathbf{T}(a)$ denotes the tabled value at a.

We can use these tables to determine the probabilities of more complex events. Let's evaluate the $\Pr\{\mathbf{Z} \le 1.25\}$ depicted in Figure 28.

$$\begin{aligned}\Pr\{\mathbf{Z} \le 1.25\} &= \Pr\{\mathbf{Z} < 0.00\} + \Pr\{0 \le \mathbf{Z} \le 1.25\} \\ &= 0.5000 + \mathbf{T}(1.25) \\ &= 0.5000 + .3944 \\ &= 0.8944\end{aligned}$$

FIGURE 28: A Standard Normal region less than or equal to 1.25.

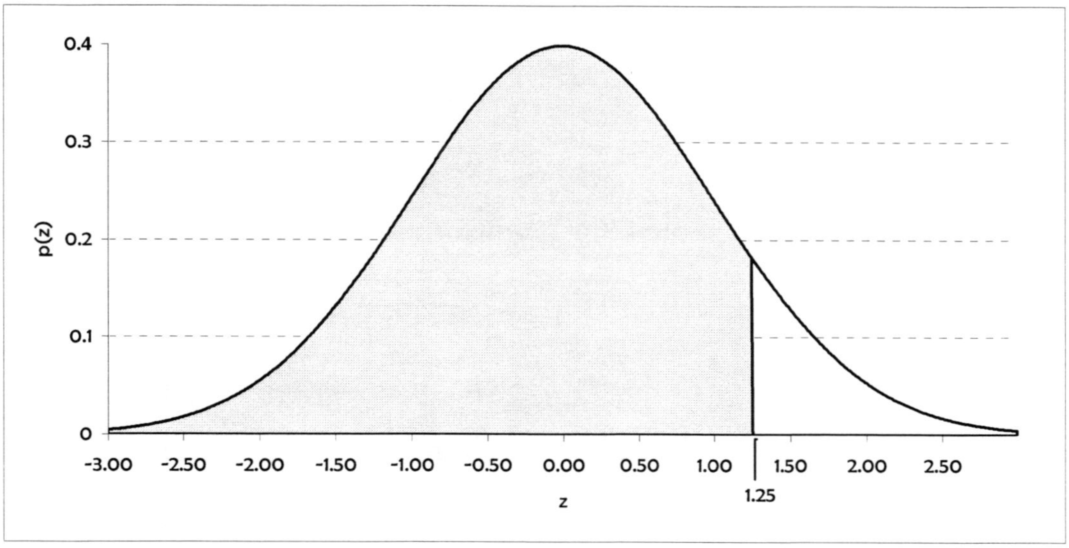

More complex computations may be required to evaluate events such as $\Pr\{\mathbf{Z} \ge 0.75\}$ depicted in Figure 29.

FIGURE 29: A Standard Normal region greater than or equal to 0.75.

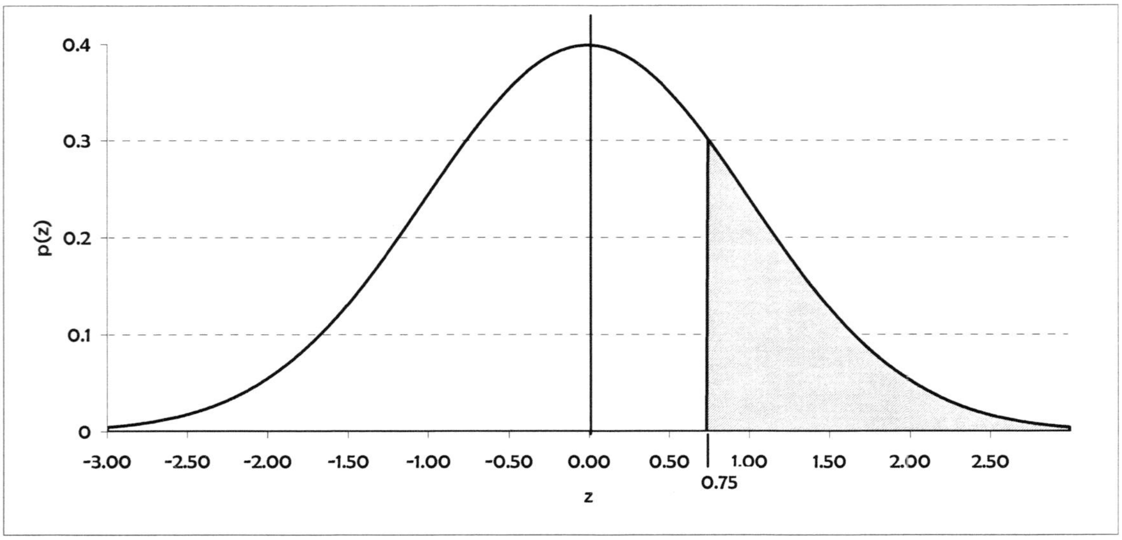

To use the table we recognize that $\Pr\{\mathbf{Z} > 0.00\} = 0.5000$ by **symmetry** of the standard normal graph **about the y – axis**. We use **axiom 3 of Kolmogorov** to rewrite $\{\mathbf{Z} \geq 0\}$ into **mutually exclusive events**.

$$\{\mathbf{Z} > 0\} = \{0 < \mathbf{Z} < 0.75\} \cup \{\mathbf{Z} \geq 0.75\}$$

So that,

$$\begin{aligned} \Pr\{\mathbf{Z} > 0\} &= \Pr\{0 < \mathbf{Z} < 0.75\} + \Pr\{\mathbf{Z} \geq 0.75\} \\ 0.5000 &= \mathrm{T}(0.75) + \Pr\{\mathbf{Z} \geq 0.75\} \\ 0.5000 &= 0.2734 + \Pr\{\mathbf{Z} \geq 0.75\} \\ 0.2266 &= \Pr\{\mathbf{Z} \geq 0.75\} \end{aligned}$$

TABLE 25B: An excerpted Standard Normal table for positive $\mathbf{z}$-values

z	**0.00**	**0.01**	**0.02**	**0.03**	**0.04**	**0.05**	**0.06**	**0.07**	**0.08**	**0.09**
.60	.2257	.2291	.2324	.2357	.2389	.2422	.2454	.2486	.2517	.2549
.70	.2580	.2611	.2642	.2673	.2704	**.2734**	.2764	.2794	.2823	.2852
.80	.2881	.2910	.2939	.2967	.2995	.3023	.3051	.3078	.3106	.3133

Note that $\Pr\{\mathbf{Z} \geq a\} = \Pr\{\mathbf{Z} \leq -a\}$ by **symmetry of the graph** of $p(\mathbf{z})$ in the y – axis. So the $\Pr\{\mathbf{Z} \leq -0.75\} = 0.2266$ as well

In a more complicated situation, we want to evaluate $\Pr\{-1.65 < \mathbf{Z} < 0.35\}$. We rewrite the event as the union of two mutually exclusive events in the following way:

$$\{-1.65 < \mathbf{Z} < 0.35\} = \{-1.65 < \mathbf{Z} < 0.00\} \cup \{0.00 \leq \mathbf{Z} < 0.35\}$$

This **union partitions the event into two intervals**, one, which is to the **left of the origin** and one to the **right of the origin** as depicted in Figure 30.

FIGURE 30: A Standard Normal region between –1.65 and 0.35.

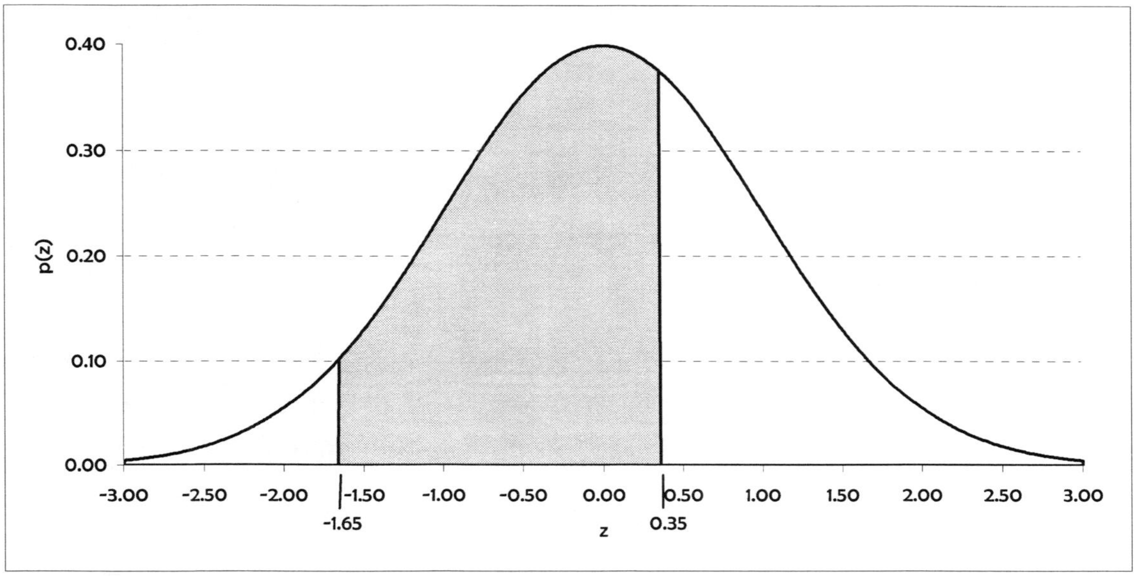

Then using **axiom 3 of Kolmogorov** and the following table we have:

TABLE 25C: An excerpted Standard Normal table for positive $\mathbf{z}-$ values

z	0.00	0.01	0.02	0.03	0.04	0.05	0.06	0.07	0.08	0.09
.20	.0793	.0832	.0871	.0910	.0948	.0987	.1026	.1064	.1103	.1141
.30	.1179	.1217	.1255	.1293	.1331	**.1368**	.1406	.1443	.1480	.1517
.40	.1554	.1591	.1628	.1664	.1700	.1736	.1772	.1808	.1844	.1879
-	-	-	-	-	-	-	-	-	-	-
1.50	.4332	.4345	.4357	.4370	.4382	.4394	.4406	.4418	.4429	.4441
1.60	.4452	.4463	.4474	.4484	.4495	**.4505**	.4515	.4525	.4535	.4545
1.70	.4554	.4564	.4573	.4582	.4591	.4599	.4608	.4616	.4625	.4633

$$\Pr\{-1.65 < \mathbf{Z} < 0.35\} = \Pr\{-1.65 < \mathbf{Z} < 0.00\} + \Pr\{0.00 \le \mathbf{Z} < 0.35\}$$
$$= \Pr\{-1.65 < \mathbf{Z} < 0.00\} + \mathbf{T}(0.35)$$
$$= \Pr\{0.00 < \mathbf{Z} < 1.65\} + 0.1368$$
$$= \mathbf{T}(1.65) + 0.1368$$
$$= 0.4505 + 0.1368$$
$$= 0.5873$$

The subsequent probability implies that 58.73% of the standard normal z-values fall between –1.65 and +0.35 or the area under the curve between the points is 0.5873.

Finding Normal Percentiles

In many cases, we want to invert the process. For example, suppose we want to determine the number a such that

$$\Pr\{0 < \mathbf{Z} < a\} = 0.2157$$

The value given is a probability. So instead reading along the rows and columns of the $\mathbf{Z}$-table, we must **follow the numbers inside the table in an increasing order** until we find **0.2157** or until we bound it above and below.

TABLE 25D: An excerpted Standard Normal table.

z	0.00	0.01	0.02	0.03	0.04	0.05	0.06	0.07	0.08	0.09
.4	.1154	.1591	.1628	.1664	.1700	.1736	.1772	.1808	.1844	.1879
.5	.1915	.1950	.1985	.2019	.2054	.2088	.2123	**.2157**	.2190	.2224
.6	.2257	.2291	.2324	.2357	.2389	.2422	.2454	.2486	.2518	.2549

Notice that $a = 0.57$ and has exactly $\mathbf{T}(0.57) = 0.2157$.

If the value does not occur exactly in the table then we would need to round the values. Suppose that we want to determine **the 80th percentile of the standard normal distribution**. Determine a so the $\Pr\{\mathbf{Z} < a\} = 0.8000$. Notice that we express the **probability to four decimal places** only to **remind us** that we are trying to **find a percentile**.

FIGURE 31: The eightieth percentile in the Standard Normal

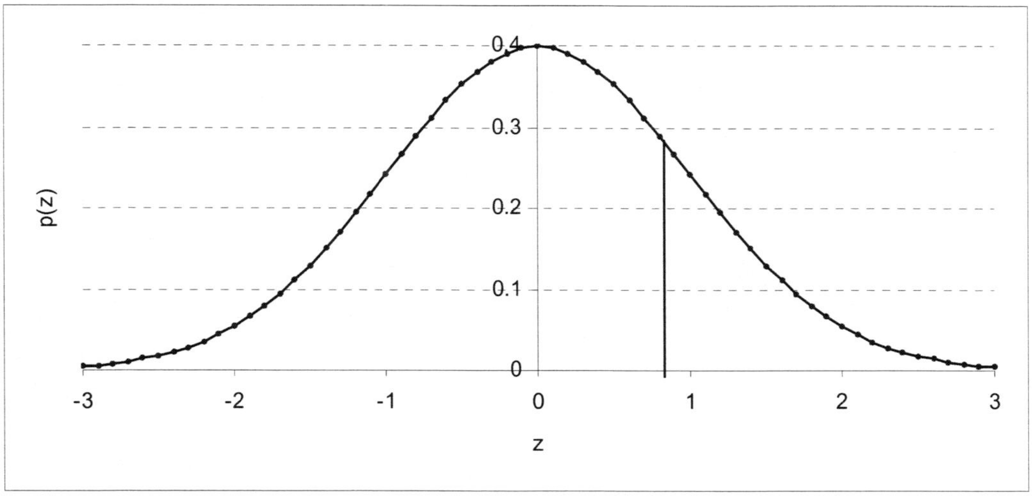

Notice that $\Pr\{\mathbf{Z} < a\} = \Pr\{\mathbf{Z} < 0\} + \Pr\{0.00 < \mathbf{Z} < a\}$, whenever $a > 0$.

$$\begin{aligned} \Pr\{\mathbf{Z} < a\} &= \Pr\{\mathbf{Z} < 0\} + \Pr\{0.00 < \mathbf{Z} < a\} \\ 0.8000 &= 0.5000 + \Pr\{0.00 < \mathbf{Z} < a\} \\ 0.3000 &= \mathbf{T}(a) \end{aligned}$$

If $\mathbf{T}(a) = 0.3000$, then

$$\begin{aligned} \mathbf{T}(0.84) &= 0.2995 \\ &\quad \} \ 0.0005 \\ \mathbf{T}(a) &= 0.3000 \\ &\quad \} \ 0.0023 \\ \mathbf{T}(0.85) &= 0.3023 \end{aligned}$$

TABLE 25E: A Standard Normal table for positive z − values

z	0.00	0.01	0.02	0.03	0.04	0.05	0.06	0.07	0.08	0.09
.70	.2580	.2611	.2642	.2673	.2704	.2734	.2764	.2794	.2823	.2852
.80	.2881	.2910	.2939	.2967	**.2995**	**.3023**	.3051	.3078	.3106	.3133
.90	.3159	.3186	.3212	.3238	.3264	.3289	.3315	.3340	.3365	.3389

Therefore, a would be closer to 0.84 than to 0.85 since the difference $\mathbf{T}(a) - \mathbf{T}(0.84) = 0.0005$, whereas $\mathbf{T}(0.85) - \mathbf{T}(a) = 0.0023$.

We use linear interpolation to arrive at a more accurate value of 0.8418. A unique straight line is determined by the two nearest tabled values (0.84, 0.2995) and (0.85, 0.3023). The slope of the straight line connecting them is given by:

$$m = \frac{\Delta y}{\Delta x} = \frac{0.3023 - 0.2995}{0.85 - 0.84} = 0.28$$

Using the point slope form for the equation of a straight line we have

$$\begin{aligned} y - y_0 &= m \times (x - x_0) \\ y - 0.2995 &= 0.28 \times (x - 0.84) \end{aligned}$$

We can then interpolate between the points by solving for x when $y = 0.3000$.

$$\begin{aligned} y - 0.2995 &= 0.28 \times (\mathbf{x} - 0.84) \\ 0.3000 - 0.2995 &= 0.28 \times (\mathbf{x} - 0.84) \\ 0.0005 &= 0.28 \times (\mathbf{x} - 0.84) \\ \frac{0.0005}{0.28} &= \mathbf{x} - 0.84 \\ 0.0018 + 0.84 &= \mathbf{x} \\ \mathbf{x} &\doteq 0.8418 \end{aligned}$$

Therefore, the **20**[th] percentile of the standard normal is given by –0.84. In other words in **80%** of the random draws from this distribution we would expect the $\mathbf{z}$–values to be less than 0.84 or in only 20% of such draws would we expect the value to exceed 0.84.

FIGURE 32: Interpolation in Standard Normal tables to find the Eightieth percentile

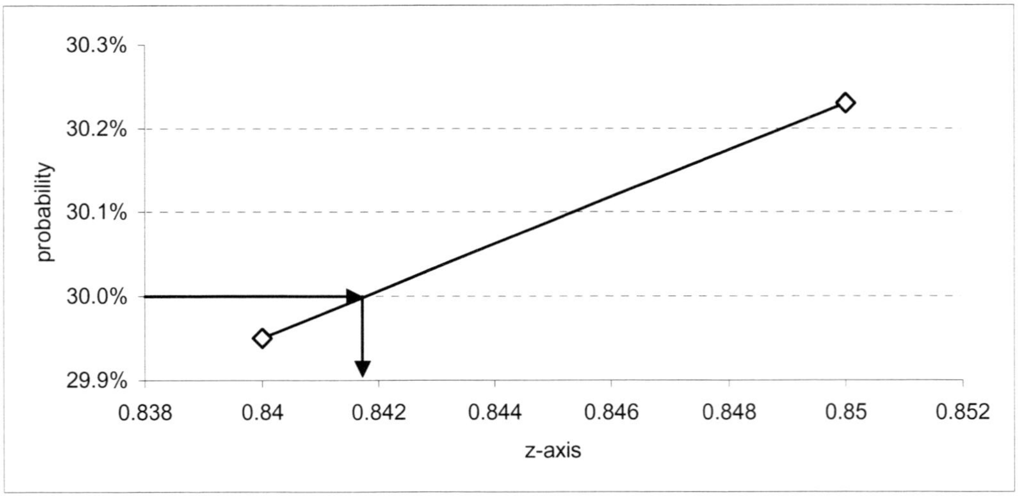

Define the $100 \times p$ percentile in the standard normal distribution as the point $\mathbf{z}(p)$ such that

$$\Pr\{\mathbf{Z} < \mathbf{z}(p)\} = p$$

So it follows that $\mathbf{z}(0.80) = 0.8418$ and by symmetry of the graph of the standard normal distribution about the origin $\mathbf{z}(0.20) = -0.8418$.

Middle Percentiles

Suppose we need to determine the **middle 50% of the standard normal distribution**. Then we want to determine a such that

$$\Pr\{-a < \mathbf{Z} < a\} = 0.5000$$

However,

$$\begin{aligned}\Pr\{-a < Z < a\} &= \Pr\{-a < \mathbf{Z} < 0.00\} + \Pr\{0.00 < \mathbf{Z} < a\} \\ &= 2 \times \Pr\{0.00 < \mathbf{Z} < a\} \\ &= 2 \times \mathbf{T}(a)\end{aligned}$$

Thus by substitution, we have:

$$\begin{aligned}\Pr\{-a < \mathbf{Z} < a\} &= 0.5000 \\ 0.5000 &= 2 \times \Pr\{0.00 < \mathbf{Z} < a\} \\ 0.5000 &= 2 \times \mathbf{T}(a) \\ 0.2500 &= \mathbf{T}(a)\end{aligned}$$

FIGURE 33: Interpolation to Find the Middle 50%

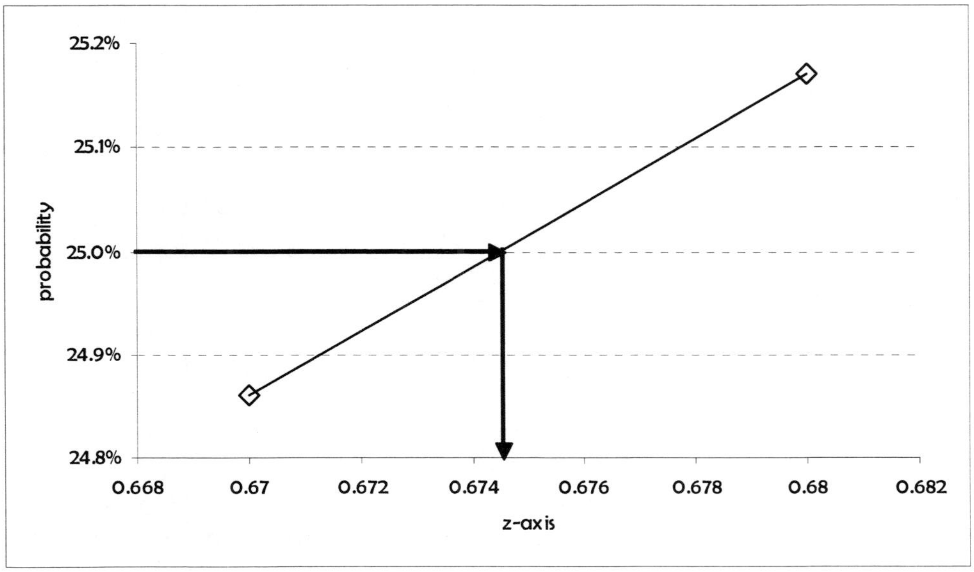

If $\mathbf{T}(a) = 0.2500$, then

$$\mathbf{T}(0.67) = 0.2486$$

$$\} \quad 0.0014$$

$$\mathbf{T}(a) = 0.2500$$

$$\} \quad 0.0017$$

$$\mathbf{T}(0.68) = 0.2517$$

We use linear interpolation to arrive at a more accurate value of 0.6745. A unique straight line is determined by the two nearest tabled values (0.67, 0.2486) and (0.68, 0.2517). The slope of the straight line connecting them is given by:

$$m = \frac{\Delta y}{\Delta x} = \frac{0.2517 - 0.2486}{0.68 - 0.67} = 0.31$$

Using the point slope form for the equation of a straight line we have

$$\begin{aligned} y - y_0 &= m \times (x - x_0) \\ y - 0.2486 &= 0.31 \times (x - 0.67) \end{aligned}$$

We can then interpolate between the points by solving for x when $y = 0.2500$.

$$\begin{aligned} y - 0.2486 &= 0.31 \times (\mathbf{x} - 0.67) \\ 0.2500 - 0.2486 &= 0.31 \times (\mathbf{x} - 0.67) \\ 0.0014 &= 0.31 \times (\mathbf{x} - 0.67) \\ \frac{0.0014}{0.31} &= \mathbf{x} - 0.67 \\ 0.0045 + 0.67 &= \mathbf{x} \\ \mathbf{x} &\doteq 0.6745 \end{aligned}$$

TABLE 25F: A Standard Normal table for positive $\mathbf{z}-$ values

z	**0.00**	**0.01**	**0.02**	**0.03**	**0.04**	**0.05**	**0.06**	**0.07**	**0.08**	**0.09**
.50	.1915	.1950	.1985	.2019	.2054	.2088	.2123	.2157	.2190	.2224
.60	.2257	.2291	.2324	.2357	.2389	.2422	.2454	**.2486**	**.2517**	.2549
.70	.2580	.2611	.2642	.2673	.2704	.2734	.2764	.2794	.2823	.2852

So a is slightly closer to 0.67 but the value obtained by interpolation would be 0.6745. The process of interpolation in this case is shown in Figure 33. Hence the middle 50% of the standard normal distribution are given by the values of **Z** that fall between ±0.6745. Notice also that **z**(0.75) = 0.6745 and **z**(0.25) = −0.6745.

Finding Normal Probabilities

The method outlined previously only allows us to determine probabilities when $\mu = 0$ and $\sigma = 1$. However, the table given allows us to compute all normal probabilities **regardless of the values** of the population **mean** and the population **standard deviation**. The mechanism that allows us to perform the computations is called **standardization**.

Standardization

When we **standardize** a normal random variable, we **subtract** off its population **mean** μ and **divide the difference** by the population **standard deviation** σ. The resulting random variable is standardized and

$$\mathbf{Z} = \frac{\mathbf{X} - \mu}{\sigma}$$

Z has a standard normal distribution, i.e., $\mathbf{Z} \sim N(0,1)$. This result means that we do not need a separate set of tables for every possible pair of values for μ and σ.

FIGURE 34: A Normal Distribution.

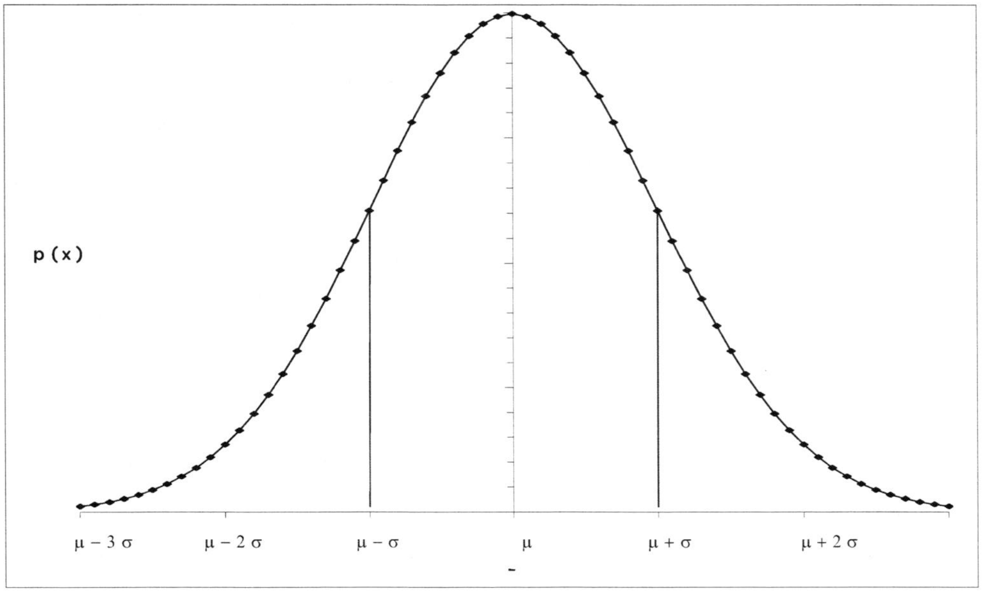

Subtracting off μ **translates the median (mean and mode)** of the distribution of $\mathbf{U} = \mathbf{X} - \mu$ **back to the origin**. The distribution of **U** is depicted in Figure 35 and is **centered over the origin**. Otherwise, **its shape is unaltered** and just the distribution is translated so that the **mode is located over the origin**.

FIGURE 35: A Normal Distribution with mean zero

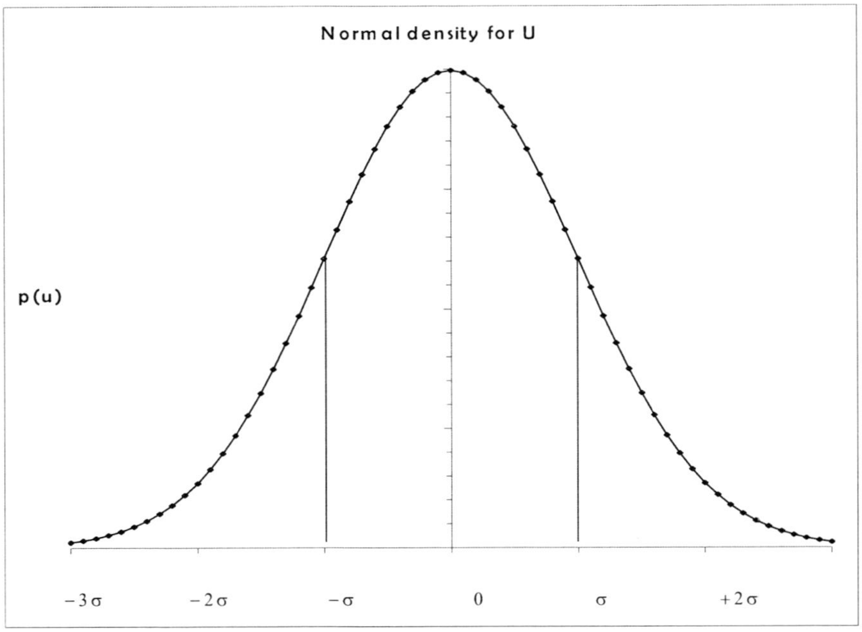

Dividing **U** by σ rescales the horizontal axis, so that **Z** has a standard deviation of **1** as depicted in Figure 36.

FIGURE 36: A Standardized Normal distribution

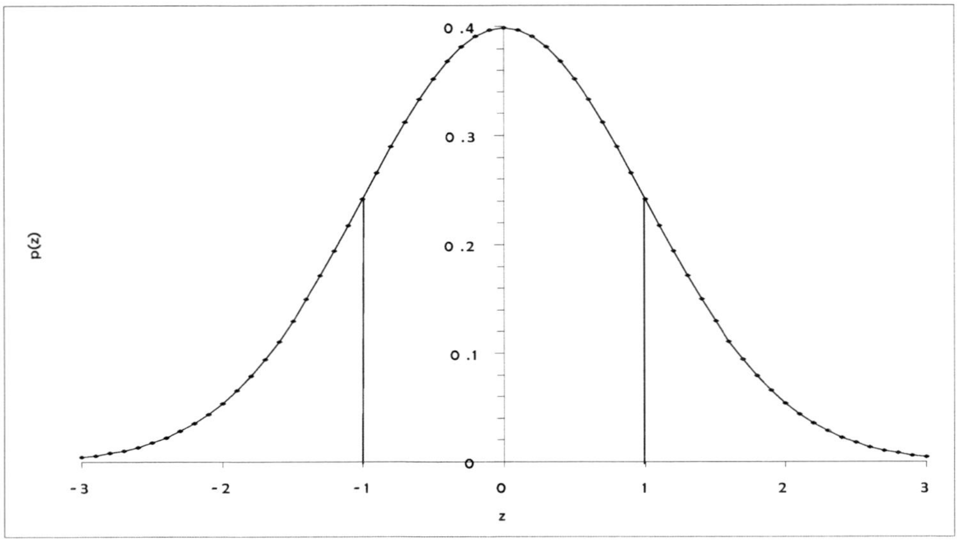

Case Study: IQ Scores

To understand the process, we use the following example based on IQ scores, which are normally distributed with a mean value of **100** and a standard deviation of **15**. Let $\mathbf{X}$ denote the random variable, which is the **IQ** score and assume that

$$\mathbf{X} \sim \mathrm{N}(100,15)$$

Problem: Determine the probability that a randomly chosen person has an IQ score less than 120.

$$\begin{aligned}
\Pr\{\mathbf{X}<120\} &= \Pr\{\mathbf{X}-100<120-100\} \\
&\quad \textit{subtract} \quad \mu=100 \quad \textit{from both sides} \\
&= \Pr\left\{\frac{\mathbf{X}-100}{15}<\frac{120-100}{15}\right\} \\
&\quad \textit{divide both sides by} \quad \sigma=15 \\
&= \Pr\{\mathbf{Z}<1.33\} \\
&= \Pr\{\mathbf{Z}<0.00\} + \Pr\{0.00\le\mathbf{Z}<1.33\} \\
&= 0.5000 + \mathbf{T}(1.33) \\
&= 0.5000 + 0.4082 \\
&= 0.9082
\end{aligned}$$

TABLE 25G: A Standard Normal table for positive $\mathbf{z}-$ values.

z	0.00	0.01	0.02	0.03	0.04	0.05	0.06	0.07	0.08	0.09
1.2	.3849	.3869	.3888	.3907	.3925	.3944	.3962	.3980	.3997	.4015
1.3	.4032	.4049	.4066	**.4082**	.4099	.4115	.4131	.4147	.4162	.4177
1.4	.4192	.4207	.4222	.4236	.4251	.4265	.4279	.4292	.4306	.4319

The probability that $\mathbf{X}<120$ is equivalent to the event of: **being less than 1.33 standard deviations above the mean in the standard normal distribution.** Thus, we expect 90.82% of the population with scores below 120.

Problem: What's the probability that a randomly chosen person in the population will have an IQ between 104 and 132?

$$\Pr\{104 < \mathbf{X} < 132\} = \Pr\{104 - 100 < \mathbf{X} - 100 < 132 - 100\}$$

$$\textit{subtract} \quad \mu = 100 \quad \textit{from} \quad \textit{both} \quad \textit{sides}$$

$$= \Pr\left\{\frac{104-100}{15} < \frac{\mathbf{X}-100}{15} < \frac{132-100}{15}\right\}$$

$$\textit{divide} \quad \textit{both} \quad \textit{sides} \quad \textit{by} \quad \sigma = 15$$

$$= \Pr\{0.27 < \mathbf{Z} < 2.13\}$$

$$= \Pr\{0.00 < \mathbf{Z} < 2.13\} - \Pr\{\mathbf{Z} < 0.27\}$$

$$= \mathbf{T}(2.13) - \mathbf{T}(0.27)$$

$$= 0.4834 - 0.1064$$

$$= 0.3770$$

Thus we expect 37.7% of the population with IQ's between 104 and 132.

FIGURE 37: Area under a Standard Normal distribution between 0.27 and 2.13

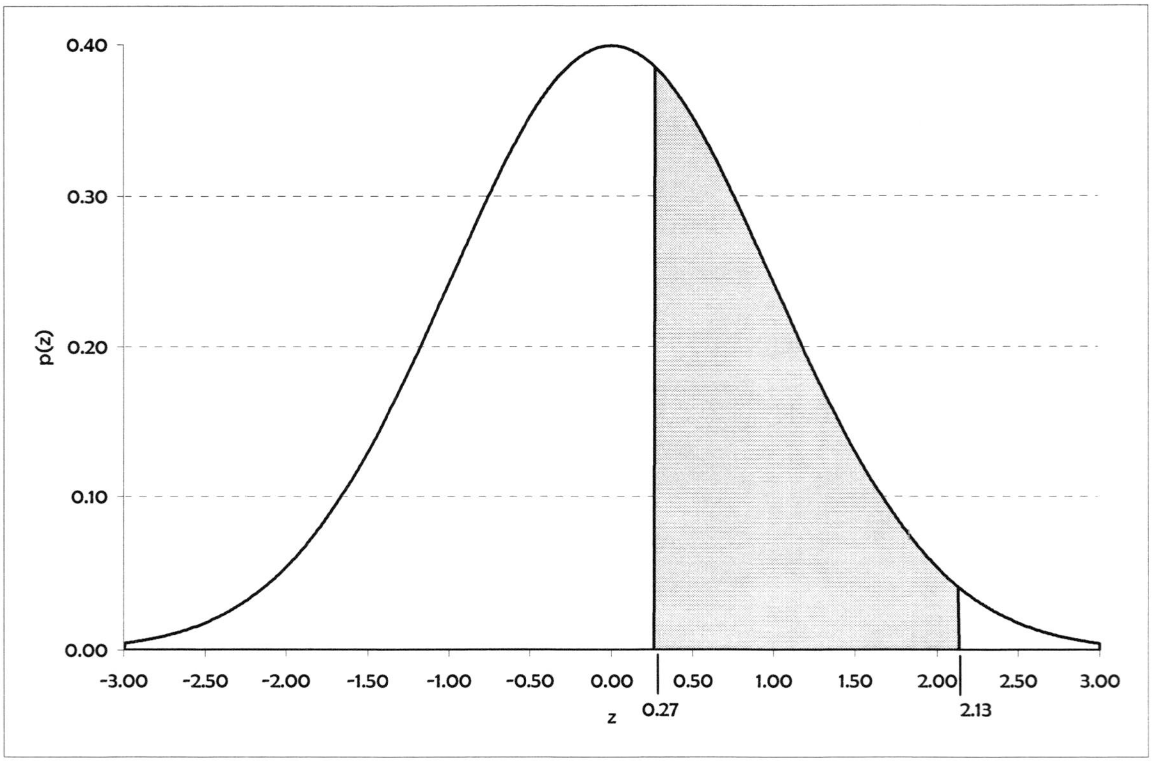

Problem: Someone tells you that he has an IQ of 150. Should you be skeptical?

$$\begin{aligned}
\Pr\{\mathbf{X} < 150\} &= \Pr\{\mathbf{X} - 100 < 150 - 100\} \\
&\quad \textit{subtract} \quad \mu = 100 \quad \textit{from both sides} \\
&= \Pr\left\{\frac{\mathbf{X} - 100}{15} < \frac{150 - 100}{15}\right\} \\
&\quad \textit{divide both sides by} \quad \sigma = 15 \\
&= \Pr\{\mathbf{Z} < 3.33\} \\
&= \Pr\{\mathbf{Z} < 0.00\} + \Pr\{0.00 < \mathbf{Z} < 3.33\} \\
&= 0.5000 + \mathbf{T}(3.33)^{**} \\
&= 0.5000 + 0.499566 \\
&= 0.999566
\end{aligned}$$

TABLE 25H: A Standard Normal table for positive $\mathbf{z}$ -values.

z	0.00	0.01	0.02	0.03	0.04	0.05	0.06	0.07	0.08	0.09
3.2	.4993	.4993	.4994	.4994	.4994	.4994	.4994	.4995	.4995	.4995
3.3	.4995	.4995	.4995	**.4996**	.4996	.4996	.4996	.4996	.4996	.4997
3.4	.4997	.4997	.4997	.4997	.4997	.4997	.4997	.4997	.4997	.4998

This means that only 434 out of every 1 million persons should have an IQ in excess of 150. So in San Antonio about 434 persons have an IQ in excess of 150 and they are distributed across all age groups, genders, etc.

Normal Percentiles

Percentiles of the normal distribution can be determined from percentiles of the standard normal distribution. Let $\mathbf{x}(p)$ denote the $100 \times p\%$ **percentile of the normal distribution** and it is given by:

$$\mathbf{x}(p) = \mu + \mathbf{z}(p) \times \sigma$$

where $\mathbf{z}(p)$ is the $100 \times p\%$ **percentile** in the **standard normal** distribution.

Problem: What is the 70th **percentile of the IQ scores**? Determine

$$\begin{aligned}
\mathbf{x}(0.70) &= 100 + \mathbf{z}(0.70) \times 15 \\
&= 100 + 0.52 \times 15 \\
&= 100 + 7.80 \\
&= 107.8
\end{aligned}$$

If one has an **IQ less than 107.8** then his or her **IQ is below the** 70th **percentile**. If your IQ exceeds 107.8 then his or her IQ is above the 70th percentile.

The 70th Percentile of IQ Scores

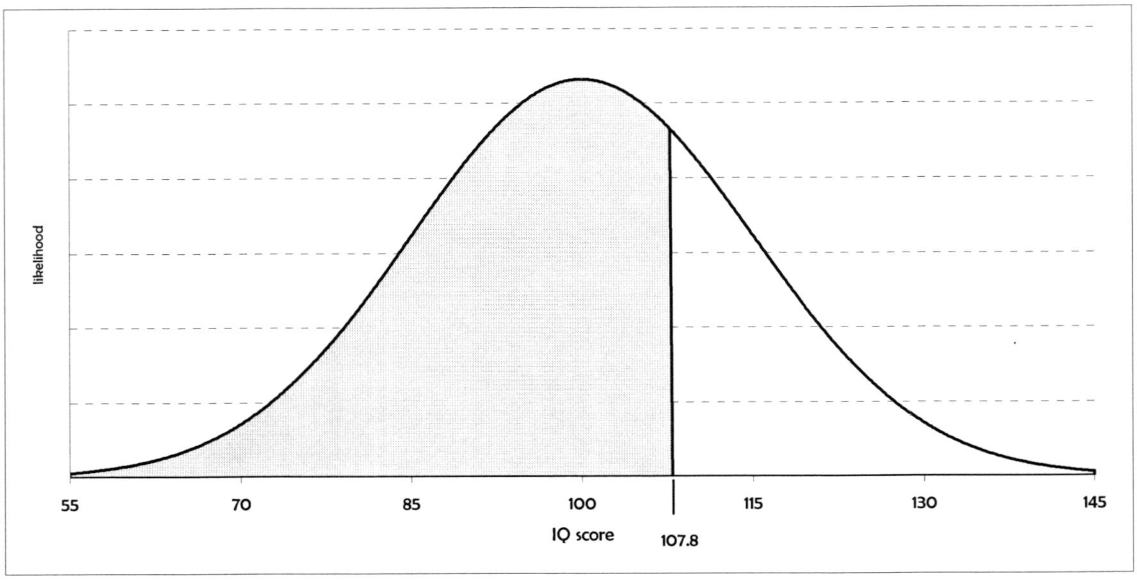

Case Study: Jean Sizes

Assume that the fashion industry knows that **waist sizes of teenage girls in the US have a mean value of 27 inches with a standard deviation 3 inches**. Determine the middle 60% of the waist sizes of US teenage girls.

The middle 60% of waist sizes are bounded by their 20th and 80th percentiles.

$$\begin{aligned}\mathbf{x}(0.80) &= 27 + \mathbf{z}(0.80) \times 3 \\ &= 27 + 0.84 \times 3 \\ &= 27 + 2.52 \\ &= 29.52\end{aligned}$$

$$\begin{aligned}\mathbf{x}(0.20) &= 27 + \mathbf{z}(0.20) \times 3 \\ &= 27 - 0.84 \times 3 \\ &= 27 - 2.52 \\ &= 24.48\end{aligned}$$

Thus if we made women's apparel and we wanted to target the middle of this population, we could introduce jean sizes with waists between 24.48 inches and 29.52 inches and we could still sell to **60% of the market**. Moreover, we could **minimize our costs** by producing fewer jean sizes and thereby **reduce our exposure to risk**.

This is precisely the highly successful technique used by **Chic Jeans** when they introduced a modest number of sizes onto the American market. They also created demand by **targeting their audience just near or below the mean**. Thus being able to wear **Chic Jeans meant you were fit**.

The middle 60% of Jean sizes for Teenage girls

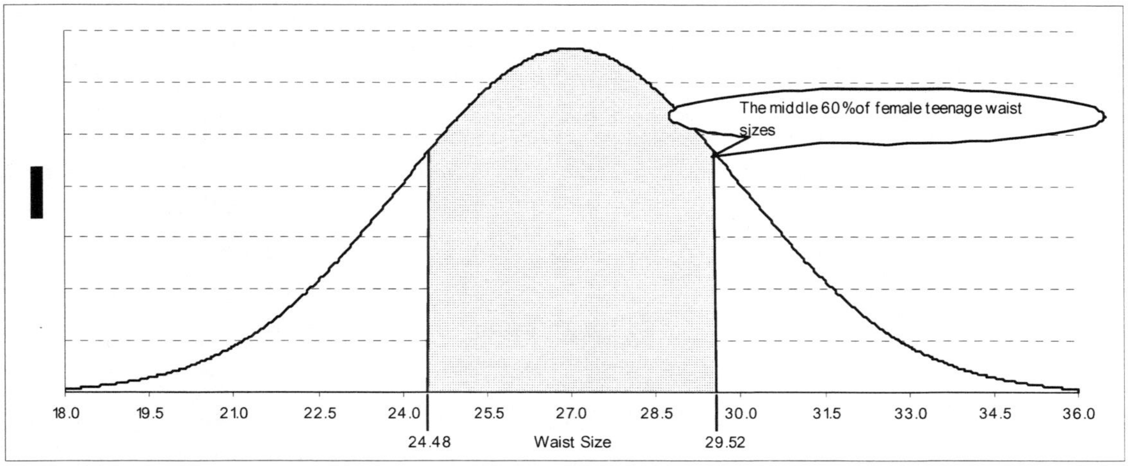

TABLE 25: A Standard Normal table for positive *z*-values

z	0.00	0.01	0.02	0.03	0.04	0.05	0.06	0.07	0.08	0.09
0.0	0.0000	0.0040	0.0080	0.0120	0.0160	0.0199	0.0239	0.0279	0.0319	0.0359
0.1	0.0398	0.0438	0.0478	0.0517	0.0557	0.0596	0.0636	0.0675	0.0714	0.0753
0.2	0.0793	0.0832	0.0871	0.0910	0.0948	0.0987	0.1026	0.1064	0.1103	0.1141
0.3	0.1179	0.1217	0.1255	0.1293	0.1331	0.1368	0.1406	0.1443	0.1480	0.1517
0.4	0.1554	0.1591	0.1628	0.1664	0.1700	0.1736	0.1772	0.1808	0.1844	0.1879
0.5	0.1915	0.1950	0.1985	0.2019	0.2054	0.2088	0.2123	0.2157	0.2190	0.2224
0.6	0.2257	0.2291	0.2324	0.2357	0.2389	0.2422	0.2454	0.2486	0.2517	0.2549
0.7	0.2580	0.2611	0.2642	0.2673	0.2704	0.2734	0.2764	0.2794	0.2823	0.2852
0.8	0.2881	0.2910	0.2939	0.2967	0.2995	0.3023	0.3051	0.3078	0.3106	0.3133
0.9	0.3159	0.3186	0.3212	0.3238	0.3264	0.3289	0.3315	0.3340	0.3365	0.3389
1.0	0.3413	0.3438	0.3461	0.3485	0.3508	0.3531	0.3554	0.3577	0.3599	0.3621
1.1	0.3643	0.3665	0.3686	0.3708	0.3729	0.3749	0.3770	0.3790	0.3810	0.3830
1.2	0.3849	0.3869	0.3888	0.3907	0.3925	0.3944	0.3962	0.3980	0.3997	0.4015
1.3	0.4032	0.4049	0.4066	0.4082	0.4099	0.4115	0.4131	0.4147	0.4162	0.4177
1.4	0.4192	0.4207	0.4222	0.4236	0.4251	0.4265	0.4279	0.4292	0.4306	0.4319
1.5	0.4332	0.4345	0.4357	0.4370	0.4382	0.4394	0.4406	0.4418	0.4429	0.4441
1.6	0.4452	0.4463	0.4474	0.4484	0.4495	0.4505	0.4515	0.4525	0.4535	0.4545
1.7	0.4554	0.4564	0.4573	0.4582	0.4591	0.4599	0.4608	0.4616	0.4625	0.4633
1.8	0.4641	0.4649	0.4656	0.4664	0.4671	0.4678	0.4686	0.4693	0.4699	0.4706
1.9	0.4713	0.4719	0.4726	0.4732	0.4738	0.4744	0.4750	0.4756	0.4761	0.4767
2.0	0.4772	0.4778	0.4783	0.4788	0.4793	0.4798	0.4803	0.4808	0.4812	0.4817
2.1	0.4821	0.4826	0.4830	0.4834	0.4838	0.4842	0.4846	0.4850	0.4854	0.4857
2.2	0.4861	0.4864	0.4868	0.4871	0.4875	0.4878	0.4881	0.4884	0.4887	0.4890
2.3	0.4893	0.4896	0.4898	0.4901	0.4904	0.4906	0.4909	0.4911	0.4913	0.4916
2.4	0.4918	0.4920	0.4922	0.4925	0.4927	0.4929	0.4931	0.4932	0.4934	0.4936
2.5	0.4938	0.4940	0.4941	0.4943	0.4945	0.4946	0.4948	0.4949	0.4951	0.4952
2.6	0.4953	0.4955	0.4956	0.4957	0.4959	0.4960	0.4961	0.4962	0.4963	0.4964
2.7	0.4965	0.4966	0.4967	0.4968	0.4969	0.4970	0.4971	0.4972	0.4973	0.4974
2.8	0.4974	0.4975	0.4976	0.4977	0.4977	0.4978	0.4979	0.4979	0.4980	0.4981
2.9	0.4981	0.4982	0.4982	0.4983	0.4984	0.4984	0.4985	0.4985	0.4986	0.4986
3.0	0.4987	0.4987	0.4987	0.4988	0.4988	0.4989	0.4989	0.4989	0.4990	0.4990
3.1	0.4990	0.4991	0.4991	0.4991	0.4992	0.4992	0.4992	0.4992	0.4993	0.4993
3.2	0.4993	0.4993	0.4994	0.4994	0.4994	0.4994	0.4994	0.4995	0.4995	0.4995
3.3	0.4995	0.4995	0.4995	0.4996	0.4996	0.4996	0.4996	0.4996	0.4996	0.4997
3.4	0.4997	0.4997	0.4997	0.4997	0.4997	0.4997	0.4997	0.4997	0.4997	0.4998
3.5	0.4998	0.4998	0.4998	0.4998	0.4998	0.4998	0.4998	0.4998	0.4998	0.4998

Problem Set 2

(33-35) All 420 employees of a company were asked whether they smoke and whether they are college graduates. The following table lists the results:

	College Grad	Not College Grad	Total
Smoker	35	80	115
Non-Smoker	130	175	305
Total	165	255	420

33) What is the probability that a randomly chosen person is a smoker *and* has not graduated from college?
a) 0.6905 b) 0.1905 c) 0.2738 d) 0.6071 e) 0.6957

34) What is the probability that a randomly chosen person is a college graduate *or* a non-smoker?
a) 0.4262 b) 0.8095 c) 0.5833 d) 0.3043 e) 0.2121

35) What is the probability that a randomly chosen person in this population smokes given that the person is a college graduate?
a) 0.2121 b) 0.5833 c) 0.3043 d) 0.1212 e) 0.2738

36) What is the probability that a randomly chosen person in this population is a college graduate given that the person does not smoke?
a) 0.5833 b) 0.7878 c) 0.3929 d) 0.3103 e) 0.4262

37) A small company has an applicant pool of 40 qualified persons of whom 22 are Latinos. If the company hires two persons from this pool, what is the probability due to chance alone that both will be non-Latinos?
a) 0.05 b) 0.296 c) 0.196 d) 0.203 e) 0.25

(38-40) A judge calls 36 citizens of whom 24 are men and 12 are women. He must empanel a jury of 6 persons.

38) How many different groups of three women can be chosen for jury duty from the 12 in the pool?
a) 33 b) 69 c) 220 d) 2,024 e) 1,320

39) How many different groups of 3 men can be chosen to serve on the jury from the 24 in the pool?
a) 33 b) 69 c) 220 d) 2,024 e) 12,144

40) What is the probability that due to chance alone the judge chooses a jury of exactly 3 men and 3 women?
a) 0.2286 b) 0.6667 c) 0.0007 d) 0.0012 e) 0.50

(41-43) A population of UTSA students is such that 20% are unemployed, 70% work part-time at Bill Miller Bar BQ for \$6 per hr. and 10% work at West Telemarketing at \$10 per hour. Let the random variable **X** denote the salary of a student in this population.

x	\$0	\$6	\$10
$p(x)$	0.2	0.7	0.1

41) What is the mean salary of this student population?
a) \$5.20 b) \$5.33 c) 0.325 d) \$6.00 e) \$7.21

42) What is the *population variance* of the earnings of theses students?
a) 9.07 b) 0.08 c) 8.16 d) 0.09 e) 2.86

$(0-5.2)^2 \cdot .2 + (6-5.2)^2 \cdot .7 + (10-5.2)^2 \cdot 0.1 = 5.408 + .448 + 2.304$

43) What is the probability that a student in this population makes at least minimum wage?
a) 0.70 b) 1.00 c) 0.80 d) 0.90 e) 0.875

$0.7 + 0.1 = 0.8$

(44-46) A US News and World Report study found only 10% of US citizens under-report their incomes to the IRS. Consider a random sample of 20 US citizens to answer the following questions.

44) What's the probability that more than two persons in this sample underreported their incomes to the IRS?
$Y>2$ or $1-\{Y\le 2\}$ a) 0.2852 b) 0.3230 c) 0.6770 d) 0.7148 e) 0.3594

$1-.1216-.2702-.2852=$

45) What's the probability that at most 4 persons in this sample underreported their incomes to the IRS?
a) 0.0431 b) 0.9569 c) 0.8671 d) 0.1329 e) 0.4238

$Y \le 4$

46) What's the probability that at least one but no more than three 3 persons in the sample underreported their incomes to the IRS?
a) 0.1216 b) 0.2852 c) 0.7148 d) 0.7455 e) 0.8739

$P(1)+P(2)+P(3)=$

47) A car dealer found that 35% of the vehicles of a particular model would have problems while the car is under warranty. If we randomly sample 18 owners of this model, what is the probability that exactly 7 will have problems while the car is still under warranty?
7, 18, .35
a) 0.1634 b) 0.1792 c) 0.3889 d) 0.8165

$_{18}C_7(.35)^7(1-.35)^{11}$ .65

48) What is $\Pr\{-1.37 < \mathbf{Z} < 1.09\}$ where **Z** has a standard normal distribution?
a) 0.9474 b) 0.0853 c) 0.7768 d) 0.8621

49) Determine the values of **Z** that bound the middle 60% of the standard normal distribution.
a) ± 0.675 b) ± 0.84 c) ± 0.525 d) ± 0.7258

(50-52) Assume that Math SAT scores have a normal distribution with a mean of 455 and a standard deviation of 75.

50) What's the probability that a student makes more than 600 or less than 300?
a) 0.9732 b) 0.0460 c) 0.9540 d) 0.0268

51) What's the probability that a randomly selected student from this population makes less than 488?
a) 0.3300 b) 0.6293 c) 0.3707 d) 0.6700

52) What is the 86th percentile of the Math SAT scores?
a) 374 b) 536 c) 543.5 d) 515

(53-56) A government census of unemployed homeless persons in Denton was taken. The people were classified by skill level and gender below.

Skill-Level	Female	Male
Skilled	10	113
Semi-skilled	51	97
Unskilled	85	220

53) What is the probability that a randomly chosen person from this population is female or semi-skilled?
a) 0.0885 b) 0.3607 c) 0.4219 d) 0.5104

54) What is the probability that a randomly chosen person from this population is male and skilled?
a) 0.0174 b) 0.1962 c) 0.7639 d) 0.9601

55) What is the probability that a randomly chosen person is female given that the person is skilled?
a) 0.0174 b) 0.0685 c) 0.0813 d) 0.2135

56) What is the probability that the person is unskilled given that the person is a man?
a) 0.3819 b) 0.5116 c) 0.7213 d) 0.7465

(57-60) A university has 32 applicants from qualified students for its masters program. Among the applicants, are 20 women and 12 men. However, the school can only admit 10 students.

57) How many different ways are there of choosing the 8 men from the 12 men, who applied?
a) 19,958,400 b) 10,158,300 c) 40,320 d) 495

58) How many ways are there of choosing exactly 2 women from the 20 women, who applied?

a) 380 b) 190 c) 225,792,840 d) 496

59) How many different ways are there of admitting 10 students from the 32 persons, who applied?

a) 66 b) 3,628,800 c) 64,512,240 d) 184,756

60) What is the probability that the school admitted 8 men and 2 women for the 10 openings?

a) 0.0015 b) 0.0667 c) 0.7667 d) 0.0439

495·190/$_{32}C_{10}$

(61-64) Let the discrete random variable **X** be defined by the probability distribution $p(x)$ given in the table below:

x	1	4	10
$p(x)$	0.3	0.5	0.2

61) What is the population mean, μ, of the discrete random variable **X** ?

a) 5 b) 4.00 c) 7.33 d) 4.30 e) 5.21

62) What is the population mode of the discrete random variable?

a) 5 b) 4.00 c) 7.33 d) 4.30 e) 5.21

63) What is the population standard deviation, σ, of the discrete random variable?

a) 10.90 b) 3.13 c) 3.30 d) 14.00 e) 9.81

64) What is $\Pr\{\mathbf{X} > 7\}$?

a) 0.00 b) 0.35 c) 0.50 d) 0.20 e) none of these

65) In a test of ESP, a subject is asked to identify the color of a randomly drawn but unseen card as red or black. After each try the card is replaced and the deck is shuffled, and continues until the person has 20 tries. If one guesses, what is the probability that he or she gets at least 8 but not more than 12 correct?

a) 0.252 b) 0.497 c) 0.617 d) 0.737 e) 0.868

66) The probability that a battery fails on a space mission is 0.07. The space shuttle has 14 such batteries. Assuming that they fail independently, what is the probability that exactly 2 fail?

a) 0.0049 b) 0.1229 c) 0.1867 d) 0.2570 e) 0.9302

(67-69) The probability that a company under fills an individual cereal box is 0.30. A random sample of 12 boxes is taken from different stores in the San Antonio.

67) What is the probability that at least four boxes will be under-filled?

a) 0.231 b) 0.276 c) 0.493 d) 0.507 e) 0.724

68) What is the probability that exactly four boxes will be under-filled?
a) 0.231 b) 0.276 c) 0.333 d) 0.493 e) 0.507

69) What is the expected number of under-filled boxes in the sample of size 12?
a) 3 b) 3.6 c) 4 d) 4.17 e) 5

70) What is the population variance of the number of failed batteries in problem # 66?
a) 0.9114 b) 0.9547 c) 0.9815 d) 0.9907 e) none of these

71) Find the area under the standard normal curve between **a = -1.83** and **b = 2.29**.
a) 0.0226 b) 0.4664 c) 0.4890 d) 0.9554

72) Let **Z** denote a standard normal random variable. Determine $\Pr\{\mathbf{Z} > -1.45\}$
a) 0.1264 b) 0.9265 c) 0.6736 d) 0.0735

73) Determine the 98th percentile of the standard normal distribution.
a) 0.3133 b) 2.05 c) 1.23 d) 0.3365

(74-76) The IQ scores of Asian-Americans students have a normal distribution (according to Herrnstein & Murray) with a population mean of 110 points and a population standard deviation of 12.

74) What is the probability that a randomly chosen Asian-American student has an IQ in excess of 120?
a) 0.7486 b) 0.7967 c) 0.2033 d) 0.4213 e) 0.2514

75) What's the probability that a randomly chosen Asian-American student makes between 107 and 137?
a) 0.1844 b) 0.1985 c) 0.3829 d) 0.6171 e) 0.5865

76) What is the 91st percentile of their IQ's?
a) 121 b) 114 c) 120 d) 116 e) 126

Central Limit Theorem

In the beginning of the semester we discussed measures of central tendency such as the sample mean, the sample median, and the sample mode, as components of exploratory data analysis. We illustrated their relative ordering through graphical procedures whenever the distributions were unimodal. It was easy to see the applicability of such analyses and the meanings of the measures of central tendency. We then moved into discussions about probability and onto the topic of probability distributions, which were primarily the binomial and the normal distributions. Today we start to unify the concepts from our

1) exploratory data analytic work with

2) mathematical discussions of the normal distribution

3) to form the Central Limit Theorem

Central Limit Theorem (CLT):

Let $\mathbf{X}$ be a random variable with a population mean μ and standard deviation σ. Let $\mathbf{X}_1, \mathbf{X}_2, \cdots, \mathbf{X}_n$ be a random sample of n observations chosen from this population. Then the **sampling distribution** of the **sample average** $\bar{\mathbf{x}}$ satisfies the following three properties:

- ❖ The **expected value** of the **sampling distribution** of $\bar{\mathbf{x}}$ is denoted by $\mu_{\bar{\mathbf{x}}}$ and given by μ.

- ❖ The **variance** of the **sampling distribution** of $\bar{\mathbf{x}}$ is denoted by $\sigma_{\bar{\mathbf{x}}}^2$ and given by σ^2/n. This means that the **corresponding standard deviation** is:

$$\sigma_{\bar{\mathbf{x}}} = \sigma / \sqrt{n}$$

  This term is also known as the **standard error** of the **sample average**.

- ❖ If $n \geq 30$ then $\bar{\mathbf{x}}$ has a **normal distribution**.

$$\bar{\mathbf{x}} \sim \mathbf{N}\left(\mu, \frac{\sigma}{\sqrt{n}}\right)$$

- **Remark 1**

  The first two results of the CLT are true **regardless of the size** of the sample. The **only assumptions** in the CLT are that the population **mean and variance exist**.

- **Remark 2**

  Part 3 of the CLT is extremely powerful. In preceding sections, how did you know that a random variable had a normal distribution? In all cases, we had to state that as an assumption or cite a reference from a scientific study. The **strength of the CLT** resides in this third property that is true **regardless of the underlying distribution** of $\mathbf{X}$. The result is **an approximation** that improves with the increases in sample size. The value of $n = 30$ is a **rule of thumb** that works in most cases but not all.

- **Remark 3**

  If the **original data** $\mathbf{X}_1, \mathbf{X}_2, \cdots, \mathbf{X}_n$ come from a random variable $\mathbf{X} \sim \mathrm{N}(\mu, \sigma)$ with a normal distribution then part 3 of the **CLT is true even if** $n < 30$.

- **Remark 4**

  It is **not necessary** that $\mathbf{X}$ has a **continuous distribution**.

Statistical Simulation

While the preceding rationale seems plausible, the skeptical student will no doubt wonder about the result. To demonstrate the remarkable nature of these results we generated 50 samples of size 30 from a uniform distribution on the interval (0, 1). See the uniform distribution depicted below and notice that it does not look bell-shaped and has very little if any resemblance to a normal random variable.

Figure: Uniform Distribution

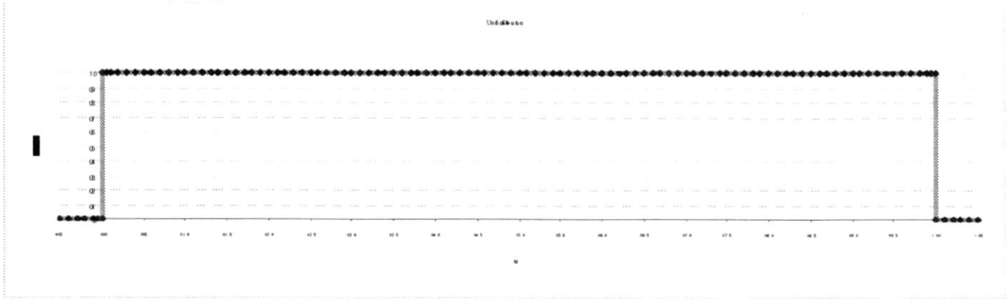

We computed sample averages of these 50 random samples of size 30 from this simulation and the 50 sample averages are given below:

0.611	0.427	0.513	0.549	0.388	0.457	0.508	0.567	0.549	0.625
0.495	0.602	0.461	0.513	0.474	0.617	0.527	0.498	0.486	0.631
0.470	0.403	0.586	0.528	0.392	0.484	0.506	0.442	0.495	0.570
0.605	0.513	0.502	0.509	0.437	0.503	0.534	0.565	0.448	0.528
0.433	0.444	0.534	0.571	0.577	0.565	0.505	0.478	0.452	0.424

The width based on **Scott's formula** is

$$w = \frac{2.15 \times \mathbf{s}}{n^{1/5}} = 0.047$$

Scott's width can be used to create relative frequency polygons as before based on these sample averages. While the frequency polygon does not perfectly fit a bell-shaped curve, it is clear that the values are distributed symmetrically around 0.50 and that one can see the tails becoming concave upward as in the normal.

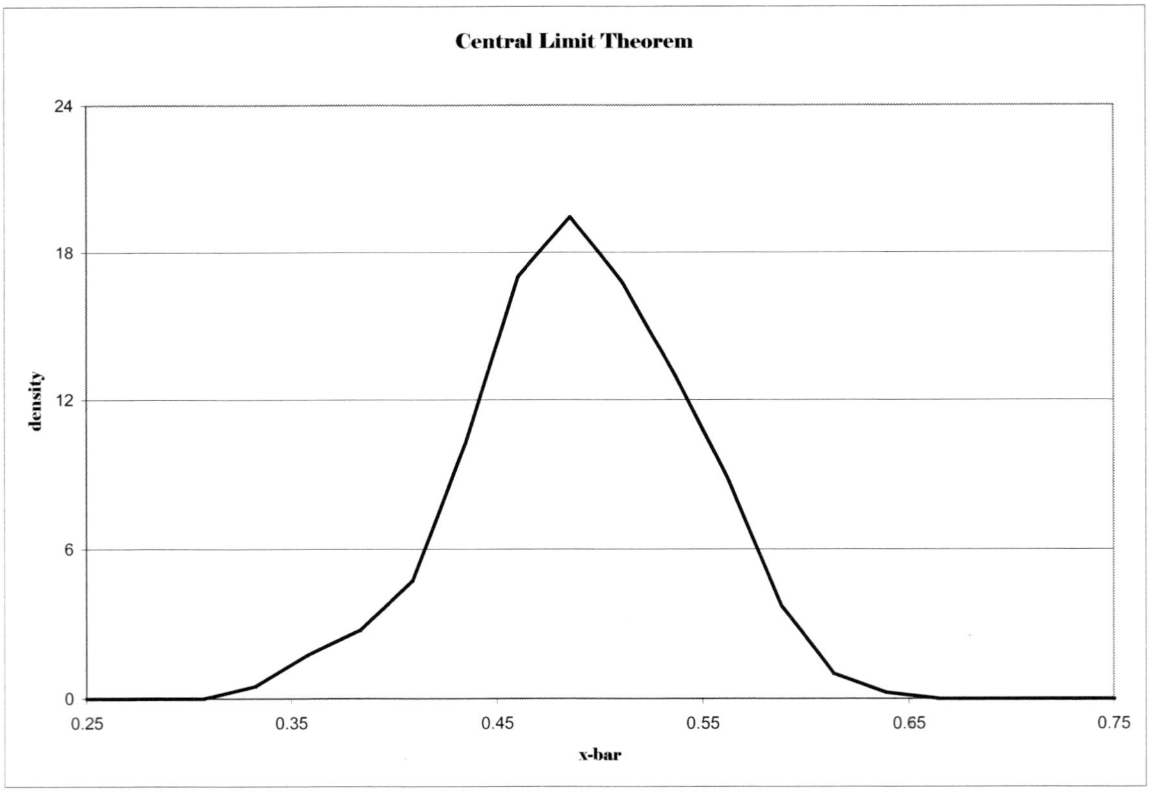

If one selects larger samples the curve improves toward a bell-shape as the sample size increases. We can see in the graph that for such extreme distributions as the uniform, the CLT **does not provide a perfect or even nearly perfect fit for samples of size 30**.

Application:

In order to further illustrate the concept of the **CLT**, suppose that there are 50 sections of ENG 1013 and that there are **30 students in each section**. The English Department gives a common first test. Assume that the **mean** of this population (all ENG 1013 students) is **72** with a **standard deviation** of **9** points.

Consider the scores on the first test for each section and compute a sample average $\bar{x}_1, \bar{x}_2, \ldots, \bar{x}_{50}$ for each section. Part 1 of the CLT states that population of the sampling distribution of samples of size 30 is given by

$$\mu_{\bar{x}} = \mu = 72$$

Part 2 states that the **standard deviation** of the sampling distribution of the sample average is **inversely related to sample size**. This result implies that there is **less variation** in the **sample averages from section to section** than there is in the **original scores** of the entire population.

$$\sigma_{\bar{x}} = \sigma/\sqrt{n} = \frac{9}{\sqrt{30}} = 1.643$$

Part 3 implies that

$$\bar{x} \sim N(72, 1.643)$$

We can use our previous results to **determine probabilities** and **percentiles** for the **sampling distribution** of the **sample average**.

Example 1

Let X denote the score on an ENG 1013 test 1. What is the probability that a section would have a **class average below 70** on the first test?

The population mean of the sampling distribution of the sample average is $\mu_{\bar{x}} = 72$ and the population standard deviation is $\sigma_{\bar{x}} = 1.643$ by parts 1 and 2, respectively, of the central limit theorem. Since the size of the section (i.e., the sample) is 30 then we can apply **part 3 of the CLT**. So we can compute probabilities by **standardizing** the sample average.

$$\Pr\{\bar{\mathbf{x}} < 70\} = \Pr\{\bar{\mathbf{x}} - 72 < 70 - 72\}$$

subtract $\mu_{\bar{x}} = 72$ *from both sides*

$$= \Pr\left\{\frac{\bar{\mathbf{x}} - 72}{1.643} < \frac{70 - 72}{1.643}\right\}$$

divide both sides by $\sigma_{\bar{x}} = 1.643$

$$= \Pr\{\mathbf{Z} < -1.22\}$$
$$= \Pr\{\mathbf{Z} > 1.22\}$$
$$= \Pr\{\mathbf{Z} > 0.00\} - \Pr\{0.00 < \mathbf{Z} < 1.22\}$$
$$= 0.5000 - \mathbf{T}(1.22)$$
$$= 0.5000 - 0.3888$$
$$= 0.1112$$

FIGURE 38: Region for **Z**<-1.22

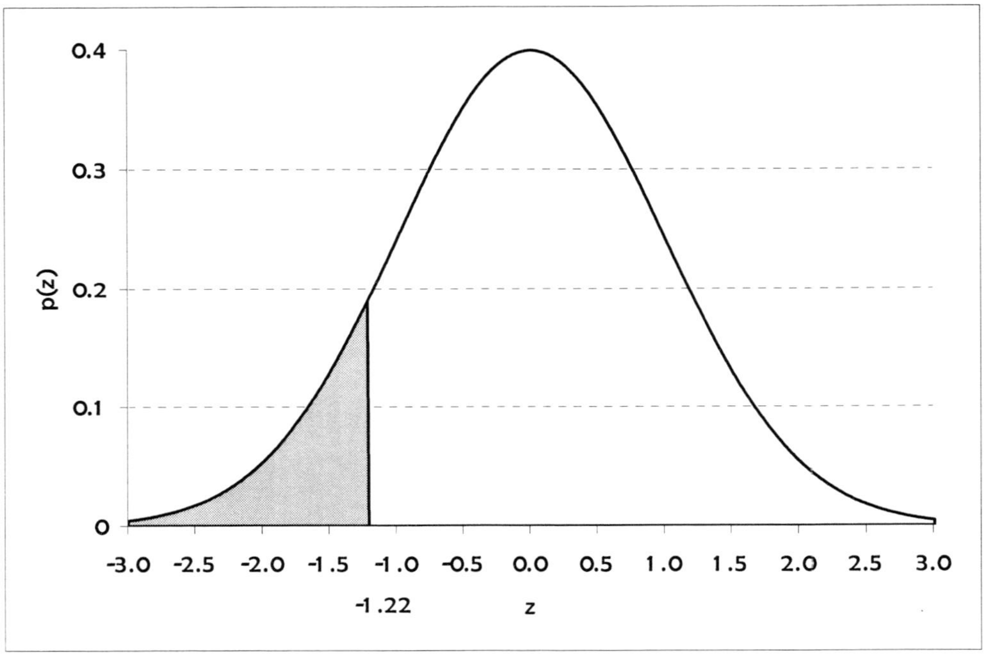

Thus in only **11.12% of the sections of ENG 1013 of size 30** would one expect **section averages below 70**.

In the same context as the previous example, what is the probability that **a section would have a class average above 75** on the first test?

The population mean of the sampling distribution of the sample average is $\mu_{\bar{x}} = 72$ and the population standard deviation is $\sigma_{\bar{x}} = 1.643$ as discussed earlier and since the size of the section is 30 we can apply part 3 of the CLT.

$$\Pr\{\overline{\mathbf{x}} > 75\} = \Pr\{\overline{\mathbf{x}} - 72 > 75 - 72\}$$

subtract $\mu_{\overline{\mathbf{x}}} = 72$ *from both sides*

$$= \Pr\left\{\frac{\overline{\mathbf{x}} - 72}{1.643} > \frac{75 - 72}{1.643}\right\}$$

divide both sides by $\sigma_{\overline{\mathbf{x}}} = 1.643$

$$= \Pr\{\mathbf{Z} > 1.83\}$$

$$= \Pr\{\mathbf{Z} > 0.00\} - \Pr\{0.00 < \mathbf{Z} < 1.83\}$$

$$= 0.5000 - \mathbf{T}(1.83)$$

$$= 0.5000 - 0.4664$$

$$= 0.0336$$

FIGURE 39: Region for $\mathbf{Z} > 1.83$

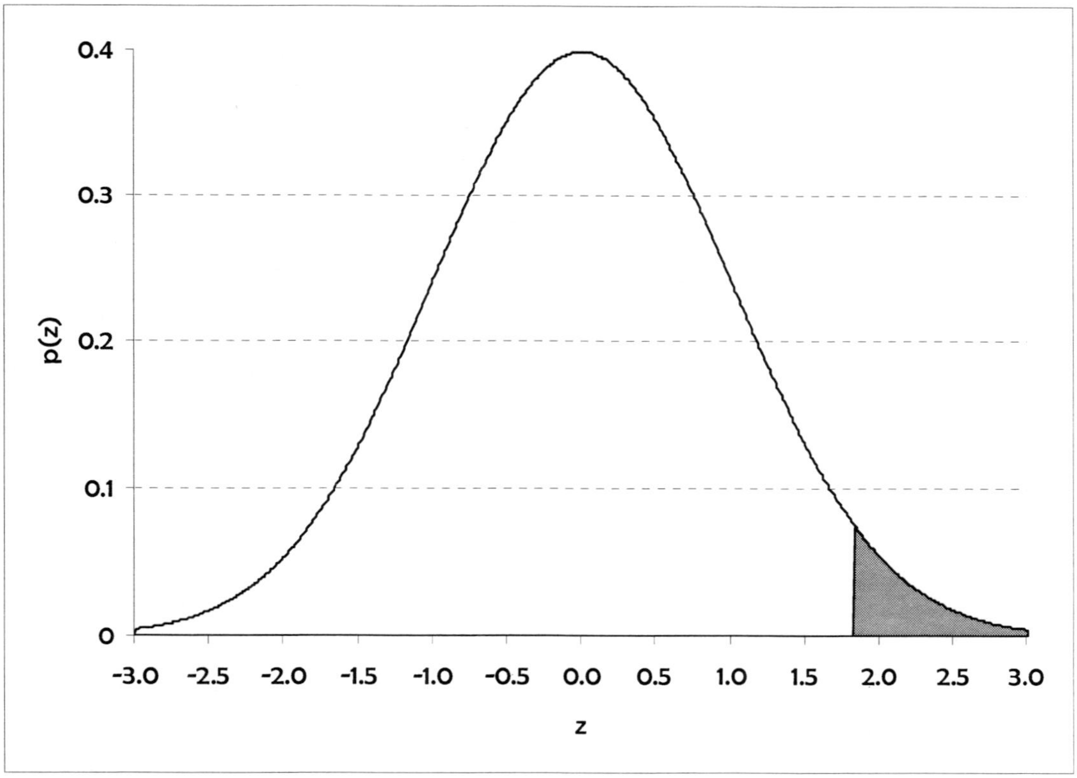

In only 3.36% of the sections would one expect **section averages** of size 30 above 75.

Group IQ Example

Let **X** denote the IQ of a UTSA Business major with a population **mean** of **115** and a **standard deviation** of **12** points. If we randomly select a section of MS 1013 with 64 students, what is the probability that the **average IQ of the section** will exceed 119?

The population mean of the **sampling distribution** of the **sample average** is $\mu_{\bar{x}} = 115$ and the population **standard deviation** is $\sigma_{\bar{x}} = \frac{12}{\sqrt{64}} = \frac{12}{8} = 1.5$ by parts 1 and 2 respectively of the **central limit theorem**. Since the size of the section (i.e., the sample) is **64** then we can **apply part 3 of the CLT**.

$$
\begin{aligned}
\Pr\{\bar{x} > 119\} &= \Pr\{\bar{x} - 115 > 119 - 115\} \\
&\quad \textit{subtract} \quad \mu_{\bar{x}} = 115 \quad \textit{from both sides} \\
&= \Pr\left\{\frac{\bar{x} - 115}{1.50} > \frac{119 - 115}{1.50}\right\} \\
&\quad \textit{divide both sides by} \quad \sigma_{\bar{x}} = 1.50 \\
&= \Pr\{\mathbf{Z} > 2.67\} \\
&= \Pr\{\mathbf{Z} > 0.00\} - \Pr\{0.00 < \mathbf{Z} < 2.67\} \\
&= 0.5000 - \mathbf{T}(2.67) = 0.5000 - 0.4962 = 0.0038
\end{aligned}
$$

FIGURE 37: Region for $\mathbf{Z} > 2.67$

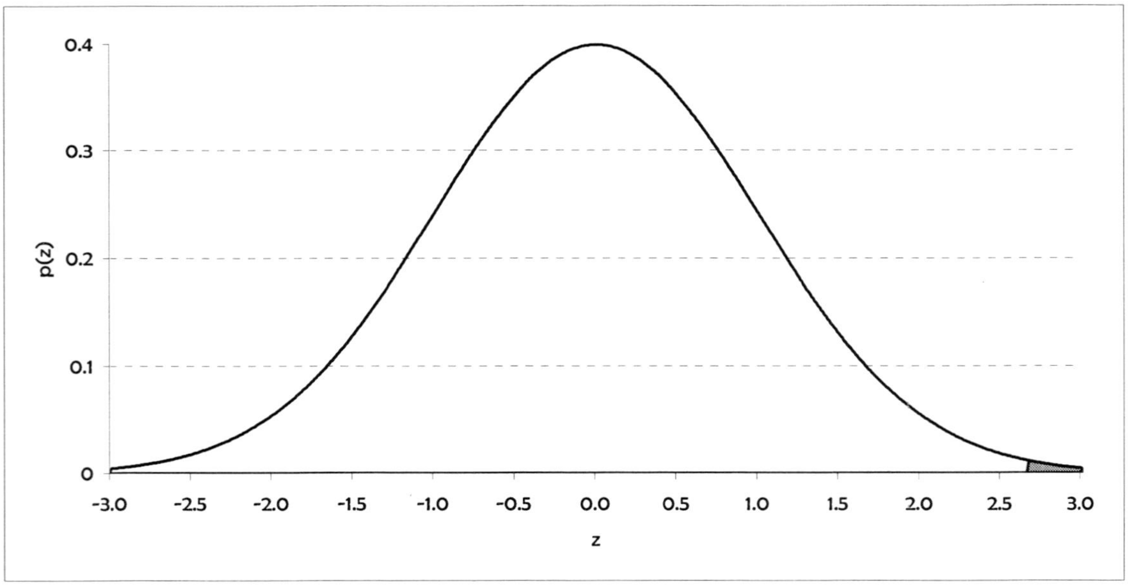

So 0.38% of the sections of MS 1013 of size 64 would have section IQ averages above 119.

Finding Percentiles on Sample Averages

What is the **90th percentile** of the section averages of ENG 1013 of size 30? The formula given for the **normal percentile** is still appropriate even in this case because it falls within the normal distribution. The $100 \times p\%$ percentile of the **sampling distribution of the sample average** is given by:

$$\begin{aligned} \bar{\mathbf{x}}(p) &= \mu_{\bar{\mathbf{x}}} + \mathbf{z}(p) \times \sigma_{\bar{\mathbf{x}}} \\ &= \mu + \mathbf{z}(p) \times \frac{\sigma}{\sqrt{n}} \quad \rightarrow \sigma = \textit{population standard deviation} \end{aligned}$$

In this case, we use the **population mean** for the **sampling distribution** of $\bar{\mathbf{x}}$ and the **standard deviation** of the sampling distribution of $\bar{\mathbf{x}}$ known as **the standard error.**

Note that $\mathbf{z}(0.90) = 1.282$ and thus it follows that the 90th **percentile** of the **section averages** ENG 1013 of size 30 is given by

$$\begin{aligned} \bar{\mathbf{x}}(0.90) &= \mu_{\bar{\mathbf{x}}} + \mathbf{z}(0.90) \times \sigma_{\bar{\mathbf{x}}} \\ &= 72 + 1.282 \times 1.643 \\ &= 72 + 2.11 \\ &= 74.11 \end{aligned}$$

Department Chairs could use such standards to check for grade inequities across sections. If the exam is standardized, teachers whose students make better scores could be perceived as better teachers.

What is the 95th **percentile** of the **section averages of IQ's** of MS 1013 students of size 64?

Since $\mathbf{z}(0.95) = 1.645$ it follows that the 95th **percentile of sample average IQ's** by section MS 1013 of size 64 is given by

$$\begin{aligned} \bar{\mathbf{x}}(0.95) &= \mu_{\bar{\mathbf{x}}} + \mathbf{z}(0.95) \times \sigma_{\bar{\mathbf{x}}} \\ &= 115 + 1.645 \times 1.50 \\ &= 115 + 2.47 \\ &= 117.47 \end{aligned}$$

Suppose I teach a section of Business Statistics with 64 students, I should only expect for the average IQ of that section to exceed 117.47 once out of twenty times.

A Special Application of the CLT
The Normal Approximation to the Binomial

The Central Limit Theorem can be applied in several ways but its most frequent use in discrete distribution involves the binomial distribution. Earlier in the semester we observed that the binomial distribution tables were limited for sample sizes in excess of 20. The **Central Limit Theorem** allows us to complete these calculations for $n \geq 30$ but with some constraints on the possible values for p. For extremely large values of n the restrictions on p vanish.

Framework for CLT:

Consider a **binomial experiment** in which the values of $\mathbf{X}_1, \mathbf{X}_2, \cdots, \mathbf{X}_n$ are the individual zeros (i.e., **failures**) or ones (i.e., **successes**) for an experiment with a success probability of p per trial. Each random variable $\mathbf{X}_i$ has a **binomial distribution** with $n = 1$ and success probability p. It follows that each element sample comes from a population with a **mean value** of

- $\mu = n \times p = 1 \times p = p$

and a **population variance** of

- $\sigma^2 = n \times p \times (1-p) = 1 \times p \times (1-p) = p \times (1-p)$

or the **standard deviation** is

- $\sigma = \sqrt{p \times (1-p)}$.

These are the conditions needed to satisfy the CLT. To apply the CLT we introduce some new notation. Since the sum of the $\mathbf{X}'s$ is the count of the number of successes in n trials, then the success rate estimate is just the count $\mathbf{Y}$ of the number of successes divided by the number of trials, n.

$$\hat{\mathbf{p}} = \frac{\sum_{i=1}^{n} \mathbf{X}_i}{n} = \overline{\mathbf{X}} = \frac{\mathbf{Y}}{n}.$$

Recall that $\mathbf{Y}$ was the symbol we used to denote the number of successes in n independent trials of a binomial experiment. So the symbol $\hat{\mathbf{p}}$ is an estimate of the true success-proportion p and it is also the sample average $\overline{\mathbf{X}}$ of the $\mathbf{X}'s$ successes and failures. By the third part of the CLT, we have

$\hat{\mathbf{p}}$ =*estimated proportion of successes*

$$\hat{\mathbf{p}} = \overline{\mathbf{x}} \sim \mathbf{N}\left(p, \frac{\sqrt{p \times (1-p)}}{\sqrt{n}} \right) \quad p \text{ is the population mean}$$

Example: Preference Polls

In a random sample of 80 persons, we want to see how many would vote for **Rick Perry for Governor**. A recent TV poll showed that **64%** of the persons polled would vote for him. If the poll represents the entire population then **64%** of the population **would support his candidacy** (i.e., $p = 0.64$).

What is the probability that **more than** 55 **persons in the sample** would vote for Mr. Perry? To answer the question, we first rephrase it in terms of a sample average by dividing the number successes by n.

$$\begin{aligned} \Pr\{\mathbf{Y} > 55\} &= \Pr\left\{ \frac{\mathbf{Y}}{80} > \frac{55}{80} \right\} \\ &= \Pr\{\overline{\mathbf{x}} > 0.6875\} \end{aligned}$$

Now $\overline{\mathbf{x}} = \hat{\mathbf{p}}$ has a normal distribution with a **mean** of $p = 0.64$ and a **standard deviation** or **standard error** of

$$\sqrt{\frac{p \times (1-p)}{n}} = \sqrt{\frac{0.64 \times (1-0.64)}{80}} = \sqrt{\frac{0.64 \times 0.36}{80}} = 0.0537.$$

Now we standardize the last probability statement using part 3 - CLT.

$$\begin{aligned} \Pr\{\mathbf{Y} > 55\} &= \Pr\{\overline{\mathbf{x}} > 0.6875\} \\ &= \Pr\{\overline{\mathbf{x}} - 0.64 > 0.6875 - 0.64\} \\ &\quad \textit{subtract} \quad \mu_{\overline{\mathbf{x}}} = p = 0.64 \quad \textit{from both sides} \\ &= \Pr\left\{ \frac{\overline{\mathbf{x}} - 0.64}{0.0537} > \frac{0.6875 - 0.64}{0.0537} \right\} \\ &\quad \textit{divide both sides by} \quad \sigma_{\overline{\mathbf{x}}} = 0.0537 \\ &= \Pr\{\mathbf{Z} > 0.88\} \\ &= \Pr\{\mathbf{Z} > 0.00\} - \Pr\{0.00 < \mathbf{Z} < 0.88\} \\ &= 0.5000 - \mathrm{T}(0.88) \\ &= 0.5000 - 0.3106 \\ &= 0.1894 \end{aligned}$$

FIGURE 40: Region for $\mathbf{Z} > 0.88$

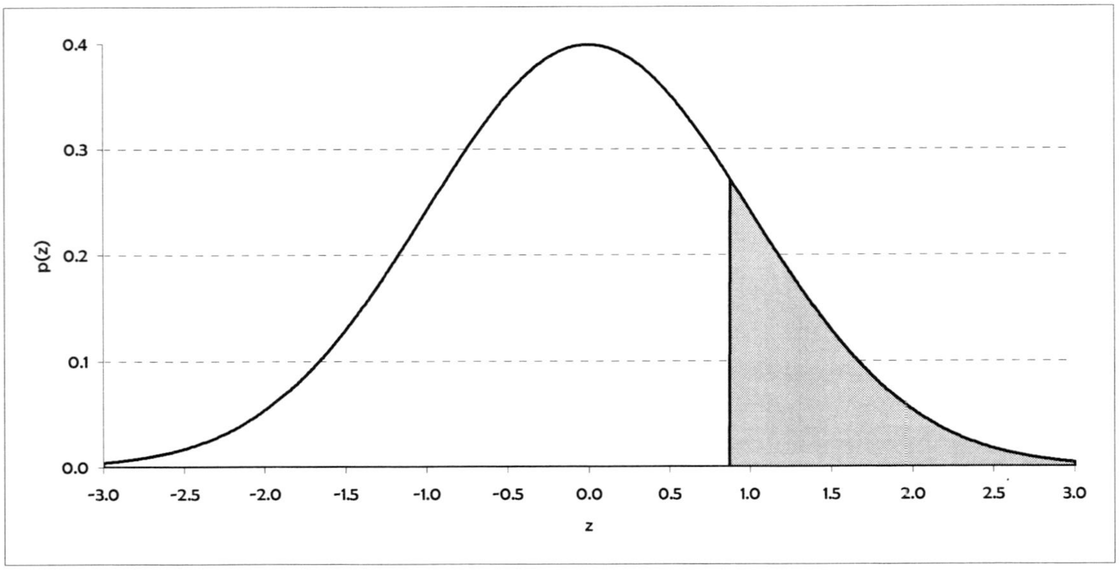

We would anticipate that only 18.94% of such samples of size 80 would have preference ratings for Mr. Perry as high as 68.75%. What would it mean if we observed several polls of this type? Would we be inclined to believe that Mr. Perry's approval rating is perhaps greater than 64%?

Example: Advertising

Sonic Boom has 34% of the CD market in San Antonio. After an ad campaign, **100 persons were polled** and asked where they purchased their CD's. Assuming the **ad campaign had no effect**, what is the probability that more than 40 persons in the survey named Sonic Boom due to chance alone?

If the ad campaign had no effect then $p = 0.34$ and therefore

- $\mu_{\bar{\mathbf{x}}} = p = 0.34$ and
- $\sigma_{\bar{\mathbf{x}}} = \sqrt{\dfrac{p \times (1-p)}{n}} = \sqrt{\dfrac{0.34 \times (1-0.34)}{100}} = \sqrt{\dfrac{0.34 \times 0.66}{100}} = 0.0474$

Let $\mathbf{Y}$ denote the number of persons in the survey that who bought CD's at **Sonic Boom**. We rephrase the question in terms of a sample average by dividing the number successes $n = 100$.

$$\begin{aligned} \Pr\{\mathbf{Y} > 40\} &= \Pr\left\{\frac{\mathbf{Y}}{100} > \frac{40}{100}\right\} \\ &= \Pr\{\bar{\mathbf{x}} > 0.40\} \end{aligned}$$

Now $\overline{\mathbf{x}} = \hat{\mathbf{p}}$ has a normal distribution with a **mean** of $p = 0.34$ and a **standard deviation** of 0.0474. So standardize the last probability statement using **part 3 - CLT**.

$$\begin{aligned}
\Pr\{\mathbf{Y} > 40\} &= \Pr\{\overline{\mathbf{x}} > 0.40\} \\
&= \Pr\{\overline{\mathbf{x}} - 0.34 > 0.40 - 0.34\} \\
&\textit{subtract} \quad \mu_{\overline{\mathbf{x}}} = p = 0.34 \quad \textit{from both sides} \\
&= \Pr\left\{\frac{\overline{\mathbf{x}} - 0.34}{0.0474} > \frac{0.40 - 0.34}{0.0474}\right\} \\
&\textit{divide both sides by} \quad \sigma_{\overline{\mathbf{x}}} = 0.0474 \\
&= \Pr\{\mathbf{Z} > 1.27\} = \Pr\{\mathbf{Z} > 0.00\} - \Pr\{0.00 < \mathbf{Z} < 1.27\} \\
&= 0.5000 - \mathbf{T}(1.27) = 0.5000 - 0.3980 = 0.1020
\end{aligned}$$

FIGURE 41: Region for $\mathbf{Z} > 1.27$

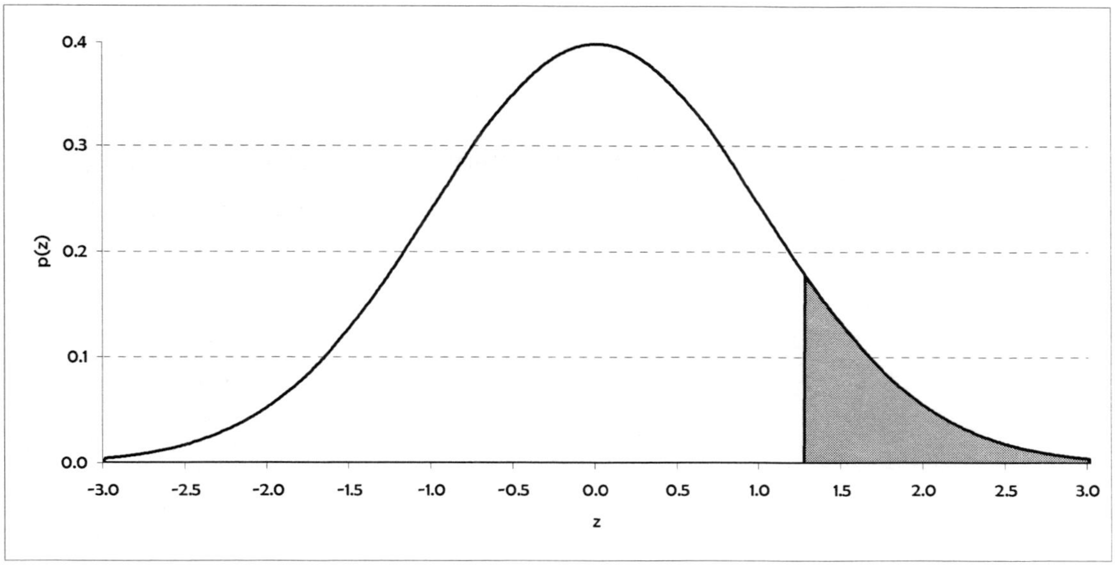

In this way we can begin to **assess the effectiveness** of the ad campaign. In other words, if the **ad campaign had no beneficial effect**, we would expect such a **favorable response** in only 10.2% of such surveys.

Example: Newer and Better Products

Large doses of an antibiotic traditionally reduce the presence of adolescent acne in 60% of the patients treated. A new medication **Accutane** is given to 100 teenage patients who have severe acne. What is the probability that at least 75 persons in the sample improved significantly if the new medication is no better than the old?

The **assumption that the new medication is no better than the old** medication implies that $p \le 0.60$ and therefore $\mu_{\bar{x}} = p = 0.60$ and

$$\sigma_{\bar{x}} = \sqrt{\frac{p \times (1-p)}{n}} = \sqrt{\frac{0.60 \times (1-0.60)}{100}} = \sqrt{\frac{0.60 \times 0.40}{100}} = 0.0490.$$

Let **Y** denote the number of teenagers in the study that improved significantly. We rephrase the question in terms of a sample average by dividing by the number successes $n = 100$.

$$\begin{aligned} \Pr\{\mathbf{Y} > 75\} &= \Pr\left\{\frac{\mathbf{Y}}{100} > \frac{75}{100}\right\} \\ &= \Pr\{\bar{\mathbf{x}} > 0.75\} \end{aligned}$$

Now $\bar{\mathbf{x}} = \hat{\mathbf{p}}$ has an approximate normal distribution with a **mean** of $p = 0.60$ and a **standard deviation** of 0.0490. So **standardize** the last probability statement using **part 3 - CLT**.

$$\begin{aligned} \Pr\{\mathbf{Y} > 75\} &= \Pr\{\bar{\mathbf{x}} > 0.75\} \\ &= \Pr\{\bar{\mathbf{x}} - 0.60 > 0.75 - 0.60\} \\ &\quad \textit{subtract} \quad \mu_{\bar{x}} = p = 0.60 \quad \textit{from both sides} \\ &= \Pr\left\{\frac{\bar{\mathbf{x}} - 0.60}{0.0490} > \frac{0.75 - 0.60}{0.0490}\right\} \\ &\quad \textit{divide both sides by} \quad \sigma_{\bar{x}} = 0.0490 \\ &= \Pr\{\mathbf{Z} > 3.06\} \\ &= \Pr\{\mathbf{Z} > 0.00\} - \Pr\{0.00 < \mathbf{Z} < 3.06\} \\ &= 0.5000 - \mathbf{T}(3.06) = 0.5000 - 0.4989 = 0.0011 \end{aligned}$$

In this way, we quantify the effectiveness of the new medication. In only **11 out of 10,000 such medical trials** would we expect to see such significant improvement due to the **antibiotic** by chance. **At what point does one begin to believe that the new medication simply works better than the old medication**?

Hypothesis Testing

Statistics has become an integral part of the scientific method in:

- the formation of hypothesis tests,
- the conduct of the experiment and
- the statement of conclusions based on the outcomes of the experiments.

Hypothesis testing involves all three phases of the scientific method in making practical business decisions, better social choices, better medications, etc. These hypotheses may span the spectrum of human endeavors, which require statistical inference to make meaningful and quantifiable decisions.

- Is a new product *"significantly" better* than an industry standard?
- Do women walk *"significantly faster"* than men in the workplace?
- Does a warning label *"better"* inform teens than a competitor's?

Case Study: Warning Labels

Scotchgard contains a chemical 1, 1, 1-**trichloroethane**, a psychoactive component. Deaths of, or permanent damage to several pre-teens were attributed to intentional inhalation of the contents (or *"huffing"*). The product was used among pre-teens as **an alternative to other drugs** because of its accessibility. The warning label for years was placed on the back of the can in fine print in the middle and is given below:

> *"Intentional misuse by deliberately concentrating and inhaling or swallowing contents can be harmful or fatal."*

Increasing concern by the company prompted research into better warning labels:

a) Pre-teens were asked to read and explain the above warning label. Most could not read all the words and words that they could annunciate phonetically were frequently mispronounced because accent was misplaced on the wrong syllable.

b) Juvenile users and other drug offenders were questioned on what wording be effective in alarming pre-teens to the dangers of misusing this product. A detailed study resulted in the following warning label.

> *"Intentionally sniffing the contents to get high can cause brain damage or death."*

The pre-teens in part a) were asked to read the second warning label with the same directions. A majority of pre-teens were much more alarmed by the second warning because the language used was accessible. However, such warning labels because of their graphic nature were not used because it could scare the customers, such as women with children, grandmothers, etc. from using the product. If one sprays the cloth seats of a car with this product, would she or he inadvertently inhale some of the spray and thereby suffer some form of brain damage?

By Margot Higgins / ENN April 11, 2001

http://www.mindfully.org/Plastic/Scotchgard-PFOS-Environment.htm

> “The researchers found traces of **PFOS** in wildlife throughout the world, **even in remote areas**. It may help keep the red wine stains out of your carpet, but **Scotchgard**, a popular water and stain repellant, is **leaving its mark on the environment**. A chemical compound known as perfluoro-octanyl sulfonate, (**PFOS**) found in the product is more prevalent in the environment than previously thought, a recent study finds. In May 2001, **3M**, which is the sole manufacturer of **Scotchgard**, decided to reformulate the product due to concerns that **PFOS** can build up in the tissue of humans and animals. The compound has been found at **widespread levels** in mammals, fish and birds, **even in remote areas** of the world that are far from where the product is manufactured.”
>
> “What we've done is a **global survey** that shows you for the first time that this compound is out there," said lead author of the study **John Giesy**, a chemist at Michigan State University. "We found a good testing method and discovered **small amounts of PFOS** in remote areas." The researchers collected more than 2,000 animal tissue samples, from the **Pacific Rim to Antarctica**, and analyzed more than 400 for PFOS. **Concentrations** of the compound in **wildlife were 10 times greater in urbanized** industrial areas than in **less populated coastal areas**, according to the results.”

FIGURE 42 : **Worldwide Presence of PFOS**

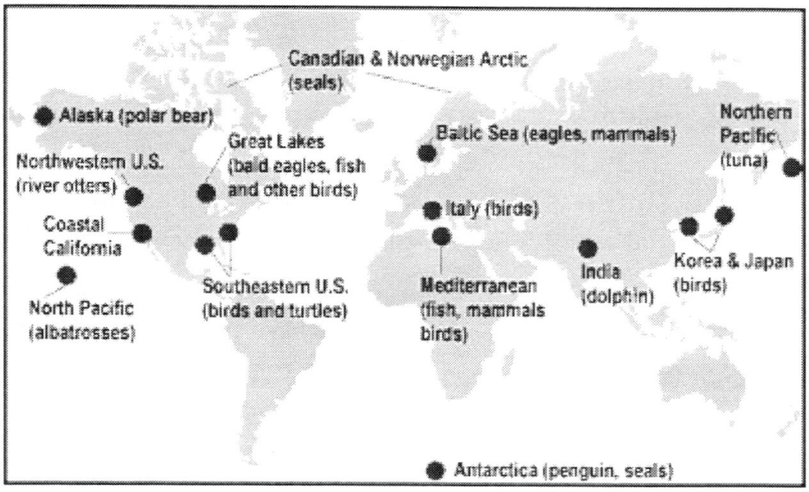

"While so far there are no data to suggest adverse health effects in humans, previous research has found that high concentrations of PFOS can cause reproductive problems in rats. (At the levels we detected in our research) we have about a **fourfold level of safety**, which is not as great as we would like to see," Giesy said."

"PFOS have been difficult to study because the **molecules are larger** and more difficult for scientific instruments to detect than other known **environmental toxins** such as **PCBs** or **DDT**. Giesy believes it is necessary to conduct more research on the health risks associated with **PFOS**, although the prospect is unlikely now that **Scotchgard** containing the compound has been pulled from the shelves."

"I think this is going to change the way we look at chemicals because PFOS were not studied very much and **they were not expected to move in the environment**," he said. "We don't know how PFOS might interact with other chemicals. From an **academic standpoint** it would be useful for this entire class of compounds, to know more about other similar chemicals that might be in the environment or might be made in the future."

Formation of Hypotheses

The first aspect of the **scientific method** involves the formation of hypotheses about the application in question. The **traditional framework** of **hypothesis testing** begins with the formation of **two hypotheses**:

The first hypothesis, known as the **null hypothesis**, is a statement about a product, person, or issue involved with the problem. The statement **may specify the value of a parameter** of a distribution under investigation. The statement may be that a **new product is no better than the industry standard**. The null hypothesis is **usually a reflection of the "status quo,"** i.e., nothing has changed.

For example, we may expect the typical family of four to spend $380 on Christmas presents. The value of $380 represents our **a priori belief** in the value of μ the **mean** of the distribution of **spending habits of these families**. The random variable $\mathbf{X}$ in question is the **amount of money spent** by such families **on Christmas presents**.

The statement may be that a new product is no better than the industry standard: e.g.,

- Tylenol is no better than Bayer in relieving headaches!
- The Energizer lasts as long as the Coppertop in children's toys!
- The Volkswagen Jetta is not a better buy than a Toyota Camry!

A second hypothesis, known as the **alternative hypothesis**, is formed in **opposition to the null**. For example, the average family of four spends **"more than $380"** on Christmas presents, or **Tylenol relieves** headaches **faster than Bayer** aspirin, or the **Energizer lasts longer** than the **Coppertop in children's toys**. In this case we stated alternatives that said a **"new product is better than an industry standard, or we could state that the newer product is "actually inferior."** With respect to spending habits a true **negation of the null** would imply that families of size four **do not spend $380** on Christmas presents. This would **not say whether** they **spent more or less** but would accommodate any change in spending habits. The **alternative hypothesis** can be made **in several ways** and the one used is based on the problem.

The **null hypothesis** is denoted by $\mathbf{H_0}$ and the alternative hypothesis by $\mathbf{H_a}$. Statistical methods suggest that **an experiment** should **be conducted**, the second step, in which:

i. the target **population** is **sampled** and
ii. the subsequent **data are collected**.

Usually **data from an experiment** are **summarized into a** descriptive statistic, known as a **test statistic**. **Depending upon** the result of an experiment and thus the **value of the test statistic**, we may decide to **reject the null hypothesis** or we may decide that **there is a lack of sufficient evidence** to **reject the null** or imply that is false. **The values of** the test **statistic** that would **cause us to reject the null** hypothesis **form the critical region** of the test.

In **hypothesis testing**, we **proceed systematically** in the following way:

1. **<u>Form the hypotheses</u>**
2. **<u>Conduct the experiment</u>**
3. **<u>Select a test statistic</u>**
4. **<u>Determine a critical region and</u>**
   (which is the point where to decide change has occurred or not.)
5. **<u>Make a decision.</u>**

In the decision making process, four possible outcomes can occur and are identified in the following table, Table 26:

TABLE 26: **Decisions, Experimental Outcomes, and their Consequences**

	Null Hypothesis	
Decision	**True**	**False**
ACCEPT $\mathbf{H_0}$	**Correct**	**Type II Error** (Consumer's Risk) {Accept $\mathbf{H_0}$ when it is false}
REJECT $\mathbf{H_0}$	**Type I Error** (Producer's Risk) {Reject $\mathbf{H_0}$ when it is true}	**Correct**

If we **accept the null** hypothesis **when it is true**, we make a **"correct decision."** If we **reject the null** hypothesis $\mathbf{H_0}$ **when it is true** we make a **mistake**, known as a **Type I Error**. If we **accept** $\mathbf{H_0}$ **when it is false**, we make another **mistake** known as **a Type II Error**. If we **reject H_0 when it is false**, we again make a **"correct decision."**

Unfortunately, we **cannot guarantee** that we will always **make correct decisions** or that we can avoid making mistakes. **However**, we can **control** the **frequency (or probability) of making such mistakes**.

1) The **probability** of making a **Type I Error** is denoted by α. and known as the **level of significance of the test**. From the manner in which hypothesis testing started, the value of α is often called the **producer's risk**: the **probability** that an **acceptable product is rejected**.

2) The **probability** of making a **Type II Error** is denoted by β and known as the **consumer's risk**: the probability that a **defective product is accepted**, which is based solely on evidence.

Don't confuse the hypothesis-testing framework with the concepts of truth. If you came here looking for truth, I need to send you back to Philosophy class. Statistical hypothesis testing can be likened to scientific gossip. The statistician on any given hypothesis test does not know whether he or she made the right conclusion, (i.e., arrived at the truth). However, he or she does know how frequently that the right decision is made. Conducting a census can give reasonable evidence.

Standard Notation

Earlier we introduced the notation of a **standard normal percentile** $\mathbf{z}(p)$ where $\mathbf{z}(p)$ is the point on the standard normal axis so that **the area to its left is** p. A more common convention is to use the notation $\mathbf{z}_\alpha$ where $\mathbf{z}_\alpha$ **is the point on the** $\mathbf{z}$**-axis** so that **the area to its right is** α. Figure 43 graphically **depicts** this upper percentile.

In this regard the value $\mathbf{z}_\alpha$ forms a $100 \times \alpha\%$ **upper-percentile** for the **standard normal** distribution. Hence, it follows that

$$\mathbf{z}_\alpha = \mathbf{z}(1-\alpha)$$

FIGURE 43: Upper percentiles in the Standard Normal Distribution

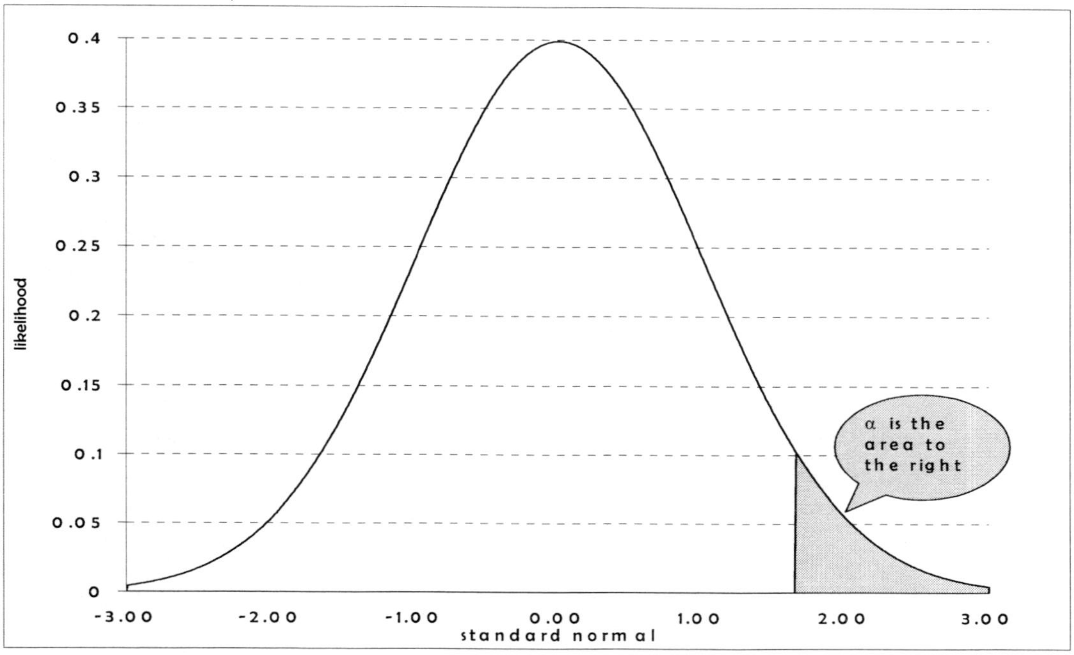

Earlier that we found the **eightieth percentile** to be 0.8418, so

$$\mathbf{z}_{0.20} = \mathbf{z}(1-0.20) = \mathbf{z}(0.80) = 0.8418$$

In the same way, the **ninetieth percentile** is 1.282, so

$$\mathbf{z}_{0.10} = \mathbf{z}(1-0.10) = \mathbf{z}(0.90) = 1.282$$

We can also find the **ninety-fifth percentile** to be 1.645 so that

$$\mathbf{z}_{0.05} = \mathbf{z}(1-0.05) = \mathbf{z}(0.95) = 1.645$$

A list of frequently used upper and lower percentiles is given in Table 27.

TABLE 27: Table of Upper and Lower Percentiles for the Standard Normal

p	$\mathbf{z}(p)$	α	$\mathbf{z}_\alpha$
1.0%	-2.326	0.010	2.326
2.5%	-1.960	0.025	1.960
5.0%	-1.645	0.050	1.645
10.0%	-1.282	0.100	1.282
20.0%	-0.842	0.200	0.842
30.0%	-0.524	0.300	0.524
40.0%	-0.253	0.400	0.253
50.0%	0.00	0.500	0.00

Example

Historical credit reports of Foley's customers indicate that families of four spent an average of \$380 on Christmas presents with a standard deviation of \$100 in 2001. Suppose that Foley's wants to test the null hypothesis that families of size four will spend more in 2002 than they did in 2001. The marketing department has funds to support a study of 64 customers. If 64 customers responded that they would spend an average of \$415 on presents, is this sufficient evidence to conclude that they will spend "significantly more" in 2002 than they did in 2001 at the 5% level of significance?

Form the hypotheses: Let the null hypothesis be that **no change** has occurred and let the **alternative** be that families of size four **will spend more** in 2002. Therefore,

- $\mathbf{H_0}: \mu = \mu_0 = \$380$
  - (i.e., there is **no change** in spending habits).
    - versus
- $\mathbf{H_a}: \mu > \mu_0 = \$380$
  - (i.e., families **will spend more**).

Conduct an experiment: Select a **random sample** of n (more than 30) families of size four from their population of customers. Request each family to project its Christmas spending for 2002. Let these values be $\mathbf{X}_1, \mathbf{X}_2, \cdots, \mathbf{X}_n$ (i.e., $n = 64$).

Test Statistic: Let $\bar{\mathbf{x}}$ denote the sample average of these n families. If the null hypothesis is true then from the Central Limit Theorem we know that the sampling distribution of the sample average, $\bar{\mathbf{x}}$, has the following properties:

- $\mu_{\bar{\mathbf{x}}} = \mu = \$380$
- $\sigma_{\bar{\mathbf{x}}} = \dfrac{\sigma}{\sqrt{n}} = \dfrac{\$100}{\sqrt{64}} = \$12.50$
- $\bar{\mathbf{x}} \sim \mathbf{N}(\$380, \$12.50)$

Determine the critical region:

We reject $\mathbf{H_0}$ **when it is true** only $100 \times \alpha\%$ of the time, in this case, 5%. The **values of the sample average** that would cause us to reject $\mathbf{H_0}$ are given by

$$\mathbf{x_0} = \mu_0 + \mathbf{z}_\alpha \times \frac{\sigma}{\sqrt{n}}$$

Make a Decision: Reject $\mathbf{H_0}$ whenever $\bar{\mathbf{x}} > \mathbf{x_0} = \mu_0 + \mathbf{z}_\alpha \times \frac{\sigma}{\sqrt{n}}$.

From the Foley's survey of 64 customers, a **sample average** of $\bar{\mathbf{x}} = \$415$ was obtained. Is this sufficient evidence at the **5% level of significance** to **reject** the claim that **this year's Christmas spending habits will be no more than last**? Remember, the **critical regions** are **values** of the **test statistic** causing **rejection of the null hypothesis.**

$$\begin{aligned}\mathbf{x_0} &= \mu_0 + \mathbf{z}_\alpha \times \frac{\sigma}{\sqrt{n}} \\ &= \mathbf{\$380} + 1.645 \times \mathbf{\$12.50} \\ &= \mathbf{\$380} + \mathbf{\$20.56} \\ &= \mathbf{\$400.56}\end{aligned}$$

Hence, if $\bar{\mathbf{x}} > \$400.56$, we **reject** $\mathbf{H_0}$ at the 5% level of significance that this year's Christmas spending **will be no more than last year's** and **accept the alternative** that these customers **will spend more** at Christmas this year. Since the **sample average** is $\bar{\mathbf{x}} = \$415 > \$400.56$, we reject $\mathbf{H_0}$ and infer that these customers **will spend more** than they did last year.

FIGURE 44: Distribution of $\bar{\mathbf{x}}$ provided $\mathbf{H_0}$ is true and critical region @ 5%

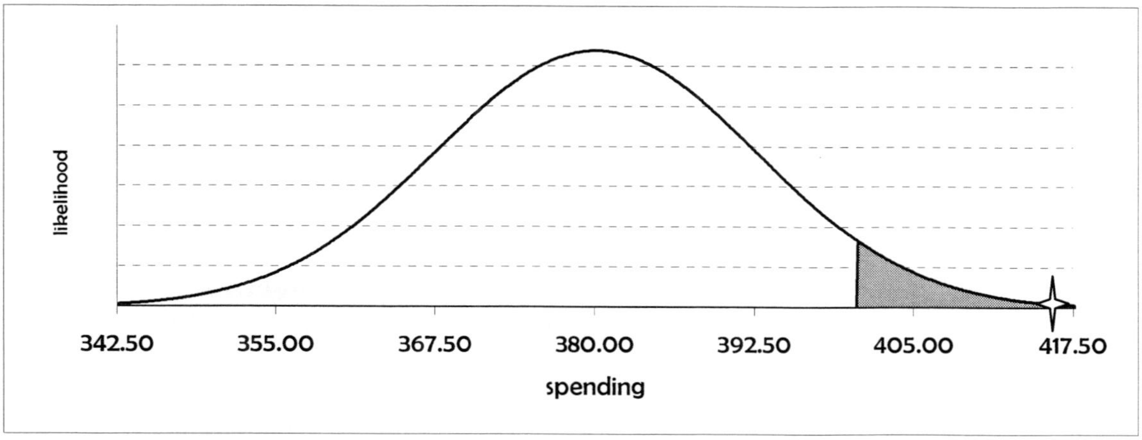

What would happen if we had been willing to only accept a Type I Error rate of 1%? In this case, $\mathbf{z}_{0.01} = 2.326 \cong 2.33$ and thus

$$\mathbf{x_0} = \mathbf{\$380} + 2.326 \times \mathbf{\$12.50} = \mathbf{\$409.08}.$$

So we reject $\mathbf{H_0}$ even if we had been willing to take a smaller risk of 1%. We can continue this process of reducing α to determine the smallest value of α, known as the $\mathbf{p}$-value, for which we would accept $\mathbf{H_0}$. It is important to choose α a priori, otherwise we can alter α so as to effect the decision.

FIGURE 44A: The distribution of $\overline{\mathbf{x}}$ when $\mathbf{H_0}$ is true and critical region @ 1%

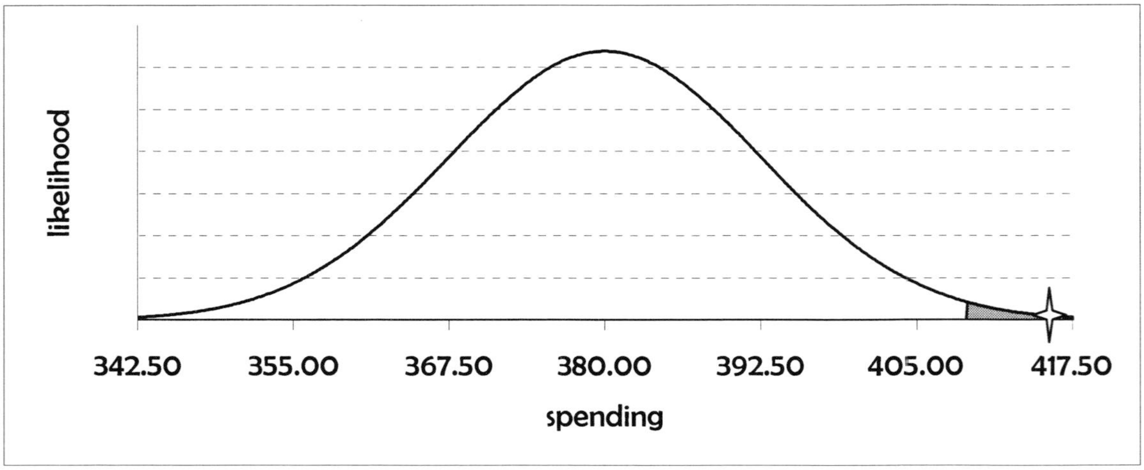

Example

A new chain of car service stores, Larry's Lube, is designed to do oil and filter changes. They claim their shops are faster than their competitors in TV advertisements. A newscaster wants to check out their claims. Based upon national figures, it takes a typical service station an average of 21 minutes ($\mu_0 = \mathbf{21}$ minutes) to do oil and filter changes with a standard deviation of 4 minutes ($\sigma = \mathbf{4}$ minutes national norm) The newscaster follows a random sample of 34 customers and times them during service and obtains their average time to complete service as 19.74 minutes. What should he report?

Formation of hypotheses

- ❖ $\mathbf{H_0}: \mu = \mu_0 = \mathbf{21}$ minutes
  - o (i.e., **there is no difference**).
    - versus
- ❖ $\mathbf{H_a}: \mu < \mu_0 = \mathbf{21}$ minutes
  - o (i.e., it **takes less time**).

Let's choose $\alpha = 0.10$ (This choice belongs to the consumer advocate).

Test Statistic: Let $\bar{\mathbf{x}}$ denote the sample average of these n service times. If the null hypothesis, $\mathbf{H_0}$, is true the sampling distribution of the sample average has the following properties:

$$\bullet \mu_{\bar{x}} = \mu = \mathbf{21} \text{ min}$$

$$\bullet \sigma_{\bar{x}} = \frac{\sigma}{\sqrt{n}} = \frac{\mathbf{4} \text{ min}}{\sqrt{34}} = \mathbf{0.686} \text{ min}$$

$$\bullet \bar{\mathbf{x}} \sim \mathbf{N(21} \text{ min}, \mathbf{0.686} \text{ min)}$$

Determine the critical region

We reject $\mathbf{H_0}$ when it is true only $100 \times \alpha\%$ of the time, in this case, 10%. The values of the sample average that would cause us to reject $\mathbf{H_0}$ are given by

$$\mathbf{x_0} = \mu_0 - \mathbf{z}_\alpha \times \frac{\sigma}{\sqrt{n}}$$

Decision Reject $\mathbf{H_0}$ whenever $\bar{\mathbf{x}} < \mathbf{x_0} = \mu_0 - \mathbf{z}_\alpha \times \frac{\sigma}{\sqrt{n}}$

From the newscaster's survey of $n = 34$ customers, a **sample average** of **19.75 minutes** was obtained. Is this **sufficient evidence** at the **10% level of significance** to **reject the claim** that Larry's Lube will be **no faster than national norms**?

$$\mathbf{x_0} = \mu_0 - \mathbf{z}_\alpha \times \frac{\sigma}{\sqrt{n}} = \mathbf{21} \text{ min} - (1.282 \times \mathbf{0.686} \text{ min}) = \mathbf{21} \text{ min} - \mathbf{0.88} \text{ min} = \mathbf{20.12} \text{ min}$$

FIGURE 45: The distribution of $\bar{\mathbf{x}}$ when $\mathbf{H_0}$ is true and critical region @ 10%

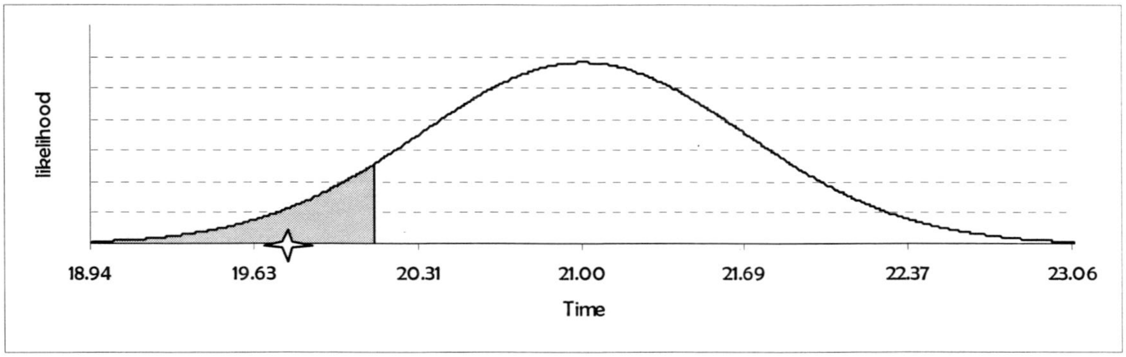

Hence, if $\bar{x} < \mathbf{20.12}$ min we would reject $\mathbf{H_0}$ that Larry's Lube is no faster than the national norm and **accept the claim that they are faster** at the **10% level of significance**. Since the sample average of the 34 customers had a mean service time of $\bar{x} = \mathbf{19.75}$ min we reject $\mathbf{H_0}$ and accept the $\mathbf{H_a}$.

What would happen if we had been willing to only **accept a Type I Error rate of 2.5%**? In this case, $z_{0.025} = 1.960$ and thus

$$\begin{aligned} x_0 &= \mathbf{21} \text{ min} - 1.96 \times \mathbf{0.686} \text{ min} \\ &= \mathbf{21} \text{ min} - \mathbf{1.34} \text{ min} \\ &= \mathbf{19.66} \text{ min} \end{aligned}$$

In his case there is not evidence to reject the null hypothesis. So we fail to reject $\mathbf{H_0}$ since we had been more conservative and were only willing to take a risk of 2.5%. We determined the smallest value of α, known as the $\mathbf{p}$-*value*, for which we would accept $\mathbf{H_0}$ is between 2.5% and 10%. We can continue this process to solve for the $\mathbf{p}$-*value*. It is important to note that the outcome of our test depended on the a priori value of α, we were willing to tolerate. Some businesses simply have smaller profit margins and higher risk taking is a by-product of a more competitive market place.

FIGURE 45A: The distribution of $\bar{x}$ when $\mathbf{H_0}$ is true and critical region @ 2.5%

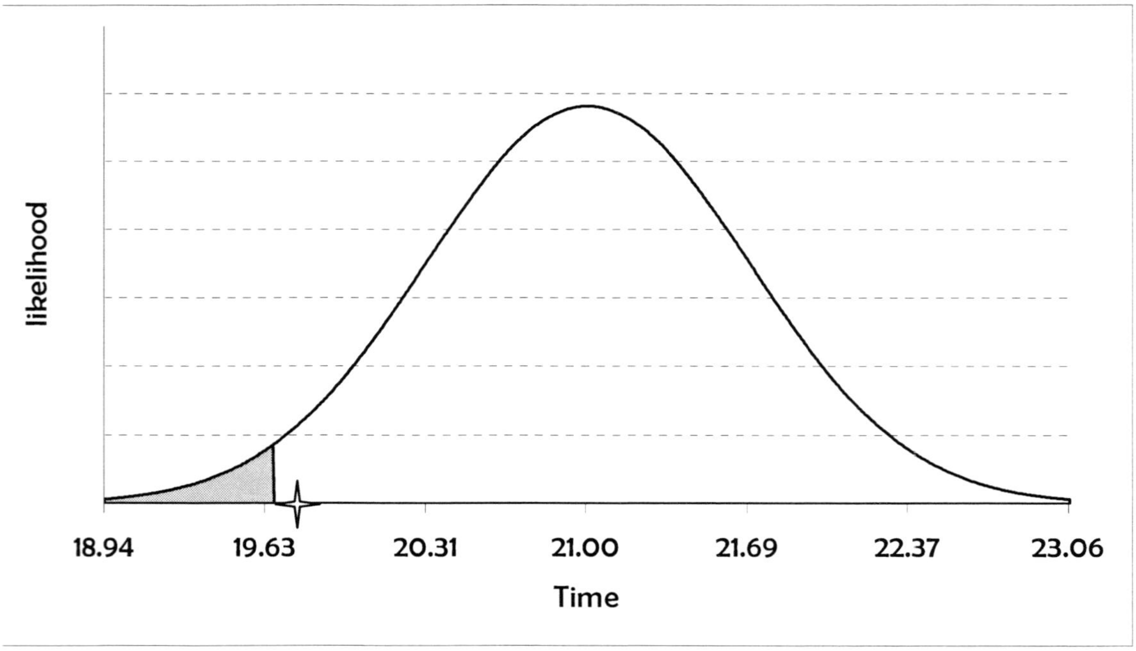

Example

Bennie's Bolts (BB) has been building **mast nuts** for **Bell Helicopter Textron (BHT)** for more than three decades. Bell requires that BB make a high precision $5''$ diameter nut. BB knows that the standard deviation of their machining process is $0.02''$. On a daily inspection, the quality inspector will measure fifty $5''$ – nuts. What bounds should he or she use in accepting or rejecting the lot? Use $\alpha = 0.05$ (5% level of significance).

FIGURE 46: **Main Rotor Mast**

Bell 427
Rotor System
Mast Nut

http://www.bellhelicopter.com/products/commercialHelicopters/427/

Formation of hypotheses

- $\mathbf{H_0}: \mu = \mu_0 = \mathbf{5''}$
  - (i.e., **nut is built to engineering specifications**).
    - versus
- $\mathbf{H_a}: \mu \neq \mu_0 = \mathbf{5''}$
  - (i.e., **the nut is either too large or too small**).

**-If the nut is too large, it will become loose due to vibration and the main rotor could become unstable. The consequences are catastrophic implying loss of aircraft and personnel. If the nut is too small, the mast may be damaged in assembly or the part may be scrapped. For these reasons, a nut that is either too large or too small is unacceptable and hence the alternative.

Test Statistic: Let $\overline{\mathbf{x}}$ denote the sample average of these $n = 50$ nuts. If the null hypothesis is true then from the Central Limit Theorem we know that the sampling distribution of the sample average has the following properties:

$$\bullet \mu_{\overline{\mathbf{x}}} = \mu = \mathbf{5''}$$

$$\bullet \sigma_{\overline{\mathbf{x}}} = \frac{\sigma}{\sqrt{n}} = \frac{0.02''}{\sqrt{50}} = 0.0028''$$

$$\bullet \overline{\mathbf{x}} \sim \mathrm{N}(\mathbf{5''}, \mathbf{0.0028''})$$

Determine the critical region

We want to reject $\mathbf{H_0}$ when it is true only $100 \times \alpha\%$ of the time, in this case: 5%. The values of the sample average that would cause us to reject $\mathbf{H_0}$ are given by

$$\mu_0 \pm \mathbf{z}_{\alpha/2} \times \frac{\sigma}{\sqrt{n}}$$

Decision Reject $\mathbf{H_0}$ whenever

$$\overline{\mathbf{x}} < x_1 = \mu_0 - \mathbf{z}_{\alpha/2} \times \frac{\sigma}{\sqrt{n}} \text{ or } \overline{\mathbf{x}} > x_2 = \mu_0 + \mathbf{z}_{\alpha/2} \times \frac{\sigma}{\sqrt{n}}$$

looking at the middle 95%)

Decision Reject $\mathbf{H_0}$ if the sample average is too large or too small.

$$\mathbf{x}_{1,2} = \mu_0 \pm \mathbf{z}_{\alpha/2} \times \frac{\sigma}{\sqrt{n}} = \mathbf{5''} \pm 1.96 \times \mathbf{0.0028''} = \mathbf{5''} \pm \mathbf{0.0055''}$$

Hence, if $\overline{\mathbf{x}} < \mathbf{4.9945''}$ or $\overline{\mathbf{x}} > \mathbf{5.0055''}$ we would reject $\mathbf{H_0}$. This interval gives Bennie's a 5% chance (**producer's risk**) of having an **acceptable lot rejected**. Notice in this scenario, we **split the producer's risk** into the two tails of the distribution. Thus **each tail** ends up with **one-half of the producer's risk**. Of course due to the different consequences the producer may want to shift more of the risk into one tail or the other because **the costs associated with the respective errors are grossly different**. From a strictly business perspective one can adjust the split according to the financial risks or consequences.

FIGURE 47: The distribution of $\overline{\mathbf{x}}$ provided $\mathbf{H_0}$ is true

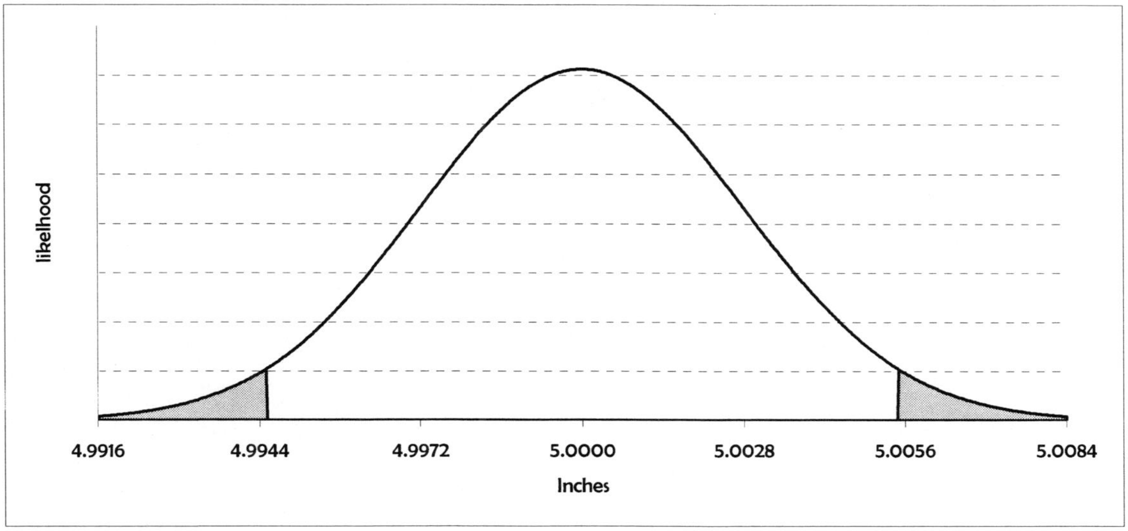

Table 28: Rejection (critical) regions large sample sizes and σ is known

Null ($\mathbf{H_0}: \mu = \mu_0$ Status Quo)

Alternative	Critical region
$\mathbf{H_a}: \mu > \mu_0$	$\left\{ \overline{\mathbf{x}} > \mathbf{x_0} = \mu_0 + \mathbf{z}_\alpha \times \frac{\sigma}{\sqrt{n}} \right.$
$\mathbf{H_a}: \mu < \mu_0$	$\left\{ \overline{\mathbf{x}} < \mathbf{x_0} = \mu_0 - \mathbf{z}_\alpha \times \frac{\sigma}{\sqrt{n}} \right.$
$\mathbf{H_a}: \mu \neq \mu_0$	$\overline{\mathbf{x}} < \mathbf{x_1} = \mu_0 - \mathbf{z}_{\alpha/2} \times \frac{\sigma}{\sqrt{n}}$ **or** $\overline{\mathbf{x}} > \mathbf{x_2} = \mu_0 + \mathbf{z}_{\alpha/2} \times \frac{\sigma}{\sqrt{n}}$

Hypothesis Tests on Binomial Proportions

We can test hypotheses about binomial proportions in the same way that we tested hypotheses on population means by using the central limit theorem. There are some differences here though:

- $\left\{ \begin{array}{l} \text{By assuming via } \mathbf{CLT} \text{ the population } \mathbf{mean} \\ \mu_{\overline{\mathbf{x}}} = p = p_0 \end{array} \right.$

- $\sigma_{\bar{x}} = \sqrt{\frac{p_0 \times (1 - p_0)}{n}}$

Thus hypothesizing the value of the proportion in the null hypothesis also makes known the population variance or standard deviation.

The sample size needs to be large and the approximation of $n = 30$ may be inadequate for extremely small values of p. Let us illustrate the process as before but in this case we provide the table of critical values first.

Table 28A: Rejection (critical) regions for proportions in large sample sizes

Null ($\mathbf{H_0} : p = p_0$ Status Quo)

Alternative	Critical region
$\mathbf{H_a} : p > p_0$	$\bar{\mathbf{x}} > \mathbf{x_0} = p_0 + \mathbf{z}_\alpha \times \sqrt{\frac{p_0 \times (1 - p_0)}{n}}$
$\mathbf{H_a} : p < p_0$	$\bar{\mathbf{x}} < \mathbf{x_0} = p_0 - \mathbf{z}_\alpha \times \sqrt{\frac{p_0 \times (1 - p_0)}{n}}$
$\mathbf{H_a} : p \neq p_0$	$\bar{\mathbf{x}} < \mathbf{x_1} = p_0 - \mathbf{z}_{\alpha/2} \times \sqrt{\frac{p_0 \times (1 - p_0)}{n}}$ **or** $\bar{\mathbf{x}} > \mathbf{x_2} = p_0 + \mathbf{z}_{\alpha/2} \times \sqrt{\frac{p_0 \times (1 - p_0)}{n}}$

Example: Advertising

Sonic Boom has 34% of the CD market in San Antonio. After an ad campaign, 100 persons were polled and asked where they purchased their CD's. Forty one persons in the survey named Sonic Boom as their store of choice. Is this sufficient evidence at the 10% level of significance to support the advertising company's claim that the ad campaign was effective?

Form the hypotheses: Let the **null hypothesis** be that **no change has occurred** and let the alternative be that Sonic boom **owns a greater share** of the market **after the ad campaign**.

- ❖ $\mathbf{H_0} : p = p_0 = 0.34$
  - o (i.e., there is **no change in preference**).
    - versus
- ❖ $\mathbf{H_a} : p > p_0 = 0.34$
  - o (i.e., **Sonic Boom's** market **share increased**).

Conduct an experiment: Select a random sample of n (more than 30) CD buyers from their population of customers. After the ad campaign, request each to state his or her preferred store of choice and let these values be $\mathbf{X}_1, \mathbf{X}_2, \cdots, \mathbf{X}_n$ (i.e., $n = 100$) be their preferences, 1 for Sonic Boom and 0 otherwise.

Test Statistic: Let $\overline{\mathbf{x}}$ denote the sample average of these n customers. If the null hypothesis is true then from the Central Limit Theorem we know that the sampling distribution of the sample average $\overline{\mathbf{x}}$ has the following properties:

$$\begin{cases} \bullet \mu_{\overline{\mathbf{x}}} = p_0 = 0.34 \\ \bullet \sigma_{\overline{\mathbf{x}}} = \sqrt{\dfrac{p_0 \times (1 - p_0)}{n}} = 0.0474 \\ \bullet \overline{\mathbf{x}} \sim \mathbf{N}(0.34, 0.0474) \end{cases}$$

Determine the critical region:

To retain a Type I error rate of α, we reject $\mathbf{H_0}$ when it is true only $(100 \times \alpha)\%$ of the time, in this case, 10%. The values of the sample average that would cause us to reject $\mathbf{H_0}$ are given by

$$\mathbf{x_0} = p_0 + \mathbf{z}_\alpha \times \sqrt{\frac{p_0 \times (1 - p_0)}{n}}$$

Decision: Reject $\mathbf{H_0}$ whenever $\overline{\mathbf{x}} > \mathbf{x_0} = p_0 + \mathbf{z}_\alpha \times \sqrt{\dfrac{p_0 \times (1 - p_0)}{n}}$.

From the survey of 100 customers, a sample average of $\overline{\mathbf{x}} = \dfrac{41}{100} = 0.41$ was obtained. Is this **sufficient evidence** at the 10% level of significance to **reject the claim that the claim that the ad campaign had no effect**?

$$\mathbf{x}_0 = p_0 + \mathbf{z}_\alpha \times \sqrt{\frac{p_0 \times (1-p_0)}{n}}$$

$$= \mathbf{0.34} + 1.282 \times \mathbf{0.0474} = \mathbf{0.34} + \mathbf{0.061} = \mathbf{0.401}$$

Hence, if $\bar{\mathbf{x}} > 0.401$ reject $\mathbf{H_0}$ at the 10% level of significance $\mathbf{H_0}$ that this Sonic Boom's share of the market will be no more than it was prior to the ad campaign and accept the alternative that their share of the market has increased. Since the sample average is $\bar{\mathbf{x}} = 0.410 > 0.401$ reject $\mathbf{H_0}$ and infer that the ad campaign was effective.

FIGURE 48: Critical region for proportion preferring Sonic Boom in the ad campaign at the 10% level of significance.

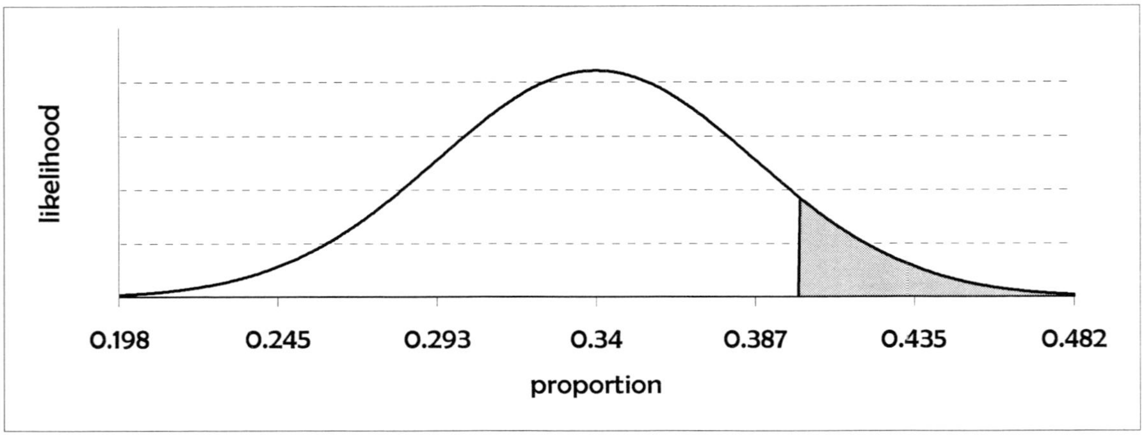

Notice that had we used a level of significance of 5%, we would fail to reject the null since:

$$\mathbf{x}_0 = p_0 + \mathbf{z}_\alpha \times \sqrt{\frac{p_0 \times (1-p_0)}{n}} = \mathbf{0.34} + 1.645 \times \mathbf{0.0474} = \mathbf{0.34} + \mathbf{0.078} = \mathbf{0.418}$$

Example: Political Polls

In a competitive election can we declare a winner? We see this happen every election night and with much interest especially in the state of Florida in 2000. Based on a random sample of n persons, we want to be able to declare a winner in a two-person election. How much evidence do we need?

Formation of hypotheses

- $\mathbf{H_0}: p = p_0 = 0.50$
  - (i.e., the **populace appears to be evenly divided** between the candidates)
    - versus
- $\mathbf{H_a}: p \neq p_0 = 0.50$
  - (i.e., the **populace is not evenly divided**)

Using the formation in this way does allow us to give a preference to either candidate.

Test Statistic: Let $\overline{\mathbf{x}}$ denote the sample average of these $n = 50$ nuts. If the null hypothesis is true then from the Central Limit Theorem we know that the sampling distribution of the sample average has the following properties:

$$\begin{cases} \bullet \mu_{\overline{\mathbf{x}}} = p = p_0 = 0.50 \\ \bullet \sigma_{\overline{\mathbf{x}}} = \sqrt{\dfrac{p_0 \times (1-p_0)}{n}} = \sqrt{\dfrac{0.5 \times (1-0.50)}{n}} = \dfrac{0.50}{\sqrt{n}} \\ \bullet \overline{\mathbf{x}} \sim \mathbf{N}\left(0.5, \dfrac{1}{2\sqrt{n}}\right) \end{cases}$$

Determine the critical region:

To preserve the stated Type I error rate, we reject $\mathbf{H_0}$ when it is true, only $(100 \times \alpha)\%$ of the time, in this case, 5%. The values of the sample average that would cause us to reject $\mathbf{H_0}$ fall outside the bounds given by

$$p_0 \pm \mathbf{z}_{\alpha/2} \times \sqrt{\frac{p_0 \times (1-p_0)}{n}}$$

Decision: Reject $\mathbf{H_0}$ whenever

$$\overline{\mathbf{x}} < \mathbf{x}_1 = p_0 - \mathbf{z}_{\alpha/2} \times \sqrt{\frac{p_0 \times (1-p_0)}{n}} \text{ or } \overline{\mathbf{x}} > \mathbf{x}_2 = p_0 + \mathbf{z}_{\alpha/2} \times \sqrt{\frac{p_0 \times (1-p_0)}{n}}$$

Reject $\mathbf{H_0}$ if the sample average is too large or too small.

$$\mathbf{x_{1,2}} = \mathbf{0.50} \pm 1.96 \times \frac{\mathbf{1}}{\mathbf{2} \times \sqrt{\mathbf{n}}} = \mathbf{0.50} \pm \frac{\mathbf{0.98}}{\sqrt{\mathbf{n}}}$$

For example suppose that we start with a sample size of 100 persons, then we would have the following bounds

$$\mathbf{x_{1,2}} = \mathbf{0.50} \pm 1.96 \times \frac{1}{2 \times \sqrt{n}} = \mathbf{0.50} \pm \frac{\mathbf{0.98}}{\sqrt{n}} = \mathbf{0.50} \pm \frac{\mathbf{0.98}}{\mathbf{10}} = \mathbf{0.50} \pm \mathbf{0.098}$$

So if the sample fraction preferring a candidate is between 40.2% and 59.8%, we do not have enough evidence at the 5% level of significance to declare a winner. In close elections, can we declare winners without knowing the final count?

If the election is close then the closer the true proportion favoring a candidate will be to 50%. This point emphasizes the ability to detect a false null depends upon how far the true value is from the hypothetical one. In this context the only factor that we change is the size of the sample n. By increasing the size of the sample we can diminish the spread about 50%. The following graph shows how the bounds above and below the mean diminish with increases in sample size. Notice that for samples of **1,000** we obtain bound about p of $\pm\mathbf{0.03} \cong \pm\mathbf{3\%}$. When you hear that a poll has a margin of error of **±3%** then we know that the size of the sample was approximately 1,000. Furthermore notice that, one would need to increase the sample size from 1,000 to about **2,500** to reduce the margin of error to $\pm\mathbf{2\%}$. In the marketing one would need to weigh the cost of increasing the sample size from 1,000 to 2,500 with the value of the added information.

FIGURE 49: Margin of error as a function of sample size

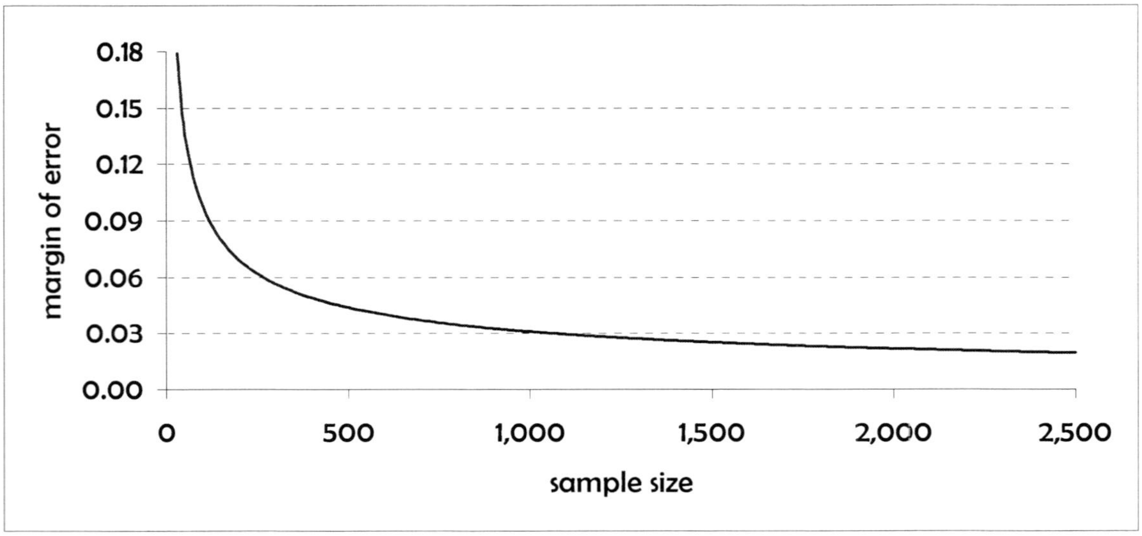

Student's t-distribution

In our previous discussion, we assumed that we had some knowledge of the population variance. This assumption was usually supported by industry research, historical records, or other opinions. However, in many practical settings, we may have hypothesis tests in which we have little if any knowledge of the population variance. Because of this frequent occurrence, we introduce **Student's t-distribution**. W.S. Gossett first discovered this distribution in 1908 while he worked on **controlling errors in the brewing process** at the **Guinness Brewery in Dublin, Ireland**: see Johnson and Kotz (1997) pg 327. The brewery objected to the dissemination of his results because of their utility in maintaining consistency in the brewing process. He published his work anonymously under the pen name: **"Student."**

Let $\mathbf{X}_1, \mathbf{X}_2, \ldots, \mathbf{X}_n$ be a random sample of size n from a **normal distribution** with mean μ and standard deviation σ. Then it follows that

$$\sqrt{n}\left(\frac{\overline{\mathbf{X}} - \mu}{\mathbf{S}}\right) \sim t(n-1)$$

has a t-distribution with $n-1$ degrees of freedom. Notice in the $\mathbf{Z}$-statistic, we have replaced the known standard deviation, σ, with the **sample standard deviation** $\mathbf{S}$. Since the sample standard deviation is a statistic with its own distribution, we see the need for new results.

Characteristics of the t-distribution:

1. The population mean of the t-distribution is 0 (provided the parameter, known as the degrees of freedom exceeds 1) and its probability distribution is symmetric about the origin as in the standard normal distribution.

2. The population variance is a decreasing function of the parameter, f (in this case $n-1$), which is known as the degrees of freedom. Asymptotically, (while n increases) the variance of the t-distribution approaches 1, that of the standard normal distribution.

3. From Figure 50, the distribution is flatter in the center and thicker in the tails than the standard normal distribution. The wider spread in the t-values compared to those in the standard normal is due to the imprecision in using s to estimate σ.

4. As $n \to \infty$ the t-distribution approaches the standard normal. (CLT: improves as n increases)

5. Gossett's results are robust to the assumption that the sample values follow a normal distribution. See the article by George Box (1953).

FIGURE 50: The t-distribution for Various Degrees of Freedom

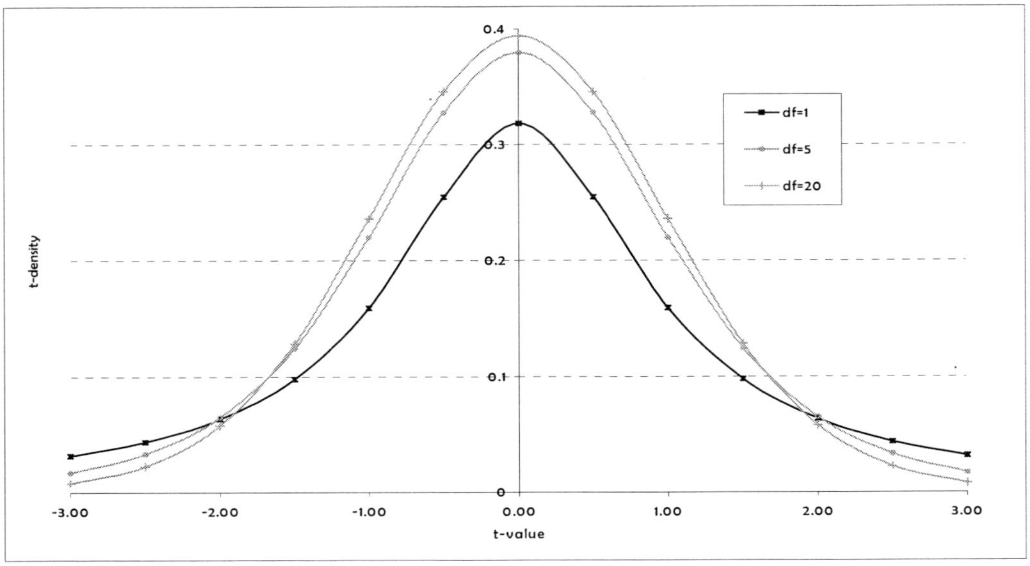

6. The percentiles of the t – distribution are indexed by the degrees of freedom parameter, f. Again we use similar notation as in the standard normal distribution for upper percentiles of the t – distribution.

$$\Pr\left\{ t(f) > t_{\alpha;f} \right\} = \alpha$$

Table 25: Upper Percentiles of a *t*-distribution

	α						α						α				
f	.100	.050	.025	.010	.005	*f*	.100	.050	.025	.010	.005	*f*	.100	.050	.025	.010	.005
1	3.078	6.314	12.706	31.821	63.656	**12**	1.356	1.782	2.179	2.681	3.055	**23**	1.319	1.714	2.069	2.500	2.807
2	1.886	2.920	4.303	6.965	9.925	**13**	1.350	1.771	2.160	2.650	3.012	**24**	1.318	1.711	2.064	2.492	2.797
3	1.638	2.353	3.182	4.541	5.841	**14**	1.345	1.761	2.145	2.624	2.977	**25**	1.316	1.708	2.060	2.485	2.787
4	1.533	2.132	2.776	3.747	4.604	**15**	1.341	1.753	2.131	2.602	2.947	**26**	1.315	1.706	2.056	2.479	2.779
5	1.476	2.015	2.571	3.365	4.032	**16**	1.337	1.746	2.120	2.583	2.921	**27**	1.314	1.703	2.052	2.473	2.771
6	1.440	1.943	2.447	3.143	3.707	**17**	1.333	1.740	2.110	2.567	2.898	**28**	1.313	1.701	2.048	2.467	2.763
7	1.415	1.895	2.365	2.998	3.499	**18**	1.330	1.734	2.101	2.552	2.878	**29**	1.311	1.699	2.045	2.462	2.756
8	1.397	1.860	2.306	2.896	3.355	**19**	1.328	1.729	2.093	2.539	2.861	**30**	1.310	1.697	2.042	2.457	2.750
9	1.383	1.833	2.262	2.821	3.250	**20**	1.325	1.725	2.086	2.528	2.845						
10	1.372	1.812	2.228	2.764	3.169	**21**	1.323	1.721	2.080	2.518	2.831						
11	1.363	1.796	2.201	2.718	3.106	**22**	1.321	1.717	2.074	2.508	2.819	∞	1.282	1.645	1.960	2.326	2.575

7. The percentiles of the t-distribution as $n \to \infty$ approach those of the standard normal as given in Table 25 for the row headed by ∞. Notice that these values agree with the 90th, 95th, 97.5th, 99th, and 99.5th percentiles in the standard normal distribution.

There is a simple transfer of the critical values for tests of hypotheses when the standard deviation is known to this case when it is unknown and must be estimated from the sample data. In the table of critical values given for large sample sizes, we merely replace σ with $\mathbf{s}$ and $\mathbf{z}_\alpha$ with $t_{\alpha;n-1}$.

Table 26: Rejection (critical) regions small sample sizes and σ estimated

Null ($\mathbf{H_0} : \mu = \mu_0$ Status Quo)

Alternative	Critical region
$\mathbf{H_a} : \mu > \mu_0$	$\left\{ \overline{\mathbf{x}} > \mathbf{x_0} = \mu_0 + t_{\alpha;n-1} \times \frac{\mathbf{s}}{\sqrt{n}} \right.$
$\mathbf{H_a} : \mu < \mu_0$	$\left\{ \overline{\mathbf{x}} < \mathbf{x_0} = \mu_0 - t_{\alpha;n-1} \times \frac{\mathbf{s}}{\sqrt{n}} \right.$
$\mathbf{H_a} : \mu \neq \mu_0$	$\overline{\mathbf{x}} < \mathbf{x_0} = \mu_0 - t_{\alpha/2;n-1} \times \frac{\mathbf{s}}{\sqrt{n}}$ **or** $\overline{\mathbf{x}} > \mathbf{x_0} = \mu_0 + t_{\alpha/2;n-1} \times \frac{\mathbf{s}}{\sqrt{n}}$

Example: On April 10th chemists for Diamond Shamrock were asked to analyze molecular weights of $n = 15$ samples of Super Unleaded taken from 15 randomly chosen stations in San Antonio. The company wants to determine whether the refinery (at Three Rivers) has raised the molecular weight from the winter blend of 102.

The following data in the form of molecular weights were obtained from the chemical assays of the 15 samples obtained from 15 different sites across the city of San Antonio.

104	105	103	104	104	102	106	104
104	104	103	104	105	105	104	

Do these data provide sufficient evidence at the 5% level of significance to support the claim that the refineries have raised the molecular weights of their blends?

Here we compute the sample descriptive statistics from this random sample to make inferences about the value of the population mean, the molecular weight of the gasoline at the refinery.

$\bar{\mathbf{x}} = 104.0667$, and $\mathbf{s} = 0.9612$

Formation of hypotheses

- $\mathbf{H_0}: \mu = \mu_0 = 102$
  - (i.e., the **refineries have not changed**).
    - versus
- $\mathbf{H_a}: \mu > \mu_0 = 102$
  - (i.e., the refineries have **changed** from the **winter to the summer** blend, which is 106).

Using the Table 26, the table of critical values, we calculate

$$\begin{aligned}
\mathbf{x_0} &= \mu_0 + t_{\alpha;n-1} \times \frac{\mathbf{s}}{\sqrt{n}} \\
&= \mathbf{102} + t_{0.05;14} \times \frac{0.9612}{\sqrt{15}} \\
&= \mathbf{102} + 1.761 \times \mathbf{0.2482} \\
&= \mathbf{102} + \mathbf{0.437} \\
&= \mathbf{102.437}
\end{aligned}$$

The value of $t_{0.05,14} = 1.761$ was found in Table 25 by going to the row headed by 14 and moving to the column headed by 0.05.

If $\bar{\mathbf{x}} > 102.437$ reject $\mathbf{H_0}$ that the refineries have made no changes in **favor of the alternative that the refineries have changed the process** at the 5% **level of significance**.

$\bar{\mathbf{x}} = 104.067 > 102.437$

FIGURE 51: The distribution if $\mathbf{H_0}$ is true for refinery data

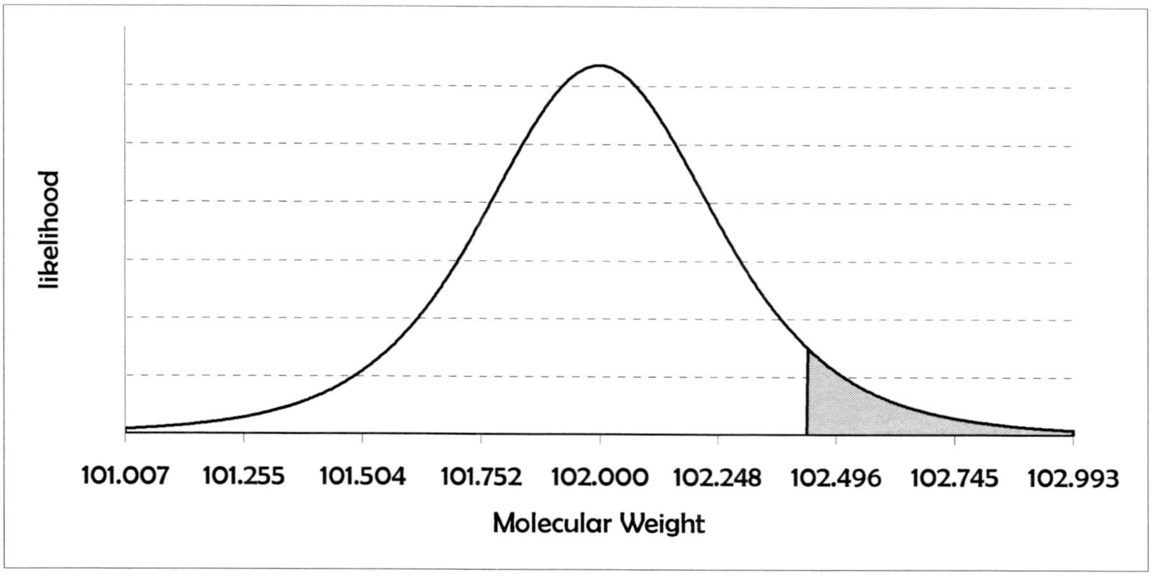

We reject $\mathbf{H_0}$ and infer that the refineries are changing the process. Such values are important in complying with EPA regulations. on Reid Vapor Pressure (RVP).

Example: A wing attachment clevis is the structural component for the wing stores on an AH-1J helicopter. The wing stores are TOW missiles, which are optically wire-guided missiles. When a missile is fired, a force is exerted on the clevis of 1,650 psi. Material engineers need to know whether the clevis is substantially stronger than the firing stress. If the clevis is weak and breaks, the pilot may be left defenseless or the clevis may break off and damage the rotor system.

FIGURE 52: Cross-Sectional View of AH-1J Aircraft

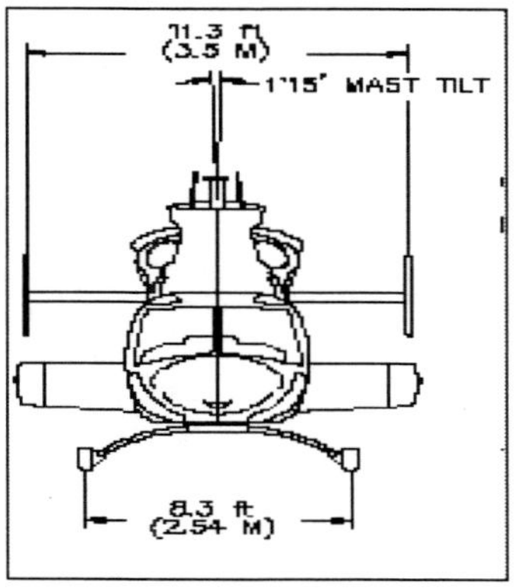

DATA: Six wing attachment clevises, located just below the extensions shown in Figure 52, were tested with the following strengths (psi): See Keating (1976).

3434 3109 2913 2854 3087 2642

Do these data provide sufficient evidence at the 5% level of significance to support the **BHT claim that the clevises are stronger than needed**?

Again we compute the **sample descriptive statistics** from this **random sample** to **make inferences about the value** of the **population mean**, the material fatigue strength of these clevises.

$\overline{\mathbf{x}} = 3,006.5$ psi and $\mathbf{s} = 270.04$ psi

Formation of hypotheses:

- $\mathbf{H_0} : \mu = \mu_0 = 1,950$ psi
  - (i.e., the part is barely strong enough at 1,650+300 psi, the 300 psi is a margin of safety added by engineers to avoid worst case scenarios).
    - versus
- $\mathbf{H_a} : \mu > \mu_0 = 1,950$ psi
  - (i.e., the clevises are more than adequate).

Using the Table 26, the table of critical values we calculate

$$\begin{aligned} \mathbf{x_0} &= \mu_0 + t_{\alpha;n-1} \times \frac{\mathbf{s}}{\sqrt{n}} \\ &= \mathbf{1,950} + t_{0.05;5} \times \frac{\mathbf{270.04}}{\sqrt{\mathbf{6}}} \\ &= \mathbf{1,950} + 2.015 \times \mathbf{110.227} \\ &= \mathbf{1,950} + \mathbf{222.107} \\ &= \mathbf{2,172.107} \text{ psi} \end{aligned}$$

Hence, if $\overline{\mathbf{x}} > 2,172.107$ psi reject $\mathbf{H_0}$ that the clevises are suspect in favor of the alternative that **they are more than adequate** at the **5% level of significance**. A detailed report of the use of these clevises within a context for which they were not designed is given below under the section on history.

FIGURE 53: The distribution if $\mathbf{H_0}$ is true for AH-1J wing attachment clevis data

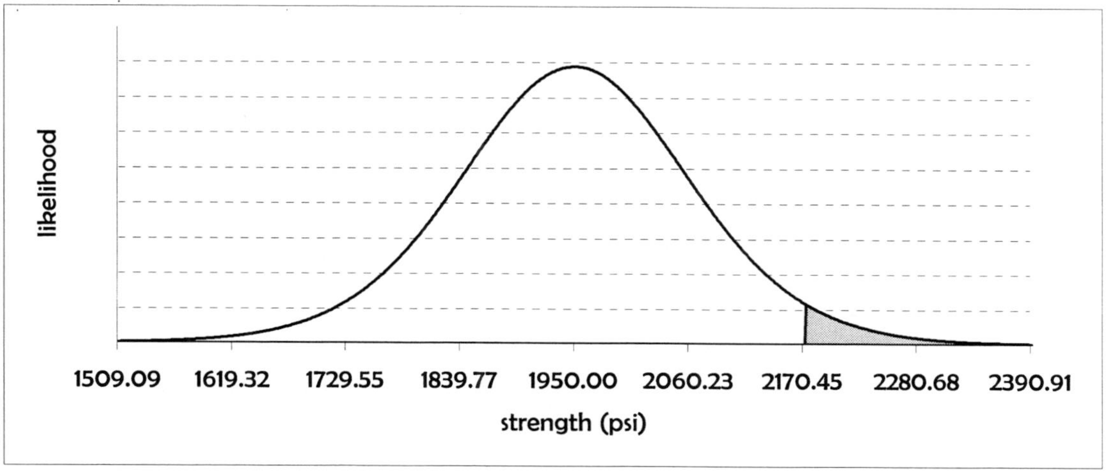

History: During the Tet offensive of 1968, the Viet Cong engaged US troops at many sites inside what was South Vietnam. One such battle took place at Bien Hoa during February 1968. As Viet Cong troops were about to overrun an airbase, some pilots decided to load their wing stores and fire them at the invading troops as they came onto the base. Several AH series helicopters, started a sequence in which pilots would load their wing stores, rise to an elevation of 50′, fire their missiles, descend, reload and repeat.

FIGURE 54: The Hydra 70 Rocket

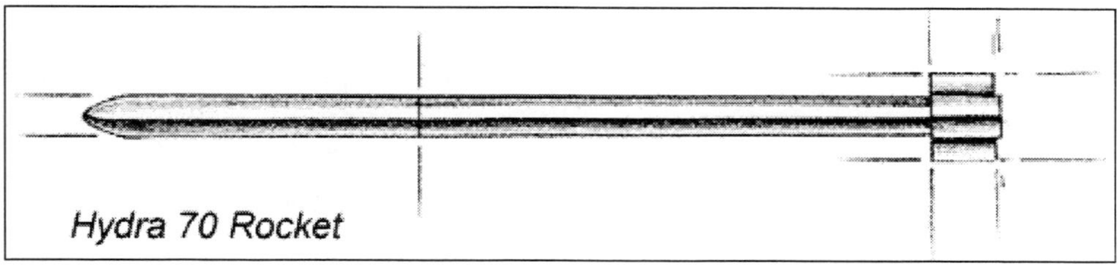

When we looked at the laboratory test data, we felt the parts were more than adequate for their designed use, which was to fly to a site, fire four externally loaded rockets (and later TOW missiles) and return to base. No one envisioned scenarios in which helicopters would fire more than four rockets (or missiles) in a two-hour mission. After this battle, several AH wing attachment clevises showed cracks, which caused a review of the part.

There are many cases in which parts are used for purposes that they were not designed to perform. The OH-58 helicopter was first used in spraying crops. In the Korean war, it was used to evacuate wounded personnel to MASH units for triage or surgery. In the

Vietnam conflict, these helicopters flew nap of the earth maneuvers, which were extremely dangerous for this model and resulted in many unintended deaths of military personnel.

Problem Set 3

(77-80) The distribution of Exam I-scores made by students in an introductory class has a population mean of 76 with a population standard deviation of 14. These grades are skewed to the left. This semester there are 100 students in this introductory class.

77) What is the probability that the sample average of this class will be less than 72 on Exam I?
a) 0.3859 b) 0.0021 c) 0.6141 d) 0.9979

78) What is the probability that the sample average of this class will be between 73 and 79?
a) 0.4676 b) 0.8154 c) 0.1782 d) 0.9676

79) What is the 99th percentile of sample averages of samples of size 100 taken from this population?
a) 77.95 b) 78.30 c) 79.26 d) 82.56

80) Determine the middle 80% of sample averages of samples of size 100 taken from the population.
a) 76 ± 1.79 b) 76 ± 1.18 c) 76 ± 2.30 d) 82.56

(81-84) 55% of statisticians prefer Dr. Pepper to other sodas. An exit poll of 200 statisticians at the annual convention in 2002 is done.

81) What is the probability that no more than 99 persons in this sample will prefer Dr. Pepper?
a) 0.0582 b) 0.2611 c) 0.2389 d) 0.9418

82) What is the probability that between 101 and 108 persons in this sample will prefer Dr. Pepper?
a) 0.0985 b) 0.2874 c) 0.3859 d) 0.4844 e) 0.6179

83) Determine the middle 95% bounds on the proportion of this sample that would favor Dr. Pepper.
a) $55\% \pm 4\%$ b) $55\% \pm 5.7\%$ c) $55\% \pm 6.9\%$ d) 59 %

84) Determine the 99th percentile of the percentage of this sample that would prefer Dr. Pepper.
a) 26.7% b) 58.5% c) 63.2% d) 67.2%

85) If one rejects the null hypothesis when its false one makes ___________.
a) a Type I error b) a Type II error
c) a producer error d) a correct decision

(86-88) Families of size four spent a population mean of $170 on a Spurs' game with a standard deviation of $40 last year. In an exit poll from the SBC Center, 50 randomly selected families of size four were interviewed in December 2002. As a result, the average spent by these families is $182. Is this sufficient evidence at the 5% level of significance to indicate that these families spent more this year?

86) The alternative hypothesis is that families of size four spent: ___________.
a) more than $182 this year b) no more than $170 this year
c) more than $170 this year d) less than $170 this year

87) The critical region is given by the values of the sample average which _______.
a) exceed $170.00 b) exceed $179.31
c) are less than $160.69 d) exceed $183.16

88) Based on these results one concludes that families of size four spent _______.
a) more than $170 this year b) less than $170 this year
c) a mean of $182 this year d) a mean of $170 this year

89) When testing the null hypothesis, if you reject H_0, then ___________.
a) a Type II error may be made b) H_0 is false
c) a Type I error is made d) H_0 may be false

(90-92) A brace on an AH-1J helicopter provides structural support to the airframe. The force exerted on the brace during action is 2000 psi. A test of six braces results in the following strengths: 2734, 2409, 2213, 2154, 2387, and 1942 pounds. Do these data provide sufficient evidence at the 1% level of significance to support the claim that the brace is stronger than the 2000-psi force?

90) The alternative hypothesis is that the braces are ______________.
a) stronger than 2306 psi b) no stronger than 2000 psi
c) stronger than 2000 psi d) weaker than 2000 psi

91) The critical region is given by the values of the sample average which _______.
a) exceed 2222-psi b) exceed 2163 psi c) are less than 1629 psi
d) exceed 2371-psi e) exceed 2257 psi

92) Based on these results one concludes that these braces have a population mean strength ____________.

a) no greater than 2000 psi　　b) less than 2000 psi
c) of 2306.50 psi　　d) greater than 2000 psi

93) The probability that a hypothesis results in a decision to accept a defective product is ____________.

a) the level of significance　　b) the consumer's risk
c) the producer's risk　　d) a Type II error

(94-96) Sonic Boom (SB) has 40% of the CD market in San Antonio. SB conducted an extensive ad campaign to increase its share of the market. A post ad campaign of 100 randomly chosen persons revealed that 47 said they purchased their CD's at Sonic Boom. Is this sufficient evidence at the 10% level of significance to indicate that SB's share of the market has increased?

94) The alternative hypothesis is that Sonic Boom's share of the CD market _______.

a) has increased above 40%　　b) has changed
c) remains unchanged　　d) has decreased below 40%

95) The critical region is given by the number of Sonic Boom patrons that are:

a) greater than 48　　b) greater than 46
c) greater than 41　　d) greater than 40

96) Based on these results one concludes that SB's share of the CD market has _______.

a) decreased below 40%　　b) changed from 40%
c) not changed from 40%　　d) increased above 40%

(97-99) Thirty-five percent of the Accounting majors at UTSA are Hispanic descendants. A random sample of 100 Accounting majors is taken.

97) Approximate the probability that at least 37 are Hispanic?

a) 0.837　　b) 0.663　　c) 0.337　　d) 0.163

98) Approximate the probability that at most 32 are Hispanic?

a) 0.764　　b) 0.736　　c) 0.264　　d) 0.236

99) Approximate the probability that the number of Hispanics in the sample is between 30 and 40?

a) 0.084　　b) 0.353　　c) 0.706　　d) 0.859

100) The alternative hypothesis ________________________.

a) uses the level of significance b) opposes the status quo
c) supports the status quo d) uses the sample size

(101-103) The annual salaries of CEO's in TEXAS in 1994 had a normal distribution with a population mean of $250,000 and a population standard deviation of $40,000.

101) What's the probability that a randomly chosen Texas CEO makes more than $235,600?

a) 0.1406 b) 0.3594 c) 0.6406 d) 0.8594

102) What's the probability that a randomly chosen Texas CEO makes between $234,400 and $260,000?

a) 0.053 b) 0.2504 c) 0.3483 d) 0.6517

103) What is the 95th percentile of their salaries?

a) $367,100 b) $288,000 c) $301,280 d)$315,800

104) When testing the null hypothesis, if you reject Ho, then __________.

a) a Type I error was made b) a Type II error is not made
c) H_o is false d) H_o is true

(105-107) The average family of four spent a mean of $160 on a visit to Sea World with a standard deviation of $25 in 1993. In an exit poll from the park, 44 randomly selected families of size four were interviewed in May 1994. The results of the sample revealed that the average amount spent by these families was $168.43. Is this sufficient evidence at the 5% level of significance to indicate that families of size four will spend more at Sea World in 1994?

105) The alternative hypothesis is that families of size four will spend ____________ in 1994.

a) $160 b) less than $160 c) more than $168.43
d) more than $160 e) exactly $168.43

106) The critical region is given by the values of the sample average which ________.

a)exceed $160.00 b) exceed $166.20 c) are less than $168.43
d) exceed $201.13 e) less than $153.80

107) Based on these results, one concludes that families of size four will spend _____.

a) more than $160 b) less than $160 c) a mean of $168.43
d) not spend more than $160 e) $160

108) The probability that a hypothesis test ends in a decision to accept a defective product is _____.

a) the producer's risk b) the consumer's risk
c) the law of averages d) a Type II error e) a Type I error

(109-111) The shelf life of a vaccine is monitored by hospitals. The manufacturer in a test of 8 randomly selected vials observes the following lifetimes in days: 108, 124, 124, 106, 138, 163, 159, and 134. Assume that the shelf lives are normally distributed. Is there sufficient evidence to support the manufacturer's claim that the mean shelf life of the vaccine is more than 125 days at the 5% level of significance?

109) The alternative hypothesis is that the shelf life is ____________ days.

a) 132 b) less than 125 c) more than 125 d) no more than 125

110) The critical region is given by the values of the sample average which ______________ days.

a) exceed 125 b) exceed 165 c) exceed 160
d) exceed 172 e) exceed 139

111) Based on these results, one concludes that these batteries will last _________ days.

a) more than 125 b) less than 125 c) a mean of 132 d) 125

112) When one accepts a true null hypothesis, one makes a ____________.

a) a Type I error b) a Type II error c) a correct decision d) a and b

(113-115) The annual salaries of College Presidents in 1993 had a population mean of \$150,000 and standard deviation of \$20,000. A random sample of 37 college Presidents is chosen from this population.

113) What's the probability that the sample average salary of this randomly chosen sample is less than \$143,400?

a) 0.0222 b) 0.3707 c) 0.4778 d) 0.6293

114) What's the probability that the sample average salary of this randomly chosen sample is between \$146,800 and \$152,900?

a) 0.1212 b) 0.4776 c) 0.5753 d) 0.6446

115) What is the 90th percentile of the average salaries from random samples of size 37?

a) \$152,959 b) \$154,215 c) \$168,000 d) \$175,640

Multinomial Experiment

Earlier in the semester we discussed the concept of a **binomial experiment**. Today we generalize that notion to a multinomial experiment.

1) A **multinomial experiment** generalizes a **binomial experiment in that the outcome can occur in several mutually exclusive ways**. Consider an experiment, which has r **mutually exclusive possible outcomes** $\mathbf{A}_1, \mathbf{A}_2, \cdots, \mathbf{A}_r$. For example a person, who chooses a new car, has many possible choices: General Motors, Ford, Chrysler, or Foreign.

2) The experiment is repeated in n **independent trials via a random sample**. For example, several individuals, who purchased new cars, are polled about their preferences. It seems reasonable that the choices are made independently unless the purchasers are related.

3) The probability that an outcome of the experiment concludes with the ith possible outcome is denoted by p_i, which **remains constant from trial to trial** of the experiment. So the probability of selecting the ith alternative from among the choices is simply p_i and that value remains constant from trial to trial.

4) The observed number $\mathbf{O}_i$ is the count of the number of occurrences of the ith alternative in the random sample. Each $\mathbf{O}_i$ has a **binomial distribution** with **success probability** p_i and a sample of n trials. The parameters of the respective distributions are:

   - $\mathbf{E}_i = \mu_i = np_i$ for each $i = 1, \cdots, r$ (expected) and
   - $\mathbf{V}_i = \mathbf{Var}\{\ \mathbf{O}_i\} = \sigma_i^2 = np_i \times (1 - p_i)$ (variance).

   The term $\mathbf{E}_i$ for each $i = 1, \cdots, r$ is the expected number of choices for the ith alternative in a sample of n trials. The parameters are useful in understanding how the distribution is approximated.

   The purpose of this lecture is to form hypothesis test about the true values of the parameters $p_1, p_2, \cdots, p_r$ where

$$\sum_{i=1}^{r} p_i = 1$$

Notice that in our example these values $p_1, p_2, \cdots, p_r$ would represent each manufacturer's share of the market place. In the 1988 Ward's Automotive Reports, each maker had the following share of the market place,

$$p_1 = 0.352, p_2 = 0.237, p_3 = 0.139, \text{ and } p_4 = 0.272$$

These values may be based on actual sales of 1988 model cars as in this case. The manufacturers are interested in testing hypotheses that the mix of the market place is the same for the new cars against the alternative that there has been a shift in buyer preference.

Formation of Hypotheses: Thus we want to test

$$\blacksquare \quad \begin{cases} \mathbf{H_0}: p_1 = \mathbf{c}_1, p_2 = \mathbf{c}_2, \cdots, p_r = \mathbf{c}_r \\ \qquad\qquad \text{versus} \\ \mathbf{H_a}: p_i \neq \mathbf{c}_i \text{ for some i=1, ..., r} \end{cases}$$

The values of $\mathbf{c}_1, \mathbf{c}_2, \cdots, \mathbf{c}_r$ represent the hypothesized mix of the market place or the mix based on historical data. If $\mathbf{H_0}$ is true, then $\mathbf{E}_i = n \times \mathbf{c}_i$: the expected number for each $i = 1, \cdots, r$ and we expect good agreement between $\mathbf{O}_i$ and $\mathbf{E}_i$ for each $i = 1, \cdots, r$.

The test statistic for this hypothesis is called the **Pearson, χ^2 , chi-square test statistic** and given by

$$\mathbb{R} = \sum_{i=1}^{r} \left[\frac{(\mathbf{O}_i - \mathbf{E}_i)^2}{\mathbf{E}_i} \right].$$

Notice that if $\mathbf{H_0}$ is true, the numerator of each term should be small due to good agreement between $\mathbf{O}_i$ and $\mathbf{E}_i$. $\mathbf{E}_i$ would make this term smaller through division. **Small values of the test statistic indicate good agreement** with the **null hypothesis** and **large values** of the test statistic **indicate disagreement** with the null hypothesis. To determine how large the test statistic is, we need the distribution of the test statistics when $\mathbf{H_0}$ is true

$$\mathbb{R} \sim \chi^2(r-1)$$

When $\mathbf{H_0}$ is true, the test statistic has a **chi-square distribution** with $r-1$ **degrees of freedom**. This result is due to Karl Pearson (1898) (see Johnson and Kotz (1997) page 150) and **Ian Hacking (1984)** has referred to it as one of the

ten greatest achievements of science in the last century. **Karl Pearson** is often known as the **father of modern statistics**.

Properties of the chi-square Distribution

- The χ^2 – distribution like the t – distribution has a distribution, which is **indexed by a parameter**, f, known as the **degrees of freedom**.

- From Figure 55, the **chi-square distribution** is **positive** and **skewed to the right**. The **mean** of the distribution **equals the degrees of freedom**, f, and its **variance** equals **twice the degrees of freedom** or $2 \times f$.

FIGURE 55: The χ^2 – distribution for various degrees of freedom

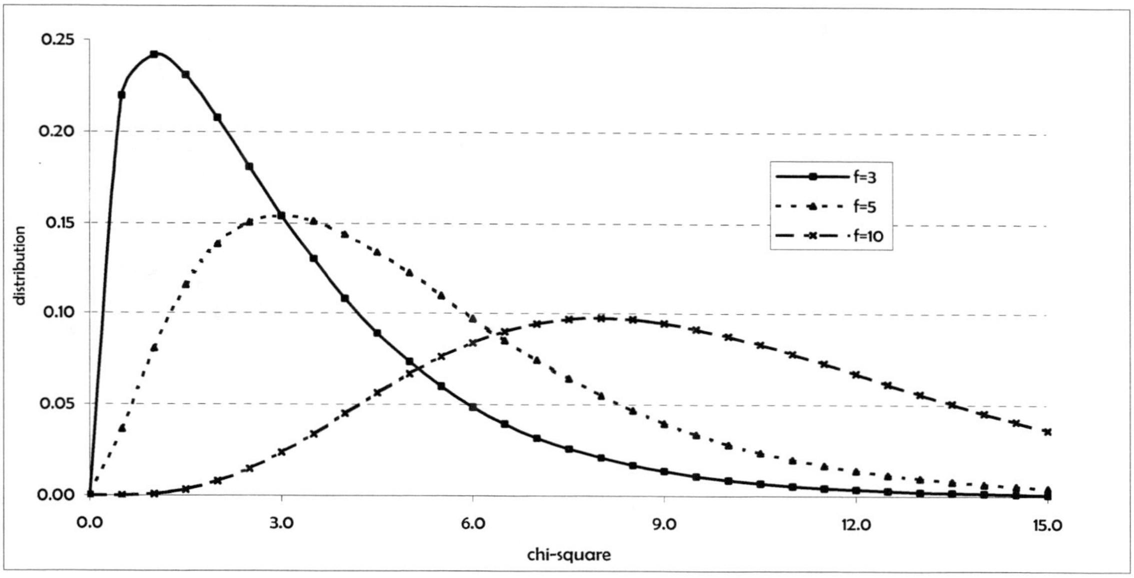

- **Upper percentiles** of the chi-square distribution with f **degrees of freedom** are denoted in a manner similar to the t – distribution.

$$\Pr\left\{ \chi^2(f) > \chi^2_{\alpha;f} \right\} = \alpha .$$

The tabled value, Table 27, is the value so that **the area to its right is** α. The tables form **the upper percentiles of the chi-square distribution**.

For example, if we have three degrees of freedom and $\alpha = 0.05$, then

$$\Pr\left\{ \chi^2(3) > 7.815 \right\} = 0.05 \Leftrightarrow \chi^2_{0.05;3} = 7.815$$

This result is depicted in Figure 56 below.

TABLE 27: Upper-Percentiles of χ^2 – distributions
for various degrees of freedom and values of α

	α				
f	0.10	0.05	0.025	0.01	0.005
1	2.706	3.841	5.024	6.635	7.879
2	4.605	5.991	7.378	9.210	10.597
3	6.251	7.815	9.348	11.345	12.838
4	7.779	9.488	11.143	13.277	14.860
5	9.236	11.070	12.832	15.086	16.750
6	10.645	12.592	14.449	16.812	18.548
7	12.017	14.067	16.013	18.475	20.278
8	13.362	15.507	17.535	20.090	21.955
9	14.684	16.919	19.023	21.666	23.589
10	15.987	18.307	20.483	23.209	25.188

FIGURE 56: Upper Percentile for χ^2 – with 3 degrees of freedom and $\alpha = 0.05$

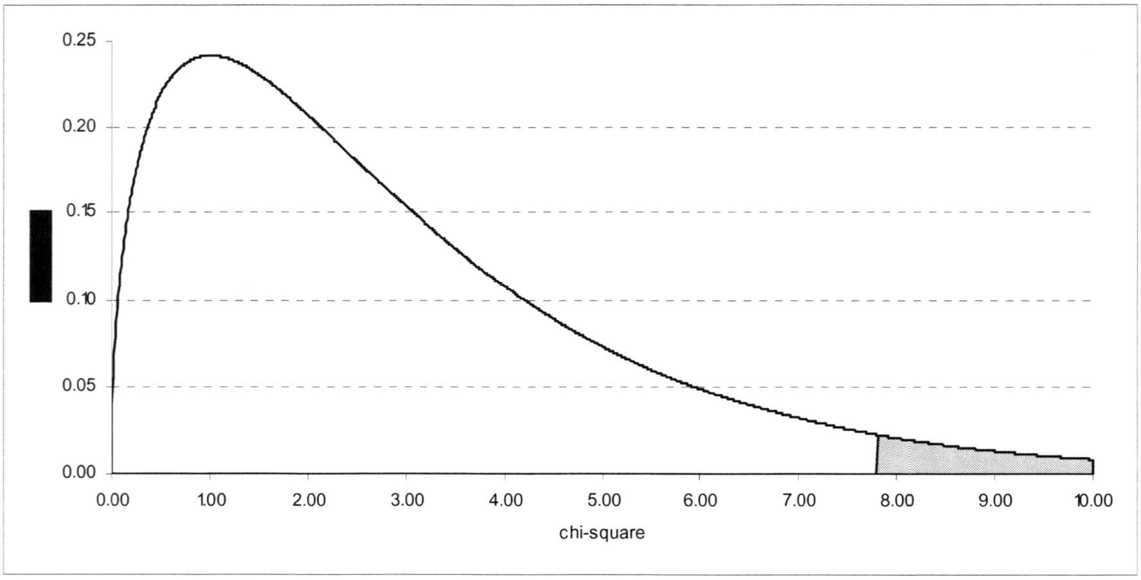

Rejection Region: We reject H_0 whenever

$$\mathbb{R} = \sum_{i=1}^{r} \frac{\left(\mathbf{O}_i - \mathbf{E}_i\right)^2}{\mathbf{E}_i} > \chi^2_{\alpha;r-1}$$

Example: Market Share Changes

In 1988, **GM had 35.2%** of the market share of new cars. **Ford had 23.7%** of the market share, **Chrysler had 13.9%** and **foreign manufacturers had 27.2%** of the market. The companies are interested in the mix of sales for the 1989 models. Such results are important to these companies in making mid-year production adjustments. The producers are willing to take a 5% risk.

A random sample of 100 new car buyers produced the following results:

TABLE 28: Observed number of new car purchases by Manufacturer based on a survey

GM	Ford	Chrysler	Foreign	Total
26	24	17	33	100

We want to test:

❖ $\mathbf{H_0}: p_1 = \mathbf{0.352}, p_2 = \mathbf{0.237}, p_3 = \mathbf{0.139}, \text{ and } p_r = \mathbf{0.272}$

against

$\mathbf{H_a}$: Some p_i has changed, i.e.,

The mix of sales of '89 models differs from '88

If $\mathbf{H_0}$ is true then

$$\mathbf{E}_1 = n \times \mathbf{c}_1 = 100 \times \mathbf{0.352} = \mathbf{35.2}, \qquad \mathbf{E}_2 = n \times \mathbf{c}_2 = 100 \times \mathbf{0.237} = \mathbf{23.7},$$
$$\mathbf{E}_3 = n \times \mathbf{c}_3 = 100 \times \mathbf{0.139} = \mathbf{13.9} \text{ and } \mathbf{E}_4 = n \times \mathbf{c}_4 = 100 \times \mathbf{0.272} = \mathbf{27.2}.$$

TABLE 29: Observed and (Expected) Number of New Car Purchases by Manufacturer

GM	Ford	Chrysler	Foreign	Total
26 (35.2)	24 (23.7)	17 (13.9)	33 (27.2)	100 (100)

$$\begin{aligned}\mathbb{R} &= \sum_{i=1}^{r} \frac{(\mathbf{O}_i - \mathbf{E}_i)^2}{\mathbf{E}_i} \\ &= \frac{(26-\mathbf{35.2})^2}{\mathbf{35.2}} + \frac{(24-\mathbf{23.7})^2}{\mathbf{23.7}} + \frac{(17-\mathbf{13.9})^2}{\mathbf{13.9}} + \frac{(33-\mathbf{27.2})^2}{\mathbf{27.2}} \\ &= 2.4045 + 0.0038 + 0.6914 + 1.2368 \\ &= 4.3365\end{aligned}$$

The value of this test statistic is compared with a percentile from a chi-square distribution with $r-1=4-1=3$ degrees of freedom. Since the level of significance was chosen to be 5%, then the tabled value of the upper percentile is given in Table 27 by $\chi^2_{r-1}=\chi^2_{0.05;3}=7.815$.

Since $\mathbb{R}=4.3365<\chi^2_{0.05;3}=7.815$ then we fail to reject $\mathbf{H_0}$ that the mix of sales remains unchanged.

To recognize the affect of survey size, assume that proportional results occur for a sample of 200 instead of 100. This means that both the expected and observed numbers are doubled

TABLE 30: Observed and (Expected) Number of New Car Purchases by Manufacturer (Larger Survey)

GM	Ford	Chrysler	Foreign	Total
52 (70.4)	48 (47.4)	34 (27.8)	66 (54.4)	200 (200)

The value of **Pearson's chi-square test statistic** is calculated as:

$$\begin{aligned}\mathbb{R} &= \sum_{i=1}^{r}\frac{(\mathbf{O}_i-\mathbf{E}_i)^2}{\mathbf{E}_i}\\ &= \frac{(52-\mathbf{70.4})^2}{\mathbf{70.4}}+\frac{(48-\mathbf{47.4})^2}{\mathbf{47.4}}+\frac{(34-\mathbf{27.8})^2}{\mathbf{27.8}}+\frac{(66-\mathbf{54.4})^2}{\mathbf{54.4}}\\ &= 4.8091+0.0076+1.3827+2.4735\\ &= 8.6729\end{aligned}$$

Since $\mathbb{R}=8.6729>\chi^2_{0.05;3}=7.815$ then we **reject** $\mathbf{H_0}$ that the mix of sales remains the same and **accept the alternative that a change has taken place**. In this scenario, one can see that **Ford** seems to have been **hardly affected** by the change and it appears that **Chrysler and Foreign manufacturers** have **gained at GM's loss**.

Example: Mendelian Genetics

Consider those families with two children. We question Mendel's theory of genetics based on the data from 39 families with two children. These data revealed that 7 families had no girls, 15 had two girls with the remaining 17 families having 1 girl. **Are these data sufficient evidence to reject Mendel's laws** at the 10% level of significance from this population of families?

Let the first class consist of those families with no girls, class 2 be the families with one girl and class 3 be those families with two girls. Under Mendel's genetics, we assume that births boys and girls are equally likely. So the corresponding classes have the following probabilities given that the births are independent and equally likely.

$$\underbrace{\mathbf{BB}}_{1} \qquad \underbrace{\mathbf{BG} \quad \mathbf{GB}}_{2} \qquad \underbrace{\mathbf{GG}}_{3}$$

$$\overbrace{\mathbf{p_1 = 0.25}} \qquad \overbrace{\mathbf{p_2 = 0.50}} \qquad \overbrace{\mathbf{p_3 = 0.25}}$$

Formation of hypotheses: Hence we want to test

❖
$$\begin{cases} \mathbf{H_0} : p_1 = 0.25,\ p_2 = 0.50,\ \text{and}\ p_3 = 0.25 \\ \quad \text{against} \\ \mathbf{H_a} : \text{Some } p_i \text{ has changed or the mix of} \\ \quad \text{births does not follow Mendel's laws.} \end{cases}$$

If $\mathbf{H_0}$ is true then

$$\begin{cases} \mathbf{E}_1 = n \times \mathbf{c}_1 = 39 \times \mathbf{0.25} = \ 9.75 \\ \mathbf{E}_2 = n \times \mathbf{c}_2 = 39 \times \mathbf{0.50} = 19.50 \\ \quad \textbf{and} \\ \mathbf{E}_3 = n \times \mathbf{c}_3 = 39 \times \mathbf{0.25} = \ 9.75 \end{cases},$$

TABLE 31: Observed and (Expected) Number of Girls
In families with Two Children

No Girls	One Girl	Two Girls	Total
7 (9.75)	17 (19.5)	15 (9.75)	39 (39)

The value of **Pearson's chi-square test statistic** can be calculated as:

$$\begin{aligned} \mathbb{R} &= \sum_{i=1}^{r} \frac{(\mathbf{O}_i - \mathbf{E}_i)^2}{\mathbf{E}_i} \\ &= \frac{(7 - \mathbf{9.75})^2}{\mathbf{9.75}} + \frac{(17 - \mathbf{19.5})^2}{\mathbf{19.5}} + \frac{(15 - \mathbf{9.75})^2}{\mathbf{9.75}} \\ &= 0.7756 + 0.3205 + 2.8269 \\ &= 3.923 \end{aligned}$$

The **corresponding critical value** is found in Table 27 as:

$$\chi^2_{\alpha:r-1} = \chi^2_{0.10;2} = 4.605$$

There is a **lack of evidence at the 10% level of significance** to reject Mendel's laws in this setting.

Case Study: Worker Productivity by Day

In every industry worker productivity is scrutinized to minimize waste and yet some anomalies remain despite all intervention methods. Among these anomalies is, the cycle of worker productivity within a week. Workers seem to produce more products and ones of higher quality in the middle of the workweek than in the extremes of the workweek. The Hawthorne Effect mentioned earlier was but one experiment to focus on the phenomenon of worker productivity. To illustrate this phenomenon a company produces items over a two-week period with the number of completed items listed by day of the week in Table 32.

TABLE 32: Observed Number of Production Items by Day of the Week

M	TU	W	TH	F	Total
42	49	58	55	46	250

While the table tends to lend some evidence to the variation in worker productivity during the workweek, is the variation large enough to be statistically significant at the 5% level of significance.

We want to test the naïve assumption that worker productivity is the same by day of the week against an alternative that workers are more productive on some days than others. Since we have five alternatives and if each day's production is the same, we would anticipate that 20% of the production would be completed on each day. We want to test:

❖ $$\begin{cases} \mathbf{H_0}: p_1 = 0.20,\ p_2 = 0.20,\ p_3 = 0.20,\ p_4 = 0.20, \text{ and } p_5 = 0.20 \\ \qquad \text{against} \\ \mathbf{H_a}: \text{Some } p_i \neq 0.20 \end{cases}$$

Based on this uniform production hypothesis by day of the week, all the expected values will be the same since the hypothesized proportions are the same.

$$\mathbf{E}_i = n \times \mathbf{c}_i = 250 \times \mathbf{0.20} = \mathbf{50}$$

$\forall$ i=1, 2, 3, 4 and 5

TABLE 33: Observed and (Expected) Number of Production Items by Day of the Week

M	TU	W	TH	F	Total
42 (50)	49 (50)	58 (50)	55 (50)	46 (50)	250 (250)

We then compute **Pearson's chi-square statistic** as:

$$\mathbb{R} = \sum_{i=1}^{r} \frac{(\mathbf{O}_i - \mathbf{E}_i)^2}{\mathbf{E}_i}$$

$$= \frac{(42-\mathbf{50})^2}{\mathbf{50}} + \frac{(49-\mathbf{50})^2}{\mathbf{50}} + \frac{(58-\mathbf{50})^2}{\mathbf{50}} + \frac{(55-\mathbf{50})^2}{\mathbf{50}} + \frac{(46-\mathbf{50})^2}{\mathbf{50}}$$

$$= 1.28 + 0.02 + 1.28 + 0.50 + 0.32$$

$$= 3.40$$

The critical value for this number of alternatives and level of significance is found in Table 27 as:

$$\chi^2_{\alpha;r-1} = \chi^2_{0.05;5-1} = 9.48773$$

Since $\Re = 3.4 < \chi^2_{0.05;3} = 9.48773$ then we fail reject H_0 and fail to conclude that worker productivity differs by day of the week. At this point the observed differences are within acceptable statistical variation and the phenomenon in this case seems little more than anecdotal.

Tests for Independence

Earlier in the semester we discussed the concepts of independent events and independent random variables. In some experimental settings, we need to test the hypothesis that the variables are independent against the alternative that they are not. In other words, based on empirical data obtained from an experiment, we need not make a blind assumption. The test for independence is also based on the chi-square distribution.

Let $\mathbf{X}$ and $\mathbf{Y}$ be two variables, which we want to study to determine whether it is reasonable to assume independence between them. Assume that $\mathbf{X}$ has $\utilde{\mathbf{r}}$ (rows) possible values, whereas $\mathbf{Y}$ has $\utilde{\mathbf{c}}$ (columns) possible values. We assume that each value of $\mathbf{X}$ can occur with each possible value of $\mathbf{Y}$. The pattern of cross-tabulation is known as an $\utilde{\mathbf{r}} \times \utilde{\mathbf{c}}$ contingency table as shown in Table 34 below.

Table 34: $\underset{\sim}{\mathbf{r}} \times \underset{\sim}{\mathbf{c}}$ Contingency Table

			Y			Row
		1	**2**		$\underset{\sim}{\mathbf{c}}$	total
	1	$\mathbf{O}_{11}$ $\mathbf{E}_{11}$	$\mathbf{O}_{12}$ $\mathbf{E}_{12}$	$\cdots$ $\cdots$	$\mathbf{O}_{1\underset{\sim}{c}}$ $\mathbf{E}_{1\underset{\sim}{c}}$	n_1
X	**2**	$\mathbf{O}_{21}$ $\mathbf{E}_{21}$	$\mathbf{O}_{22}$ $\mathbf{E}_{22}$	$\cdots$	$\mathbf{O}_{2\underset{\sim}{c}}$ $\mathbf{E}_{2\underset{\sim}{c}}$	n_2
		$\vdots$	$\vdots$		$\vdots$	
	$\underset{\sim}{\mathbf{r}}$	$\mathbf{O}_{\underset{\sim}{r}1}$ $\mathbf{E}_{\underset{\sim}{r}1}$	$\mathbf{O}_{\underset{\sim}{r}2}$ $\mathbf{E}_{\underset{\sim}{r}2}$	$\cdots$	$\mathbf{O}_{\underset{\sim}{r}\underset{\sim}{c}}$ $\mathbf{E}_{\underset{\sim}{r}\underset{\sim}{c}}$	$n_{\underset{\sim}{r}}$
Column	Total	m_1	m_2	$\cdots$	$m_{\underset{\sim}{c}}$	**N**

Note that $\underset{\sim}{\mathbf{r}}$ is the number of rows in the $\underset{\sim}{\mathbf{r}} \times \underset{\sim}{\mathbf{c}}$ contingency table and $\underset{\sim}{\mathbf{c}}$ is the corresponding number of columns. The random variable $\mathbf{O}_{ij}$ is the observed number in the cell formed by the ith row and j^{th} column or the count of the number of concurrences for which $\{\ \mathbf{X} = i\ \}$ and $\{\ \mathbf{Y} = j\ \}$. We assume that n_i is fixed for each $i = 1, \cdots, \underset{\sim}{\mathbf{r}}$. So that

$$\mathbf{Pr}\{\ \mathbf{X} = i\ \} = \frac{n_i}{\mathbf{N}} \text{ and } \mathbf{Pr}\{\ \mathbf{Y} = j\ \} = \frac{m_j}{\mathbf{N}}$$

where $\mathbf{N}$ is the total number of observations. The values $n_1, n_2, \cdots, n_{\underset{\sim}{r}}$ are known as the marginal totals for $\mathbf{X}$ whereas $m_1, m_2, \cdots, m_{\underset{\sim}{c}}$ are the marginal totals for $\mathbf{Y}$

If $\mathbf{X}$ and $\mathbf{Y}$ were independent, the expected number of observations in the ith row and j^{th} column is denoted by $\mathbf{E}_{ij}$. If $\mathbf{H_0}$ is true then

$$\begin{aligned} \mathbf{E}_{ij} &= \mathbf{N} \times \mathbf{Pr}\{(\mathbf{X} = i) \cap (\mathbf{Y} = j)\} \\ &= \mathbf{N} \times \mathbf{Pr}\{\ \mathbf{X} = i\ \} \times \mathbf{Pr}\{\ \mathbf{Y} = j\ \} \\ &= \mathbf{N} \times \frac{n_i}{\mathbf{N}} \times \frac{m_j}{\mathbf{N}} \\ &= \frac{n_i \times m_j}{\mathbf{N}} \end{aligned}$$

The number n_i is the **marginal total** for the ith **row** of the $r \times c$ **contingency table** and m_j is the **marginal total** for the jth **column**.

Formation of Hypotheses: We want to test

❖ $\begin{cases} \mathbf{H_0} : \mathbf{X} \text{ and } \mathbf{Y} \text{ are independent} \\ \quad \text{against} \\ \mathbf{H_a} : \mathbf{X} \text{ and } \mathbf{Y} \text{ are dependent} \end{cases}$

If $\mathbf{H_0}$ is true then we **would expect good agreement** between $\mathbf{O}_{ij}$ and $\mathbf{E}_{ij}$ for each $i = 1, \cdots, \underset{\sim}{\mathbf{r}}$ and each $j = 1, \cdots, \underset{\sim}{\mathbf{c}}$. The **test statistic** for this hypothesis is also called a **chi-square test statistic** and given by:

$$\mathbb{R} = \sum_{i=1}^{\underset{\sim}{\mathbf{r}}} \sum_{j=1}^{\underset{\sim}{\mathbf{c}}} \frac{\left(\mathbf{O}_{ij} - \mathbf{E}_{ij}\right)^2}{\mathbf{E}_{ij}}$$

Notice that if $\mathbf{H_0}$ $\mathrm{H_0}$ is true then the numerator of each term should be small and thus each would be made smaller though division by $\mathbf{E}_{ij}$. Thus **small values** of the test statistic **indicate good agreement** with the null hypothesis, whereas **large values indicate disagreement with the null**. In order to determine how large the test statistic must become we need to know the distribution of the test statistic when $\mathbf{H_0}$ is true. Under this assumption, it can be established that $\mathbb{R}$ has a chi-square distribution with $(\underset{\sim}{\mathbf{r}} - 1) \times (\underset{\sim}{\mathbf{c}} - 1)$ degrees of freedom. Consequently we reject $\mathbf{H_0}$ whenever

$$\mathbb{R} = \sum_{i=1}^{\underset{\sim}{\mathbf{r}}} \sum_{j=1}^{\underset{\sim}{\mathbf{c}}} \frac{\left(\mathbf{O}_{ij} - \mathbf{E}_{ij}\right)^2}{\mathbf{E}_{ij}} > \chi^2_{\alpha;(\underset{\sim}{\mathbf{r}}-1)\times(\underset{\sim}{\mathbf{c}}-1)} .$$

Example: Oil and Gas Lease Bids

In an effort to encourage bidding on leases on the Outer Continental Shelf (OCS), the US Geological Survey introduced a restriction known as the **three-bid rule**. If a lease does not have at least three bids, the USGS can withdraw the lease from sale when the **largest bid does not exceed a proxy value** set by the USGS.

The USGS began to suspect that **large oil companies were soliciting bids** from **smaller companies in order to circumvent the three-bid rule**. In other words, a large oil company might tender an offer on a lease and **solicit two smaller companies to submit token bids to evade the three-bid rule**. In 1984, the USGS conducted a major sale in the Gulf of Mexico. Suspicious bidding behavior was observed between Union Oil and Murphy-Odeco. In the 2×2 contingency table given below, we see the number of times that Union and Murphy bid on leases from the 1984 OCS lease in the Gulf of Mexico.

TABLE 35: Observed number of bids on oil & gas leases
Gulf of Mexico for Union Oil and Murphy-Odeco

		UNION		
		Bid	No Bid	Total
MURPHY	Bid	4	2	6
	No Bid	7	44	51
	Total	11	46	57

Thus $\mathbf{O}_{11} = 4$, $\mathbf{O}_{12} = 2$, $\mathbf{O}_{21} = 7$, and $\mathbf{O}_{22} = 44$ are the observed numbers of bids for each of the four bidding combinations. The totals $n_1 = 6$ and $n_2 = 51$ are the marginal totals for **Murphy** and $m_1 = 11$ and $m_2 = 46$ are the marginal totals for **Union Oil**.

Under the assumption that the **companies are bidding independently** we can calculated the **expected number of bids** for each of the 4 options.

$$\mathbf{E}_{11} = \frac{n_1 \times m_1}{\mathbf{N}} = \frac{6 \times 11}{57} = 1.16,\quad \mathbf{E}_{12} = \frac{n_1 \times m_2}{\mathbf{N}} = \frac{6 \times 46}{57} = 4.84,$$

$$\mathbf{E}_{21} = \frac{n_2 \times m_1}{\mathbf{N}} = \frac{51 \times 11}{57} = 9.84, \text{ and } \mathbf{E}_{22} = \frac{n_2 \times m_2}{\mathbf{N}} = \frac{51 \times 46}{57} = 41.16.$$

This produces the following **contingency table** that contains the **observed and the expected values** with the latter ones listed in parentheses.

TABLE 36: Observed and (Expected) number of bids on oil & gas leases
Gulf of Mexico for Union Oil and Murphy-Odeco

		UNION		
		Bid	No Bid	Total
MURPHY	Bid	4	2	6
		(1.16)	(4.84)	(6)
	No Bid	7	44	51
		(9.84)	(41.16)	(51)
	Total	11	46	57
		(11)	(46)	

Observe that the sum of the expected values for Murphy when bidding is (6), which is the marginal total. Notice that the expected numbers have the very nice aspect that the marginal totals for the expected numbers are the same as for the observed values. Since this always occurs, we could have simply found the first expected value and found the others by subtraction.

From these values, we can **compute the value of the chi-square test statistic** and compare the result with an **upper percentile** from a **chi-square distribution**.

$$\mathbb{R} = \sum_{i=1}^{2}\sum_{j=1}^{2}\frac{\left(\mathbf{O}_{ij}-\mathbf{E}_{ij}\right)^2}{\mathbf{E}_{ij}}$$

$$= \frac{(4-\mathbf{1.16})^2}{\mathbf{1.16}}+\frac{(2-\mathbf{4.84})^2}{\mathbf{4.84}}+\frac{(7-\mathbf{9.84})^2}{\mathbf{9.84}}+\frac{(44-\mathbf{41.16})^2}{\mathbf{41.16}}$$

$$= 6.95 + 1.67 + 0.82 + 0.20$$

$$= 9.64$$

This test statistic is to be compared with **an upper percentile** from the χ^2 distribution with $\mathbf{(\underset{\sim}{r}-1)\times(\underset{\sim}{c}-1)=(2-1)\times(2-1)=1}$ degree of freedom. Since the **level of significance was** chosen to be **5%**, then the **critical value** from Table 27 becomes $\chi^2_{0.05;1} = 3.841$.

Since $\mathbb{R} = 9.64 > \chi^2_{0.05;1} = 3.841$ then we **reject $\mathbf{H_0}$**, the null hypothesis that the bids of **Union Oil and Murphy are independent**. This conclusion **does not imply** that there is **collusion between Union and Murphy** but it certainly says that the **probability of that this bidding scheme occurred due to chance alone is less than 5%**.

Case Study: Pension Plan Preference

A company has three available pension plans for its employees. Management wants to determine whether the preference for plans is independent of job classification. The choices of 500 employees are shown below in Table 37.

TABLE 37: Cross Tabulation of Choice of Pension Plan by Job Classification

Classification\Plan	A	B	C	Total
Salaried Workers	160	140	40	340
Hourly Workers	40	60	60	160
Total	200	200	100	

Formation of hypotheses: We test the following hypotheses:

❖ $\mathbf{H_0}$: Choice of pension plan is independent of worker status
against
$\mathbf{H_a}$: Choice of pension plan depends on worker status

$$\mathbf{E}_{11} = \frac{340 \times 200}{500} = 136, \quad \mathbf{E}_{12} = \frac{340 \times 200}{500} = 136, \quad \mathbf{E}_{13} = \frac{340 \times 100}{500} = 68$$

$$\mathbf{E}_{21} = \frac{160 \times 200}{500} = 64, \quad \mathbf{E}_{22} = \frac{160 \times 200}{500} = 64, \text{ and } \mathbf{E}_{23} = \frac{160 \times 100}{500} = 32$$

TABLE 38: Cross Tabulation of Choice of Pension Plan (Observed and Expected) by Job Classification

Classification\Plan	A	B	C	Total
Salaried Workers	160 (136)	140 (136)	40 (68)	340 (340)
Hourly Workers	40 (64)	60 (64)	60 (32)	160 (160)
Total	200 (200)	200 (200)	100 (100)	

From these values, we compute the **value of the chi-square test statistic** as:

$$\sum_{i=1}^{\mathbf{r}} \sum_{j=1}^{\mathbf{c}} \frac{\left(\mathbf{O}_{ij} - \mathbf{E}_{ij}\right)^2}{\mathbf{E}_{ij}} = \frac{(160-136)^2}{136} + \frac{(140-136)^2}{136} + \frac{(40-68)^2}{68}$$

$$+ \frac{(40-64)^2}{64} + \frac{(60-64)^2}{64} + \frac{(60-32)^2}{32}$$

$$= 4.235 + 0.118 + 11.529$$

$$+ 9.000 + 0.250 + 24.500$$

$$= 49.632$$

This **test statistic** is **compared with an upper percentile** from the χ^2 **distribution** with $(\underset{\sim}{\mathbf{r}} - \mathbf{1}) \times (\underset{\sim}{\mathbf{c}} - \mathbf{1}) = (2-1) \times (3-1) = 2$ degrees of freedom. Since the **level of significance was chosen to be 5%** the critical value from Table 27 becomes $\chi^2_{0.05;2} = 5.991$. Since $\mathbb{R} = 49.632 > 5.991 = \chi^2_{0.05;2}$, we **reject $\mathbf{H_0}$ that choice of pension plan is independent of job classification** and **accept the alternative at the 5% level of significance**. We conclude that the **profile of pension plan preferences differs by job classification**.

Analysis of Variance

The technique known as analysis of variance (**ANOVA**) examines the variation in a response variable **Y** as a function of other variables known as factors, dosage levels, or treatment regimens. In essence, we want to determine the amount of **variation** in the **Y** – variable **that can be explained** by **knowing the factors** or treatments. These treatments may just be different levels of the same medication or they may be different medications altogether. This technique is used **when two or more groups are compared**.

This topic had its origins in agricultural experiments at the **Roth Amsted Experimental Station** in England and at **Iowa State University**. R.A. Fisher (1925) (see Johnson and Kotz (1997) page 99) pioneered the efforts in Great Britain while George Snedecor (see Johnson and Kotz (1997) page 339) pioneered efforts at Iowa State. It is a great tribute to the **creative genius of Fisher** that he developed almost all of his ideas in **experimental design** based on his scientific intuition. Much of the **mathematical foundation** of his ideas was later completed by **Jerzy Neyman** (see Johnson and Kotz (1997) page 137) and **Egon S. Pearson** (see Johnson and Kotz (1997) page 146), the son of the founder of modern statistical inference, Karl Pearson (see Johnson and Kotz (1997) page 150). It is now a widely used procedure in studies worldwide.

Consider an experiment in which the effectiveness of different levels of glucose on insulin release is tested among a cohort of animals, who are essentially homogeneous. Specimens of pancreatic tissue from these animals were treated with five (5) levels of glucose. A later determination was made to calculate the amount of insulin released.

Let **a** denote the number of treatments, in this case: the number of glucose levels; and let n_i denote the number of replicates per treatment.

TABLE 39: Rectangular plot layout columns - $\max\{n_i\}$

Rows (**a**)	Replicate **1**	Replicate **2**		Replicate n_i
Treatment **1**				
Treatment **2**				
⋮				
Treatment **a**				

We will test the experimental units, which are assigned randomly to the glucose levels. We **assume** that the animals, persons, or items **are homogeneous by important characteristics**, such weight, BMI, etc.

Let $\mathbf{Y}_{ij}$ represent the response, e.g., the **amount of insulin released**, from the pancreatic tissue of the jth **animal given** the ith **level of glucose**. We describe the observations from the preceding example by a **linear model**:

$$\mathbf{Y}_{ij} = \mu + \boldsymbol{\tau}_i + \boldsymbol{\varepsilon}_{ij}$$

for each $i = 1, \cdots, \mathbf{a}$ and $j = 1, \cdots, n_i$. The term $\boldsymbol{\varepsilon}_{ij}$ is the **random** or **experimental error** associated with using the ith treatment (glucose level), on the jth animal. The parameter μ represents the **overall (grand) mean effect** of all the treatments, e.g., glucose levels. The parameter $\mu + \boldsymbol{\tau}_i$ represents the **mean effect** of the ith **treatment** (glucose level). So the parameter $\boldsymbol{\tau}_i$ is the **differential effect**, i.e., above or below, of the ith **treatment with respect to the overall mean effect** μ. The differential treatment effects $\boldsymbol{\tau}_1, \boldsymbol{\tau}_2, \ldots, \boldsymbol{\tau}_\mathbf{a}$ are subject to the following constraint:

$$\sum_{i=1}^{\mathbf{a}} \boldsymbol{\tau}_i = 0$$

This constraint means that the parameter space of the differences is restricted and is at most of dimension $\mathbf{a}-\mathbf{1}$ or equivalently if one knows $\mathbf{a}-\mathbf{1}$ of the $\boldsymbol{\tau}_i^{'}\mathrm{s}$, the other can be obtained by **negating the sum** of the given $\boldsymbol{\tau}_i^{'}\mathrm{s}$. If there are no differences among the $\mathbf{a}$ treatments (i.e., the null hypothesis $\mathbf{H_0}$ that there are **no differences among the mean effects** of the blood glucose levels), then we would want to test:

$$\begin{cases} \bullet\ \mathbf{H_0} : \boldsymbol{\tau}_1 = \boldsymbol{\tau}_2 = \cdots = \boldsymbol{\tau}_\mathbf{a} = 0 \\ \qquad \text{versus} \\ \bullet\ \mathbf{H_a} : \boldsymbol{\tau}_i \neq 0 \text{ for some i} = \mathbf{1}, \ldots, \mathbf{a} \end{cases}$$

If we **fail to reject the null hypothesis, no further comparisons** can be made. However, if $\mathbf{H_0}$ is **rejected** then we proceed to **determine the differences among the groups**. This process is known as the **multiple comparisons procedure**.

ANOVA Assumptions

To test these hypotheses, we make certain assumptions about the random variables $\boldsymbol{\varepsilon}_{ij}$

- ε_{ij} are **independent** and **identically distributed** random variables

- ε_{ij} are normally distributed with mean zero
  - $\varepsilon_{ij} \sim N(0, \sigma)$

- **constant variance** σ^2 for each treatment group, known as the **homogeneity of variances** principle.

The **linear statistical model** given below is known as a **one-way classification model** for the analysis of variance:

$$Y_{ij} = \mu + \tau_i + \varepsilon_{ij}$$

The effects of the group may be fixed or random. The following presentation assumes that the effects are fixed.

The term $\bar{y}_{i\bullet}$ is the **sample mean** for the ith **treatment group**: the sample average of the **insulin releases** for the group given the ith level of glucose. The term $\bar{y}_{\bullet\bullet}$ is the **sample grand mean**, which is the **sample average** of **all the observations** regardless of group.

TABLE 40: **ANOVA Table**

Source	**df**	**SS**	**MS**	**F-ratio**
Treatment	a − 1	$\sum_{i=1}^{a} n_i(\bar{y}_{i\bullet} - \bar{y}_{\bullet\bullet})^2$	$\frac{SST}{(a-1)}$	$\frac{MST}{MSE}$
Error	N − a	$\sum_{i=1}^{a}\sum_{j=1}^{n_i}(y_{ij} - \bar{y}_{i\bullet})^2$	$\frac{SSE}{(N-a)}$	
Total	N − 1			

The **total sum of squares** $TSS = \sum_{i=1}^{a}\sum_{j=1}^{n_i}\left(y_{ij} - \bar{y}_{\bullet\bullet}\right)^2$ is the **total amount of variation in the responses**, the insulin releases, in the entire data set. In statistical circles, we say that this is the **amount of information** about the insulin releases contained in these data. The term **TSS** can be decomposed in two sums.

$$TSS = SST + SSE$$

All **the variation in the data** can be attributed to **effects between treatments** SST and **effects within treatments** SSE. The term SST quantifies the amount of variation in the *y*-values that can be **attributed to differences in group-means**, where **each group is weighted by the number**, n_i, of **observations** per group.

$$\mathbf{SST} = \sum_{i=1}^{\mathbf{a}} n_i (\bar{y}_{i\bullet} - \bar{y}_{\bullet\bullet})^2$$

So in the example of insulin releases, the **SST** quantifies the amount of variation that can be explained by knowing the (blood glucose) group. The other component of the total sum of squares is known as the **Sum of Squares for Error** (SSE). It is formally defined as:

$$\mathbf{SSE} = \sum_{i=1}^{\mathbf{a}} \sum_{j=1}^{n_i} (y_{ij} - \bar{y}_{i\bullet})^2 = \sum_{i=1}^{\mathbf{a}} (n_i - 1)\mathbf{s}_i^2$$

In this way, the term SSE sums the **variation within the groups**. The variation within the groups **does not explain differences among the sample averages of the groups**. Under the ANOVA assumptions, it follows that

$$\frac{\mathbf{SSE}}{\sigma^2} \sim \chi^2(\mathbf{N}-\mathbf{a})$$

has a **chi-square distribution** with $\mathbf{N}-\mathbf{a}$ degrees of freedom. This distribution for SSE is valid under the ANOVA assumptions **whether the means are different by group or not**. The term mean squares for error MSE is found by **dividing the sum of squares for error** by the corresponding **degrees of freedom** $\mathbf{N}-\mathbf{a}$. If $\mathbf{H}_0$ is true $\boldsymbol{\tau}_1 = \boldsymbol{\tau}_2 = \cdots = \boldsymbol{\tau}_{\mathbf{a}} = 0$ then it also follows that:

$$\frac{\mathbf{SST}}{\sigma^2} \sim \chi^2(\mathbf{a}-\mathbf{1})$$

SST has a chi-square distribution with $\mathbf{a}-\mathbf{1}$ degrees of freedom. The MST term mean squares for treatments is found by **dividing the sum of squares for treatments** SST by the **corresponding degrees of freedom** $\mathbf{a}-\mathbf{1}$.

From Cochran's theorem, it follows that SST and SSE are **independently distributed**. Snedecor (1937) derived the distribution known as the **F-ratio**, which is the **quotient of the mean squares**:

$$\mathbf{F\text{-}ratio} = \frac{\mathbf{MST}}{\mathbf{MSE}} \sim F(\mathbf{a}-\mathbf{1}; \mathbf{N}-\mathbf{a})$$

The $\mathbf{F\text{-}ratio}$ has Snedecor's (1937) F – distribution with $\mathbf{a-1}$ numerator and $\mathbf{N-a}$ denominator degrees of freedom. We reject $\mathbf{H_0}$ that all groups have the same mean provided:

$$\mathbf{F\text{-}ratio} = \frac{\mathbf{MST}}{\mathbf{MSE}} > F_{\alpha;\,\mathbf{a\text{-}1,\,N\text{-}a}}$$

Notice that α is the **level of significance of the test**. This value is the probability of rejecting the null hypothesis $\mathbf{H_0}$ when it is true.

If $\mathbf{H_0}$ is false, the **mean squares** for **treatments** would be **significantly greater than the mean squares** for **error** implying that the **dispersion among the treatment means** was **significantly larger** than the **dispersion within the treatment groups**. Examining the expected mean squares for treatments and for errors, one can also see this:

$$\mathbf{E}\left[\mathbf{MSE}\right] = \sigma^2 \quad \text{and} \quad \mathbf{E}[\mathbf{MST}] = \sigma^2 + \frac{\sum_{i=1}^{\mathbf{a}} n_i \boldsymbol{\tau}_i^2}{\mathbf{a-1}}$$

Under $\mathbf{H_0}$ both expected mean squares would be σ^2. However, if $\mathbf{H_0}$ is false then we would expect that $\mathbf{E}\left[\mathbf{MSE}\right] << \mathbf{E}[\mathbf{MST}]$

Example: Insulin Analysis

Consider an experiment in which insulin releases from pancreatic tissues are measured as a response to a glucose level. The data in Table 41 form a data set:

TABLE 41: Insulin release data as function of each of 5 glucose level

n\a	1	2	3	4	5
1	1.53	3.15	3.89	8.18	5.86
2	1.61	3.96	4.80	5.64	5.46
3	3.75	3.59	3.69	7.36	5.69
4	2.89	1.89	5.70	5.33	6.49
5	3.26	1.45	5.62	5.26	7.81
6	2.83	3.49	5.79	.	9.03
7	2.86	1.56	4.75	.	.
8	2.59	2.44	.	.	.
$\bar{y}_{i\bullet}$	2.665	2.691	4.891	6.354	6.723
s_i^2	0.579	0.970	0.744	1.775	1.993
n_i	8	8	7	5	6

These data produce the following ANOVA Table:

TABLE 42: ANOVA table Insulin release values by glucose level

Source	**df**	**SS**	**MS**	**F-ratio**	**F-critical**
Glucose	4	100.6041	25.1510	22.53	2.7014
Error	29	32.3788	1.1165		
Total	33				

The 95th **percentile** from an $F-$**distribution with 4 and 29 degrees of freedom** is given as $F_{0.05;4,29} = 2.7014$ and called the **critical value of the** $F-$**test** or $F-$**critical**. The $\mathbf{p}-\text{value}$ is the smallest value of α for which we would reject $\mathbf{H_0}$. An algorithm was used to estimate the $\mathbf{p}-\text{value} = 1.5\times10^{-8}$ and allows us to quantify *"how likely the groups are significantly different."*

At this point, there are significant differences in insulin releases among the glucose levels. Our next step is to determine where the differences occur.

Multiple Comparisons Problem

Provided the null hypothesis $\mathbf{H_0}: \boldsymbol{\tau}_1 = \boldsymbol{\tau}_2 = \cdots = \boldsymbol{\tau}_a = 0$ is rejected, the clinician would like to determine **which treatments are different** and which ones are indistinguishable at the **5% level of significance**. The traditional method of **comparing differences in means** is conducted via a $t-$test.

To test $\mathbf{H_0}: \boldsymbol{\tau}_m = \boldsymbol{\tau}_k$ versus $\mathbf{H_a}: \boldsymbol{\tau}_m \neq \boldsymbol{\tau}_k$ for some m and k, $m \neq k$, reject $\mathbf{H_0}$ provided:

$$\left|\bar{y}_{m\bullet} - \bar{y}_{k\bullet}\right| > t_{\alpha/2;\mathbf{N-a}} \times \sqrt{\mathbf{MSE} \times \left(\frac{1}{n_m} + \frac{1}{n_k}\right)} = \mathbf{LSD}$$

The term involving the **upper** $100\times(1-\alpha/2)\%$ **percentile from a** $t-$**distribution** and the **principal square root is** known as the **least significant difference** ($\mathbf{LSD}$). The $\mathbf{LSD}$ technique works as follows. If the **absolute difference between** two **treatment means exceeds the** $\mathbf{LSD}$, then the **two effects judged to be significantly different**. The $\mathbf{LSD}$ technique has a **Type I error rate of** α **per comparison**. When the **method is applied to all possible paired comparisons, the experiment-wide Type I error rate is uncontrolled**. Arrange the groups in decreasing order of by sample averages and then forming an upper triangular table, Table 43, of paired comparisons.

TABLE 43: Upper Triangular Paired Mean Differences

m/k	5	4	3	2	1
5		0.369	**1.832**	**4.032**	**4.058**
4			**1.463**	**3.663**	**3.689**
3				**2.200**	**2.226**
2					0.026
1					

The term in the ith row and j^{th} column of Table 43 is:

$$\overline{y}_{m\bullet} - \overline{y}_{k\bullet}, \text{ for } m > k$$

To compute **LSD** in this setting, we compute that $t_{0.025;29} = 2.0452$ and $\sqrt{\mathbf{MSE}} = 1.05665$. The **LSD** only varies according to the sample sizes of the two groups as shown in Table 44 below. The **absolute differences that exceed the corresponding LSD thresholds** are shaded and boldfaced in Table 43.

TABLE 44: Paired t-Test Critical values (LSD)

m/k	4	3	2	1
5	1.309	1.202	1.167	1.167
4		1.265	1.232	1.232
3			1.118	1.118
2				1.081

These paired comparisons produce the following summary results that break the groups into three significantly different groups:

Groups 5 and 4, Group 3, and Groups 2 and 1, can be treated as being indistinguishable based on the LSD comparisons.

<u>5 4</u> <u>3</u> <u>2 1</u>

In the process of making these *10*-paired comparisons, we lost control of the experiment-wide Type I error rate. We made ten paired comparisons each if which had a 5% level of significance.

We can compare all the differences and maintain control on the experiment-wide Type I error rate using an adaptation of the t – test in conjunction with *Bonferroni's inequality*. Suppose that α is the overall (experiment-wide) Type I error rate of all k paired tests. Then if α_0 is the individual level of significance of each paired comparison then

$$1-\alpha \le (1-\alpha_0)^k$$

$$\alpha_0 \le 1-(1-\alpha)^{1/k}$$

In our example, $\alpha = 0.05$ and $k = 10$ then

$$\alpha_0 \le 1-(1-\alpha)^{1/k} = 1-(1-0.05)^{1/10} = 0.0051162$$

The **Bonferroni LSD** is then formed by

$$\mathbf{BLSD} = t_{\alpha_0/2;\mathbf{N\text{-}a}} \times \sqrt{\mathbf{MSE} \times \left(\frac{1}{n_m} + \frac{1}{n_k}\right)}$$

This test is also known as **Dunn's test**. Using her adaptation to **adjust the individual significance level** of the paired comparisons so as to limit the **experiment-wide Type I error rate** to 5%, we determine that the t – value should be adjusted to ***3.038**** as opposed to 2.045 without adjustment.

The subsequent BLSD threshold values for different paired comparisons are:

TABLE 45: Critical Values for Dunn's Test (**BLSD**)

m/k	4	3	2	1
5	1.945	1.786	1.734	1.734
4		1.879	1.830	1.830
3			1.661	1.661
2				1.606

TABLE 46: Significant upper triangular paired mean differences based on an experiment wide level of significance

m/k	5	4	3	2	1
5		0.369	**1.832**	**4.032**	**4.058**
4			1.463	**3.663**	**3.689**
3				**2.200**	**2.226**
2					0.026
1					

This more conservative approach separates the data into larger groups formed by Groups 5, 4, and 3 and Groups 2 and 1. Herein, we conclude that *Group 3 is indistinguishable from Group 4 and as are Groups 5 and 4*, thus producing a more conservative result.

5 4 3 2 1

Note: A shortcut formula for the Bonferroni adjustment can be found by using

$$\alpha_0 \cong \frac{\alpha}{k}$$

used by many major statistical packages such as SAS. The differences in population mean by glucose level can be demonstrated through the following boxplot of the data. In Figure 57, the Glucose Levels 4 and 5 have been connected by their common means, since the multiple comparisons indicated no difference. The same is true for Levels 1 and 2. Notice that the quartile boxes overlap for Levels 3 and 4 and the issue of whether insulin levels differ or not levels 3 and 4.

FIGURE 57: Boxplot of Insulin response data by glucose level

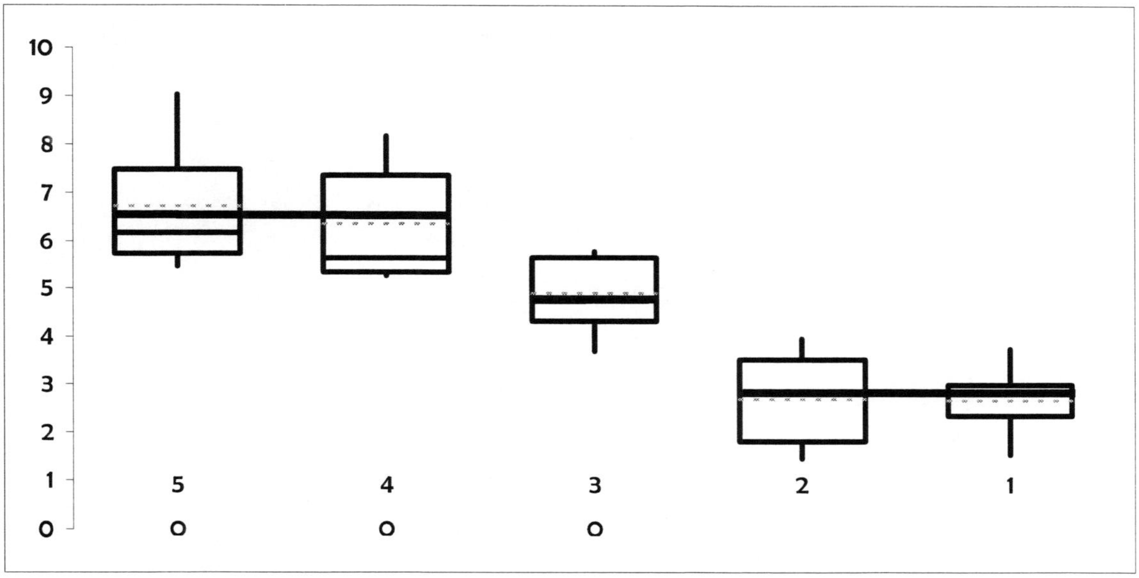

Checking ANOVA Assumptions

The assumption of equal variances for each treatment group may cause serious problems if violated. The test for "*homogeneity of variances*" is known as **Bartlett's test**. Suppose that there are **a** treatment groups and we test

$$\begin{cases} \bullet\ \mathbf{H_0}: \sigma_1^2 = \sigma_2^2 = \cdots = \sigma_{\mathbf{a}}^2 \\ \textbf{against} \\ \bullet\ \mathbf{H_a}: \sigma_m^2 \neq \sigma_k^2 \text{ for some } m \neq k \end{cases}$$

The uniformly most powerful test of size α for testing for equality of variance is Bartlett's test and its test statistic is given by

$$\ell_1^* = \frac{\prod_{i=1}^{a} (S_i^2)^{r_i}}{\sum_{i=1}^{a} r_i S_i^2}$$

where $r_i = (n_i - 1)/(\mathbf{N} - \mathbf{a})$. The complex expression for the test statistic is the ratio of the **weighted geometric mean** of the **sample variances** of the treatments to their **weighted arithmetic mean**. For the insulin data, the following useful summary of values used in the computation of Bartlett's test statistic.

TABLE 47: Sample variances and weights for the Insulin response data

i	s_i^2	r_i
5	0.579143	0.241379
4	0.970212	0.241379
3	0.744448	0.206897
2	1.77538	0.137931
1	1.993027	0.172414

By substituting these values into the formula, we obtain

$$\ell_1^* = \frac{0.9979}{1.1165} = 0.8938$$

Critical values $\mathbf{b}_\alpha(\mathbf{a}, n)$ of Bartlett's test are given in Table 54 for cases in which the **sample sizes are equal**. These values are taken from Dyer and Keating (1980) for various values of $\mathbf{a}$, the number of groups, and n, the **common sample size**. If the sample sizes are not equal, we can use the **Dyer-Keating approximation** to the critical values (see Madansky 1989)

$$\mathbf{b}_\alpha(\mathbf{a}; n_1, \cdots, n_\mathbf{a}) \doteq \sum_{i=1}^{\mathbf{a}} \frac{n_i}{\mathbf{N}} \times \mathbf{b}_\alpha(\mathbf{a}, n_i)$$

So for the insulin release data, we have the following values:

$$\begin{aligned}\mathbf{b}_{0.05}(\mathbf{5}; 6,5,7,8,8) &\doteq \frac{6}{34}\mathbf{b}_{0.05}(\mathbf{5};6) + \frac{5}{34}\mathbf{b}_{0.05}(\mathbf{5};5) + \frac{7}{34}\mathbf{b}_{0.05}(\mathbf{5};7) + \frac{8}{34}\mathbf{b}_{0.05}(\mathbf{5};8) + \frac{8}{34}\mathbf{b}_{0.05}(\mathbf{5};8) \\ &= \frac{6}{34}0.6646 + \frac{5}{34}0.5952 + \frac{7}{34}0.7142 + \frac{8}{34}0.7512 + \frac{8}{34}0.7512 \\ &= 0.7054\end{aligned}$$

Since $\ell_1^* = 0.8938 > 0.7054 = \mathbf{b}_{0.05}(\mathbf{5}; 6,5,7,8,8)$ there is not enough evidence to reject the null hypothesis of equal variances at the 5% level of significance.

Example: Material Transfer Methods

Three methods are available to transfer materials from one location to another. Each approach is tried several different times and observed times in hours are listed below:

TABLE 48: Transfer Times by Method

	A	B	C
1	8.2	7.9	7.1
2	7.1	8.1	7.4
3	7.8	8.3	6.9
4	8.9	8.5	6.8
5	8.8	7.6	
6		8.5	
$\bar{y}_{i\bullet}$	8.16	8.15	7.05
s_i^2	0.553	0.127	0.070
n_i	5	6	4

Using the formulas given earlier we produce the following ANOVA table:

TABLE 49: ANOVA Table by Transfer Method

Source	**df**	**SS**	**MS**	**F-ratio**	**F-critical**
Method	2	3.579	1.7895	7.025	5.096
Error	12	3.057	0.25475		
Total	14				

The 95th percentile from an $F-$distribution with *2* and *12* degrees of freedom is given as $F-critical = 5.09587$. The $p-value$ is the smallest value of alpha for which we would reject $\mathbf{H_0}$ with $p-value$ is 0.01911. At this point, there are significant differences in mean times among the three methods. Our next step is to determine where the differences occur.

Multiple Comparisons Problem

To test $\mathbf{H_0}: \boldsymbol{\tau}_m = \boldsymbol{\tau}_k$ versus $\mathbf{H_a}: \boldsymbol{\tau}_m \neq \boldsymbol{\tau}_k$ for some m and k, $m \neq k$, reject $\mathbf{H_0}$ if:

$$\left|\bar{y}_{m\bullet} - \bar{y}_{k\bullet}\right| > t_{\alpha/2;\mathbf{N\text{-}a}} \times \sqrt{\mathbf{MSE} \times \left(\frac{1}{n_m} + \frac{1}{n_k}\right)} = \mathbf{LSD}$$

We begin by arranging the groups in decreasing order of by sample averages and then forming an upper triangular table of paired comparisons.

Table 50: Paired mean differences of transfer times by method

m/k	A	B	C
A	-	0.01	**1.11**
B		-	**1.10**
C			-

To compute **Fisher's LSD** in this setting, note that $t_{0.025;12} = 2.56$ from Table 27 and $\sqrt{\mathbf{MSE}} = 0.5047$. The LSD varies according to the sample sizes of the compared groups as shown in the table below. The absolute differences that exceed the corresponding LSD thresholds are shaded and in **bold** type in Table 50.

TABLE 51: LSD critical values for different paired comparisons

m/k	B	C
A	0.7824	0.8668
B		0.8341

These paired comparisons produce the following summary results, that break the groups into three significantly different groups: Groups A and B, and Group C, can be treated as being indistinguishable based on the LSD comparisons.

A B C

In the process of making these *3*-paired comparisons, we lost control of the experiment-wide Type I error rate. We made three paired comparisons, each which had a 5% level of significance.

We can compare all the differences and maintain control on the **experiment-wide Type I error rate** using an adaptation of the *t*-test in conjunction with the **Bonferroni inequality**. In our example, $\alpha = 0.05$ and $k = 3$ then

$$\alpha_0 \leq 1-(1-\alpha)^{1/k} = 1-(1-0.05)^{1/3} = 0.01695$$

The Bonferroni-(**LSD**) is then formed for each pair of methods by

$$\mathbf{BLSD} = t_{\alpha_0/2;\mathbf{N\text{-}a}} \times \sqrt{\mathbf{MSE} \times \left(\frac{1}{n_m} + \frac{1}{n_k}\right)}$$

To limit the Type I error rate to 5%, we determine that the t-value should be adjusted to **3.1435** as opposed to 2.56 without adjustment.

TABLE 52: **BLSD** critical values for different paired comparisons

m/k	B	C
A	0.9608	1.0643
B		1.0242

This more conservative approach separates the data into the same two groups but does so by more conservative means.

A B C (A and B underlined together; C underlined separately)

We conclude at the 5% level of significance that method C uses less time than methods A or B. Checking assumption of equal variances, we see in Table 53:

TABLE 53: Variances and weights by method of transfer

i	S_i^2	r_i
A	0.553	0.33333
B	0.127	0.41667
C	0.070	0.25000

By substituting these values into the formula for the test statistic, we obtain

$$\ell_1^* = \frac{(0.553)^{0.33333} \times (0.127)^{0.41667} \times (0.07)^{0.25}}{0.33333 \times (0.553) + (0.41667) \times (0.127) + (0.25) \times (0.07)}$$

$$= \frac{0.1787}{0.2547}$$

$$= 0.7016$$

Since the sample sizes are unequal, one can use the **Dyer-Keating approximation** and for the time-to-transfer method data, the following values from Table 54:

$$\mathbf{b}_{0.05}(\mathbf{3}; 5, 6, 4) \doteq \frac{5}{15}\mathbf{b}_{0.05}(\mathbf{3}; 5) + \frac{6}{15}\mathbf{b}_{0.05}(\mathbf{3}; 6) + \frac{4}{15}\mathbf{b}_{0.05}(\mathbf{3}; 4)$$

$$= \frac{1}{3}0.5762 + \frac{2}{5}0.6483 + \frac{4}{15}0.4699$$

$$= 0.5767$$

At the 5% level of significance, there is not enough evidence to reject the null hypothesis of equal variances.

Case Study: Keating Power Consumption

From page 32, we asked if you could detect any patterns in these data based on the descriptive statistics. Try plotting the sample average by month. The descriptive statistics are given in the Table A1 below.

TABLE A1: Descriptive statistics for power consumption by month Keating electrical data 1983-1998

Statistic	JAN	FEB	MAR	APR	MAY	JUN	JUL	AUG	SEP	OCT	NOV	DEC
Mean	47.99	42.74	31.45	29.69	38.38	50.74	57.02	54.10	46.18	32.18	28.51	39.83
Median	46.11	40.93	30.98	30.09	37.78	50.09	57.18	52.71	46.60	33.02	28.28	37.22
Standard Deviation	5.96	5.18	3.28	3.27	5.07	6.82	5.98	4.66	4.02	4.82	4.40	8.87
Sample Variance	35.57	26.82	10.73	10.72	25.65	46.50	35.73	21.70	16.14	23.19	19.39	78.63
Range	19.68	18.39	13.38	13.50	21.58	24.17	21.04	16.00	11.62	17.93	19.74	30.20
Minimum	37.00	37.03	25.52	24.43	27.90	38.93	45.09	47.72	40.07	23.79	19.91	30.90
Maximum	56.68	55.42	38.90	37.93	49.48	63.09	66.13	63.72	51.69	41.72	39.645	61.10
Size	16	16	16	16	16	16	16	16	16	16	16	16

We plot the sample average and sample median by month in Figure A1. We found a typical seasonal pattern of electrical usage, in which power consumption increases in the summer months (June, July August, and September), declines in the fall months (October & November) increases again in the winter months, (December and January) and declines again in the spring months (March & April). You would not be surprised to know then that our house is equipped to heat with electricity. This would explain the increase in electrical usage in the winter months. Had we heated with another source such as natural gas, we would not anticipate such an increase in our electrical use during winter months.

FIGURE A1: Plot of average and median power consumption by month:

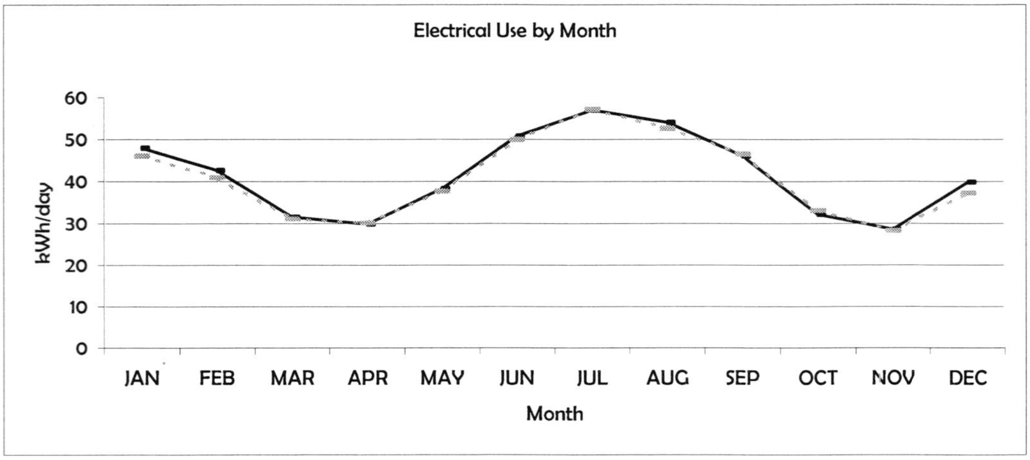

The seasonal pattern is virtually identical whether one uses the sample mean or sample median. In this regard it is clearer to see that these measures of central tendency produce the same monthly pattern. A boxplot adds further evidence to the analysis of these data.

FIGURE A2: Boxplots of power consumption by month

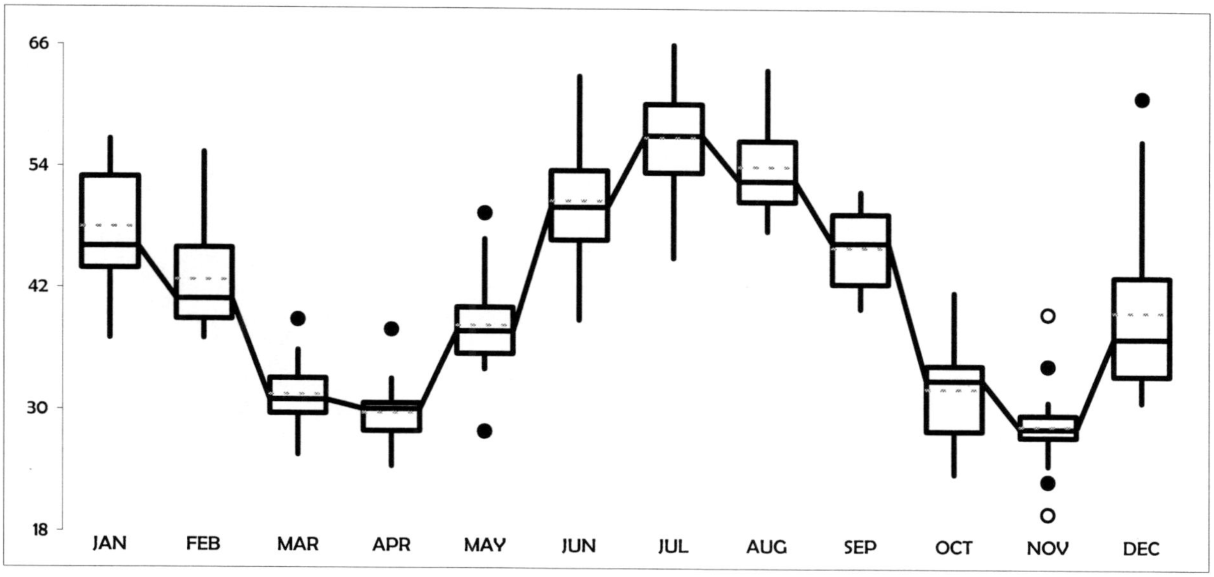

These plots would be very useful to the energy provider, City Public Service (CPS), in estimating demand and therefore production capacity on daily basis. Since inadequate power consumption might result in black out conditions, wherein everyone would be without electricity, the power company will focus on maximum power consumption. The City of San Antonio owns part of the South Texas Nuclear Plant, a source that augments supply especially during peak usage periods such as June through September. The facility must be shout down annually for inspection and cleanup. The months of March, April, October, or November would be good candidates for the closure. The month with the smallest maximum would be the choice of CPS.

FIGURE A3: Electrical Use by Year Keating Data 1983-1998

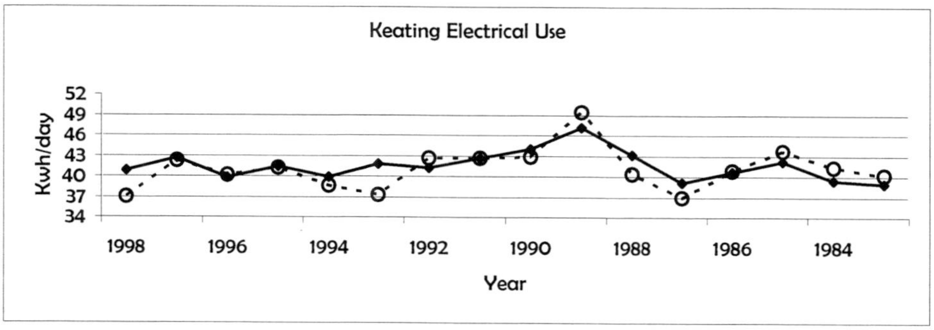

FIGURE A4: Scott's Frequency Polygon: Keating Data

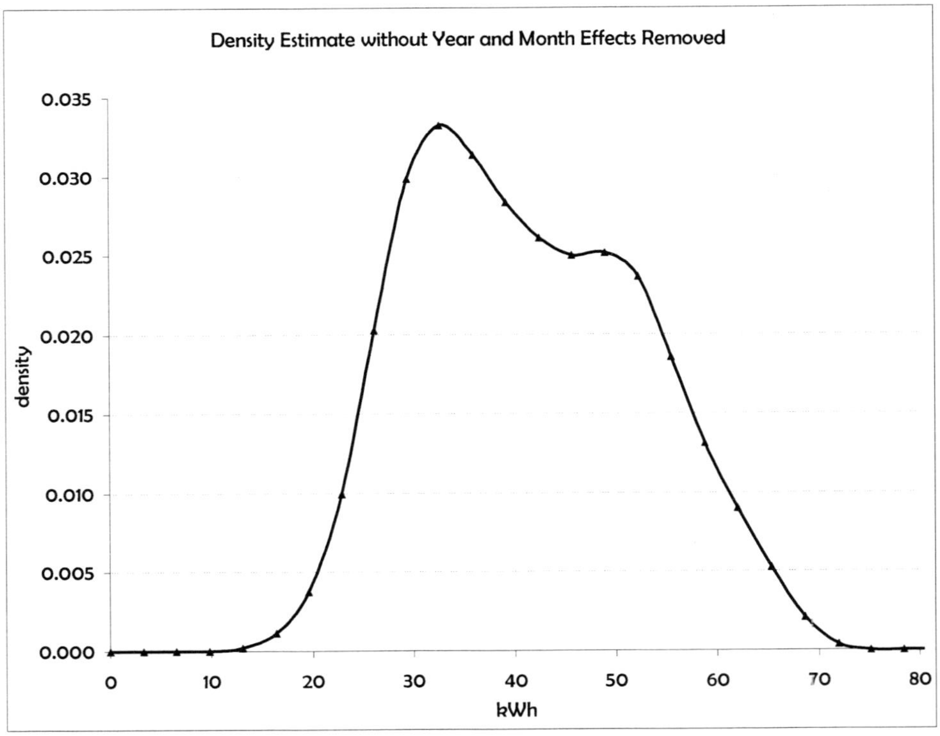

We produce the following ANOVA table:

TABLE A2: ANOVA Table by Month

Source	**df**	**SS**	**MS**	**F-ratio**	**F-critical**
Month	11	18,425.27	1,674.115	51.509	1.839
Error	192	6,240.32	32.502		
Total	203	24,655.58			

The 95th percentile from an $F-$distribution with *11* and *192* **degrees of freedom** is given as $F-critical=1.839$. The $p-value$ is 2.56×10^{-51}. At this point, there are significant differences in mean electrical use among the twelve months.

Multiple Comparisons by Month

We can compare all the differences and maintain control on the **experiment-wide Type I error rate** using an adaptation of the *t*-test in conjunction with the **Bonferroni inequality**. In our example, $\alpha=0.05$ and $k=66$ then

$$\alpha_0\leq1-(1-\alpha)^{1/k}=1-(1-0.05)^{1/66}=0.000777$$

The Bonferroni-$(\mathbf{LSD})$ is then formed for each pair of methods by

$$\text{BLSD} = t_{0.000388;192} \times \sqrt{\text{MSE} \times \left(\frac{1}{16} + \frac{1}{16}\right)}$$

$$= 3.4155 \times 5.701 \times 0.35355$$

$$= 6.884$$

This more conservative approach separates the data into multiple groups by conservative means in the ordered hierarchical fashion given below.

1) JUL – AUG – JUN

2) JUN – JAN – SEP

3) **JAN – SEP – FEB**

4) **SEP – FEB – DEC**

5) **FEB – DEC – MAY**

6) **MAY – OCT**

7) OCT – MAR – APR – NOV

We conclude at the 5% level of significance that the household electrical use is not significantly different for July, August and June, for June, January and September, for January, September and February, for September, February and December, for February, December and May, for May and October, and for October, March, April and November.

Months	JUL	AUG	JUN	JAN	SEP	FEB	DEC	MAY	OCT	MAR	APR	NOV
JUL	-	2.38	5.82	9.56	10.63	15.15	17.25	18.30	24.72	25.85	27.27	28.78
AUG		-	3.44	7.18	8.25	12.77	14.87	15.92	22.34	23.47	24.89	26.40
JUN			-	3.74	4.81	9.33	11.43	12.48	18.90	20.03	21.45	22.96
JAN				-	1.07	5.59	7.69	8.74	15.16	16.29	17.71	19.22
SEP					-	4.52	6.62	7.67	14.10	15.23	16.65	18.15
FEB						-	2.10	3.15	9.57	10.70	12.12	13.63
DEC							-	1.05	7.47	8.60	10.02	11.53
MAY								-	6.42	7.55	8.97	10.48
OCT									-	1.13	2.55	4.06
MAR										-	1.42	2.93
APR											-	1.51

Notice that the primary group of March, April, October, and November form the first mode in Scott's frequency polygon around an average electrical use of 30 kWh/day. These are months when we did not use heating or air conditioning. The secondary mode in the frequency polygon is due mostly to the summer months of July, August and June.

TABLE 54: **Bartlett Test Critical Values** (5% level)

	Number of Populations, a								
n	**2**	**3**	**4**	**5**	**6**	**7**	**8**	**9**	**10**
3	.3123	.3058	.3173	.3299	.	.	.	.	.
4	.4780	.4699	.4803	.4921	.5028	.5122	.5204	.5277	.5341
5	.5845	.5762	.5850	.5952	.6045	.6126	.6197	.6260	.6315
6	.6563	.6483	.6559	.6646	.6727	.6798	.6860	.6914	.6961
7	.7075	.7000	.7065	.7142	.7213	.7275	.7329	.7376	.7418
8	.7456	.7387	.7444	.7512	.7574	.7629	.7677	.7719	.7757
9	.7751	.7686	.7737	.7798	.7854	.7903	.7946	.7984	.8017
10	.7984	.7924	.7970	.8025	.8076	.8121	.8160	.8194	.8224
11	.8175	.8118	.8160	.8210	.8257	.8298	.8333	.8365	.8392
12	.8332	.8280	.8317	.8364	.8407	.8444	.8477	.8506	.8531
13	.8465	.8415	.8450	.8493	.8533	.8568	.8598	.8625	.8648
14	.8578	.8532	.8564	.8604	.8641	.8673	.8701	.8726	.8748
15	.8676	.8632	.8662	.8699	.8734	.8764	.8790	.8814	.8834
16	.8761	.8719	.8747	.8782	.8815	.8843	.8868	.8890	.8909
17	.8836	.8796	.8823	.8856	.8886	.8913	.8936	.8957	.8975
18	.8902	.8865	.8890	.8921	.8949	.8975	.8997	.9016	.9033
19	.8961	.8926	.8949	.8979	.9006	.9030	.9051	.9069	.9086
20	.9015	.8980	.9003	.9031	.9057	.9080	.9100	.9117	.9132
21	.9063	.9030	.9051	.9078	.9103	.9124	.9143	.9160	.9175
22	.9106	.9075	.9095	.9120	.9144	.9165	.9183	.9199	.9213
23	.9146	.9116	.9135	.9159	.9182	.9202	.9219	.9235	.9248
24	.9182	.9153	.9172	.9195	.9217	.9236	.9253	.9267	.9280
25	.9216	.9187	.9205	.9228	.9249	.9267	.9283	.9297	.9309
26	.9246	.9219	.9236	.9258	.9278	.9296	.9311	.9325	.9336
27	.9275	.9249	.9265	.9286	.9305	.9322	.9337	.9350	.9361
28	.9301	.9276	.9292	.9312	.9330	.9347	.9361	.9374	.9385
29	.9326	.9301	.9316	.9336	.9354	.9370	.9383	.9396	.9406
30	.9348	.9325	.9340	.9358	.9376	.9391	.9404	.9416	.9426
40	.9513	.9495	.9506	.9520	.9533	.9545	.9555	.9564	.9572
50	.9612	.9597	.9606	.9617	.9628	.9637	.9645	.9652	.9658
60	.9677	.9665	.9672	.9681	.9690	.9698	.9705	.9710	.9716
80	.9758	.9749	.9754	.9761	.9768	.9774	.9779	.9783	.9787
100	.9807	.9799	.9804	.9809	.9815	.9819	.9823	.9827	.9830

Regression Analysis

The regression problem dates back to the beginning of the 19th century. Adrian Marie Legendre (1805) is credited with the first published article on this method. Karl Friedrich Gauss (see Johnson and Kotz (1997) page 361) later claimed that he invented the method a decade earlier in 1795. Since Gauss did not publish his works such a claim was difficult to dispute. However, Stephen Stigler (1986), based on an examination of Gauss's private papers, acknowledges that Gauss dabbled with the method but did not complete his ideas until 1809.

The regression problem stems from a fundamental question: Given a set of paired observations:

$$(x_1, y_1),\ (x_2, y_2),\ \ldots,\ (x_n, y_n)$$

Can we reasonably fit a straight line to these data?

It is conventional in these methods to use the slope-intercept form for the equation of a straight line:

$$y = \boldsymbol{\beta}_0 + \boldsymbol{\beta}_1 x + \boldsymbol{\varepsilon}$$

where $\boldsymbol{\beta}_0$ is the $y-$intercept $\boldsymbol{\beta}_1$ is the slope of the straight line and $\boldsymbol{\varepsilon}$ is the random or unexplained error.

Regression Assumptions

To test hypotheses and make inferences, we make certain assumptions about the random errors or variables $\boldsymbol{\varepsilon}_i$ where $\boldsymbol{\varepsilon}_i$ is the random error

$$y_i = \boldsymbol{\beta}_0 + \boldsymbol{\beta}_1 x_i + \boldsymbol{\varepsilon}_i$$

- $\boldsymbol{\varepsilon}_i$ are **independent and identically** distributed random variables
- $\boldsymbol{\varepsilon}_i$ are **normally distributed** with mean zero and
  - $\boldsymbol{\varepsilon}_i \sim \mathrm{N}(0, \sigma)$
- **constant variance**, σ^2, the variance remains constant across all values of x and is known as the **homogeneity of variances principle**.

Recall that the $y-$intercept $\boldsymbol{\beta}_0$ is simply the value of y when $x = 0$. Also the slope is

FIGURE 58: A Straight Line Plot

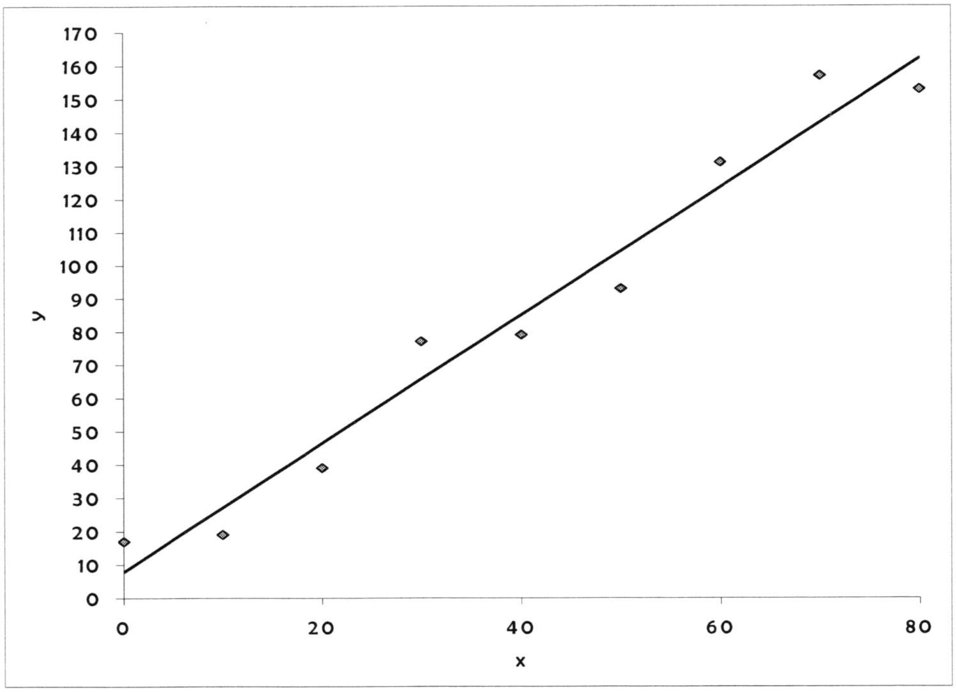

$$\boldsymbol{\beta}_1 = \frac{\Delta y}{\Delta x}$$

If we plotted the points and drew lines through the points, we would have many different lines, perhaps a unique one for each of us. So not only is there a way to draw a straight line, but also is there a way to do so objectively?

Method of Least Squares

The method for choosing the best line follows the "method of least squares." The technique says to choose estimates $\mathbf{b}_0$ and $\mathbf{b}_1$ of $\boldsymbol{\beta}_0$ and $\boldsymbol{\beta}_1$ to minimize the sum of squares for error. The **estimated error**, or **residual**, made for the ith-ordered pair (x_i, y_i) in using a prediction line $\hat{y} = \mathbf{b}_0 + \mathbf{b}_1 x$ will be the difference between the **observed value of** y_i **and the predicted value of** $\hat{y}_i$, which is $\mathbf{b}_0 + \mathbf{b}_1 x_i$ (vertical difference).

$$r_i = y_i - \hat{y}_i = y_i - \left(\mathbf{b}_0 + \mathbf{b}_1 x_i\right)$$

This magnitude $|r_i|$ is the **vertical difference** in the **observed** and **predicted** y – values or the **vertical deviation of the point from the line**. This error can either be positive or negative depending upon whether the observed value of y lies above the value predicted by the line of best fit or below that line. In order for these errors not to cancel, we square each error and thus make them additive. The **sum of these squared errors**, known as $\mathbf{SSE}$, is given by

$$\mathbf{SSE} = \sum \left(y_i - \left[\mathbf{b}_0 + \mathbf{b}_1 x_i \right] \right)^{\mathbf{2}}$$

Since the size of $\mathbf{SSE}$ is dependent upon our choices of $\mathbf{b}_0$ and $\mathbf{b}_1$, we choose them to minimize the sum of squares for errors. Consequently the estimators are the "least squares" estimators. We could use methods of the calculus to solve for these best estimates. So we would:

- take the partial derivatives of $\mathbf{SSE}$ with respect to $\mathbf{b}_0$ and $\mathbf{b}_1$ respectively
- set these partial derivatives equal to zero, and
- solve the subsequent system of two equations in two unknowns.

In this case, we state the results as follows:

$$\mathbf{b}_1 = \frac{\sum_{i=1}^{n} (x_i - \bar{x})(y_i - \bar{y})}{\sum_{i=1}^{n} (x_i - \bar{x})^2} = \frac{\mathbf{S}_{xy}}{\mathbf{S}_{xx}}$$

and

$$\mathbf{b}_0 = \bar{y} - \mathbf{b}_1 \bar{x}$$

The line formed with this estimated intercept and slope,

$$\hat{y} = \mathbf{b}_0 + \mathbf{b}_1 x$$

is called the "prediction" or "regression" line. From the solution given above, we observe that the point $(\bar{x}, \bar{y})$, lies on the regression line.

Example: A car dealer wants to associate the number of cars sold and the number of salespersons employed at the time. The following data represent sales figures for five randomly chosen weeks in 1999.

TABLE 55: Dealership Sales Data

x (sales persons)	6	6	4	3	2
y (cars sold)	20	18	10	11	6

First plot these data on a $x - y$ scatter plot to determine whether the proposed straight line is even plausible. In industry, we often conducted these plots to pass the "laugh test" (i.e., not to be laughed out of a meeting because you had not done your background work).

FIGURE 59: Scatterplot of Sales Data versus Personnel

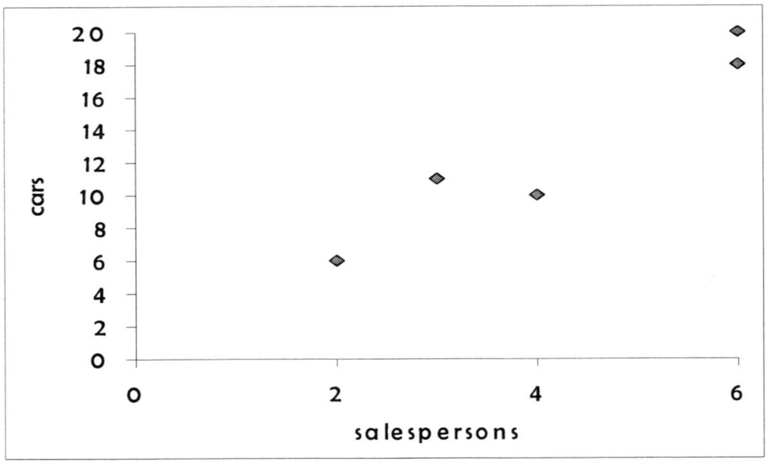

In Figure 59, a straight line might reasonably pass through these data and provide a reasonable model for car sales and it's reasonable to proceed. The least squares method provides an objective way of drawing the straight line through data.

Least Squares Calculations

TABLE 56: Least Squares Calculations for Sales Data

x_i	$(x_i - \bar{x})$	$(x_i - \bar{x})^2$	y_i	$(y_i - \bar{y})$	$(x_i - \bar{x}) \times (y_i - \bar{y})$
6	+1.8	3.24	20	+7	12.6
6	+1.8	3.24	18	+5	9.0
4	-0.2	0.04	10	-3	0.6
3	-1.2	1.44	11	-2	2.4
2	-2.2	4.84	6	-7	15.4
21	0	12.8	65	0	40.0
$\sum x_i$		S_{xx}	$\sum y_i$		S_{xy}

Thus the estimates for the sales data are given by:

$$\mathbf{b}_1 = \frac{\sum_{i=1}^{n} (x_i - \bar{x})(y_i - \bar{y})}{\sum_{i=1}^{n} (x_i - \bar{x})^2} = \frac{S_{xy}}{S_{xx}} = \frac{40.0}{12.8} = 3.125$$

and

$$\mathbf{b}_0 = \bar{y} - b_1\bar{x} = 13 - 3.125 \times 4.2 = -0.125$$

These values provide the following linear fit to the observed data.

FIGURE 60: Regression line of Sales as a function of the number of salespersons

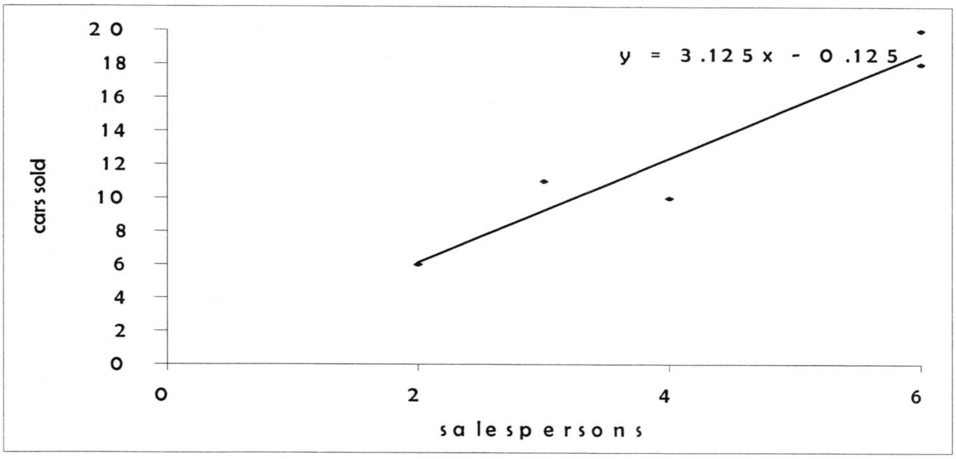

Interpretations

The estimated slope $\mathbf{b}_1 = 3.125 = \Delta y / \Delta x$ is the change in y divided by the change in x. If we **increase the number of salesmen by 1**, then $\Delta x = 1 \Rightarrow \Delta y = 3.125$. If we add 1 more salesperson, we estimate or expect to sell 3.125 more cars.

The intercept is the value of y when $x = 0$. So this is the number of cars, we expect or predict to sell if with no salespersons. The value of -0.125 cars makes little sense but we expect the predicted number to be near zero but not negative.

If we had 4 salespersons, how many cars would we expect to sell? Notice that $x = 4$ so that we predict the number of cars sold as:

$$\begin{aligned} \hat{y} &= -0.125 + 3.125 \times 4 \\ &= -0.125 + 12.500 \\ &= 12.375 \end{aligned}$$

If we needed to sell 11 cars per week to be profitable, how many salespersons should we need? In this case $y = 11$, so the number of salespersons needed is:

$$\begin{aligned} 11 &= -0.125 + 3.125 \times \hat{x} \\ 11.125 &= 3.125 \times \hat{x} \\ \frac{11.125}{3.125} &= \hat{x} \\ \hat{x} &= 3.56 \end{aligned}$$

So the dealer would need 3.56 salespersons! Obviously, we cannot employ 3.56 salespersons but we could keep a staff of 3 and hire another person during busier times of the season.

Caveat

We should not predict how many cars we could sell with 10 or 15 sales persons. The model was based on the observed data and the farther that you extrapolate outside the x-space, the observed values of x, the less reliable our inference is.

Beware of predicting outside the values of the x-space!

Francis Galton (1889) coined the phrase "regression" when he used this method to quantify that the heights of sons tended to be regressed toward the average height regardless of the father's stature. If the father were short then the son should be taller and if the father were tall then the son should be shorter. He perceived regression toward a mean as a regression to mediocrity.

Goodness of Fit

Obviously, we can carry out these calculations but we need to quantify how well the data fit the equation of a straight line. In order to assess the "goodness of fit" we introduce the coefficient of determination $\mathbf{R}^2$

$$\mathbf{R}^2 = \frac{\sum_{i=1}^{n}(\hat{y}_i - \bar{y})^2}{\sum_{i=1}^{n}(y_i - \bar{y})^2} = \frac{\textbf{SSR}}{\textbf{TSS}}$$

The numerator **SSR** is a measure of the amount of variation in the predicted values, $\hat{y}_i$, based on the regression line, whereas the denominator **TSS** is a measure of the amount of variation in observed values of y just as in ANOVA.

TABLE 57: Goodness of Fit Calculations for Sales Data

x_i	y_i	$y_i - \bar{y}$	$(y_i - \bar{y})^2$	$\hat{y}_i$	$\hat{y}_i - \bar{y}$	$(\hat{y}_i - \bar{y})^2$
6	20	+7	49	18.625	+5.625	31.641
6	18	+5	25	18.625	+5.625	31.641
4	10	-3	9	12.375	-0.625	0.391
3	11	-2	4	9.25	-3.750	14.063
2	6	-7	49	6.125	-6.875	47.266
		0	136	65	0	124.964

The computed coefficient of determination $\mathbf{R}^2$ is given by:

$$\mathbf{R}^2 = \frac{124.964}{136} = 0.919$$

This means that 91.9% of the variation in the y – values can be explained by knowing the x – values. $\mathbf{R}^2$ is a measure of how well the data fit the regression line. If the fit were **perfect**, then $\mathbf{R}^2$ should be **exactly 1** (that is, the points are collinear). If there is **no correlation** between the variables then the **coefficient determination should be 0**. $0 \le \mathbf{R}^2 \le 1$

Example: The following data are the weights (kg's) and blood glucose levels of 16 healthy adult males. Can we associate weights of males with their glucose levels?

TABLE 58: Weight and Glucose Levels for 16 Adult Males

Weight (x)	Glucose (y)	Weight (x)	Glucose (y)
64.0	108	82.1	101
75.3	109	78.9	85
73.0	104	76.7	99
82.1	102	82.1	100
76.2	105	83.9	108
95.7	121	73.0	104
59.4	79	64.4	102
93.4	107	77.6	87

In this case it makes sense that weight would effect blood glucose level, so we consider weight x to be the independent variable and glucose level y to be the dependent variable.

$$\hat{y} = \mathbf{b}_0 + \mathbf{b}_1 x$$

Using calculators, spreadsheets or hand calculations, we obtain the following estimate of the slope:

$$\mathbf{b}_1 = 0.51$$

The blood glucose level is predicted to increase 0.51 units for each additional kg:

$$\mathbf{b}_0 = 61.88$$

Furthermore, the y – intercept is the estimate of the glucose level of a person whose weight is zero.

FIGURE 61: Regression Line of Glucose Levels as a Function of Weight

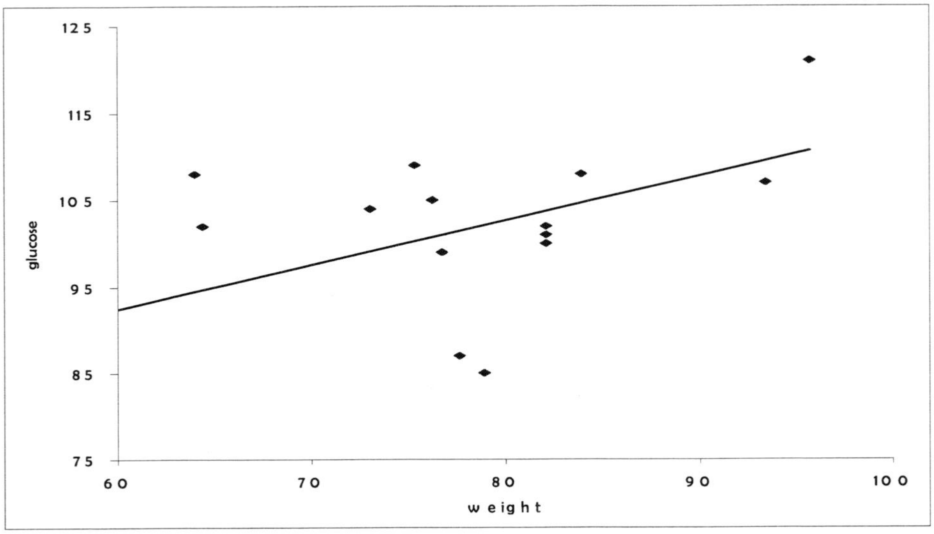

The value of $\mathbf{R}^2 = 0.2344$ implies that weight is useful in explaining 23.44% of the variation in the sugar or glucose levels. Notice in the scatterplot, we see less of a linear trend in the data and more scatter than in the car sales data. These observations are quantified in part through the small value of $\mathbf{R}^2$.

This straight line is a primitive step in model building. In this capacity, the statistician is called upon to help quantify the relationship between variables. There are many types of regression analysis that involve equations, which are more complex than the linear model given here.

Properties of Regression Estimators

The regression estimators of the slope, intercept, and variance have optimal properties in they are **unbiased estimators** of their respective parameters just as $\overline{\mathbf{x}}$ is an unbiased estimator of μ. The **estimators** of the slope and intercept **are normally distributed** and the estimator of σ^2 is a function of a chi-square.

TABLE 59: **Properties of Regression Estimators**

Slope	**Intercept**	**Variance**
$E(b_1) = \beta_1$ and $V(b_1) = \frac{\sigma^2}{S_{xx}}$ $b_1 \sim N\left(\beta_1, \frac{\sigma}{\sqrt{S_{xx}}}\right)$	$E(b_0) = \beta_0$ and $V(b_0) = \sigma^2 \times \left\{\frac{1}{n} + \frac{\overline{x}^2}{S_{xx}}\right\}$ $b_0 \sim N\left(\beta_0, \sigma\sqrt{\frac{1}{n} + \frac{\overline{x}^2}{S_{xx}}}\right)$	$SSE = S_{yy} - b_1 \times S_{xy}$ $E(SSE) = (n-2) \times \sigma^2$ $E(MSE) = \sigma^2$ $\frac{SSE}{\sigma^2} \sim \chi^2_{n-2}$

These properties enable us to test hypotheses on the respective parameters. To test $\mathbf{H_0}$ on the slope and intercept we follow the same procedure as in the t – tests.

TABLE 62: Inferences on Regression Estimators

$\mathbf{H_0} : \boldsymbol{\beta}_1 = \mathbf{c}_1$	$\mathbf{H_0} : \boldsymbol{\beta}_0 = \mathbf{c}_0$
versus	versus
$\mathbf{H_a} : \boldsymbol{\beta}_1 \neq \mathbf{c}_1$	$\mathbf{H_a} : \boldsymbol{\beta}_0 \neq \mathbf{c}_0$

Reject $\mathbf{H_0}$ in these respective scenarios provided:

$$|\mathbf{b}_1 - \mathbf{c}_1| > t_{\alpha/2;n-2}\sqrt{\frac{\mathbf{MSE}}{\mathbf{S}_{xx}}} \qquad |\mathbf{b}_0 - \mathbf{c}_0| > t_{\alpha/2;n-2}\sqrt{\mathbf{MSE}\left\{\frac{1}{n}+\frac{\overline{\mathbf{x}}^2}{\mathbf{S}_{xx}}\right\}}$$

Confidence intervals are useful in placing bounds on the values of the parameters with a certain degree of confidence. They can be used to test hypotheses about the respective parameters as well. They are formed from the t-distribution as well:

TABLE 63: Confidence Intervals on Regression Estimators

Slope	**Intercept**
$\mathbf{b}_1 \pm t_{\alpha/2;n-2}\sqrt{\frac{\mathbf{MSE}}{\mathbf{S}_{xx}}}$	$\mathbf{b}_0 \pm t_{\alpha/2;n-2}\sqrt{\mathbf{MSE}\left\{\frac{1}{n}+\frac{\overline{\mathbf{x}}^2}{\mathbf{S}_{xx}}\right\}}$

ANOVA Table for Regression

The ANOVA table in regression analysis plays very much the same role that it did earlier. It attempts to determine the importance of individual factors. In this case there is only one predictor and we are only estimating the slope and intercept and not multiple $\boldsymbol{\tau}_i$'s as we did in the previous section. Hence regression has only 1 degree of freedom, i.e., one less than the number of parameters to be estimated.

TABLE 64: ANOVA Table

Source	df	SS	MS	F-ratio
Regression	1	SSR	$\frac{\mathbf{SSR}}{\mathbf{1}}$	$\frac{\mathbf{MSR}}{\mathbf{MSE}}$
Error	$n-2$	SSE	$\frac{\mathbf{SSE}}{(n-2)}$	
Total	$n-1$			

$$\mathbf{SSR} = \sum_{i=1}^{n} (\hat{y}_i - \bar{y})^2 \text{ and } \mathbf{SSE} = \sum_{i=1}^{n} (y_i - \hat{y}_i)^2$$

The term $\mathbf{SSR}$ measures the variation in the $y-$values predicted by the regression line and is the numerator for $\mathbf{R}^2$, the **coefficient of determination**. This term measures the **amount of variation** in the $y-$values that can be explained by knowing the regression or predictor variable. The term $\mathbf{SSE}$ compares, in the Pearson sense, the observed and predicted (or expected) and quantifies the amount of **total variation** that **cannot be explained** by knowing the predictor variable. These values lead us to an $F-$test that checks whether the regression model has predictive ability.

$F-ratio = \dfrac{\mathbf{MSR}}{\mathbf{MSE}} \sim F_{1,n-2}$. We reject $\mathbf{H_0}:\boldsymbol{\beta}_1 = 0 - \mathbf{vs} - \mathbf{H_a}:\boldsymbol{\beta}_1 \neq 0$, provided

$F-ratio = \dfrac{\mathbf{MSR}}{\mathbf{MSE}} > F_{\alpha;1,n-2}$, where $F_{\alpha;r,s}$ is an upper percentile of an $F-$distribution.

In many practical scenarios, we extend our observations and draw confidence bands about the predicted line. This is done by using the distributional properties of the predicted value.

Properties of Predicted y-values

TABLE 65: Properties of Predicted Values ANOVA Table

$\mathbf{E}(\hat{y}_0) = y_0$	
$\mathbf{V}(\hat{y}_0) = \sigma^2 \times \left\{ \dfrac{1}{n} + \dfrac{(\bar{\mathbf{x}} - \mathbf{x_0})^2}{\mathbf{S}_{xx}} \right\}$	$\hat{y}_0 \pm t_{\alpha/2;n-2} \sqrt{\mathbf{MSE}\left(\dfrac{1}{n} + \dfrac{(\bar{\mathbf{x}} - \mathbf{x_0})^2}{\mathbf{S}_{xx}} \right)}$
$\hat{y}_0 \sim \mathbf{N}\left(y_0, \sigma\sqrt{1 + \dfrac{1}{n} + \dfrac{(\bar{\mathbf{x}} - \mathbf{x_0})^2}{\mathbf{S}_{xx}}} \right)$	

Case Study: Detecting Leaks in Underground Storage Tanks

As discussed earlier, EPA studies cited the propensity for leaks in underground storage tanks; these findings precipitated government action, which was codified into leak detection protocol in **The Federal Register** (1988): The EPA requires that every service station be equipped with a leak detection system and that the system must **detect leaks of 0.2 gallons per hour, with a detection probability of 95% and a probability of a false alarm of 5% per month**. In statistical terms, if the tank is not leaking the system should signify a leak in no more than 5% of the cases. If the null hypothesis, that the tank is not leaking is true, then the EPA has set $\alpha = 0.05$. If the alternative hypothesis is true that the tank is leaking and leaking as much as **0.2 GPH** or **4.8 gallons per day**, then the system must have the capacity to detect a leak of this magnitude with a consumer's risk of 5%.

FIGURE 62: Typical UST Installation at a Service Station

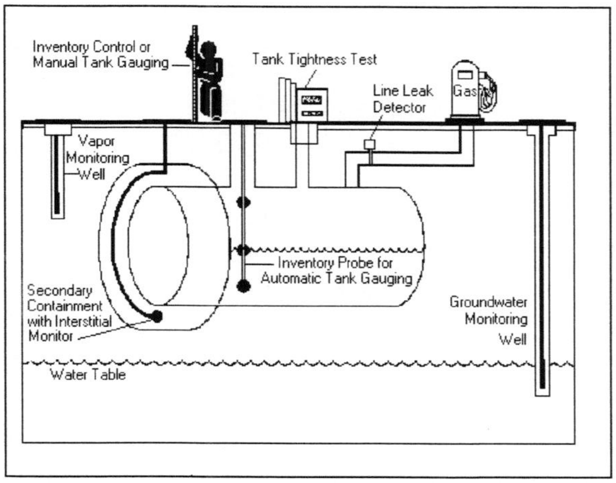

http://www.epa.nsw.gov.au/mao/servicestation.htm

Most modern service stations are equipped with electronic systems that download meter readings, $x's$, from the pumps through the cashier's console, see Keating, Dunn, and Dunn (1994). The tanks also contain an internal level-measuring device that electronically detects the level of the gasoline in the underground storage tank. Given the tank-geometry, one can use the level readings between successive measurements to determine the volumes, $y's$. We place these terms in an inventory model as:

$$y = \boldsymbol{\beta}_0 + \boldsymbol{\beta}_1 x + \boldsymbol{\varepsilon}$$

where y is the volume displaced from the underground storage tank, x, is the volume of gasoline dispensed through the meters. The intercept is the value of y when $x = 0$, i.e., $\boldsymbol{\beta}_0$ is the amount of gasoline displaced from the UST when no gasoline has been dispensed through the meters. If the readings are taken on a daily basis, then $\boldsymbol{\beta}_0$, is tantamount to a daily leak rate. The slope $\boldsymbol{\beta}_1 = \boldsymbol{\Delta} y / \boldsymbol{\Delta} x$ is the change in y, $\boldsymbol{\Delta} y$ for a given change in x, $\boldsymbol{\Delta} x$. Thus for each gallon , $\boldsymbol{\Delta} x = \mathbf{1}$, of gasoline dispensed $\boldsymbol{\Delta} y$ is the corresponding amount displaced from the UST. Thus the slope $\boldsymbol{\beta}_1$ is actually the meter calibration value, which we hope is 1 but by law must fall between $\mathbf{1 \pm 0.005}$.

Consider the following data, which are daily tank and meter readings chosen from the data in Krueger, et al. (1996).

TABLE 66: Unleaded plus tank and meter readings: Judson Road service station

Met-Tot (x)	Tank (y)
798.75	803.64
625.06	631.28
597.01	589.92
712.41	708.48
507.53	508.29
583.57	576.05
909.92	905.31
693.54	687.85
395.00	394.94
528.76	528.48
392.13	387.88
498.61	498.80
456.05	454.59
770.78	766.20
692.26	689.18

The data are plotted in the scatter plot given below in Figure 63. From the graph it is apparent that the data are well approximated by a straight line fit.

TABLE 67: **ANOVA** Table for Gasoline Service Station Data

	df	SS	MS	*F*-ratio
Regression	1	321,985.37	321,985.37	18,543.91
Residual	13	225.72	17.36	
Total	14	322,211.10		

From Table 67, the total sum of squares in the displaced volumes is 322,211.10, and that 321,985.37 can be explained by knowing the meter readings and thus $\mathbf{R}^2 = 0.9993$. So that **99.93% of the variation in** the $y-$ values, the **tank displacements, can be explained by knowing** the $x-$ values, **the meter readings**.

FIGURE 63: Scatter plot of Tank and Meter Readings

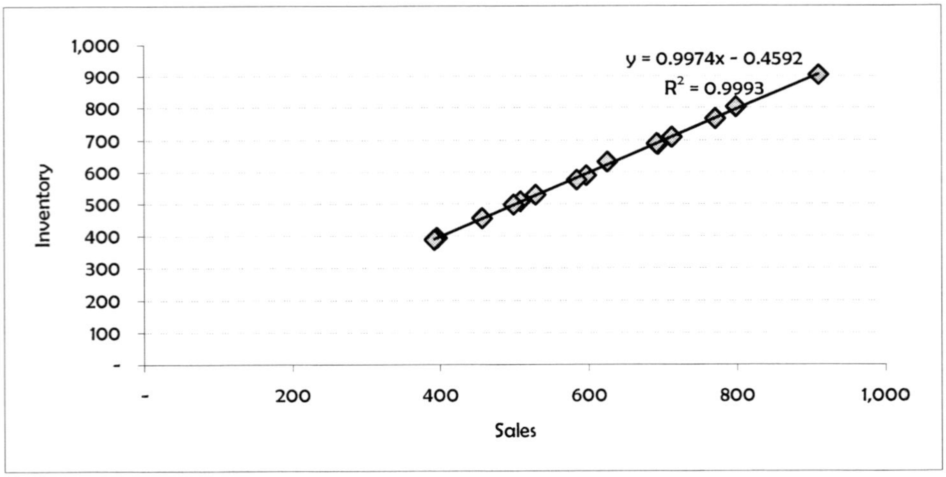

Using least squares, estimates for the slope and intercept are given in Table 65.

TABLE 68: Coefficients Table for Gasoline Service Station Data

	Coefficients	Standard Error	t Stat	p-value
Intercept	-0.45923	4.60107138	-0.09980991	0.922018
Met-Tot (x)	0.997424	0.00732452	136.176031	6.794E-22

The slope implies that the estimated meter calibration is not 1 but rather 0.997 and that the estimated intercept is not 0 but rather –0.45923. The slope tells us for each 1,000 gallons of gasoline dispensed, 997.424 gallons are displaced from the UST.

$$\mathbf{b}_1 = 0.997424 = \frac{\mathbf{S}_{xy}}{\mathbf{S}_{xx}} \text{ and } \mathbf{b}_0 = -0.45923$$

The intercept of –0.45923 estimates that the tank is taking on volume, most likely water, at a rate 0.45923 gallons per day or 0.19 gallons per hour. Are these values significantly different than the hypothetical or ideal values?

TABLE 69: Inferences on Regression Estimators

$\mathbf{H_0}: \beta_1 = 1$	$\mathbf{H_0}: \beta_0 = 0$
versus	**versus**
$\mathbf{H_a}: \beta_1 \neq 1$	$\mathbf{H_a}: \beta_0 \neq 0$

We test these null hypotheses, $\mathbf{H_0}$, in these respective scenarios as:

$$|\mathbf{b}_1 - 1| = |0.997424 - 1| = 0.02576$$

$$t_{0.025;13}\sqrt{\frac{17.36}{323,650.79}} = 2.160 \times 0.00732 = 0.0158$$

$$Since - |\mathbf{b}_1 - 1| < t_{0.025;13}\sqrt{\frac{17.36}{323,650.79}}$$

$$we - fail - to - reject - \mathbf{H}_0$$

Notice that the standard error, 0.007, given in the coefficient table is the value of the principal square root in this formula. At the 5% level of significance, we fail to reject $\mathbf{H_0}: \beta_1 = 1$, i.e., the **meters are calibrated**. Hypothesis tests in EXCEL test whether the slope is zero and clearly rejects that notion with a $p - value = 6.794 \times 10^{-22}$.

$$|\mathbf{b}_0 - 0| = |-0.45923 - 0| = 0.45923$$

$$t_{0.025;13}\sqrt{17.36\left\{\frac{1}{15}+\frac{373,025.77}{323,650.79}\right\}} = 2.160 \times 4.6006 = 9.9373$$

$$Since - |\mathbf{b}_0 - 0| < t_{0.025;13}\sqrt{17.36\left\{\frac{1}{15}+\frac{373,025.77}{323,650.79}\right\}}$$

$$we - fail - to - reject - \mathbf{H_0}$$

Notice that the standard error, 4.601, given in the coefficient table is the value of the principal square root in this formula as well. We fail to reject $\mathbf{H_0} : \boldsymbol{\beta}_0 = 0$, i.e., there is not enough evidence at a false alarm rate of 5%, to indicate that the tank is leaking. The hypothesis test from EXCEL tests whether the intercept is zero and it clearly does not reject it with a $p - value = 0.922$, i.e., we would need to live with a false alarm rate of 92.2% to indicate that the tank is leaking.

Finally we add the confidence bands about the predicted values of $y -$ values. These curves provide bands about the regression line by the confidence level:

$$\hat{y}_0 \pm t_{\alpha/2;n-2}\sqrt{\mathbf{MSE}\left(\frac{1}{n}+\frac{(\bar{\mathbf{x}}-\mathbf{x_0})^2}{\mathbf{S}_{xx}}\right)}$$

$$\hat{y}_0 \pm t_{0.025;13}\sqrt{17.36\left(\frac{1}{15}+\frac{(610.76-\mathbf{x_0})^2}{323,65.79}\right)}$$

These lines vary with the value of $\mathbf{x_0}$ and provide lower and upper bounds about the prediction line and values are tabled in Table 66 below. Note that as $\mathbf{x_0}$ moves away from $\bar{\mathbf{x}}$, the confidence bands widen in Figure 64 and reinforce the notion that one must be careful in predicting outside the observed $x -$ values.

TABLE 70: Confidence Bounds about the Prediction Line

Meters	Lower	Pred	Upper	Meters	Lower	Pred	Upper
	380.74	390.66	400.58		613.69	622.99	632.29
	383.62	393.53	403.43		680.64	690.02	699.41
	444.80	454.41	464.03		681.90	691.29	700.68
	487.40	496.87	506.33		700.68	710.11	719.55
	496.32	505.76	515.20		758.70	768.34	777.98
	517.55	526.94	536.32		786.47	796.24	806.00
	572.30	581.61	590.92		896.68	907.12	917.55
	585.71	595.01	604.31				

FIGURE 64: Confidence Intervals about The Predicted Values

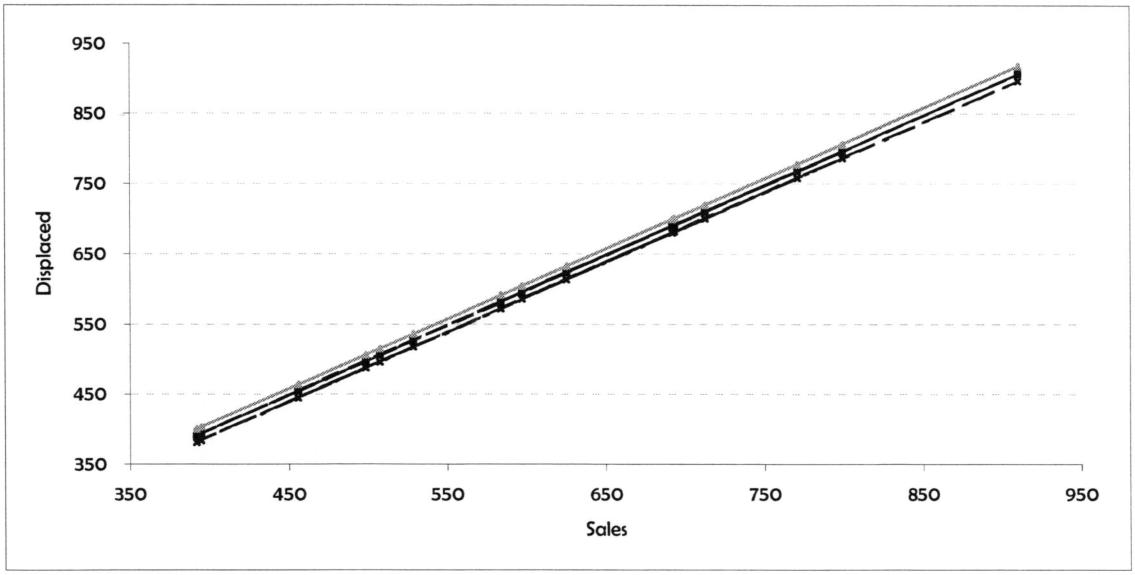

Case Study: Keating Power Consumption A Closer Examination

From the first analysis, see page 216, of the Keating Electrical Use Data, see page 32, we noticed significant differences in electrical use by month. The cyclical nature of the graph produced a seasonal trend wherein electrical was high in winter and summer months but low in spring and autumn months. One might well conjecture that electrical use is a function of temperature. Further, the months of December in 1983 and 1989 showed very high electrical use as compared to other December months. These were in fact the two coldest months on record in San Antonio not just the two coldest Decembers on record.

To pursue the conjecture, we collected the average temperature in San Antonio for each month during the 16 year period. These values are given in degrees Fahrenheit in Table B1.

Table B1: San Antonio Average Temperatures by Month 1983-1998

Year	*Jan*	*Feb*	*Mar*	*Apr*	*May*	*Jun*	*Jul*	*Aug*	*Sep*	*Oct*	*Nov*	*Dec*
1983	48.9	52.1	58.7	65.2	73.6	79.2	82.9	84.5	78.5	70.9	62.5	43.0
1984	46.7	54.1	64.2	69.7	77.1	82.8	85.0	84.7	77.6	71.2	58.8	59.6
1985	44.2	50.5	64.1	69.4	76.7	80.2	82.2	85.5	79.4	71.7	64.4	49.9
1986	53.4	58.0	62.9	72.6	74.6	81.5	85.8	85.7	83.7	69.7	59.4	51.6
1987	50.7	55.9	57.8	66.1	75.8	80.5	83.8	86.0	79.2	71.2	60.6	54.2
1988	47.6	54.3	61.3	69.1	76.1	81.2	84.6	86.4	80.7	73.2	65.1	56.0
1989	56.2	51.6	61.9	70.4	81.7	83.3	86.6	86.0	79.1	71.3	61.8	43.4
1990	56.4	58.9	61.5	69.7	79.3	87.5	83.4	85.3	80.0	69.3	63.0	51.9
1991	48.9	56.6	64.0	72.4	77.7	82.8	84.5	85.8	77.8	73.3	57.4	55.5
1992	50.8	59.1	63.3	69.0	73.7	82.5	84.7	82.2	81.7	73.4	57.3	56.3
1993	51.2	55.5	61.5	67.3	73.9	81.6	86.1	87.3	81.5	70.7	56.3	55.1
1994	52.3	56.2	63.9	69.8	76.0	84.5	87.9	86.1	78.4	72.7	64.8	57.0
1995	53.5	57.4	61.9	69.8	78.6	79.3	84.3	85.5	80.1	69.8	59.5	55.7
1996	51.1	57.9	57.6	69.5	81.9	84.1	87.3	84.4	78.4	71.1	61.3	54.5
1997	49.2	53.1	63.3	63.9	74.0	79.8	85.1	86.1	82.2	70.2	57.3	50.2
1998	56.4	55.3	59.8	66.7	79.8	86.3	88.1	83.6	80.5	71.3	62.4	52.7

Notice the average temperature of December 1983 was 43 degrees and that of 1989 was 43.4. The next coldest month was January 1985 in which the average temperature was 44.2 degrees. Also January 17, 1985 was the last time San Antonio had a measurable snowfall and the total amount was 13 inches.

As in regression analysis, we obtain a scatter plot of electrical use versus temperature. The scatter plot depicted in Figure B2 does not indicate a linear relationship but it does support the notion that both warm and cold months produce higher electrical use than more moderate spring and autumn months. From the graph it appears that electrical use reaches a minimum around 65 degrees and increase in V-shaped fashion as the temperature moves away 65 degrees. This graph is quite reminiscent of the absolute value function and thus we can put forth a new model:

$$y = \boldsymbol{\beta}_0 + \boldsymbol{\beta}_1 \mathbf{x}' + \boldsymbol{\delta}$$

where

$$\mathbf{x}' = |\mathbf{t} - 65|$$

Figure B1: Scatter plot of Electrical Use as a Function of Temperature

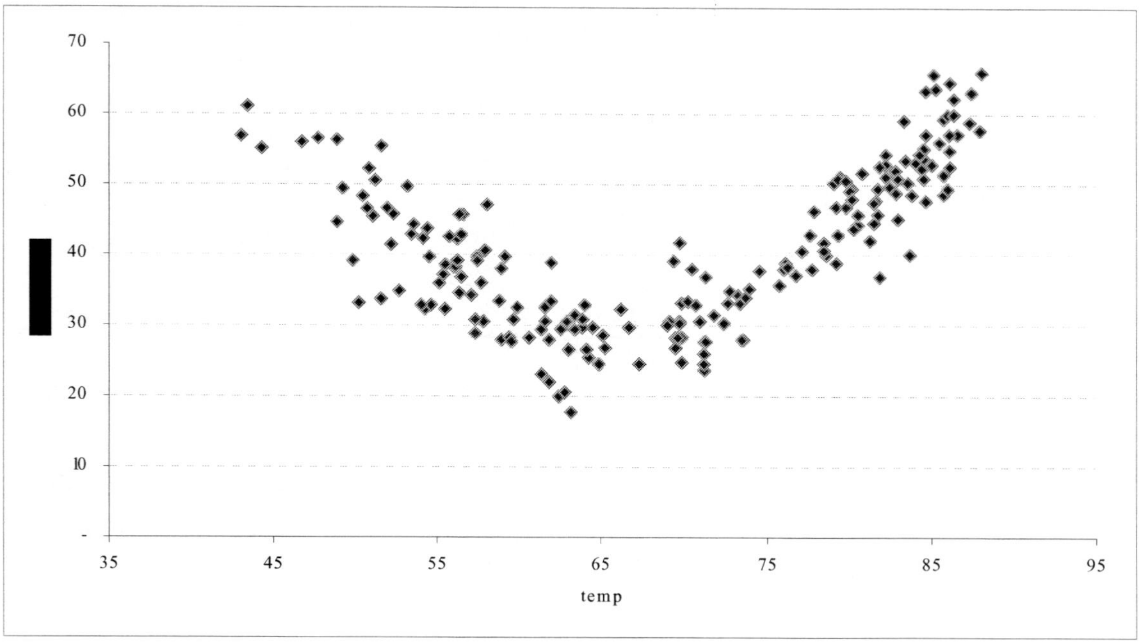

Notice also that there are many more extremely hot months than there are extremely cold months by looking at the cluster of months near the vertex of each part of the "V".

Consider the scatter plot of the electrical use as function of the modified temperature, which is the absolute temperature deviation form 65.

Figure B2: Scatter plot of electrical use against the modified temperature

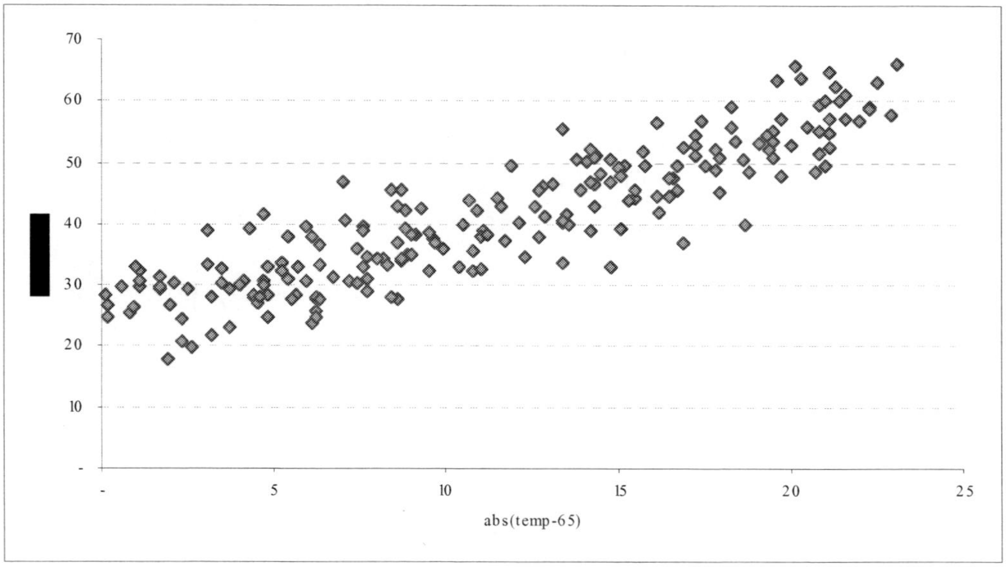

In the new scatter plot of electrical use against temperature deviation from 65, we can now see a distinct linear pattern. So we proceed with regression using the value of temperature minus 65 as the predictor or independent variable.

Table B2: ANOVA table for regression model using modified temperature.

Source	*Df*	*SS*	*MS*	*F-ratio*
New-Temp	1	17,663.87	17,663.87	738.32
Error	190	4,545.63	23.92	
Total	191	22,209.49		

This model produces an excellent fit in that the F-ratio is highly significant with a p-value of 2.3×10^{-67}. From Table B2, the total sum of squares in electrical use is 22,209.49 units of which 17, 663.87 cab explained knowing the new temperature. This model produces a coefficient of determination of

$$\mathbf{R}^2 = \frac{17,663.87}{22,209.49} = 0.7953$$

So 79.53% of the variation in electrical use can be explained by knowing the absolute temperature difference from 65.

Table B3: Coefficient Table

Parameters	*Estimates*	*Std-Error*	*t Stat*	*P-value*
Intercept	24.265	0.728	33.328	2.68E-81
New-temp	1.505	0.055	27.172	2.3E-67

The model estimates that when the temperature is 65 degrees the Keating household will still use an average of 24.265 kWh/day. This electrical use is attributed to costs other than heating or cooling. Likewise for each additional increase in temperature above 65 degrees we expect to use an additional 1.505 kWh/day. For temperature decrements below 65 degrees, each additional drop of one degree corresponds to an increase in electrical use of 1.505 kWh/day.

So in a month with a mean temperature of 75 degrees, we would predict electrical use based on the model as:

$$\begin{aligned}\hat{y} &= \boldsymbol{\beta}_0 + \boldsymbol{\beta}_1\mathbf{x}' \\ &= 24.265 + 1.505\times|\mathbf{t} - 65| \\ &= 24.265 + 1.505\times|75 - 65| \\ &= 24.265 + 15.048 \\ &= 39.313\end{aligned}$$

So in a month with a mean temperature of 75 degrees, the electrical use is predicted to be 39.313 kWh/day.

If we are given an electrical use of 45 kWh/day for a month, we would have two choice: one that would correspond to a month in which the electrical use is above 65 and another in which the temperature is below 65 degrees.

$$y = \boldsymbol{\beta}_0 + \boldsymbol{\beta}_1 \hat{\mathbf{x}}'$$

$$45 = 24.265 + 1.505 \times |\mathbf{t} - 65|$$

$$45 - 24.265 = 1.505 \times |\mathbf{t} - 65|$$

$$\frac{45 - 24.265}{1.505} = |\mathbf{t} - 65|$$

$$\mathbf{t} = 65 \pm 13.78 \Rightarrow \begin{cases} \mathbf{t}_1 = 78.78 \\ \mathbf{t}_2 = 51.22 \end{cases}$$

As in the calculations, we would have a month with an average temperature of 78.78 degrees or 51.22 degrees.
The best estimate of the standard deviation in the daily electrical use is given by

$$\hat{\sigma} = \sqrt{\mathbf{MSE}} = 4.891$$

So this estimates that the model residuals should follow a normal distribution with a mean of zero and a standard deviation of 4.891 kWh/day. By one part of the empirical rule, we would expect 95% of the residuals to fall within $\pm\, 2\times$standard deviations or $\pm$ 9.782 kWh/day.

The residual plot given in Figure B3 is customarily used to diagnose model problems. Notice in this case, there are roughly ten observations that fall outside the two-standard deviation bands and none outside the three-standard deviation bands, as one would expect in a sample of almost 200.

Figure B3: Residual Plot

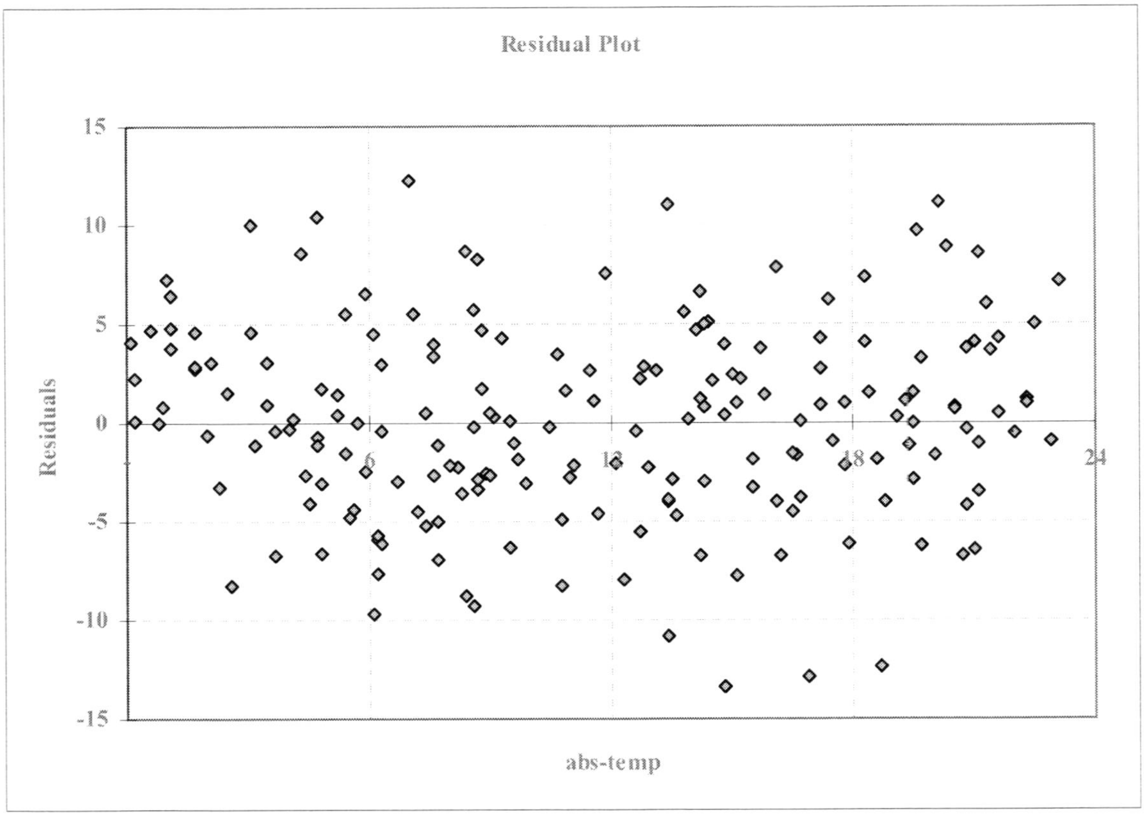

Problem Set 4

{115-120} These data are ages (years) and systolic blood pressures of healthy adults:

Age	**20**	**43**	**63**	**26**	**53**	**31**	**58**	**46**	**70**	**19**
BP	**120**	**128**	**141**	**126**	**134**	**128**	**136**	**132**	**144**	**121**

Fit a linear regression line to these data. From the prediction equation answer the following questions.

116) What is the predicted increase in systolic BP for each year a person ages?
a) 112.80 b) 2.241 c) 0.448 d) 0.424

117) What is the predicted systolic BP of a healthy newborn child?
a) 111.86 b) 112.80 c) 0.424 d) 250.67

118) If one is a healthy 30 year-old, what does the regression predict for his or her systolic BP?
a) 125.53 b) 125.54 c) 131.00 d) 195.19

119) If one's systolic BP is 120, how old does the regression line predict the person to be?
a) 19.50 b) 18.25 c) 16.97 d) 20 e) 20.7

120) What is the coefficient of determination?
a) 0.975 b) 0.904 c) 0.951 d) 0.987 e) 1.050

{121-125} These data are the meter readings (gallons) and tank volumes (gallons) displaced on 6 days at a Diamond Shamrock Corner Store.

Day	**1**	**2**	**3**	**4**	**5**	**6**
Meter	770.8	712.4	909.9	395.0	528.8	456.0
Tank	766.2	708.5	905.3	394.9	528.5	454.6

Fit a linear regression line to the data. From the prediction equation answer the following questions.

121) What is the predicted amount of gasoline displaced from the tank when one gallon of gasoline is dispensed through the meters?
a) 0.990 b) 1.010 c) 0.996 d) 1.004 e) 1.000

122) What is the predicted amount of gasoline displaced when none is dispensed through the meters?
a) -3.740 b) 3.710 c) 0 d) 0.414 e) -0.414

123) If a station dispenses 800 gallons through its meters, what does the regression line predict for the number of gallons displaced from the tank?

a) 788.45 b) 791.84 c) 795.83 d) 796.80 e) 804.21

124) If a station measures its underground tanks and determines that 594 gallons have been displaced from the tank, what does the regression line predict for the number of gallons dispensed through the meters?

a) 588.06 b) 591.86 c) 594.00 d) 596.16 e) 600

125) What is the coefficient of determination?

a) 0.904 b) 0.951 c) 0.975 d) 0.997 e) 1.000

{126-129} 100 TV's were sampled and the weekday the TV was made was determined from manufacturing records based on the inventory number. The data are summarized in the table below by classes, Monday and Friday (M_F), Tuesday and Thursday (T_T), and Wednesday. Are these data sufficient at the 5% level of significance to indicate that production does not occur uniformly over weekdays?

W	T_T	M_F
28	42	30

126) The value of the chi-square test statistic is given by

a) 12.60 b) 3.92 c) 5.80 d) 3.44

127) The critical value from the chi-square table is given by:

a) 7.815 b) 9.488 c) 5.991 d) 3.841

128) The expected number of TV's made on Monday-Friday based on the uniformity assumption is:

a) 33.33 b) 40 c) 20 d) 30

129) Based on these results, we conclude production of TV's by week-day is:

a) not different b) different
c) are best on Wednesday d) worst on Monday-Friday.

{130-134} The data, in the table below, come form Karl Pearson in 1909. At the five-percent level of significance, does the type of crime appear to be related to whether the criminal was drunken or sober?

	Arson	Rape	Assault	Theft	Fraud	
Drunken	50	88	155	379	63	735
Sober	45	62	110	301	147	665
	95	150	265	680	210	1,400

130) The alternative hypothesis is that:

a) type of crime and state of sobriety are independent
b) fraud requires sobriety
c) types of crime are equally likely to be committed
d) type of crime is dependent upon state of sobriety
e) types of crime are not equally likely to be committed

131) If state of sobriety and type of crime are independent, what is the expected number of criminals, who commit assault while inebriated?

a) 110.25 b) 125.875 c) 139.125 d) 155 e) 357

132) If state of sobriety and type of crime are independent, what is the contribution to the test statistic made by criminals, who commit fraud while sober?

a) 110.25 b) 22.38 c) 20.25 d) 33.075 e) 144

133) What is the critical value of the chi-square test?

a) 51.587 b) 49.731 c) 11.143 d) 9.488 e) 11.071

134) Based on the evidence at the 5% level of significance, we conclude that:

a) type of crime is independent of state of sobriety
b) for each type of crime, the proportion drunk is the same
c) you better be sober to commit fraud
d) state of sobriety of the offender depends upon the crime

{135-139} A highway has 4 inbound lanes and traffic analysts want to know whether drivers prefer some lanes. 100 cars on the inbound lanes were observed in early morning traffic. The lane and count of the number of cars by lane:

Lane	1	2	3	4
# of Cars	29	28	24	19

Do these data provide sufficient evidence at the 5% level of significance to indicate that some lanes are preferred over others?

135) The value of the multinomial test statistic is:

a) 2.48 b) 2.70 c) 3.841 d) 6.251 e) 6.95

136) What is the expected number of cars for Lane 2, if the null is true?

a) 29 b) 20 c) 16.67 d) 25 e) 28

137) What is the contribution of Lane 4 to the value of the test statistic?

a) 36 b) 1.44 c) 1.89 d) 0.64 e) 19

138) The critical region of the test is given by the values of the test statistic which exceed:
a) 2.70 b) 5.991 c) 7.779 d) 7.815 e) 9.488

139) Based on these results, we conclude that:
a) drivers prefer lanes 1 & 2 b) drivers dislike lane 4
c) lanes 1 & 2 are preferred over lane 4 d) there's not enough evidence to indicate a preference

{140-144} A small company would like to quantify the relationship between its monthly promotional costs and net gains. The data for 8 consecutive months are given below in thousands of dollars each:

Month	1	2	3	4	5	6	7	8
Promotional Costs	10	15	40	100	90	230	30	50
Net Gains	155	160	140	334	195	530	155	244

140) What is the additional net gain expected for each additional dollar of promotional cost expended?
a) 0.51 b) 0.57 c) 1.76 d) 1.64 e) 1.39

141) What is the expected net gain (thousands) if no promotional costs are expended?
a) 137.74 b) 114.74 c) -51.28 d) -65.15 e) 31.13

142) If one expends $80 (thousand) in promotional costs, what is his predicted net gain (thousands)?
a) 255.64 b) 257.51 c) -10.50 d) -19.72 e) 127.42

143) If one makes net gains of $250 (thousand), what is the amount one is predicted to expend in promotional costs?
a) 555.03 b) 590.97 c) 67.76 d) 76.80 e) 316.49

144) What percentage of the net gains can be explained by knowing the promotional costs?
a) 94.75% b) 89.78% c) 97.34% d) 16.33% e) 46.21%

{145-148} An insurance company surveyed 1,000 employees about their pension funds. Do the data below contradict the claim of independence between age and investment preference at the 5% level of significance?

Age	**All Stock**	**All Annuities**	**Mixed**
Over 45	196	131	158
Under 45	223	116	176

145) The alternative hypothesis is that:

a) investment preference and age of investor are independent
b) investment in stocks is for the young
c) investment preferences are equally likely to be chosen
d) investment preference is dependent upon age of investor
e) age groups are evenly distributed

146) If investor age and investment preferences are independent, what is the expected number of investors under 45 that prefer all annuities?

a) 119.795 b) 127.205 c) 139.125 d) 161.991 e) 157

147) If investment type and age of investor are independent, what is the contribution to the test statistic made by under-45 investors, who put all funds in stocks?

a) 127.205 b) 215.785 c) 0.987 d) 0.235 e) 0.256

148) What is the critical value of the chi-square test statistic?

a) 7.815 b) 2.72 c) 5.991 d) 9.488 e) 12.59

149) What is the value of the chi-square test statistic?

a) 1.67 b) 2.72 c) 6.00 d) 7.841 e) 8.94

150) Based on the evidence at the 5% level of significance, we conclude that:

a) investment preference is independent of age of investor
b) for each age group, the proportion using mixed investments is the same
c) for each investment preference, the proportion under 45 is the same
d) investment preference depends upon age of investor

References

1. Bayes, T (1763), "*An Essay Towards Solving a Problem in the Doctrine of Chances,*" **Philosophical Transactions of the Royal Society**, **53**, 370-418.

2. Chentsov, NN (1990) "*The Unfathomable Influence of Kolmogorov,*" **Annals of Statistics**, **18**, 987-998.

3. Clark, D (2002), "*Hawthorne Effect*" http://www.nwlink.com/~donclark/hrd/history/hawthorne.html

4. DeMoivre, A (1733) **Miscellenea Analytica de Seriebus et Quadraruris**.

5. Dyer, D and Keating, JP (1980), "*On the Determination of Critical Values for Bartlett's Test,*" **Journal of the American Statistical Association, 75**, 313-319.

6. Fienberg, SE (1971) "*Randomization and Social Affairs,*" **Science, 171**, 255-261

7. Fisher, RA (1925) **Statistical Methods for Research Workers**, Oliver & Boyd, Edinburgh.

8. Fisher, RA (1936) "*Has Mendel's Work Been Rediscovered?*" **Science, 171**, 255-261.

9. Galton, F (1889) **Natural Inheritance**, Macmillan Publishing, London.

10. Gauss, KF (1809) *Disquisitiones de Elementis Ellipticus Pallidis*, **Werke, 6**, 1-24.

11. Hacking, I (1984), "*Trial by Number,*" **Science, 84**, 69-70.

12. Herrnstein, RJ and Murray, C (1994) **The Bell Curve**, The Free Press, New York.

13. Higgins, M. Scotchgard and PFOS, ENN, April 11, 2001 http://www.mindfully.org/Plastic/Scotchgard-PFOS-Environment.htm

14. Johnson, NL and Kotz, S (1997) **Leading Personalities in Statistical Sciences**, John Wiley and Sons, New York.

15. Keating, JP (1976) "*Handbook for Determining Lower Confidence Bounds on Reliability and Reliable Loads from Fatigue Data,*" **BHT Report: 299-099-859**

16. Keating, JP, Dunn, W and Dunn, D (1994) "*Storage Tank and Line Leak Detection and Inventory Reconciliation Process,*" **Patent Number 5,297,423**.

17. Keating, JP and Mason, RL (1988) "*Preference Regions and Their Probabilities Based on Rectangular Grids,*" **Communications in Statistics, A17**, 1973-1983.

18. Keating, JP and Scott, DW (1999) "*A Primer on Density Estimation for the Great Home Run Race of 1998,*" **STATS, 25**, 16-22.

19. Kolmogorov, AN (1956) **Foundations of the Theory of Probability**, Chelsea Publishing Company, New York.

20. Krueger, C, Keating, JP, Kannan, N and Mason, RL (1996) "*Calibration of Gasoline Flow Meters,*" **Statistics of Quality**, Marcel-Dekker, Inc, New York.

21. Legendre, AM (1805), *Nouvelles Méthodes pour la Determination des Orbits des Cométes*, Appendix to **Sur la Méthode des Monde Carrés**.

22. Madansky, A (1989) **Prescriptions for Working Statisticians**, Springer-Verlag, New York.

23. Meier, P, Sacks, J, and Zabell, S (1986), "*What Happened in Hazelwood?*" **Statistics and the Law**, 1-40, John Wiley & Sons Co., New York.

24. Montgomery, DC (2001) **Introduction to Statistical Quality Control**, John Wiley & Sons, New York, 43-44.

25. Mosteller, F and Tukey, JW (1968) "*Data Analysis Including Statistics,*" **Handbook of Social Psychology**, Volume 2, Addison-Wesley, Boston.

26. Munford, AG (1977) "*A Note on the Uniformity Assumption in the Birthday Problem,*" **The American Statistician, 31**, 119.

27. "National Survey of Underground Storage Tanks," **Environmental Protection Agency (EPA) Report 560/5-86-013**, Page 42, May 1986.

28. Pareto, V (1897) **Cours d'Economie Politique**, Paris: Rouge et Cie.

29. Pascal, B (1665) **Traité du Triangle Arithmétique**.

30. "*Preliminary Results: 3 in 1,000 Have AIDS Virus,*" **U., The National College Newsletter**, Volume 2, Page 1, February 1989.

31. Rao, CR (1989) **Statistics and Truth**, Council of Scientific and Industrial Research, New Delhi.

32. "*Rules and Regulations,*" **Federal Register, 53**, Number 185, page 37,144, 9/23/1988.

33. Scott, DW (1979) "*On Optimal and Data Based Histograms,*" **Biometrika, 66**, 605-610.

34. Scott, DW (1984) "*Frequency Polygons: Theory and Application,*" **Journal of the American Statistical Association, 80**, 348-354.

35. Silverman, BW (1986) **Density Estimation for Statistics and Data Analysis**, Chapman & Hall, London.

36. Snedecor, GW (1937) **Statistical Methods**, Iowa State Press.

37. Sparks, T. (2001), **Statistics in Ecotoxicology**, John Wiley & Sons, New York.

38. Stigler, S (1986) **The History of Statistics: The Measurement of Uncertainty before 1900**, Belknap Press, Cambridge.

39. Student, <Gossett, WS>, (1908) "*The Probable Error of the Mean,*" **Biometrika, 6**, 1-25.

40. "*Topics of the Day: Final Returns in The Digest's Poll of Ten Million Voters,*" **Literary Digest**, October 31, 1936, 5-6.

41. "*Topics of the Day: What Went Wrong with the Polls?*" **Literary Digest**, November 14, 1936, 7-8.

42. Tukey, JW (1977) **Exploratory Data Analysis**, Addison-Wesley, Boston.

43. Wand, M (1997) "*Data-Based Choice of Histogram Bin Width,*" **The American Statistician, 51**, 59-64.

Case Studies

Answers

Complete the following sentences with the most appropriate answer.

1. The goal of statistics involves ____________.
   a) representative samples b) appropriate sample statistics
   c) inference about population parameters **d) all of these**

2. A __________ is a numerical measure of a population.
   a) statistic **b) parameter** c) sample mean d) sample

3. Sampling errors cannot arise from ______________________.
   a) personal bias b) inadvertent omission of a subset of the population
   c) large samples **d) none of these**

4. The population is always a ______.
   a) sample space b) set of UTSA students
   c) sample d) set of real numbers

5. Which of the following data are often discretized?
   a) height b) weight c) age **d) all of these** e) none of these

The following data are the low temperatures of 17 major cities in Texas taken on Saturday February 12, 1994. A meteorologist wants to use these data to make inferences about the low temperature in the state.

45, 39, 33, 26, 38, 39, 46, 48, 53, 57, 56, 46, 47, 38, 46, 43, 47

6. The average low temperature of the sample is __ .
   a) 41.50 **b) 43.94** c) 46.00 d) 44.06

7. The mode of the sample of low temperatures is _ .
   a) 38 b) 39 **c) 46** d) 47

8. The range of the sample of low temperatures is _ .
   a) 7.70 b) 7.75 c) 7.94 **d) 31.00**

9. The standard deviation of the sample of low temperatures is __ .
   a) 7.70 b) 7.75 **c) 7.94** d) 63.06

10. The median low temperature of the sample data is ____ .
    a) 43 **b) 46** c) 53 d) 57

11. In order to construct a frequency polygon for these low temperatures, Scott would suggest using an interval width of size ___.
    a) 4.02 b) 4.14 c) 9.39 **d) 9.69**

12. Based on the measures of central tendency one would conclude that the data are___
a) skewed to the right b) symmetric
c) skewed to the left d) cannot be determined.

The following table shows the monthly water use (in hundreds of ft^3) of the Keating household for three consecutive years.

Monthly Use	Frequency	Monthly Use	Frequency
8-14	23	15-21	10
22-28	1	29-35	1
36-42	1		

13. The grouped average of the sample of water use is _________ .
a) 14.63 b) 16.53 c) 25.00 **d) 14.69**

14. The grouped standard deviation of the sample of water use is ______ .
a) 7.11 b) 6.28 c) 39.43 **d) 6.37**

15. The grouped mode of the sample of water use is ___________.
a) 23 b) 14.63 c) 25 **d) 11**

16. Plot Scott's frequency polygon for the temperature data: (25 points)

Table for Scott's Frequency Polygon

(i)	b	e	m	f
1	0.00	9.69	4.845	0
2	9.69	19.38	14.535	0
3	19.38	29.07	24.225	1
4	29.07	38.76	33.915	3
5	38.76	48.45	43.605	10
6	48.45	58.14	53.295	3
7	58.14	67.83	62.985	0
8	67.83	77.52	72.675	0

Figure for Scott's Frequency Polygon

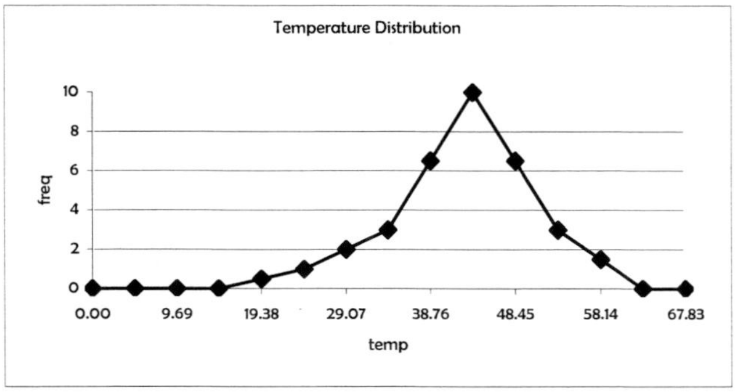

Consider the following sample that contains 5 observations: 12 17 20 30 36

17. If we delete an observation from this sample to produce a sample of size 4, which observation should we delete to **change** the sample average the most?
a) 12 b) 17 c) 20 d) 30 **e) 36**

18. If we delete an observation from this sample to produce a sample of size 4, which observation should we delete to **decrease** the sample standard deviation the most?
a) 12 b) 17 c) 20 d) 30 **e) 36**

19. Let a population consist of all UTSA Business majors. If we select a sample of Accounting majors from this population, their average GPA is a:
a) parameter **b) statistic**
c) measure of dispersion d) response variable

Complete the following sentence, which is in two parts:

I. The goal of statistics is to make meaningful inferences about the values of:

20. **a) population parameters** b) measures of central tendency
c) measures of dispersion d) response variables

II. based on descriptive statistics chosen from ________.

21. a) random samples b) the population
c) representative samples d) surveys

(22-27) The following data are the electrical uses of a household for the month of February in seven years. Consider these values as a sample of size 7.

1,150 1,323 1,176 1,718 1,358 1,110 1,364

22. The sample average electrical use for the month of February is:
a) 1,314.14 b) 1,323 c) 1,718 d) 1,414

23. The sample median electrical use for the month of February is:
a) 1,414 b) 1,718 c) 1,314.14 **d) 1,323**

24. The sample range of electrical use for the month of February is:
a) 825.09 **b) 608.00** c) 395.00 d) 214.00

25. The sample standard deviation of electrical use for the month of February is:
a) 152.00 b) 190.97 **c) 206.27** d) 214.00

26. The width of Scott's frequency polygon for these data is:
a) 300.51 b) 278.217 c) 167.621 d) 9.051

27. Which observation in this sample contributes most to the sample standard deviation?
a) 1,110 b) 1,176 c) 1,364 **d) 1,718**

In a class of 50 students, the teacher reported the grades in the following way:

Grade	Frequency	Grade	Frequency
40-49	1	50-59	4
60-69	8	70-79	12
80-89	15	90-99	10

28. The grouped mode of these data is given by:
a) 15 b) 79.5 **c) 84.5** d) 44.5

29. The grouped mean of these data is given by:
a) 69.5 **b) 77.7** c) 79.5 d) 84.5

30. The grouped standard deviation of these data is given by:
a) 13.01 b) 12.87 c) 11.80 d) 14

31. These data are:
a) skewed to the right **b) skewed to the left**
c) symmetric d) none of these

32. Plot Scott's frequency polygon for the February electrical data (25 points). Scale and label the axes. Start the plot at zero!

Figure for Scott's Frequency Polygon

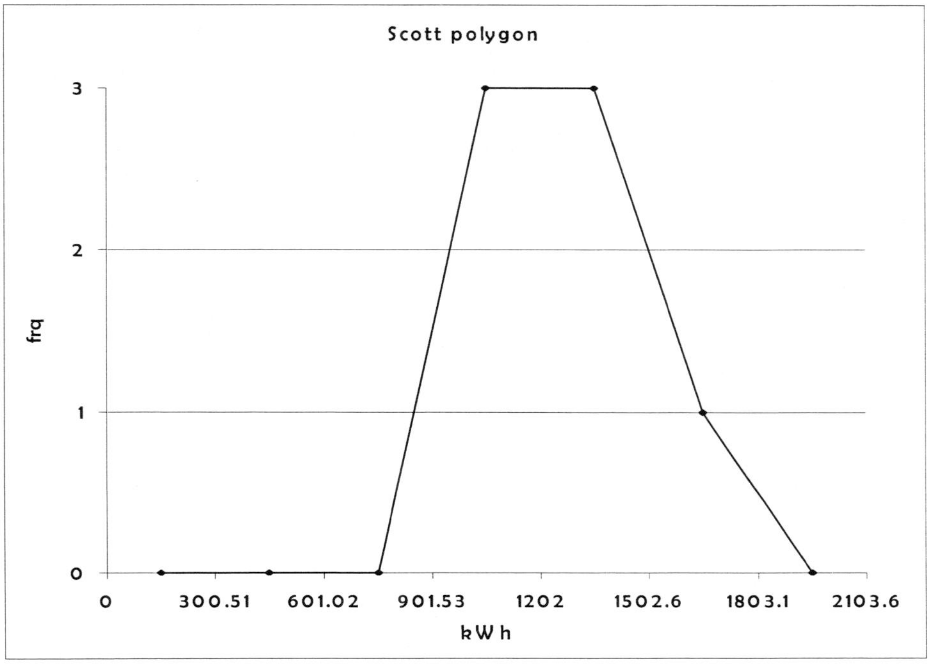

Table for Scott's Frequency Polygon

beg	end	mid	Frq
0.00	300.51	150.255	0
300.51	601.02	450.765	0
601.02	901.53	751.275	0
901.53	1202.04	1051.785	3
1202.04	1502.55	1352.295	3
1502.55	1803.06	1652.805	1
1803.06	2103.57	1953.315	0

(33-36). All 420 employees of a company were asked whether they smoke and whether they are college graduates. The following table lists the results:

	College Grad	*Not College Grad*	*Total*
Smoker	*35*	*80*	*115*
Non-Smoker	*130*	*175*	*305*
Total	*165*	*255*	*420*

33. What is the probability that a randomly chosen person is a smoker *and* has not graduated from college?
a) 0.6905 **b) 0.1905** c) 0.2738 d) 0.6071 e) 0.6957

$$P(S \cap NCG) = \frac{80}{420} = 0.1905$$

34. What is the probability that a randomly chosen person is a college graduate *or* a non-smoker?
a) 0.4262 **b) 0.8095** c) 0.5833 d) 0.3043 e) 0.2121

$$\begin{aligned} P(CG \cup NS) &= P(CG) + P(NS) - P(CG \cap NS) \\ &= \frac{165}{420} + \frac{305}{420} - \frac{130}{420} \\ &= 0.3929 + 0.7262 - 0.3095 \\ &= 0.8095 \end{aligned}$$

35. What is the probability that a randomly chosen person in this population smokes given that the person is a college graduate?
a) 0.2121 b) 0.5833 c) 0.3043 d) 0.1212 e) 0.2738

$$P(S \mid CG) = \frac{35}{165} = 0.2121$$

36. What is the probability that a randomly chosen person in this population is a college graduate given that the person does not smoke?
a) 0.5833 b) 0.7878 c) 0.3929 d) 0.3103 **e) 0.4262**

$$P(CG \mid NS) = \frac{130}{305} = 0.4262$$

37. A small company has an applicant pool of 40 qualified persons of whom 22 are Latinos. If the company hires two persons from this pool, what is the probability due to chance alone that both will be non-Latinos?
a) 0.05 b) 0.296 **c) 0.196** d) 0.203 e) 0.25

$$P(\overline{L}_2 \cap \overline{L}_1) = P(\overline{L}_2 \mid \overline{L}_1) \times P(\overline{L}_1) = \frac{17}{39} \times \frac{18}{40} = 0.1962$$

(38-40) A judge calls 36 citizens of whom 24 are men and 12 are women. He must empanel a jury of 6 persons.

38. How many different groups of three women can be chosen for jury duty from the 12 in the pool?
a) 33 b) 69 **c) 220** d) 2,024 e) 1,320

$$n_1 = {}_{12}C_3 = 220$$

39. How many different groups of 3 men can be chosen to serve on the jury from the 24 in the pool?
a) 33 b) 69 c) 220 **d) 2,024** e) 12,144

$$n_2 = {}_{24}C_3 = 2{,}024$$

40. What is the probability that due to chance alone the judge chooses a jury of exactly 3 men and 3 women?
a) 0.2286 b) 0.6667 c) 0.0007 d) 0.0012 e) 0.50

$$\Pr(3 - women \cap 3 - men) = \frac{n_1 \times n_2}{{}_{36}C_6} = \frac{220 \times 2{,}024}{1{,}947{,}792} = 0.2286$$

(41-43) A population of UTSA students is such that 20% are unemployed, 70% work part-time at Bill Miller Bar BQ for \$6/hr. and 10% work at West Telemarketing at \$10/hour. Let the random variable X denote the salary of a student in this population.

x	\$0	\$6	\$10
p(x)	0.2	0.7	0.1

41. What is the mean salary of this student population?
a) \$5.20 b) \$5.33 c) 0.325 d) \$6.00 e) \$7.21

$$\mu = \left(0 \times \frac{2}{10}\right) + \left(6 \times \frac{7}{10}\right) + \left(10 \times \frac{1}{10}\right) = 0 + 4.2 + 1.0 = 5.2$$

42. What is the <u>*population variance*</u> of the earnings of these students?
a) 9.07 b) 0.08 **c) 8.16** d) 0.09 e) 2.86

$$\sigma^2 = \left(0 - \frac{52}{10}\right)^2 \times \frac{2}{10} + \left(6 - \frac{52}{10}\right)^2 \times \frac{7}{10} + \left(10 - \frac{52}{10}\right)^2 \times \frac{1}{10}$$
$$= \frac{5{,}408}{1{,}000} + \frac{448}{1{,}000} + \frac{2{,}304}{1{,}000} = 8.16$$

43. What is the probability that a student in this population makes at least minimum wage?
a) 0.70 b) 1.00 **c) 0.80** d) 0.90 e) 0.875

$$\Pr(X > \$5.75) = p(6) + p(10) = \frac{7}{10} + \frac{1}{10} = 0.80$$

(44-46) A US News and World Report study found only 10% of US citizens underreport their incomes to the IRS. Consider a random sample of 20 US citizens to answer the following questions.

44. What's the probability that more than two persons in this sample underreported their incomes to the IRS?
a) 0.2852 **b) 0.3230** c) 0.6770 d) 0.7148 e) 0.3594

$$\Pr\{Y > 2\} = 1 - \Pr(Y \le 2) = 1 - \{p(0) + p(1) + p(2)\} =$$
$$1 - \{0.1216 + 0.2702 + 0.2852\} = 1 - 0.6770 = 0.3230$$

45. What's the probability that at most 4 persons in this sample underreported their incomes to the IRS?
a) 0.0431 **b) 0.9569** c) 0.8671 d) 0.1329 e) 0.4238

$$\Pr\{Y \le 4\} = p(0) + p(1) + p(2) + p(3) + p(4) =$$
$$0.1216 + 0.2702 + 0.2852 + 0.1901 + 0.0898 = 0.9569$$

46. What's the probability that at least one but no more than three 3 persons in the sample underreported their incomes to the IRS?
a) 0.1216 b) 0.2852 c) 0.7148 **d) 0.7455** e) 0.8739

$$\Pr\{1 \leq Y \leq 3\} = p(1) + p(2) + p(3) = 0.2702 + 0.2852 + 0.1901 = 0.7455$$

47. A car dealer found that 35% of the vehicles of a particular model have problems while the car is under warranty. If we randomly sample 18 owners of this model, what is the probability that exactly 7 will have problems while the car is still under warranty?
a) 0.1634 **b) 0.1792** c) 0.3889 d) 0.8165

$$p(7) = {}_{18}C_7 \times (0.35)^7 (1-0.35)^{18-7} = 31{,}824 \times 0.000643393 \times 0.008750783 = 0.1792$$

48. What is P[-1.37 < Z < 1.09], where Z has a standard normal distribution?
a) 0.9474 b) 0.0853 **c) 0.7768** d) 0.8621

$$P(-1.37 < Z < 1.09) = P(0 < Z < 1.09) + P(-1.37 < Z < 0)$$
$$= \underline{T}(1.09) + P(0 < Z < 1.37)$$
$$= 0.3621 + T(1.37) = 0.3621 + 0.4147 = 0.7768$$

49. Determine the values of Z that bound the middle 60% of the standard normal distribution.
a) ± 0.675 **b) ± 0.84** c) ± 0.525 d) ± 0.7258

$$\Pr(-b \leq Z \leq +b) = 0.6000 \Rightarrow \Pr(0 < Z \leq b) = 0.3000 \Rightarrow b \cong 0.84$$

(50-52) Assume that Math SAT scores have a normal distribution with a mean of 455 and a standard deviation of 75.

50. What's the probability that a student makes more than 600 or less than 300?
a) 0.9732 **b) 0.0460** c) 0.9540 d) 0.0268

$$1 - \Pr(300 < X < 600) = 1 - \Pr(-2.07 < Z < 1.93) =$$
$$1 - [T(1.93) + T(2.07)] = 1 - [0.4732 + .4808] = 0.0460$$

51. What's the probability that a randomly selected student from this population makes less than 488?
a) 0.3300 b) 0.6293 c) 0.3707 **d) 0.6700**

$$\Pr(X < 488) = \Pr(Z < 0.44) = 0.5000 + T(0.44) = 0.6700$$

52. What is the 86th percentile of the Math SAT scores?
a) 374 **b) 536** c) 543.5 d) 515

$$x_{0.86} = \mu + z_{0.86} \times \sigma = 455 + 1.08 \times 75 = 536$$

(53-56) A government census of unemployed homeless persons in Denton was taken. The people were cross-classified by skill level and gender in the table below.

Skill-Level	Female	Male
Skilled	10	113
Semi-skilled	51	97
Unskilled	85	220

53. What is the probability that a randomly chosen person from this population is female or semi-skilled?
a) 0.0885 b) 0.3607 **c) 0.4219** d) 0.5104

54. What is the probability that a randomly chosen person from this population is male and skilled?
a) 0.0174 **b) 0.1962** c) 0.7639 d) 0.9601

55. What is the probability that a randomly chosen person is female given that the person is skilled?
a) 0.0174 b) 0.0685 **c) 0.0813** d) 0.2135

56. What is the probability that the person is unskilled given that the person is a man?
a) 0.3819 **b) 0.5116** c) 0.7213 d) 0.7465

(57-60) A University has 32 applicants from qualified students for its Masters program. Among the applicants there are 20 women and 12 men. However, the school can only admit 10 students.

57. How many different ways are there of choosing the 8 men from the 12 men, who applied?
a) 19,958,400 b) 10,158,300 c) 40,320 **d) 495**

58. How many ways are there of choosing exactly 2 women from the 20 women, who applied?
a) 380 **b) 190** c) 225,792,840 d) 496

59. How many different ways are there of admitting 10 students from the 32 persons, who applied?
a) 66 b) 3,628,800 **c) 64,512,240** d) 184,756

60. What is the probability that the school admitted 8 men and 2 women for the 10 openings?
a) 0.0015 b) 0.0667 c) 0.7667 d) 0.0439

(61-64) Let the discrete random variable, X, be defined by the probability distribution, p(x), given in the table below:

x	1	4	10
p(x)	0.3	0.5	0.2

61. What is the population mean, μ, of the discrete random variable X?
a) 5 b) 4.00 c) 7.33 **d) 4.30** e) 5.21

62. What is the population mode of the discrete random variable?
a) 5 **b) 4.00** c) 7.33 d) 4.30 e) 5.21

63. What is the population standard deviation, σ, of the discrete random variable?
a) 10.90 **b) 3.13** c) 3.30 d) 14.00 e) 9.81

64. What is the P[X > 7]?
a) 0.00 b) 0.35 c) 0.50 **d) 0.20** e) none of these

65. In a test of ESP, a subject is asked to identify the color of a randomly drawn but unseen card as red or black. After each try the card is replaced and the deck is shuffled, and continues until the person has 20 tries. If one guesses, what is the probability that he or she gets at least 8 but nor more than 12 correct?
a) 0.252 b) 0.497 c) 0.617 **d) 0.737** e) 0.868

66. The probability that an individual battery fails on a space mission is 0.07. The space shuttle has 14 batteries of this type. Assume that they fail independently. What is the probability that exactly two will fail?
a) 0.0049 b) 0.1229 **c) 0.1867** d) 0.2570 e) 0.9302

(67-69) The probability that a company under fills an individual cereal box is 0.30. A random sample of 12 boxes is taken from different stores in the San Antonio area.

67. What is the probability that at least four boxes will be under-filled?
a) 0.231 b) 0.276 c) 0.493 **d) 0.507** e) 0.724

68. What is the probability that exactly four boxes will be under-filled?
a) 0.231 b) 0.276 c) 0.333 d) 0.493 e) 0.507

69. What is the expected number of under-filled boxes in the sample of size 12?
a) 3 **b) 3.6** c) 4 d) 4.17 e) 5

70. What is the population variance of the number of failed batteries in problem # 66?
a) 0.9114 b) 0.9547 c) 0.9815 d) 0.9907 e) none of these

71. Find the area under the standard normal curve between a=-1.83 and b=2.29.
a) 0.0226 b) 0.4664 c) 0.4890 **d) 0.9554**

72. Let Z denote a standard normal random variable. Determine Pr(Z > -1.45).
a) 0.1264 **b) 0.9265** c) 0.6736 d) 0.0735

73. Determine the 98th percentile of the standard normal distribution.
a) 0.3133 **b) 2.05** c) 1.23 d) 0.3365

(74-76) The IQ scores of Asian-Americans students have a normal distribution (according to Herrnstein & Murray) with a population mean of 110 points and a population standard deviation of 12.

74. What is the probability that a randomly chosen Asian-American student has an IQ in excess of 120?
a) 0.7486 b) 0.7967 **c) 0.2033** d) 0.4213 e) 0.2514

75. What's the probability that a randomly chosen Asian-American student makes between 107 and 137?
a) 0.1844 b) 0.1985 c) 0.3829 d) 0.6171 **e) 0.5865**

76. What is the 91st percentile of their IQ's?
a) 121 b) 114 c) 120 d) 116 **e) 126**

(77-80) The distribution of Exam I-scores made by students in Dr. Keating's introductory class has a population mean of 76 with a population standard deviation of 14. These grades are skewed to the left. This semester there are 100 students in the introductory statistics class.

$$\mu_{\bar{x}} = \mu = 76$$

$$\sigma_{\bar{x}} = \frac{\sigma}{\sqrt{n}} = \frac{14}{\sqrt{100}} = 1.4$$

$$\bar{x} \sim N(76, 1.40)$$

77. What is the probability that the sample average of this class will be less than 72 on Exam I?
a) 0.3859 **b) 0.0021** c) 0.6141 d) 0.9979

$$\Pr(\bar{x} < 72) = \Pr\left(\frac{\bar{x}-76}{1.4} < \frac{72-76}{1.4}\right)$$
$$= \Pr(Z < -2.86) = \Pr(Z > +2.86)$$
$$= 0.5000 - \Pr(0 < Z < 2.86)$$
$$= 0.5000 - 0.4979 = 0.0021$$

78. What is the probability that the sample average of this class will be between 73 and 79?
a) 0.4676 b) 0.8154 c) 0.1782 **d) 0.9676**

$$\Pr(73 < \bar{x} < 79) = \Pr\left(\frac{73-76}{1.4} < \frac{\bar{x}-76}{1.4} < \frac{79-76}{1.4}\right)$$
$$= \Pr(-2.14 < Z < +2.14) = 2 \times \Pr(0 < Z < +2.14)$$
$$= 2 \times 0.4838 = 0.9676$$

79. What is the 99th percentile of sample averages of samples of size 100 taken from this population?
a) 77.95 b) 78.30 **c) 79.26** d) 82.56

$$\bar{x}(0.99) = \mu_{\bar{x}} + z(0.99) \times \sigma_{\bar{x}} = 76 + 2.326 \times 1.4 = 76 + 3.26 = 79.26$$

80. Determine the middle 80% of sample averages of samples of size 100 taken from this population.
a) 76 ± 1.79 b) 76 ± 1.18 c) 76 ± 2.30 d) 82.56

$$middle = \mu_{\bar{x}} \pm z(0.90) \times \sigma_{\bar{x}} = 76 \pm 1.282 \times 1.4 = 76 \pm 1.79$$
The 10th and the 90th percentiles determine these values.

(81-84) 55% of statisticians prefer Dr. Pepper to other sodas. An exit poll of 200 statisticians at their annual convention is conducted.

$$\mu_{\bar{x}} = p = 0.55$$
$$\sigma_{\bar{x}} = \sqrt{\frac{0.55 \times 0.45}{200}} = 0.0351781182$$
$$\bar{x} \sim N(0.55, 0.035)$$

81. What is the probability that no more than 99 persons in this sample will prefer Dr. Pepper?
a) 0.0582 b) 0.2611 c) 0.2389 d) 0.9418

$$\Pr(Y \le 99) = \Pr\left(\frac{Y}{200} \le \frac{99}{200}\right)$$
$$= \Pr(\bar{x} \le 0.495) = \Pr\left(\frac{\bar{x}-0.55}{0.035} \le \frac{0.495-0.550}{0.035}\right)$$
$$= \Pr(Z \le -1.57) = \Pr(Z \ge +1.57)$$
$$= 0.5000 - 0.4418 = .0582$$

82. What is the probability that between 101 and 108 persons in this sample will prefer Dr. Pepper?
a) 0.0985 **b) 0.2874** c) 0.3859 d) 0.4844 e) 0.6179

$$\Pr(101 \le Y \le 108) = \Pr\left(\frac{101}{200} \le \frac{Y}{200} \le \frac{108}{200}\right)$$
$$= \Pr(0.505 \le \bar{x} \le 0.540)$$
$$= \Pr\left(\frac{0.505 - 0.550}{0.035} \le \frac{\bar{x} - 0.55}{0.035} \le \frac{0.54 - 0.550}{0.035}\right)$$
$$= \Pr(-1.29 \le Z \le -0.29) = \Pr(+0.29 \le Z \le +1.29)$$
$$= \Pr(0 \le Z \le 1.29) - \Pr(0 \le Z \le 0.29)$$
$$= 0.4015 - 0.1141 = 0.2874$$

83. Determine the middle 95% bounds on the proportion of this sample that would favor Dr. Pepper.
a) 55% $\pm$ 4% b) 55% $\pm$ 5.7% **c) 55% $\pm$ 6.9%** d) 59 %

$$middle = \mu_{\bar{x}} \pm z(0.975) \times \sigma_{\bar{x}} = 0.55 \pm 1.96 \times 0.035 = 0.55 \pm 0.0686$$

These values are determined by the 2.5th and the 97.5th percentiles.

84. Determine the 99th percentile of the percentage of this sample that would prefer Dr. Pepper.
a) 26.7% b) 58.5% **c) 63.2%** d) 67.2%

$$\bar{x}(0.99) = \mu_{\bar{x}} + z(0.99) \times \sigma_{\bar{x}} = 0.55 + 2.326 \times 0.035 = 0.55 + 0.0814 = 0.6314$$

85. If one rejects the null hypothesis when its false one makes ______________.
a) a Type I error b) a Type II error
c) a producer error **d) a correct decision**

(86-88) Families of size four spent a population mean of \$170 on a Spurs' game with a standard deviation of \$40 last year. In an exit poll from the dome, 50 randomly selected families of size four were interviewed in March 1997. As a result of this sample, the average amount spent by these families is \$182. Is this sufficient evidence at the 5% level of significance to indicate that these families spent more this year?

$$H_0 : \mu = 170 \qquad H_A : \mu > 170$$

$$\mu_0 = 170 \qquad \frac{\sigma}{\sqrt{n}} = \frac{40}{\sqrt{50}} = 5.657$$

$$\alpha = 0.05 \Rightarrow z_{0.05} = 1.645 \qquad \bar{x} = 182$$

86. The alternative hypothesis is that families of size four spent:__________.
a) more than \$182 this year   b) no more than \$170 this year
c) more than \$170 this year   d) less than \$170 this year

87. The critical region is given by the values of the sample average which ______.
a) exceed \$170.00   **b) exceed \$179.31**
c) are less than \$160.69   d) exceed \$183.16

$$\bar{x} > \mu_0 + z_\alpha \frac{\sigma}{\sqrt{n}} = 170 + 1.645 \times 5.657 = 170 + 9.31 = 179.31$$

88. Based on these results one concludes that families of size four spent _______.
a) more than \$170 this year   b) less than \$170 this year
c) a mean of \$182 this year   d) a mean of \$170 this year

89. When testing the null hypothesis, if you reject H_0, then __________.
a) a Type II error may be made   b) H_0 is false
c) a Type I error is made   **d) H_0 may be false**

(90-92) A brace on an AH-1J helicopter provides structural support to the airframe. The force exerted on the brace during action is 2000 psi. A test of six braces results in the following strengths: 2734, 2409, 2213, 2154, 2387, and 1942 pounds. Do these data provide sufficient evidence at the 1% level of significance to support the claim that the brace is stronger than the 2000-psi force?

$$H_0 : \mu = 2{,}000 \qquad H_A : \mu > 2{,}000$$

$$\mu_0 = 2{,}000 \qquad \frac{S}{\sqrt{n}} = \frac{270.03759}{\sqrt{6}} = 110.242$$

$$\alpha = 0.01 \cdots n = 6 \Rightarrow t_{0.01;5} = 3.365 \qquad \bar{x} = 2{,}306.5$$

90. The alternative hypothesis is that the braces are _____________.
a) stronger than 2306 psi   b) no stronger than 2000 psi
c) stronger than 2000 psi d) weaker than 2000 psi

91. The critical region is given by the values of the sample average which ______.
a) exceed 2222 psi b) exceed 2163 psi c) are less than 1629 psi
d) exceed 2371-psi e) exceed 2257 psi

$$\bar{x} > \mu_0 + t_{\alpha;n-1} \frac{S}{\sqrt{n}} = 2{,}000 + 3.365 \times 110.242 = 2{,}000 + 370.96 = 2{,}370.96$$

92. Based on these results one concludes that these braces have a population mean strength ___.

a) no greater than 2000 psi b) less than 2000 psi
c) of 2306.50 psi d) greater than 2000 psi

93. The probability that a hypothesis results in a decision to accept a defective product is _.

a) the level of significance **b) the consumer's risk**
c) the producer's risk d) a Type II error

(94-96) Sonic Boom (SB) has 40% of the CD market in San Antonio. SB conducted an extensive ad campaign to increase its share of the market. A post ad campaign of 100 randomly chosen persons revealed that 47 said they purchased their CD's at Sonic Boom. Is this sufficient evidence at the 10% level of significance to indicate that SB's share of the market has increased?

$$H_0 : p = 0.40 \quad vs \quad H_A : p > 0.40$$

$$p_0 = 0.40 \quad and \quad \sqrt{\frac{0.40 \times 0.60}{100}} = 0.04899$$

$$\alpha = 0.10 \Rightarrow z_{0.10} = 1.282$$

94. The alternative hypothesis is that Sonic Boom's share of the CD market _______.

a) has increased above 40% b) has changed
c) remains unchanged d) has decreased below 40%

95. The critical region is given by the number of Sonic Boom patrons that are ______.

a) greater than 48 **b) greater than 46** c) greater than 41 d) greater than 40

$$\bar{x} > p_0 + z_\alpha \frac{\sqrt{p_0 \times (1 - p_0)}}{\sqrt{n}} = 0.40 + 1.282 \times 0.04899 = 0.40 + 0.0628 = 0.4628$$

$$Y > 100 \times 0.4628 = 46.28$$

96. Based on these results one concludes that SB's share of the CD market has _______.

a) decreased below 40% b) changed from 40%
c) not changed from 40% **d) increased above 40%**

(97-99) Thirty-five percent of the Accounting majors at UTSA are Hispanic descendants. A random sample of 100 Accounting majors is taken.

$$\mu_{\bar{x}} = p = 0.35 \qquad \sigma_{\bar{x}} = \sqrt{\frac{0.35 \times 0.65}{100}} = 0.047697 \qquad \bar{x} \sim N(0.35, 0.047697)$$

97. Approximate the probability that at least 37 are Hispanic?
a) 0.837 b) 0.663 **c) 0.337** d) 0.163

$$\begin{aligned}\Pr(Y \geq 37) &= \Pr\left(\frac{Y}{100} \geq \frac{37}{100}\right)\\ &= \Pr(\bar{x} \geq 0.37)\\ &= \Pr\left(\frac{\bar{x}-0.35}{0.047697} \geq \frac{0.37-0.35}{0.047697}\right)\\ &= \Pr(Z \leq 0.42)\\ &= 0.5000 - \Pr(0 \leq Z \leq 0.42)\\ &= 0.5000 - 0.1628 = .3372\end{aligned}$$

98. Approximate the probability that at most 32 are Hispanic?
a) 0.764 b) 0.736 **c) 0.264** d) 0.236

$$\begin{aligned}\Pr(Y \leq 32) &= \Pr\left(\frac{Y}{100} \leq \frac{32}{100}\right)\\ &= \Pr(\bar{x} \geq 0.32)\\ &= \Pr\left(\frac{\bar{x}-0.35}{0.047697} \geq \frac{0.32-0.35}{0.047697}\right)\\ &= \Pr(Z \leq -0.63) = \Pr(Z \geq +0.63)\\ &= 0.5000 - \Pr(0 \leq Z \leq 0.63)\\ &= 0.5000 - 0.2357 = .2643\end{aligned}$$

99. Approximate the probability that the number of Hispanics in the sample is between 30 and 40?
a) 0.084 b) 0.353 **c) 0.706** d) 0.859

$$\begin{aligned}\Pr(30 \leq Y \leq 40) &= \Pr\left(\frac{30}{100} \leq \frac{Y}{100} \leq \frac{40}{100}\right)\\ &= \Pr(0.30 \leq \bar{x} \leq 0.40)\\ &= \Pr\left(\frac{0.30-0.35}{0.047697} \leq \frac{\bar{x}-0.35}{0.047697} \leq \frac{0.40-0.35}{0.047697}\right)\\ &= \Pr(-1.05 \leq Z \leq +1.05)\\ &= 2 \times \Pr(+0.00 \leq Z \leq +1.05)\\ &= 2 \times .3531 = .7062\end{aligned}$$

100. The alternative hypothesis ____________________.
a) uses the level of significance **b) opposes the status quo**
c) supports the status quo d) uses the sample size

(101-103) The annual salaries of CEO's in TEXAS in 1994 had a normal distribution with a population mean of $250,000 and a population standard deviation of $40,000.

$$\mu = \mu = \$250{,}000$$
$$\sigma = \$40{,}000$$
$$X \sim N(\$250{,}000, \$40{,}000)$$

101. What's the probability that a randomly chosen Texas CEO makes more than $235,600?
a) 0.1406 b) 0.3594 **c) 0.6406** d) 0.8594

$$\begin{aligned}\Pr(X > \$235{,}600) &= \Pr\left(\frac{X - \$250{,}000}{\$40{,}000} > \frac{\$235{,}600 - \$250{,}000}{\$40{,}000}\right)\\ &= \Pr(Z > -0.36)\\ &= \Pr(Z < +0.36)\\ &= 0.5000 + \Pr(0 < Z < 0.36)\\ &= 0.5000 + 0.1406 = 0.6406\end{aligned}$$

102. What's the probability that a randomly chosen Texas CEO makes between $234,400 and $260,000?
a) 0.053 **b) 0.2504** c) 0.3483 d) 0.6517

$$\begin{aligned}\Pr(\$234{,}400 < X < \$260{,}000) &= \Pr\left(\frac{\$234{,}400 - \$250{,}000}{\$40{,}000} < \frac{X - \$250{,}000}{\$40{,}000} < \frac{\$260{,}000 - \$250{,}000}{\$40{,}000}\right)\\ &= \Pr(-0.39 < Z < +0.25)\\ &= \Pr(0 < Z < 0.39) + \Pr(0 < Z < 0.25)\\ &= 0.1517 + 0.0987 = 0.2504\end{aligned}$$

103. What is the 95th percentile of their salaries?
a) $367,100 b) $288,000 c) $301,280 **d)$315,800**

$$X(0.95) = \mu + z(0.95) \times \sigma = \$250{,}000 + 1.645 \times \$40{,}000 = \$250{,}000 + \$65{,}800 = \$315{,}800$$

104. When testing the null hypothesis, if you reject Ho, then ____________________.

a) a Type I error was made **b)a Type II error is not made**
c) Ho is false d) Ho is true

(105-107) The average family of four spent a mean of $160 on a visit to Sea World with a standard deviation of $25 in 1993. In an exit poll from the park, 44 randomly selected families of size four were interviewed in May 1994. The results of the sample revealed that the average amount spent by these families was $168.43. Is this sufficient evidence at the 5% level of significance to indicate that families of size four will **spend more** at Sea World in 1994?

$H_0: \mu = \$160 \qquad H_A: \mu > \$160$

$\mu_0 = \$160 \qquad \frac{\sigma}{\sqrt{n}} = \frac{\$25}{\sqrt{44}} = \$3.769$

$\alpha = 0.05 \Rightarrow z_{0.05} = 1.645 \qquad \bar{x} = \$168.43$

105. The alternative hypothesis is that families of size four will spend ______________.

a) $160 in 1994 b) less than $160 in 1994 c) more than $168.43 in 1994
d) more than $160 in 1994 e) exactly $168.43 in 1994

106. The critical region is given by the values of the sample average which ________.

a)exceed $160.00 **b) exceed $166.20** c) are less than $168.43
d) exceed $201.13 e) less than $153.80

$$\bar{x} > \mu_0 + z_\alpha \frac{\sigma}{\sqrt{n}} = 160 + 1.645 \times 3.769 = 160 + 6.20 = 166.20$$

107. Based on these results, one concludes that families of size four will spend _____.

a) more than $160 b) less than $160 c) a mean of $168.43
d) not spend more than $160 e) $160

108. The probability that a hypothesis test ends in a decision to accept a defective product is _______.
a) the producer's risk **b) the consumer's risk** c) the law of averages
d) a Type II error e) a Type I error

(109-111) The shelf life of a vaccine is monitored by hospitals. The manufacturer in an independent test of 8 randomly selected vials observes the following lifetimes in days: 108, 124, 124, 106, 138, 163, 159, and 134. Assume that the shelf lives are normally distributed. Is there sufficient evidence to support the manufacturer's claim that the mean shelf life of the vaccine is **more than 125 days** at the 5% level?

$H_0: \mu = 125 \qquad H_A: \mu > 125$

$\mu_0 = 125 \qquad \frac{S}{\sqrt{n}} = \frac{21.078}{\sqrt{8}} = 7.452$

$\alpha = 0.05 \cdots n = 8 \Rightarrow t_{0.05;7} = 1.895 \qquad \bar{x} = 132.00$

109. The alternative hypothesis is that the shelf life is _____________ days.
a) 132 b) less than 125 **c) more than 125** d) no more than 125

110. The critical region is given by the values of the sample average which __________ days.

a) exceed 125 b) exceed 165 c) exceed 160
d) exceed 172 **e) exceed 139**

$$\bar{x} > \mu_0 + t_{\alpha;n-1}\frac{S}{\sqrt{n}} = 125 + 1.895 \times 7.452 = 125 + 14.12 = 139.12$$

111. Based on these results, one concludes that these batteries will last _________ days.
a) more than 125 b) less than 125 c) a mean of 132 **d) 125**

112. When one accepts a true null hypothesis, one makes a _____________.
a) a Type I error b) a Type II error **c) a correct decision** d) a and b

(113-115) The annual salaries of College Presidents in 1993 had a population mean of $150,000 and standard deviation of $20,000. A random sample of 37 college Presidents is chosen from this population.

$$\mu_{\bar{x}} = \mu = \$150,000$$
$$\sigma_{\bar{x}} = \frac{\sigma}{\sqrt{n}} = \frac{\$20,000}{\sqrt{37}} = \$3,287.98$$
$$\bar{x} \sim N(\$250,000, \$3,287.98)$$

113. What's the probability that the sample average salary of this randomly chosen sample is less than $143,400?
a) 0.0222 b) 0.3707 c) 0.4778 d) 0.6293

$$\Pr(\bar{x} < \$143,400) = \Pr\left(\frac{\bar{x} - \$150,000}{\$3,287.98} < \frac{\$143,400 - \$150,000}{\$3,287.98}\right)$$
$$= \Pr(Z < -2.01)$$
$$= \Pr(Z > +2.01)$$
$$= 0.5000 - \Pr(0 < Z < 2.01)$$
$$= 0.5000 - 0.4778 = 0.0222$$

114. What's the probability that the sample average salary of this randomly chosen sample is between $146,800 and $152,900?
a) 0.1212 b) 0.4776 c) 0.5753 **d) 0.6446**

$$\Pr(\$146,800 < \bar{x} < \$152,900) = \Pr\left(\frac{\$146,800 - \$150,000}{\$3,287.98} < \frac{\bar{x} - \$150,000}{\$3,287.98} < \frac{\$152,900 - \$150,000}{\$3,287.98}\right)$$
$$= \Pr(-0.97 < Z < +0.88)$$
$$= \Pr(-0.97 < Z < 0) + \Pr(0 < Z < 0.88)$$
$$= \Pr(0 < Z < 0.97) + \Pr(0 < Z < 0.88)$$
$$= 0.3340 + 0.3106 = 0.6446$$

115. What is the 90th percentile of the average salaries from random samples of size 37?
a) \$152,959 **b) \$154,215** c) \$168,000 d) \$175,640

$$\bar{x}(0.90) = \mu_{\bar{x}} + z(0.90) \times \sigma_{\bar{x}}$$
$$= \$150{,}000 + 1.282 \times \$3{,}287.98$$
$$= \$150{,}000 + \$4{,}215.19$$
$$= \$154{,}215.19$$

These data are the ages (in years) and systolic blood pressures of ten healthy adults:

Age	20	43	63	26	53	31	58	46	70	19
BP	120	128	141	126	134	128	136	132	144	121

Fit a linear regression line to these data. From the prediction equation answer the following questions.

Scatterplot of SBP versus Age

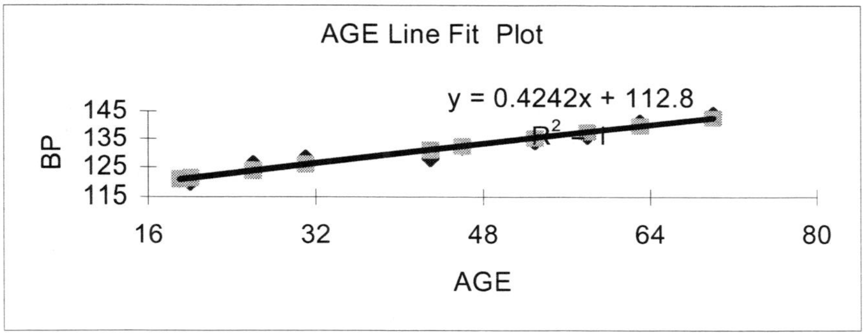

ANOVA				
	df	*SS*	*MS*	*F-ratio*
Regression	1	540.01	540.01	154.37
Residual	8	27.99	3.498	
Total	9	568		

116. What is the predicted increase in systolic BP for each year a person ages?
a) 112.80 b) 2.241 c) 0.448 **d) 0.424**

117. What is the predicted systolic BP of a healthy newborn child?
a) 111.86 **b) 112.80** c) 0.424 d) 250.67

	Coeff	*Std Error*	*t-Stat*	*p-value*
Intercept	112.802	1.5796	71.410	1.65E-12
AGE	0.4242	0.0341	12.425	1.64E-06

118. If one is a healthy 30 year-old, what does the regression predict for his or her systolic BP?
a) 125.53 b) 125.54 c) 131.00 d) 195.19

119. If one's systolic BP is 120, how old does the regression line predict that the person is?
a) 19.50 b) 18.25 **c) 16.97** d) 20 e) 20.7

120. What is the coefficient of determination?
a) 0.975 b) 0.904 **c) 0.951** d) 0.987 e) 1.050

R Square	0.950729

{121-124} These data are the meter readings (in gallons) and tank volumes (in gallons) displaced on 6 operational days at a Diamond Shamrock Corner Store.

Day	1	2	3	4	5	6
Meter	770.8	712.4	909.9	395.0	528.8	456.0
Tank	766.2	708.5	905.3	394.9	528.5	454.6

SCATTERPLOT of Tank versus Meters

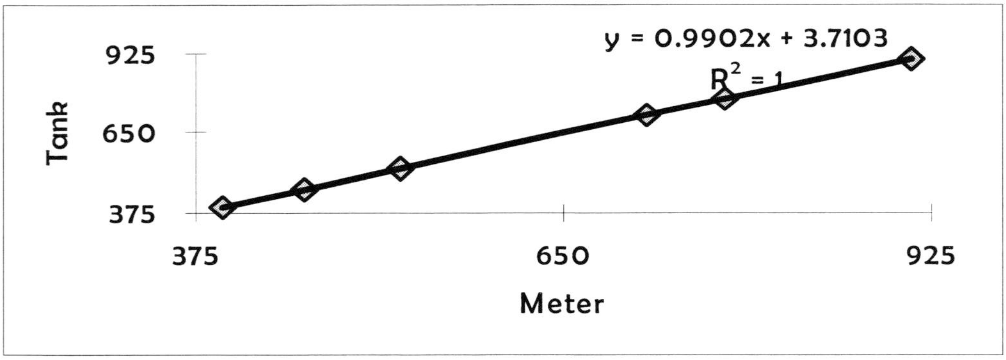

Fit a linear regression line to the data. From the prediction line answer these questions.

ANOVA				
	df	*SS*	*MS*	*F*
Regression	1	196758.4	196758.4	252415.5
Residual	4	3.118009	0.779502	
Total	5	196761.5		
	Coeff	*Std Err*	*t-stat*	*p-value*
Intercept	3.710295	1.290626	2.874802	0.045249
Meter	0.99015	0.001971	502.4097	9.42E-11

121. What is the predicted amount of gasoline displaced from the tank when one gallon of gasoline is dispensed through the meters?

a) 0.990 b) 1.010 c) 0.996 d) 1.004 e) 1.000

122. What is the predicted amount of gasoline displaced when none is dispensed through the meters?

a) -3.740 **b) 3.710** c) 0 d) 0.414 e) -0.414

123. If a station dispenses 800 gallons through its meters, what does the regression line predict for the number of gallons displaced from the tank?

a) 788.45 b) 791.84 **c) 795.83** d) 796.80 e) 804.21

124. If a station measures its underground tanks and determines that 594 gallons have been displaced from the tank, what would the regression line predict for the number of gallons dispensed through the meters?

a) 588.06 b) 591.86 c) 594.00 **d) 596.16** e) 600

125. What is the coefficient of determination?

a) 0.904 b) 0.951 c) 0.975 d) 0.997 **e) 1.000**

{126-129} 100 TV's were randomly sampled and the weekday that the TV was made was determined from manufacturing records based on the inventory number. The data are summarized in the table below by classes, Monday and Friday (M_F), Tuesday and Thursday (T_T), and Wednesday. Are these data sufficient at the 5% level of significance to indicate that production does not occur uniformly over weekdays?

W	T_T	M_F
28	42	30

$$\text{H}_0 : p_1 = 0.20, p_2 = 0.40, p_3 = 0.40$$

versus

$$\text{H}_a : some - p_i - is - misspecified$$

$$E_1 = n \times c_1 = 100 \times 0.20 = 20, \text{and } E_2 = n \times c_2 = 100 \times 0.40 = 40, \text{and } E_3 = n \times c_3 = 100 \times 0.40 = 40$$

W	T_T	M_F	Total
28 (20)	42 (40)	30 (40)	100 (100)

$$\Re = \sum_{i=1}^{r} \frac{(O_i - E_i)^2}{E_i} = \frac{(28-20)^2}{20} + \frac{(42-40)^2}{40} + \frac{(30-40)^2}{40}$$
$$= 3.20 + 0.10 + 2.50 = 5.80$$

The value of this test statistic must be compared with a percentile from a chi-square distribution with $r-1=3-1=2$ degrees of freedom. Since the level of significance was chosen to be 5%, then the tabled value of the upper percentile is given by $\chi^2_{r-1} = \chi^2_{0.05;2} = 5.991$. Since $\Re = 5.80 < \chi^2_{0.05;3} = 5.991$ then we fail to reject H_0 that production rates vary by day of the workweek.

126. The value of the chi-square test statistic is given by:
a) 12.60 b) 3.92 **c) 5.80** d) 3.44

127. The critical value from the chi-square table is given by:
a) 7.815 b) 9.488 **c) 5.991** d) 3.841

128. The expected number of TV's made on Monday-Friday based on the uniformity assumption is
a) 33.33 **b) 40** c) 20 d) 30

129. Based on these results, one concludes that production of TV's by weekday is:
a) not different b) different
c) are best on Wednesday d) worst on Monday-Friday.

{130-134} The data, in the table below, come form Karl Pearson in 1909. At the five-percent level of significance, does the type of crime appear to be related to whether the criminal was drunken or sober?

	Arson	Rape	Assault	Theft	Fraud	Total
Drunken	50	88	155	379	63	735
Sober	45	62	110	301	147	665
Total	95	150	265	680	210	1,400

$H_0: Type-of-crime-and-state-of-sobriety-are-independent$

versus

$H_a: Type-of-crime-committed-depends-upon-state-of-sobriety$

$$E_{11} = \frac{n_1 \times m_1}{N} = \frac{735 \times 95}{1,400} = 49.875 \qquad E_{21} = \frac{n_1 \times m_2}{N} = \frac{735 \times 150}{1,400} = 78.75$$

$$E_{31} = \frac{n_1 \times m_3}{N} = \frac{735 \times 265}{1,400} = 139.125 \qquad E_{41} = \frac{n_1 \times m_4}{N} = \frac{735 \times 680}{1,400} = 357.0$$

	Arson	Rape	Assault	Theft	Fraud	Total
Drunken	50 (49.875)	88 (78.75)	155 (139.125)	379 (357)	63 (110.25)	735 (735)
Sober	45 (45.125)	62 (71.25)	110 (125.875)	301 (323)	147 (99.75)	665 (665)
Total	95	150	265	680	210	1,400

$$\Re = \sum_{j=1}^{c}\sum_{i=1}^{r}\frac{(O_{ij}-E_{ij})^2}{E_{ij}}$$

$$= \frac{(50-49.875)^2}{49.875}+\frac{(88-78.75)^2}{78.75}+\frac{(155-139.125)^2}{139.125}+\frac{(379-357)^2}{357}+\frac{(63-110.25)^2}{110.25}+$$

$$\frac{(45-45.125)^2}{45.125}+\frac{(62-71.25)^2}{71.25}+\frac{(110-125.875)^2}{125.875}+\frac{(301-323)^2}{323}+\frac{(147-99.75)^2}{99.75}$$

$$= 0.0003+1.0865+1.8114+1.3557+20.25+0.0003+1.2009+2.0021+1.4985+22.3816=51.5873$$

130. The alternative hypothesis is that ___________.
   a) type of crime and state of sobriety are independent
   b) fraud requires sobriety
   c) types of crime are equally likely to be committed
   d) type of crime is dependent upon state of sobriety
   e) types of crime are not equally likely to be committed

131. If state of sobriety and type of crime are independent, what is the expected number of criminals, who commit assault while inebriated?
   a) 110.25 b) 125.875 **c) 139.125** d) 155 e) 357

132. If state of sobriety and type of crime are independent, what is the contribution to the test statistic made by the criminals who commit fraud while sober?
   a) 110.25 **b) 22.38** c) 20.25 d) 33.075 e) 144

133. What is the critical value of the chi-square test?
   a) 51.587 b) 49.731 c) 11.143 **d) 9.488** e) 11.071

134. Based on the evidence at the 5% level of significance, we conclude that:
   a) type of crime is independent of state of sobriety
   b) for each type of crime, the proportion drunk is the same
   c) you better be sober to commit fraud
   d) crime committed depends upon state of sobriety of the offender

{135-139} A City highway has 4 inbound lanes and traffic analysts want to know whether drivers prefer some lanes. 100 cars on the inbound lanes were observed in early morning traffic. The lane and count of the number of cars per lane are given below:

Lane	1	2	3	4
# of Cars	29	28	24	19

Do these data provide sufficient evidence at the 5% level of significance to indicate that some lanes are preferred over others?

$$H_0: p_1 = 0.25, p_2 = 0.25, p_3 = 0.25, p_4 = 0.25$$

versus

$$H_a: some - p_i - is - misspecified$$

$$E_1 = n \times c_1 = 100 \times 0.25 = 25, \cdots, \text{and } E_4 = n \times c_4 = 100 \times 0.25 = 25$$

1	2	3	4	Total
29 (25)	28 (25)	24 (25)	19 (25)	100 (100)

$$\Re = \sum_{i=1}^{r} \frac{(O_i - E_i)^2}{E_i}$$

$$= \frac{(29-25)^2}{25} + \frac{(28-25)^2}{25} + \frac{(24-25)^2}{25} + \frac{(19-25)^2}{25}$$

$$= 0.64 + 0.36 + 0.04 + 1.44 = 2.48$$

The value of this test statistic must be compared with a percentile from a chi-square distribution with $r-1 = 4-1 = 3$ degrees of freedom. Since the level of significance was chosen to be 5%, then the tabled value of the upper percentile is given by $\chi^2_{r-1} = \chi^2_{0.05;3} = 7.815$. Since $\Re = 2.48 < \chi^2_{0.05;3} = 7.815$ then we fail to reject H_0 that the lanes are used uniformly.

135. The value of the multinomial test statistic is:
a) 2.48 b) 2.70 c) 3.841 d) 6.251 e) 6.95

136. What is the expected number of cars for Lane 2, if the null hypothesis is true?
a) 29 b) 20 c) 16.67 **d) 25** e) 28

137. What is the contribution of Lane 4 to the value of the test statistic?
a) 36 **b) 1.44** c) 1.89 d) 0.64 e) 19

138. The critical region of the test is given by the values of the test statistic which exceed:

a) 2.70 b) 5.991 c) 7.779 **d) 7.815** e) 9.488

139. Based on these results, we conclude that:

a) drivers prefer lanes 1 & 2

b) drivers dislike lane 4

c) lanes 1 & 2 are preferred over lane 4

d) there's not enough evidence to indicate a preference

{140-144} A small company would like to quantify the relationship between its monthly promotional costs and net gains. The data for 8 consecutive months are given below in thousands of dollars each:

Month	1	2	3	4	5	6	7	8
Promotional Costs	10	15	40	100	90	230	30	50
Net Gains	155	160	140	334	195	530	155	244

ANOVA

	df	*SS*	*MS*	*F-ratio*
Regression	1	112,967.8	112,967.8	52.73521
Residual	6	12,853.03	2,142.2	
Total	7	125,820.9		

	Coeff	*Std Error*	*t-stat*	*p-value*
Intercept	114.7438	23.68832	4.843897	0.002869
Cost	1.76115	0.242519	7.261901	0.000347

SCATTERPLOT of Gain versus Cost

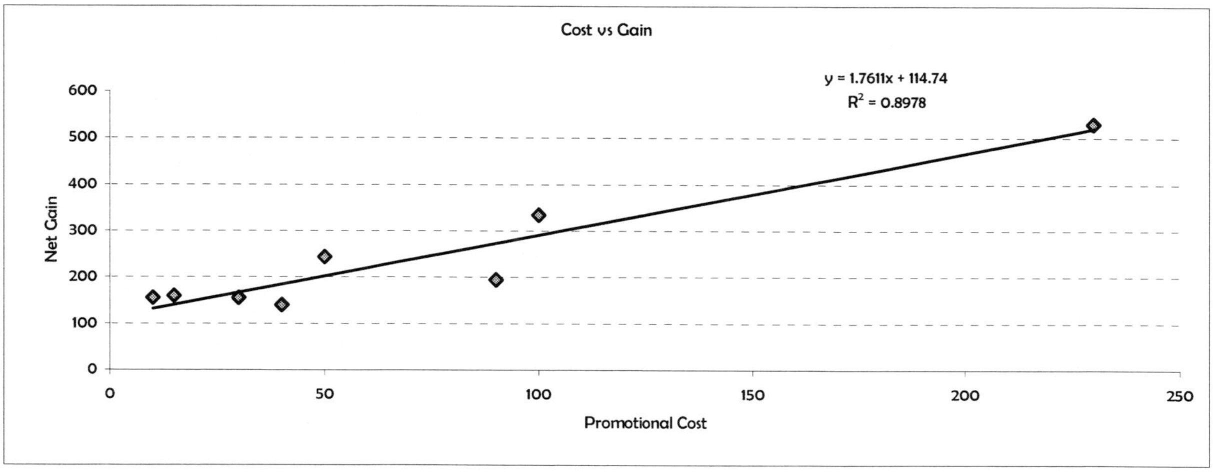

140. What is the additional net gain expected for each additional dollar of promotional cost expended?

a) 0.51 b) 0.57 **c) 1.76** d) 1.64 e) 1.39

141. What is the expected net gain (in thousands) if no promotional costs are expended?
a) 137.74 **b) 114.74** c) -51.28 d) -65.15 e) 31.13

142. If one expends $80 (thousand) in promotional costs, what is his predicted net gain (thousands)?
a) 255.64 b) 257.51 c) -10.50 d) -19.72 e) 127.42

143. If one makes net gains of $250 (thousand), what is the amount one is predicted to expend in promotional costs?
a) 555.03 b) 590.97 c) 67.76 **d) 76.80** e) 316.49

144. What percentage of the net gains can be explained by knowing the promotional costs?
a) 94.75% **b) 89.78%** c) 97.34% d) 16.33% e) 46.21%

{145-150} An insurance company surveyed 1,000 employees about their pension funds. Do the data below contradict the claim of independence between age and investment preference at the five-percent level of significance?

Age	All Stock	All Annuities	Mixed
Over 45	196	131	158
Under 45	223	116	176

H_0 : Type of investment and age of investor are independent versus

H_a : Type of investment chosen is dependent upon and age of investor

$$E_{11} = \frac{n_1 \times m_1}{N} = \frac{485 \times 419}{1{,}000} = 203.215 \text{ and } E_{12} = \frac{n_1 \times m_2}{N} = \frac{485 \times 247}{1{,}000} = 119.795$$

Age	All Stock	All Annuities	Mixed	Total
Over 45	196 (203.215)	131 (119.795)	158 (161.99)	485 (485)
Under 45	223 (215.785)	116 (127.205)	176 (172.01)	515 (515)
Total	419	247	334	1,000